Advances in Spatial Science

Titles in the Series

G. Clarke and *M. Madden* (Eds.)
Regional Science in Business
VIII, 363 pages. 2001. ISBN 978-3-540-41780-4

M. M. Fischer and *Y. Leung* (Eds.)
GeoComputational Modelling
XII, 279 pages. 2001. ISBN 978-3-540-41968-6

M. M. Fischer and *J. Fröhlich* (Eds.)
Knowledge, Complexity and Innovation Systems
XII, 477 pages. 2001. ISBN 978-3-540-41969-3

M. M. Fischer, J. Revilla Diez and *F. Snickars*
Metropolitan Innovation Systems
VIII, 270 pages. 2001. ISBN 978-3-540-41967-9

L. Lundqvist and *L.-G. Mattsson* (Eds.)
National Transport Models
VIII, 202 pages. 2002. ISBN 978-3-540-42426-0

J. R. Cuadrado-Roura and *M. Parellada* (Eds.)
Regional Convergence in the European Union
VIII, 368 pages. 2002. ISBN 978-3-540-43242-5

G. J. D. Hewings, M. Sonis and *D. Boyce* (Eds.)
Trade, Networks and Hierarchies
XI, 467 pages. 2002. ISBN 978-3-540-43087-2

G. Atalik and *M. M. Fischer* (Eds.)
Regional Development Reconsidered
X, 220 pages. 2002. ISBN 978-3-540-43610-2

Z. J. Acs, H. L. F. de Groot and *P. Nijkamp* (Eds.)
The Emergence of the Knowledge Economy
VII, 388 pages. 2002. ISBN 978-3-540-43722-2

R. J. Stimson, R. R. Stough and *B. H. Roberts*
Regional Economic Development
X, 397 pages. 2002. ISBN 978-3-540-43731-4

S. Geertman and *J. Stillwell* (Eds.)
Planning Support Systems in Practice
XII, 578 pages. 2003. ISBN 978-3-540-43719-2

B. Fingleton (Ed.)
European Regional Growth
VIII, 435 pages. 2003. ISBN 978-3-540-00366-3

T. Puu
Mathematical Location and Land Use Theory, 2nd Edition
X, 362 pages. 2003. ISBN 978-3-540-00931-3

J. Bröcker, D. Dohse and *R. Soltwedel* (Eds.)
Innovation Clusters
and Interregional Competition
VIII, 409 pages. 2003. ISBN 978-3-540-00999-3

D. A. Griffith
Spatial Autocorrelation and Spatial Filtering
XIV, 247 pages. 2003. ISBN 978-3-540-00932-0

J. R. Roy
Spatial Interaction Modelling
X, 239 pages. 2004. ISBN 978-3-540-20528-9

M. Beuthe, V. Himanen, A. Reggiani
and *L. Zamparini* (Eds.)
Transport Developments
and Innovations in an Evolving World
XIV, 346 pages. 2004. ISBN 978-3-540-00961-0

Y. Okuyama and *S. E. Chang* (Eds.)
Modeling Spatial
and Economic Impacts of Disasters
X, 323 pages. 2004. ISBN 978-3-540-21449-6

L. Anselin, R.J.G.M. Florax and *S. J. Rey*
Advances in Spatial Econometrics
XXII, 513 pages. 2004. ISBN 978-3-540-43729-1

R.J.G.M. Florax and *D. A. Plane* (Eds.)
Fifty Years of Regional Science
VIII, 400 pages. 2004. ISBN 978-3-540-22361-0

D. Felsenstein and *B.A. Portnov* (Eds.)
Regional Disparities in Small Countries
VI, 333 pages. 2005. ISBN 978-3-540-24303-8

A. Reggiani and *L.A. Schintler* (Eds.)
Methods and Models in Transport
and Telecommunications
XIII, 364 pages. 2005. ISBN 978-3-540-25859-9

H.W. Richardson and C.-H.C. Bae (Eds.)
Globalization and Urban Development
X, 321 pages. 2005. ISBN 978-3-540-22362-7

G. Arbia
Spatial Econometrics
XVII, 207 pages. 2006. ISBN 978-3-540-32304-4

B. Johansson, C. Karlsson,
R. Stough (Eds.)
The Emerging Digital Economy
X, 352 pages. 2006. ISBN 978-3-540-34487-2

H. Westlund
Social Capital in the Knowledge Economy
X, 212 pages. 2006. ISBN 978-3-540-35364-5

A.T. Murray, T.H. Grubesic (Eds.)
Critical Infrastructure
VIII, 311 pages. 2007. ISBN 978-3-540-68055-0

Åke E. Andersson · Lars Pettersson
Ulf Strömquist (Editors)

European Metropolitan Housing Markets

With 139 Figures
and 94 Tables

Springer

Professor Åke E. Andersson
Lars Pettersson PhD

Jönköping International Business School
P.O. Box 1026
551 11 Jönköping
Sweden

ake.andersson@ihh.hj.se
lars.pettersson@sjv.se

Ulf Strömquist

Temaplan
Peter Myndes backe 16
118 86 Stockholm
Sweden

ulf.stromquist@temaplan.se

Library of Congress Control Number: 2007924899

ISSN 1430-9602

ISBN 978-3-540-69891-3 Springer Berlin Heidelberg New York

Springer is a part of Springer Science+Business Media

springer.com

Production: LE-TEX Jelonek, Schmidt & Vöckler GbR, Leipzig
Cover-design: WMX Design GmbH, Heidelberg

SPIN 11978558 88/3100YL - 5 4 3 2 1 0 Printed on acid-free paper

Contents

1 European Housing Markets – An Overview

Åke E. Andersson[1], Lars Pettersson[1] and Ulf Strömquist[2]

[1]Jönköping International Business School, Jönköping University, Jönköping
[2]Temaplan, Stockholm

1.1 Introduction

The performance of the housing and the real estate markets is important for nations, regions and individuals. When major changes take place on these markets they often have impacts on other sectors of the economy. Everyday life of people is very much influenced of where and how they live and reside as well.

For any analyst entering this field of research it is evident that there are differences as well as similarities between housing markets in different countries and regions. For example, most countries in Europe have a regime of regulation of rents, but there are differences with respect to how these policies have been implemented. In general, rent regulations were introduced during the time of the World Wars with the purpose to prevent landlords from taking advantage of the problems related to extreme scarcity. This first generation of rent control aimed at freezing the rents. The second generation of rent control regimes of the 1960s and 1970s were more flexible, allowing rents to adjust with respect to changes in construction costs and inflation. A third generation of rent control, introduced in the 1980s and the 1990s, is the so-called 'tenancy rent control', where rents are regulated within a given tenure, but unregulated for new tenures. Different countries have transformed their policies to different degrees. Currently, there are countries that have rent regulation from either the second or the third generation, while some countries have abandoned rent regulation. The situation is similar for subsidies, allowances, and other policy instruments.

When looking back on the historic development of the housing markets in Europe, the influence of the World War II is evident. Firstly, a substantial new construction took place after the war had ended, which now is in ripe for renewal and upgrading. Secondly, the fear of problems that were expected to follow after the war led to a number of policy interventions during the decades following the war. Construction programmes and rent regulation are examples of the post-war policy. Many countries have developed their hard rent control into second, and even third, generations of rent regulation regimes. In some countries (for example Norway and Finland) regulations have been abandoned during recent years.

This book offers a number of studies from metropolitan regions of different European countries. The metropolitan regions belong to the same size class in order to provide a useful comparative overview. The metropolitan regions of Amsterdam, Brussels, Copenhagen, Glasgow, Hamburg, Helsinki, Milan, Munich, Oslo, Stockholm, Zurich and Vienna are included in the analysis. The size of these metropolitan regions spans from around one million to a bit less than four million inhabitants.

The case studies in this volume focus on the development during the recent decades and include both quantitative and qualitative analysis. In this way different aspects of the interactions between urban structures, the economy and the housing market is revealed.

The housing markets of the different metropolitan regions differ. The overview of the metropolitan regions included in the study reveals differences in market performance (Temaplan 2003).[1] In Vienna and Milan more than 90 per cent of all housing is found in multifamily houses. In these metropolitan regions the interaction with the single-family housing market plays a minor role. The situation is the opposite in Oslo, Amsterdam and Brussels, where multifamily houses represent only less than 45 per cent of the market. Multifamily houses dominate the housing market in the average metropolitan regions, with market shares of 60 per cent or more.

There are also substantial differences between the metropolitan regions with respect to the growth of the total number of apartments during the 1990s. Helsinki had a growth rate of 18 per cent of the number of apartments in multifamily houses between 1990 and 2000. The corresponding growth rate in the other metropolitan regions was between 7 and 12 per cent, except for Copenhagen and Milan, which had the lowest increase in the number of apartments of only 3–4 per cent in the same time period.[2] A panel of experts from the regions have indicated that there was an excess demand in all the metropolitan regions, except for Brussels and Vienna in 2001/2002.[3] The panel of experts also reported small housing construction activities in most of the metropolitan regions. Construction was judge to be in balance 'with long-term market conditions' in Brussels and Vienna only.

---

1 The descriptive comparison in this analyse is based on Temaplan's publication 'Benchmarking av Stockholms bostadsmarknad' [Benchmarking of the housing market in Stockholm] from 2003.

2 Data were not available for Brussels.

3 Local experts were contacted at the time when this project on 'European Metropolitan Housing Markets' was carried out. These experts were asked questions about regional conditions that could not be answered by analysing statistical sources. The experts were people that acted professionally on respective markets.

1.2 Market Interaction

Real estate is durable and price and production levels are determined on an asset market. The pricing of real estate depends on the demand and the supply of housing units. The quantity of the demand for housing units and the propensity to pay for housing services can be explained from the performance of the regional economy and the level of rent. The construction market supplies new real estate assets and the net marginal revenue of real estate and the cost of new construction can explain the activity in this market. The price of real estate and thus the net marginal revenue is then determined by the rental income asset owners can receive from the houses. This also means that it is important to consider that the use of real estate for housing space can be converted from one type of use to another.

DiPasquale and Wheaton (1996) have presented an illustrative model of the interactions of the markets for housing, real estate, construction and assets. This model combines demand-side dependency of the general conditions of the economy and the determination of rents (*R*), formation of asset prices (*P*), construction activities (*C*) and the stock supply of housing (*S*). Also the required internal rate of return (*i*) and the depreciation rate (δ) are considered in this model in a somewhat simplified way by use of the following asset price equation:

$$P = \int_0^T R(t) e^{-it} dt = \frac{R}{i}\left[1 - e^{-iT}\right] \tag{1.1}$$

$$\text{for } R(t) = R \text{, if } T \to \infty \text{ and } P \to \overline{\frac{R}{i}}$$

where *P* is the asset price per square metre of housing at time 0, *R* is a flow of net returns per square metre assumed to be constant, and *i* is the real rate of interest on housing. Fig. 1.1 also includes subsidies (*n*) net of tax on assets in the equation that determines the price (*P*) on the asset market. Construction activity (*C*) is assumed to be a function of the price (*P*) on the asset market; in a more general context construction is a function of Tobin's q, i.e. the ratio between the price on real estate offered on the market and the price of newly constructed real estate. $q > 1$ implies incentive to construct new housing, while $q < 1$ implies a change of ownership of usage of assets.

Fig. 1.1 shows how equilibrium is determined and the way the adjustment process on the market is carried out. If the demand for space increases (the northeast quadrant) the price level will also increase (the northwest quadrant). This stimulates the construction activity (the southwest quadrant) and increases the supply of space by stock adjustment (the southeast quadrant). The supply of space will adjust according to the initial change in demand (the northeast quadrant). The adjustment process can be assumed to make its journey around the diagram, illustrating the solution to the underlying system of equations determining the equilibrium of the markets.

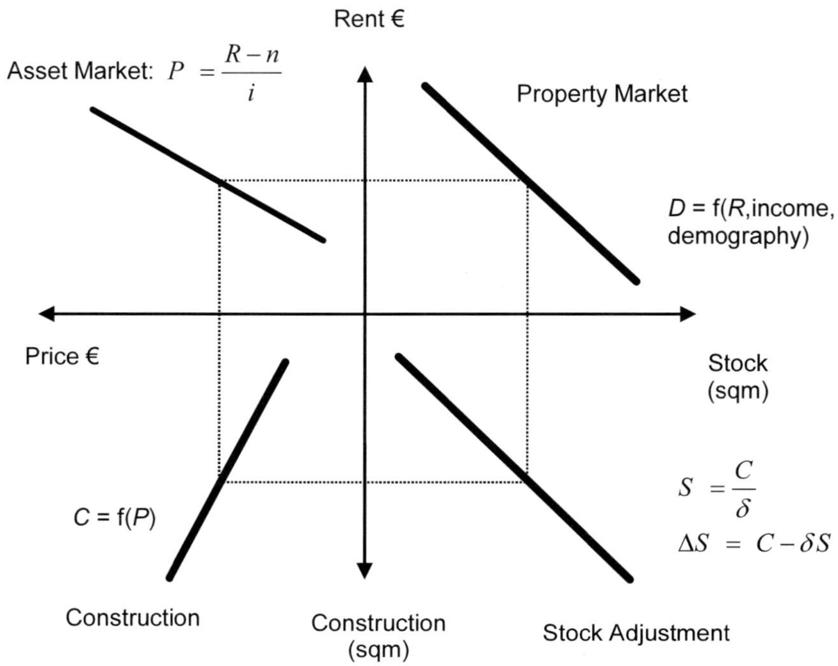

Fig. 1.1. Real estate: the property and asset markets (Source: DiPasquale and Wheaton 1996 p. 8, our modified version)

Considering a change in the demand for housing generated by a change in the regional situation, the model can be used to analyse the adjustment process and how this process is affected by e.g. a rent regulation regime. Assume an increase in the demand for housing. If the rent is not allowed to respond to this change, new construction will not be stimulated. Policy makers have tried different subsidies, e.g. subsidy on interest payments, in order to increase asset prices and construction activities. Another alternative is to subsidise construction firms. In the first case the price on the asset market will be $P = (R - n)/(i - z)$, where z is the subsidy on interest payment, making the curve that depicts the relation between price and rent less steep.

With a rent regulation equal to $\overline{R}$, there will be no change in the asset price, if the demand for housing would increase. In Fig. 1.2 a subsidy of interest payments is used as means to increase equilibrium supply of housing stock during a rent regulation regime. An alternative to interest subsidies would be construction cost subsidies, changing the construction market function.

This model demonstrates the many factors interacting in the determination of housing market equilibrium. The dependency of the housing market on asset markets, construction market and the dynamics of the regional economy and demography is analysed in the metropolitan case studies presented below. Differences in economic growth performance, real interest rates, demographic changes, growth

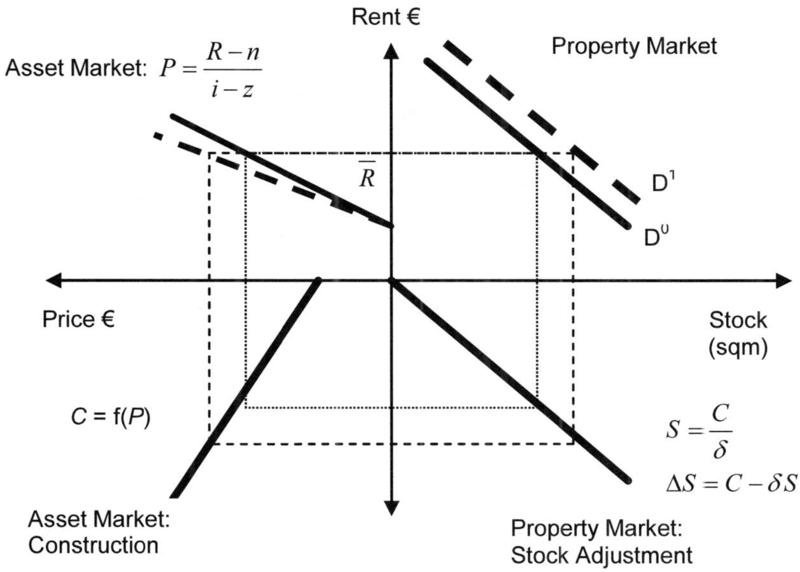

Fig. 1.2. Real estate: the property and asset markets

of household income, construction costs etc. all have significant influences on the particular regional housing market.

The model points to the complex process of adjustments in the real estate market. The presence of interdependency with other parts of the economy implies that business cycle fluctuations, as well as changes in the monetary and fiscal policies all exert influences on the real estate and housing markets. Dynamic variants of real estate market models stress the importance of the time dimension and how expectations about future economic development, especially future house prices and inflations would influence current behaviour in these markets. One way is to assume that exogenous expectation applies. Hence households believe that prices grow with the growth rate of the economy and are unaffected by regional housing market conditions. Mortgage prepayment models are used in analysis of housing prices (Deng et al. 2000). In some dynamic models adaptive or backward-looking expectations are based on past trends (Dunn and McConell 1981; Stanton 1995, 1996). There are also dynamic housing market models based on an assumption of forward-looking expectations (Patruno 1994; Chan and Russell 1997). In such models households makes their decision based on available information about all relevant operations in the market and are thus able to make correct predictions about future developments.

There are rational reasons for incorporation of both macroeconomic and regional economic conditions in an analysis of a metropolitan housing market. In the early 1990s many countries went through an economic crisis, which affected both national and regional housing markets. There are also a number of differences in macroeconomic policy regimes influencing the metropolitan regions.

1.3 Regional Housing Markets

At the micro level bid rents are related to household location and housing decisions. An early formulation of bid rent and housing choice was developed in the famous work of Alonso (1964), and was further developed by Mills (1967) and Muth (1969). The use of this model in applied studies became widely spread in the 1970s and 1980s as reviewed by Pettersson (2001). Fujita (1989) presents a unified framework for the use of the bid rent model in analysis of urban land use as well as city structure.

According to this approach, a rent gradient law can be formulated. This law claims that small households are likely to be found in the centre of an urban region, while large households are more likely to be found far away from the central parts of the urban region. Assume that the utility of a household is defined to be a function of consumption of a composite good c and the size of the housing unit b. The choice problem of the consumer is then:

$$\max U = u(c,b) \tag{1.2}$$

$$\text{st: } y = c + P(d)b + R(d)$$

where y is household income, P is the price on housing that depend on the size b at location d, and R is the rent per square metre that depends on the distance d between a location and the urban city centre. The utility-function is assumed to be concave and differentiable at least twice. The corresponding Lagrange equation for this problem is:

$$\max_{\{c,b,d,\lambda\}} L = u(c,b) - \lambda\left(c + P(d)b + R(d) - y\right) \tag{1.3}$$

where the maximisation conditions are:

$$\begin{aligned} \frac{\delta L}{\delta c} &= \frac{\delta u}{\delta c} - \lambda = 0 \\ \frac{\delta L}{\delta b} &= \frac{\delta u}{\delta b} - \lambda p(d) = 0 \\ \frac{\delta L}{\delta d} &= -\lambda\left[\frac{\delta P}{\delta d}b + \frac{\delta R}{\delta d}\right] = 0 \\ \frac{\delta \lambda}{\delta \lambda} &= c + P(d)b + R(d) - y = 0 \end{aligned} \tag{1.4}$$

Given that $\lambda \neq 0$ we can conclude that $\frac{\delta P}{\delta d} = -\frac{\delta R}{\delta d}\frac{1}{b}$. The decision made by the household is optimal, if the marginal change in housing price with respect to distance from the metropolitan centre is equal to the marginal change in rent with respect to distance divided by housing quantity. This implies that small house-

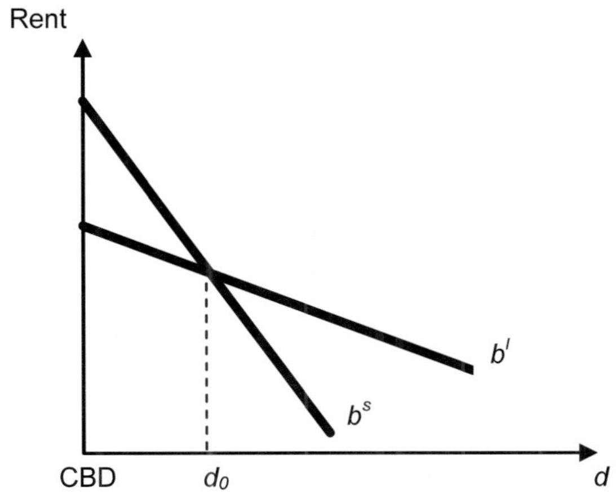

Fig. 1.3. The rent gradient for small and large households

holds, demanding little b, will tend to locate closer to the metropolitan centre compared to larger households (demanding larger quantity of housing), assuming equal household income levels. The bid-rent curves for the two types of household units are depicted in Fig. 1.3, where $b^s < b^l$.

According to the model, we could assume that small households in the normal case will be found in the central parts of an urban region, while large household units at some given income level will be found on a longer distance from the metropolitan centre. In Fig. 1.3 the interception between the two rent gradients (bid-rent curves) indicate the location (distance from CBD) that serves as a dividing point in the urban region. If $d < d_0$, b^s dominates, and beyond d_0, b^l dominates.

In reality there are a large number of bid-rent curves intersecting each other almost continuously distributed over distances. The housing rent structure of a metropolitan unregulated market would be found as the upper envelope of these bid-rent functions. An illustration is given by Fig. 1.4.

1.4 Urban Housing Markets, Rent Structure and Prices

There are both differences and similarities between the metropolitan areas included in this study. For example, rent regulation regimes have been present in all regions during the post-war era. This form of policy has also gone through different phases and today second or third generations of rent regulations are found in many of the metropolitan regions. The regulation regimes of today should be understood in a historical perspective. Rent controls on housing were introduced in most European countries during both world wars in order to prevent landlords from taking advantage of the scarcity problems (Ellingsen and Englund 2003). In general, the first generation of rent control is a ceiling on rents. Such regimes were abolished or replaced by a second generation of rent control after the wars that allowed for gradual increase of rents reflecting changes in construction costs and the general price level. In the 1980s and 1990s, several second generation rent control regimes were abolished or transformed into a third generation form of rent regulation (Turner and Malpezzi 2003). In the current regimes it is common that rents are regulated within the tenure, but unregulated for new tenants by 'tenancy rent control' (Arnott 2003).[4]

The rent control regimes on the housing markets in Europe can be characterised as more or less flexible, which is typical of the second and third generations of rent regulation. These regimes allow rents to adjust with respect to changes in the market. In several of the metropolitan regions landlords are allowed to charge market rent on newly built or vacant apartments, according to the third generation of rent control policy. This means that the rent gradient adjusts in direction towards the market level, and settles on a level between a complete regulated market and a free market. Arnott (2003) analyses the effects from the third generation of rent control. Recognising the imperfections that are likely to be found in the housing market, Arnott argues that a well-designed control regime can be welfare improving. Nevertheless, Arnott states that the economic outcome of a regulation regime will depend on the details of such programme, the situation on the market, and security of tenure. Arnott makes the important assumption of comparing an unregulated market with a third generation rent regulation system.

One can still question the use of third generation rent control from the perspective of economic efficiency. The housing markets of European metropolitan regions do not start from an unregulated situation. This means that we cannot assume that the regional housing markets are in a stable equilibrium (Wijkander 2003). Thus, the Arnott approach is not applicable. In addition, the use of a third generation rent control regime will have effects on the allocation of apartments, in particular in a dynamic perspective. Even if willingness to pay for housing is considered, when apartments are turned over on the market, there will be efficiency losses in the long run, due to the fact that tenants will stay on in their apartments, although there are other households in the market having a larger willingness to pay for the same apartment.

In two of the metropolitan regions analysed in this study, Oslo and Helsinki, the rent regulation has been removed during the last decade. Social housing as well as non-profit housing companies has different positions in different regions and countries. In Fig. 1.4 the rent gradients of the metropolitan regions are considered with distinction between regions with second and third generation of rent control, versus the free rental structure.

A free market regime is assumed to be found in e.g. Oslo and Helsinki. In Amsterdam, Milan, Vienna, Zurich there are restrictions on profits for significant parts of the rental markets i.e. a third generation type of rent control. Stockholm

[4] Our definition of first, second and third generation of rent control regimes follows Ellingsen and Englund's (2003) definitions. Not all schoolars use this destinction, some times second- and third generations are refered to as one and the same generation of rent control regimes (for example in Arnott 2003).

represents a case of second generation of rent control.

A comparison of the rent gradients for these three types of regimes reveals substantial differences in rent structure between the metropolitan regions. Fig. 1.4 shows that in the strongest regulated market – Stockholm – the rent does not change at all with respect to location. The rent level is in fact the same in the centre of the city as in peripheral parts of the region (locations in the 'C-ring' of the region). Moving to less regulated markets we find more substantial differences in the rent level, corresponding to the gradient law of bid-rent theory, which stipulate relatively lower rents in peripheral locations to compensate for the higher transportation costs.

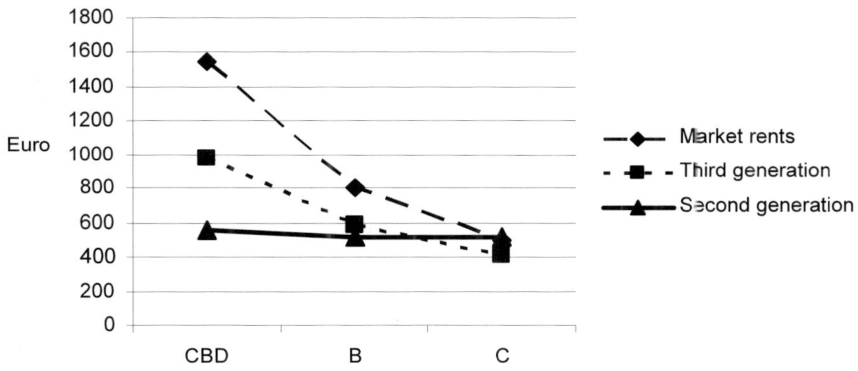

Fig. 1.4. Rent gradients for apartments with 3 rooms in a selection of European metropolitan regions 2000/2001, average rent per month (Source: Temaplan 2003)

The studies of the different cases presented in this volume show that macro- as well as microeconomic conditions are important for local and regional housing markets. In order to more clearly analyse the importance of the two levels we use an example with three different types of regions. Firstly, there are large metropolitan regions. Secondly, there are medium-sized regions, which we can refer to as 'normal regions'. Thirdly, there are small regions, especially in peripheral locations. We also assume that housing companies are locally owned and can only act on the local market. We further assume that rents are strictly regulated according to the equilibrium level of housing market of the 'normal region'. The situation in the different regions can then be illustrated as in Fig. 1.5.

If the rent is regulated to the same level in all types of regions, housing companies in each market are assumed to adjust their decisions according to the marginal revenue. Starting from a short- and long-run equilibrium, where the inelastic supply is equal to demand, an excess demand situation will be established in the large metropolitan regions. The situation will be the opposite in small regions, which means that the supply of housing will adjust towards a lower level, where marginal revenue equals marginal cost. If we assume that there is a rental housing monopoly in the small regions, profit maximisation will correspond to a lower level of supply, which means that a regulated market will yield a monopolistic outcome in the small regions.

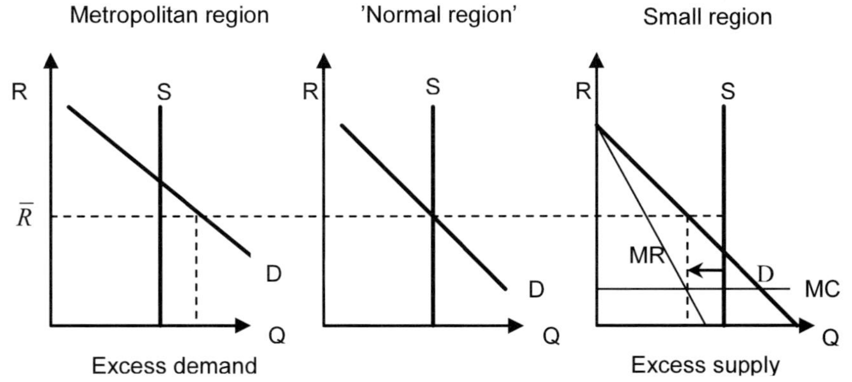

Fig. 1.5. Effect from a 'pure' rent regulation in different regions

This example shows that housing companies in both 'normal regions' and small regions could be willing to accept the outcome of rent regulation. From the point of view of housing companies rent regulation will not be harmful. Actually they may be supporters of a regulating regime as in the case of Sweden. If the housing companies in small and 'normal' regions are larger in number than the housing companies of large metropolitan regions, then the association of landlords would likely favour rent regulation. In the long run housing supply will be reduced in the small regions while there would be a permanent excess demand in the large metropolitan regions (and the possible emergence of a black market).

1.5 Size, Diversification and Risk

The presence of economies of agglomeration that is very much in focus within 'new economic geography', explains how metropolitan regions often serve as 'engines' of economic growth. There are a large number of studies that point to this phenomenon. Quigley (1998) offers an overview of the literature on how urban size and diversity causes economic growth. In their seminal book 'Economics of Agglomeration – Cities, Industrial Location and Economic Growth', Fujita and Thisse (2002) stress the impact of urban diversity on regional development. The building block for models in this field rests on considerations of monopolistic competition and the presence of increasing returns to scale. From this theoretical fundament it is clear that the size of the local market is one important factor stimulating regional development. This means that regional growth and development is to a large degree an endogenous self-reinforcing process. Large metropolitan regions can be expected to have a faster economic development, compared to small and peripheral regions, given that congestion and other diseconomies of scale are not significant problems.

According to 'economics of agglomeration' we can expect investments in the housing markets of large metropolitan regions to give a low risk, compared to housing investments in small regions. The small regions can in general be assumed to have a weaker and more risky demand for housing. This means that the risk and expected return on housing investment would be different in different size classes of regions. The required expected return on investment will thus be larger in small regions (corresponding to a higher β-value) and lower in large metropolitan regions (corresponding to a lower β-value). This is illustrated in Fig. 1.6, where the security market line is also depicted. r_m and r_f denotes the return on the market and the risk-free rate respectively. The market risk premium is defined as $(r_m - r_f)$.

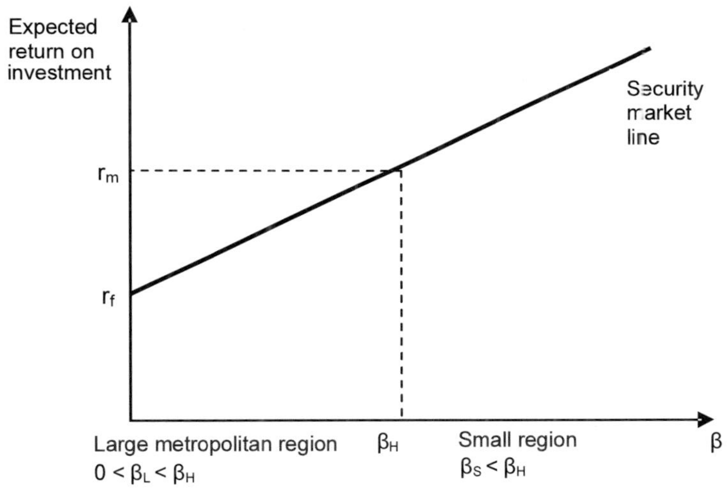

Fig. 1.6. Risk and expected rate of return

Given that housing companies are able to act on all regional markets, they will be able to adjust their portfolio of housing assets in such way that the problem of specific market risk from regional markets can be reduced. If housing companies cannot act on different regional markets they will face an enclosure-risk. This is an obvious problem of housing companies owned by local authorities. Local housing companies suffer from enclosure-risk and face higher returns, required in the markets for loans.

A housing company enclosed in the regional market will not be able to diversify the asset portfolio in the same way as a large real estate company operating in all regional markets. A large real estate company, e.g. Castellum that has a nationally diversified portfolio of real estate in Sweden, has a β-value for its share that equals 0.34 as of March 2004. If we assume that A in Fig. 1.7 corresponds to Castellums position, showing also the expected rate of return on the company's portfolio, we can conclude that a housing company that is politically enclosed into a local market will face a request of a higher expected rate of return (compare A with B).

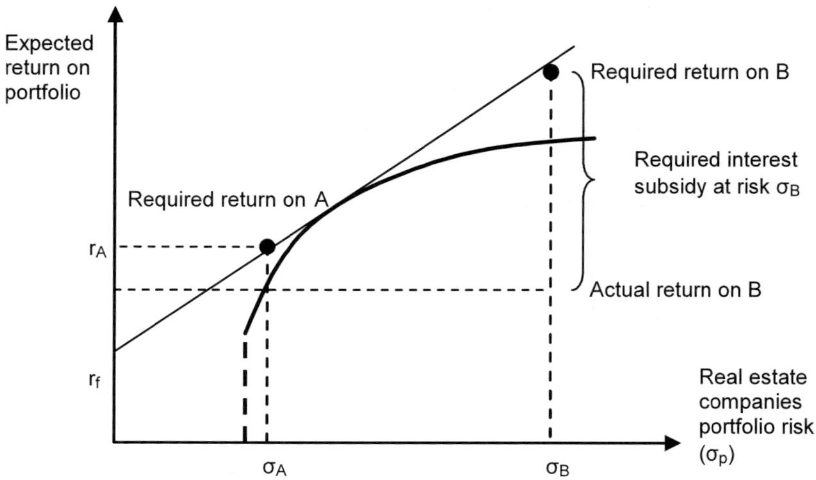

Fig. 1.7. Risk and interest

1.6 An Empirical Overview

The metropolitan studies of the twelve metropolitan regions are based on the concept of 'Functional Urban Region' (FUR). One way to define a FUR is to measure the common labour market interaction. A FUR can then be defined as the geographical area in which people are daily commuting between their homes and working places, and buy their perishable consumer goods and services (Johansson, Strömquist and Åberg 1998). A FUR can also be assumed to have a role as central place in a hierarchical order of metropolitan regions, following the central place theory and the rank size rule (Dicken and Lloyd 1990).

The geographical definitions of the metropolitan regions in this volume use the NUTS-2 level for Copenhagen, Amsterdam, Stockholm, Helsinki, Vienna, Oslo and Zurich. NUTS-1 level is used for Hamburg, and NUTS-3 level is used for Munich, Brussels (both defined as three NUTS-3 regions) Glasgow and Milan. The largest of these markets in terms of population is Milan with close to 3.8 million inhabitants and the smallest is Oslo with approximately 1 million inhabitants. The population of the twelve metropolitan regions is given in Fig. 1.8.

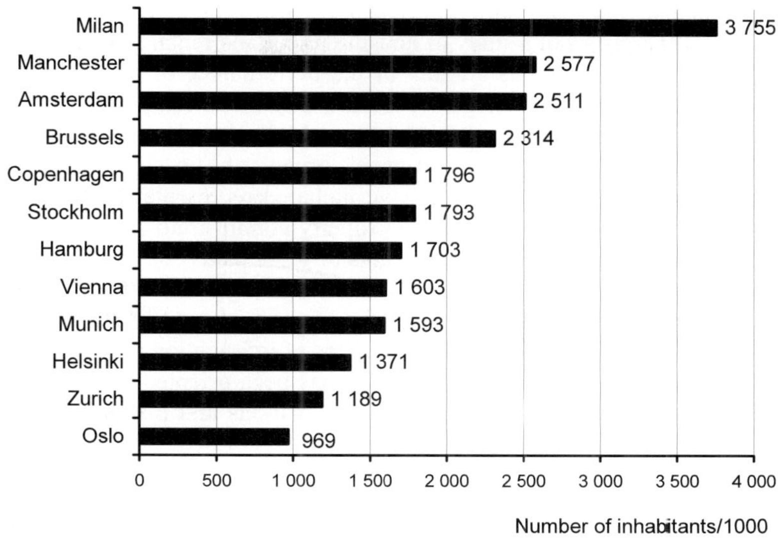

Fig. 1.8. Population of twelve metropolitan regions (Source: Eurostat)

In the comparative analysis we have abstained from includes the two largest metropolitan regions in Europe – London and Paris. Because of the size and extreme spatial density of these regions they would require special analysis, as provided in the book on London by Cheshire (2004).

In our comparative analysis we employ an approach borrowed from industrial economics with a subdivision of the analysis into three related stages structure–conduct–performance. The basic idea of this approach is that the structure of a market will influence economic behaviour by companies as well as households. The structure can be described as market conditions, market growth, forms of competition and control. The consequence of this behaviour can be observed in the form of development of prices, quantities exchanged, constructed and maintained and development of patterns of location and choice of space.

The comparative analysis is subdivided into four consecutive stages, relevant for the housing market. Stage one is focused on nationally determined constraints on the behaviour of metropolitan housing markets in general. This is based on the assumption that the metropolitan housing markets are highly dependent upon the macroeconomic conditions of the larger national environment in which the metropolitan region is embedded. More specifically, economic growth in terms of GDP and national disposable income has a major impact on housing demand. Similarly, financial conditions in terms of general inflation, rate of interest and macroeconomic policies as well as taxation and national housing policies would have an impact on the structure and performance of metropolitan regions.

The second stage focuses on special macroeconomic conditions of the metropolitan region, which in certain respects can deviate from the national characteristics. Some of the regions have experienced rapid population growth as well as rapid expansion of the human capital stocks, while other regions have experienced tendencies to stagnation.[5]

The third stage consists of a study of housing prices and rental structure.

The fourth and final stage is a study of the performance of the metropolitan markets in terms of economic efficiency, accessibility and social performance.

The basis of this comparative analysis is given by the bench-marking presented in this volume and hearings with expert panels organised in each one of the metropolitan regions. These expert panels have included representatives of regional and national broker associations, housing property administrators and regional or local chambers of commerce. The participants of these panels have independently replied to two different surveys covering the situations of their specific housing markets. A third type of information is gathered from national and regional statistical databases. As a complement to these sources of information two special studies have been conducted. One of these studies has been oriented to housing laws and other formal institutions regulating housing markets and planning in the regions. The other special study has been oriented to a study of taxes and taxation laws, regulating behaviour of the participants in the housing markets. The time-frame of these studies has been the period 1990 to 2001.

1.6.1 National Economic Conditions

There are considerable differences in the national macro-economic conditions in the countries of the compared metropolitan regions. The differences are considerable primarily in terms of national growth of population and GDP and partly as a consequence of this in the rate of inflation, interest rates and household savings. Our basic assumption is related to these variables in the sense that a fast rate of growth of population and GDP will give rise to a rapid increase in private consumption expenditures of households, possibly also in increases of household savings and reduced stability of prices. The combination of increasing household expenditures and a lowering of the real rate of interest if inflation is insufficient controlled by interest rates will stimulate housing demand as well as housing investments. A generally high rate of growth has primarily been observed in the Netherlands with its primary metropolitan region Amsterdam, in Finland (Helsinki) and in Norway (Oslo). The national rates of growth in the period 1995–2000 are given in Fig. 1.8 and the he prime importance of GDP growth for the growth of private consumption is illustrated by Fig. 1.9.

The rates of inflation have differed substantially during the time period analysed. Rates of inflation higher than 10 per cent have been observed in the three rapidly growing economies and in Italy and Britain. This has of course had an impact on the real rate of interest but not as great as one might have expected. Helsinki has for instance had a real rate of interest of around 4 per cent, while Amsterdam, also growing rapidly, has managed to keep the real rate of interest below 3 per cent. Fig. 1.10 gives the average long-term real rates of interest.

[5] NUTS-3 level data has been used for most metropolitan regions. In some cases more appropriate data was available and, hence, used.

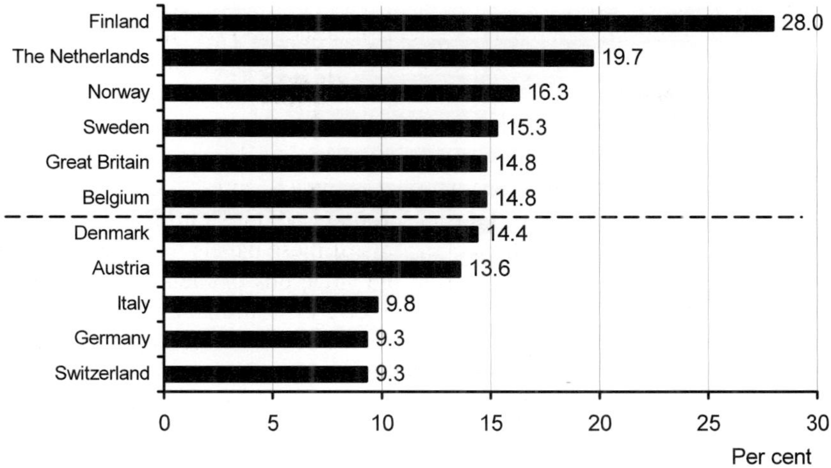

Fig. 1.9. National rates of growth of GDP 1995–2000 (Source: OECD)

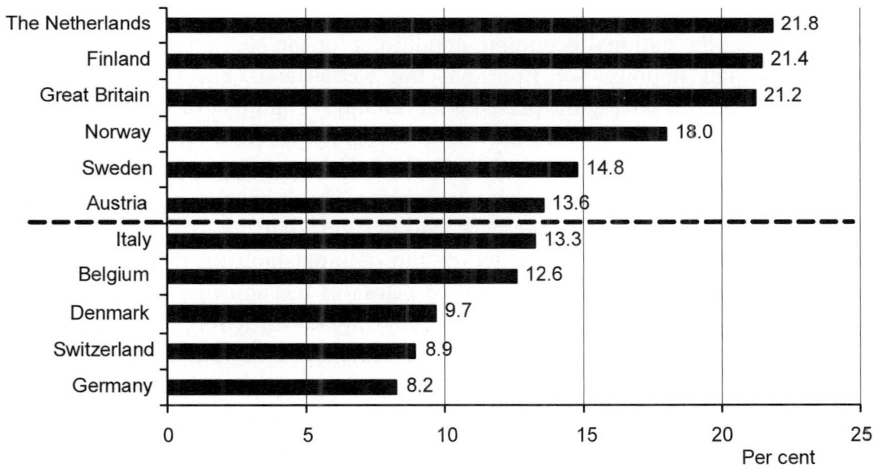

Fig. 1.10. National growth of private consumption 1995–2000 (Source OECD)

The long-term real rates of interest have an impact on the real rate of interests ruling in the housing market. Countries like Switzerland and Netherlands, keeping a low rate of real interest, also have correspondingly low real rates of interest on newly emitted mortgage loans, while Italy and Sweden have had high rates of interests on housing loans. But there are also exceptions. Belgium, with a relatively low real rate of interest, belongs to the high rate of interest countries in the mortgage loan market.

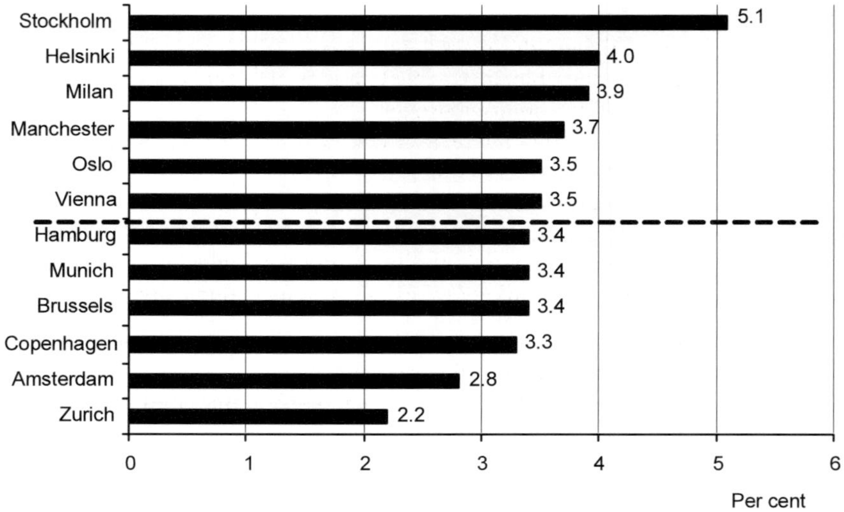

Fig. 1.11. Average long-term real rates of interest, 1995–2000 (Source: ECOWIN)

Aggregating the national economic conditions for the Netherlands and thus for the metropolitan regions, we find that the Netherlands has the best macro-economic conditions during the period with relatively high rate of growth of population, GDP, private consumption, low real rate of interest and relatively high savings rate among households. Finland and Great Britain have also been in a relatively favourable situation in these respects. The opposite macro-economic conditions have been ruling in Denmark, Sweden and Italy.

In the analysis of the performance of the national housing markets we have concentrated the study on development of prices in the housing market, transactions, and gross investments in housing and housing construction.

Amsterdam has according to the European Mortgage Federation seen the fastest growth of prices in the housing market, while Germany saw declining levels of housing prices in the period 1995–2000. Information on the development of prices has not been available for Italy and Switzerland. The activity in the housing market is not only reflected in the growth of the price level, where Netherlands, Norway, Finland and Great Britain has seen the fastest rate of growth. The dynamics of the housing market is also reflected in the transaction volumes, i.e. the rates of change of ownership of housing units. Transactions have grown the most in Italy, Finland, Sweden, Great Britain, the Netherlands and Norway, while the transaction volumes have decreased in Germany and Denmark.

The growth of the housing stock is primarily influenced by housing construction. Housing construction in terms of the number of produced housing units per thousand inhabitants has varied very much between the different countries of the study. The average number of constructed dwellings has exceeded 5 per thousand inhabitants in Austria, Germany, Netherlands and Finland, but has been as low as 1.4 dwellings per thousand inhabitants in Sweden during the study period

(European Mortgage Federation). Housing construction costs have gone up extremely much in Great Britain during the study period (58 per cent) but the expansion has also been considerable in the Netherlands, Denmark and Norway and moderate to low in the other countries studied.

There is a relatively obvious interaction between the national macroeconomic conditions of the housing markets and the development of these markets in terms of the performance indicators used. With a limited number of observations the econometric analysis of these interactions are out of the question. However, simply aggregating the macroeconomic conditions and the indicators of the activity levels of the national housing markets we can draw a few conclusions:

1. The Netherlands, UK and Finland provided the best macroeconomic conditions for their metropolitan housing markets.
2. Sweden and Italy have had the worst macroeconomic conditions for their metropolitan housing markets.
3. Belgium has had a combination of average macroeconomic conditions and very low activity on the national housing market.
4. The analysis supports the view that macroeconomic conditions and the activity in the housing markets have a positive relationship.

1.6.2 Regional Economic and Housing Development

The size of the metropolitan regions relative to the nation as a whole differs between the European countries. Metropolitan regions in small countries like Denmark and Finland have a population share around 30 per cent of the national population, while the German metropolitan regions of Hamburg and Munich only account for 2–3 per cent of the German population. This implies that the interaction between the regional and the national economic development is much stronger in the smaller countries.

In the northern and most sparsely populated countries of Europe there was a substantial change of the population distribution of the countries in favour of the metropolitan regions. During the 1990s the population of the Helsinki, Stockholm and Oslo regions increased by 12, 11 and 10 per cent, while the population of densely populated metropolitan regions in Germany and the south of Europe was more or less stagnant.

The general level of consumption prices differs between the metropolitan regions of Europe. The Union Bank of Switzerland provides consumption price indices, based on comparisons of the prices of 110 consumer goods. Fig. 1.12 presents the price index of these consumer goods in the year 2000.

As can be seen from the figure the metropolitan regions of the small Nordic countries and Switzerland had the highest consumer prices. In spite of the very high price level in Oslo, that region belongs to the highest income group of the European metropolitan regions included in the study.

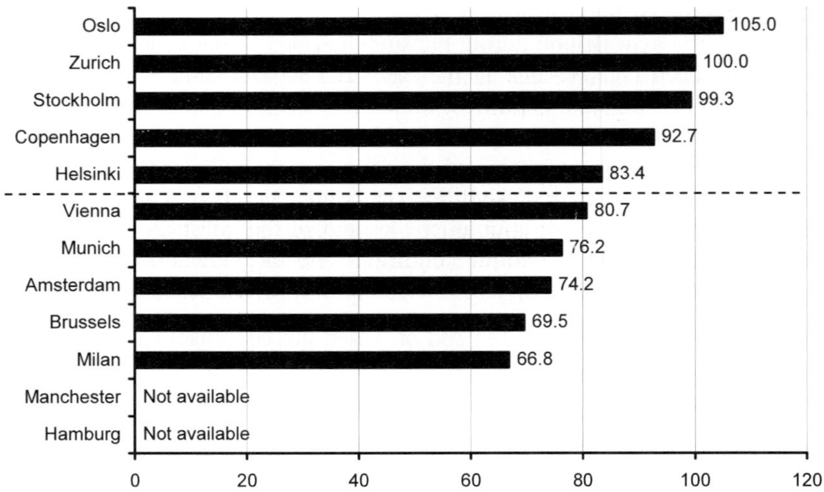

Fig. 1.12. Local price index for metropolitan regions 2000, excluding housing, Zürich=100 (Source: UBS 2001)

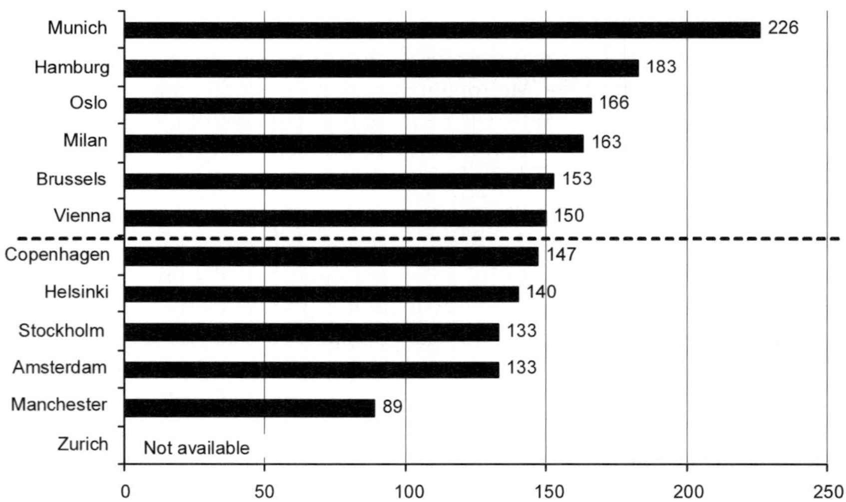

Fig. 1.13. Gross regional product per inhabitant (PPP) 1999, EU15=100 (Source: Eurostat)

Fig. 1.13 provides information on the purchasing power parity corrected estimates of gross regional product per inhabitant of the metropolitan regions at the end of the 1990s.

The economic conditions have been rapidly improving in the Nordic and Dutch metropolitan regions in the period studied. This has obviously implied a rapid expansion of the demand for housing in these regions.

1.6.3 Metropolitan Supply of Housing

There are substantial differences in the composition of housing supply in the different metropolitan regions of Europe. In some regions like Vienna, Milan, Hamburg, Zurich and Munich, multi-family housing dwellings comprise four fifths or more of the total metropolitan housing stock, while more than 50 per cent of the housing stock is in single-family housing in Amsterdam, Brussels and Oslo. This implies that the density distribution differs very much between the European metropolitan regions. The growth of housing supply has been very fast in Helsinki, a region that has had rapid economic growth supporting growth of demand. Housing supply has also grown in Oslo and Amsterdam, while the growth of supply has been rather limited in Stockholm and Manchester – two regions having seen rapid economic growth in the 1990s. In most of the metropolitan regions the supply of single-family housing units has been growing more rapidly than the general supply of housing, indicating suburbanisation of the metropolitan regions of Europe. A survey with the participants in the regional expert panels indicates that housing construction activities have been declining after the year 2000 in most of the European metropolitan regions. This is illustrated by the following figure.

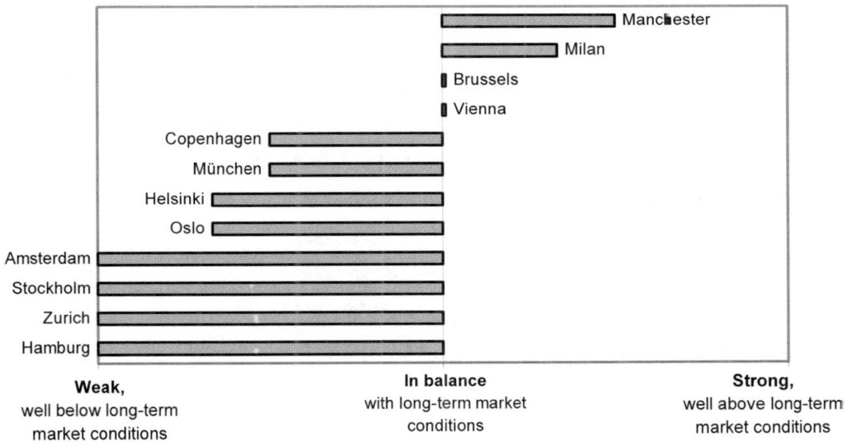

Fig. 1.14. Current housing construction activities 2001/2002 (Source: Regional panels of experts 2002)

There does not seem to be any strong relation between increasing demand by growth of real income and increases of supply of housing in the metropolitan regions. Only in the few cases where national as well as regional macroeconomic conditions have been favourable are there any clear signs of adequate supply responses in the housing market.

1.6.4 Differences in Construction Costs

Of great importance for the supply responses to increasing housing demand are the construction costs. These differ very much between different European regions according to different empirical estimates after the year 2000. A study by Gardener and Seabold (2003) indicates that building costs (excluding taxes and cost of land) ranges from €900 per square metre in Amsterdam to building cost close to €2,000 per square metre in British and German metropolitan regions. Another study by Temaplan is shown in Table 1.1.

Table 1.1. Total building costs for multi-family housing 2002, Euro per square metre excluding taxes and land costs

Metropolitan regions	Cost interval
Oslo	1700–2050
Copenhagen and Vienna	1450–1850
Stockholm	1300–1650
Helsinki and Zurich	1050–1250

Source: Housing cost study, Temaplan AB 2002.

Especially in Britain high cost of construction would dampen increases in supply by construction activity. In Cheshire (2004) the combination of high cost of construction, sluggish supply and rapid increases of housing prices in the London metropolitan region is analysed.

1.6.5 Prices and Rents

Prices of real estate are not subjected to any special regulations in Europe. As in any other asset market the level and development of real estate prices are determined by (1) the level and growth of the capital stock, (2) the level and growth of demand, and (3) expectations about future profits and dividends in the real estate market.

These three factors influencing prices of housing estates all contribute to the large variance in prices between European metropolitan regions. This large variance is illustrated by Fig. 1.15. As can be seen from Fig. 1.15, the highest prices are recorded for the high income regions of Munich and Zurich and for Helsinki, which has had a rapid economic growth in the 1990s. The prices of owner-occupied apartments show a similar pattern of variation. This is illustrated in Fig. 1.16.

Munich and Zurich are also in this case in the group of the highest prices, while Brussels has a price level of less than 40 per cent of the prices in Munich. The prices differ even more for owner-occupied apartments in the most attractive, central locations. For such apartments the price was around €6,000 per square metre in Amsterdam and Munich, while similar apartments were sold in 2001 for a price of €1,840 per square metre in Brussels.

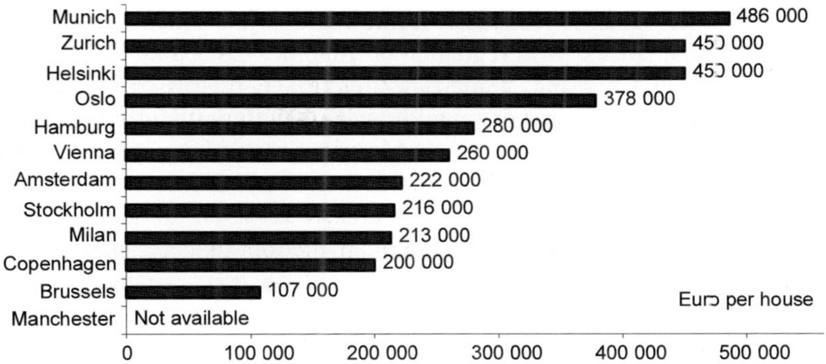

Fig. 1.15. Average price of single-family houses in Europe 2001 (Source: Regional broker organizations 2002)

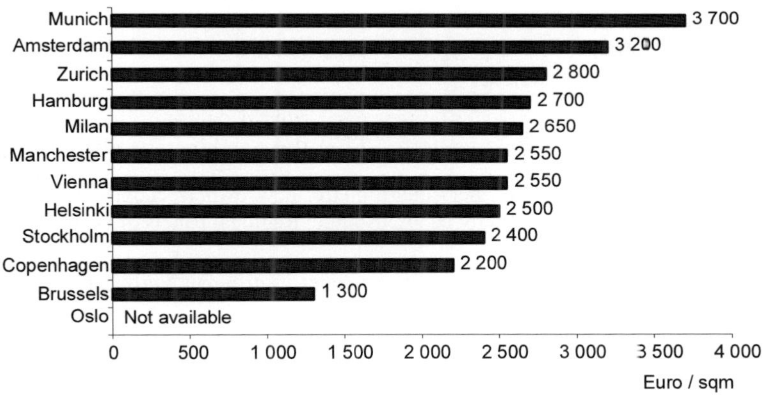

Fig. 1.16. Average price of owner-occupied apartments 2001. Three rooms and kitchen of normal standard (Source: Regional broke organizations 2002)

The dynamics of the housing market is closely related to the prices of housing units in the 'second-hand market' and the prices of new housing units. This ratio – Tobin's q – varies considerably between the different regions. This is illustrated in Fig. 1.17.

As can be seen from Fig. 1.17 the prices of new apartments is considerably smaller than the prices recorded in the second-hand market in Zurich and Munich, indicating incentives to invest in new property. The opposite is the case in e.g. Brussels and Copenhagen.

While pricing in the owner-occupied parts of the metropolitan markets are determined in the market without any price regulation the opposite is true of practically all European rental housing markets. Markets with very limited price regulation are Brussels, Helsinki, Oslo and Manchester. Stockholm is the metropolitan region in Europe with the hardest form of rent control. The metropolitan regions also differ in the relative role of non-profit rental housing suppliers, as well as regulations of profits on rental housing. Some regions like Amsterdam and Copenhagen have rental stocks, with regulated profitability exceeding 80 per cent of the total stock of rental housing, while other regions, e.g. Brussels and Helsinki have much less than 50 per cent of rental housing supply without constraints on profitability. The combination of profitability constraints and the character of rent regulation are illustrated in Table 1.2.

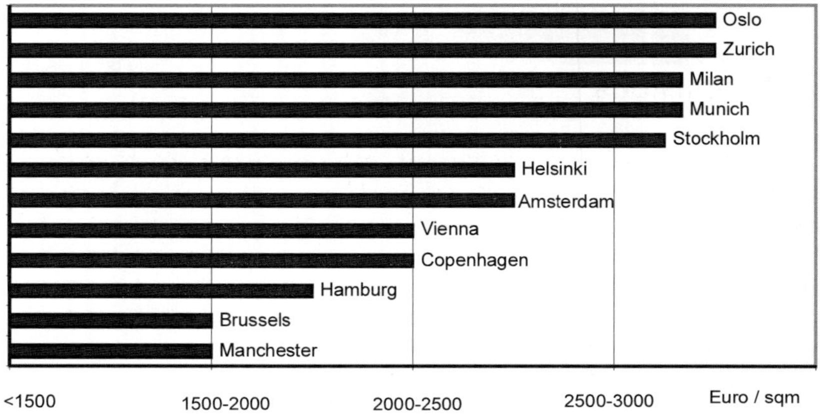

Fig. 1.17. Market price 2001/2002 per square metre, new owner-occupied two bedroom apartment middle class district, not city centre (Source: Regional panels of experts 2002)

Table 1.2. Degree of rent control and profit constraint in different European metropolitan regions

Rent control	Small relative share of profit constraint supply	Large relative share of profit constraint supply
Soft	1. Brussels, Helsinki, Oslo, Munich, Hamburg	2. Amsterdam, Manchester
Hard		3. Copenhagen, Milan, Zurich, Vienna, Stockholm

As illustrated in Table 1.2 a combination of hard rent control and a small share of profit constraint supply is virtually nonexistent.

In summary the following conclusions are warranted:

1. The analysis of the different metropolitan housing markets corresponds very well with conventional theory of housing- and urban economics.
2. There exist a European political consensus on the need for some controls in the housing the housing market.
3. However, the instruments of control differ between metropolitan regions and countries.

4. Systems for rent controls are slowly moving towards softer forms of regulation with an increasing impact of market incentives.
5. The distance gradients of rents are substantially smaller in regions with strict forms of rent control compared to regions where the rent control is more oriented toward market incentives.
6. Prices of housing units differ considerably with peaks in the regions having experienced rapid economic growth.

1.7 Conclusions

The population growth varies significantly between the metropolitan regions. Fast growth regions are Oslo, Helsinki and Stockholm during the 1990s. In these regions the population growth was around 10 per cent between the years 1990 and 1999. This growth rate was twice as large as the other metropolitan regions. In Munich and Milan there were hardly any population growths at all during the period. There was even a decrease of population in these two latter regions during the second half of the 1990s.

The growth of real GDP was similar to the population growth. However, the absolute level of purchasing income per capita in 1999 (measured as real gross regional product) was reduced for Munich (226 per cent of EU average) and Hamburg (183 per cent of EU average). The other regions of the study had a level of income between 30 and 66 per cent above the average of EU15.

Inflation figures and price comparison between regions made by Union Bank of Switzerland shows that the regional price level to a large extent correlates with the national price level. Taking into account the disposable income and the general price level of the metropolitan regions (net wages divided by price level), we find that this real income index is comparably high in Zurich, Munich, Amsterdam and Brussels before housing expenditures are accounted for. This means that the real income to be used for other goods and services, besides housing, is correspondingly high in these metropolitan regions.

Amsterdam, Oslo, Helsinki and Vienna have all had favourable macroeconomic conditions as well as relatively strong regional growth performance during the 1990s. Further more, Milan, Hamburg and Brussels have experienced weak macroeconomic development combined with weak regional growth in the 1990s. The remaining metropolitan regions of Stockholm, Copenhagen and Munich had a combination of weak macroeconomic performance at the national level and a comparable strong regional growth and other advantageous local conditions for the housing market.

An overview of the metropolitan markets of this study shows that both the national macroeconomic and the regional growth conditions appear to be important factors determining construction activities in the regions. For example, in some cases construction activity is low although the demand for housing has been expanding in the regional markets. Evidently, one must also consider construction cost, when analysis of construction activity is made. According to Gardiner and

Theobald (2003) the cost of construction was around 1600–2000 Euros per square metre in 2002 for Hamburg, Munich, Milan and Copenhagen.[6] The corresponding cost was between 1200 and 1500 Euros in Oslo, Stockholm, Helsinki, Zürich and Brussels. The lowest construction cost per square metre was found in Amsterdam 2002, and was then 900 Euros. From the observations, we can conclude that there is a significant variation between the metropolitan regions in terms of construction costs.

Data on costs of newly constructed apartments in metropolitan regions of the same size in the US range between a costs of 500 to 800 Euros per square metre. This price range is so much lower than the price range in our study that there is a reason to believe that European housing construction is inefficient. This degree of inefficiency can only be explained by market failures, such as cartelisation, excessive political constraints in physical planning and lack of competition in the building material markets.

In relation to the observation concerning differences in construction costs it is relevant to stress questions also regarding market competition within the EU. In national markets with a low degree of competition and, few dominating construction companies, one can assume construction prices to be set at monopolistic levels. Since new construction in general is a small fraction of the total housing stock, a small change in the demand for housing will then likely cause a sharp increase in the demand for new construction, given that there are no vacancies on the market. This means that a metropolitan construction market would normally be relatively sensitive to changes in the demand for housing.

Housing has attracted political attention in most countries. Much of this attention by policy makers has been focused on the metropolitan regions because of the population size and long-term growth of these regions. The durability of housing capital as well as the fixed location of houses once built has caused site rents to become an issue of political importance.

Market equilibration requires rents of attractive housing in central locations to increase with the growth of the metropolitan region as a whole. Many European policy makers have neither been in favour of the market economy nor seen any other advantages of a large spatial differentiation of housing rents. Quite to the contrary, rent control was politically introduced during the two world wars with the explicit aim of avoiding inflation and redistribution of wealth. Once introduced, rent control tended to be conserved long after the wars.

The extended rent controls turned out to generate a number of problems not associated with a housing market with free rent setting. Among these problems the following are generic:

- Black market transactions of apartment contracts.
- Inefficient choice of quality level.
- Inefficient repair and maintenance of apartments and rental houses.
- Reduced rental-housing investments.
- Urban sprawl.

[6] Construction costs, excluding VAT and costs for land.

- Discrimination of newcomers on the housing market.
- Conversion of rental units into other uses than rental housing.

A consequence of these problems has been a successive softening of the rent controls in the European metropolitan housing markets. However, the speed of softening of the control system has been highly differentiated. In a few cases – Stockholm, Copenhagen and Amsterdam – housing is still quite politically regulated, while the housing sector has become almost fully market regulated in the British, Norwegian, Belgian and Finnish metropolitan regions.

The major arguments for political controls are today oriented to the presumed reduction of segregation, caused by control of rents and assignment of apartments. However, recent studies of segregation show that rent controls have little effect on the degree of segregation (Hårsman and Quigley 2004; Glaeser 2003). The case studies reported in this book give ample evidence of the greater importance of macroeconomic factors such as income growth, working of the money markets, inflation, and employment policies for the outcome of housing consumption.

References

Alonso W (1964) Location and Land Use. Harvard University Press. Cambridge Mass.

Anas A (1997) Rent Control with Matching Economies: A Model of European Housing Market Regulation. Journal of Real Estate Finance and Economics 15(1): 111–37

Arnott R (1995) Time for Revisionism on Rent Control? Journal of Economic Perspectives 9: 99–120

Arnott R (2003) Tenancy Rent Control. In: Ellingsen and Englund (ed) (2003) Swedish Economic Policy Review. The Economic Council of Sweden

Chan YK, Russell R (1997) A Term Structure Model and the Pricing of Fixed Income Securities. Salomon Brothers

Cheshire P (2004) The British Housing Market: Contained and Exploding. Urban Policy and Research 22(1): 13–22

Cheshire P, Magrini S, Medda F, Monastiriotis V (2004) Cities are not Isolated States. In: Boddy M, Parkinson M (eds) City Matters. The Policy Press, Bristol

Deng Y, Quigley J, van Order R (2000) Mortgage Terminations, Heterogeniety and the Exercise of Mortgage Options. Econometrica 68(2): 275–307

Dicken P, Lloyd P (1990) Location in Space. Theoretical Perspectives in Economic Geography. Third edn., Harper Collins, New York

DiPasquale D, Wheaton WC (1996) Urban Economics and Real Estate Markets. Prentice Hall, New Jersey

Dunn K, McConell J (1981) Valuation of GNMA Mortgage Backed Securities. Journal of Finance 36: 599–616

EcoWin (2002) Economic data. http://www.ecowin.com

Ellingsen T, Englund P (2003) Rent Regulation: An Introduction. In: Ellingsen T, Englund P (ed) (2003) Swedish Economic Policy Review. The Economic Council of Sweden

Eurostat (2003) Regional and General Conditions. European Commission

Fujita M (1989) Urban Economic Theory, Land Use and City Size. Cambridge University Press, Cambridge

Gardiner and Theobald (2003) International Construction Cost Survey. http://www.gardiner.com/Economics/cost_papers.asp
Glaeser E (2003) Does Rent Control Reduce Segregation? In: Ellingsen T, Englund P (ed) (2003) Swedish Economic Policy Review, The Economic Council of Sweden
Glaeser E, Henry SGB (2003) The Misallocation of Housing Under Rent Control. American Economic Review 93: 1027–46
Gould JR, Henry SGB (1967) The Effects of Price Control on a Related Market. Economica 34: 42–49
Johansson B, Strömqvist U, Åberg P (1998) Regioner, Handel och Tillväxt [Regions, Trade and Growth]. Regionplane- och trafikkontoret. report 6, Stockholm
Hårsman B, Quigley J (1991) Housing Markets and Housing Institutions: An International Comparison. Kluwer, Dordrecht
Lindh H (2001) Rent Regulation: A Conceptual and Comparative Analysis. European Journal of Housing Policy 1: 41–58
Lindh H (2003) Rent Regulation and New Construction: With a Focus on Sweden 1995–2001. In: Ellingsen T, Englund P (ed) (2003) Swedish Economic Policy Review. The Economic Council of Sweden
Mills ES (1967) An Aggregate Model of Resource Allocation in a Metropolitan Area. American Economic Review 57: 197–210
Muth RF (1969) Cities and Housing. University of Chicago Press, Chicago
Nguyen TT, Whalley J (1986) Equlibrium Under Price Controls with Endogenous Transaction Costs. Journal of Economic Theory 39: 290–300
OECD (2003) World Development Indicators. Organisation for Economic Co-operation and Development
Patruno GN (1994) Mortgage Prepayment: A New Model for a New Era. The Journal of Fixed Income. December, pp 42–56
Pettersson L (2001) Location, Housing and Premises in a Dynamic Perspective. Ph.D. thesis, JIBS Dissertation Series No. 10, Jönköping International Business School
Regional Broker Organizations (2002) Survey for the Housing Cost Study. Temaplan AB Stockholm. http://www.temaplan.se
Regional panels of experts (2002) Survey for the Housing Cost Study. Temaplan AB Stockholm. http://www.temaplan.se
Stanton R (1995) Rational Prepayment and the Valuation of Mortgage-backed Securities. The Review of Financial Studies 8(3): 677–708
Stanton R (1996) Unobservable Heterogeneity and Rational Learning: Pool-specific Versus Generic Mortgage-backed Security Prices. Journal of Real Estate Finance and Economics 12(3): 243–63
Temaplan AB (2002) Housing Cost Study. Temaplan AB Stockholm. http://www.temaplan.se
Temaplan (2003) Benchmarking av Stockholms Bostadsmarknad [Benchmarking of the Housing Market in Stockholm]. Temaplan, Stockholm
Turner B, Malpezzi S (2003) A Review of Empirical Evidence on the Cost and Benefits of Rent Control. In: Ellingsen T, Englund P (ed) (2003) Swedish Economic Policy Review. The Economic Council of Sweden
UBS (2001) Annual Review 2001. UBS Switzerland
Weibull J (1983) A Dynamic Model of Trade Frictions and Disequilibrium in the Housing Market. Scandinavian Journal of Economics 85(3): 373–92
Wijkander H (2003) Comment on Richard Arnott: Tenancy Rent Control. In: Ellingsen T, Englund P (ed) (2003) Swedish Economic Policy Review. The Economic Council of Sweden

2 An Analysis of the Housing Market in Greater Brussels

Didier Baudewyns

Free University of Brussels, Brussels

2.1 Introduction

This chapter presents an analysis of the housing market in the greater Brussels area. On June 18, 1989, with the election of its first parliament, the region of Brussels-capital (19 centralised 'communes' or municipalities with almost 1 million inhabitants) was created. On January 1, 1995, it was removed from the province of Brabant in order to get more autonomy. The Parliament of BCR is in fact a regional council that may vote orders, but not decrees (or laws a fortiori). The remaining part of the old province of Brabant was itself split into two independent provinces: Flemish Brabant and Walloon Brabant that have been incorporated into, respectively, Flanders – 5.9 millions inhabitants, one of the most prosperous regions in Europe – and Wallonia (3.3 millions inhabitants), the traditional manufacturing-based region.

The area analysed in the next sections is defined as three NUTS regions (NUTS code in parenthesis): Brussels-capital region (BE 1), Flemish Brabant (BE 24) and Walloon Brabant (BE 31). The entire district of Hal-Vilvoorde and some north-western municipalities of Nivelles (such as Waterloo) are the immediate suburbs of Brussels. Leuven (eastwards) and a majority of municipalities of the district of Nivelles (southwards) are more distant outskirts of the capital city, Brussels (see the map below). For purpose of exposition, let us adopt the following notations:

- BCR = Brussels-capital region = 'central-city' (162 km^2)
- WB = Walloon Brabant = Nivelles district
- FB = Flemish Brabant = Hal-Vilvoorde district + Leuven district
- FB + WB = suburbs
- Metropolitan area analysed = BCR + FB + WB (3,358 km^2)

BCR is bilingual (French/Dutch) with a majority of French-speaking inhabitants (about 85 per cent according to some estimates). It comprises the capital city of Belgium (central commune of Brussels with 135,000 inhabitants) and also hosts the headquarters of NATO and numerous European Union institutions: the European Commission since 1958 (about 14,000 civil servants), the European Parliament since 1992, the Committee of Regions since 1994, the Council of the European Union, the European Economic and Social Committee. In total, about 20,000 international civil servants live in greater Brussels. BCR also welcomes more than 120 international governmental organisations and around 1,400 international non-governmental organisations on its territory. With 159 embassies and 2,500 diplomats, Brussels is also the second largest diplomatic city in the world only after Washington, DC. Since more and more important decisions are made at the European level, it is not surprising that many lobbying organisations have chosen to locate near the 'European' central business district.

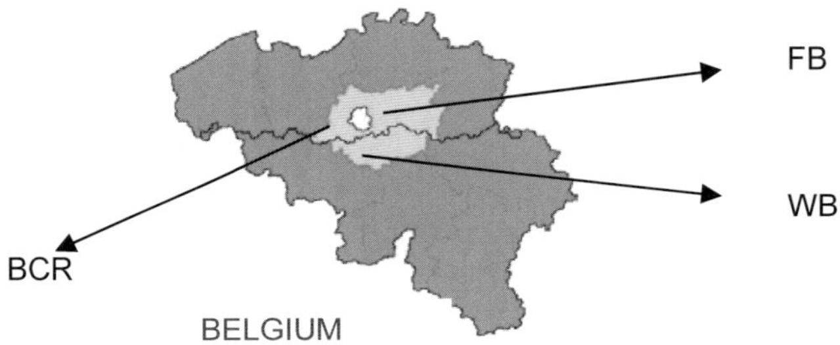

Fig. 2.1. The area analysed

Between 1961 and 1995, the share of immigrants has been multiplied by five, from 6 to 31 per cent. Among the 260 thousands foreigners living in BCR in 2001, about 54 per cent (or 140 thousands) are of an EU-country origin, 21 per cent (or 55 thousands) are Moroccans and 6 per cent (or 16 thousands) are Turks. About 90 thousands foreigners live in the suburbs (WB + FB) among whom 62 thousands are EU-foreigners and only one thousand Turks and 5.3 thousands Moroccans. On the other hand, there are more US residents in the suburbs (3,672) than in BCR (3,038). Clearly, the residential urban space is segregated by ethnic groups: from 1960 on, non-EU immigrant workers from Turkey and Morocco have gradually filled those dwellings in central areas left by middle-class Belgians. This reinforced the existing segregation by income (see next Sect.).

According to some European comparisons, BCR would be one of the most productive regions of Europe in terms of GDP per capita. However, this is misleading because the metropolitan region we must consider is larger than BCR (many central-city workers reside outside the 19 central municipalities). The correct indicator is the GDP per capita (in PPPs) for the whole metropolitan area, i.e., BCR + FB + WB; one then finds that greater Brussels has a GDP per capita equal to 1.5 times the EU15 average (see Table 2.1), i.e., below the GDPs per capita of

Hamburg, Munich or Milan.

The total labour force living in the whole metropolitan area is equal to 925 thousands workers, half of them being employed in the central city. 86 per cent of the working residents of BCR are employed in their own region. We infer that about 360 thousands people commute to the central-city. The manufacturing industry (including construction) accounts for 15 per cent of the total employment in BCR, the rest being employed in the business services sector (58 per cent) and non-business services (27 per cent) (Bayenet and de Bruycker 2003).

Table 2.1. Key indicators of the metropolitan area

	Greater Brussels (BCR+WB+FB)	Central-city (BCR)
Population 2000-12-31 (1000)	2334.8	964.4
Foreigners 2000-12-31 % (1000)	351.2 (15)	262.8 (27)
Population increase % 1979–1990	1.4	–4.8
Population increase % 1990–2000	3.6	0.4
Population increase % 1995–2000	2.2	1.5
Unemployment 2000 %	6.7a	11.1[b]
Labour force 1999 (1,000)	925	340
(% working in BCR)	(51)	(86)
Total employment in 1999 (1,000)	1128.7	660.9
Regional GDP 1999 (millions €)	76695	
Regional GDP per capita 1999 (€)	33125	
GDP per capita 1999 (in PPP) EU15=100	153	
GDP growth, constant prices % per annum 1995–99	3.4	

[a]Weighted average of different NUTS regions. The labour force is used as weights.
[b]Bayenet and de Bruycker (2003), Table 2.1.
Sources: Cambridge Econometrics, except population and labour force; own calculations made on data from National Institute of Statistics (NIS), National Bank of Belgium (NBB 2002) and IRIS–Bres (Brussels Region 2000).

The remainder of the chapter is organised as follows. The next section analyses the housing market in both the central-city and the suburbs: we present the recent evolution of the housing stock, taxation, cost of capital, spatial price structure and demography. Sect. 2.3 reviews the major housing problems facing the BCR's government while Sect. 2.4 reviews the main lines of the regional housing policy. Sect. 2.5 concludes.

2.2 The Market for Housing in Greater Brussels

Already during the rapid and impressive industrialisation of Belgium, between 1830 and 1870, the upper class of Brussels gradually left the central municipalities to reside in the immediate eastern suburbs near the Forêt de Soignes. At that time, the manufacturing industry, followed by its workers, moved from the canal area to the north-western suburbs. Between 1830 and 1846, the population of some suburban municipalities was multiplied by four (Robert and Jones 1999 p. 262). In 1900, the central city of Brussels contained 30 per cent of the 560 thousands people in its metropolitan area while in 1800 about three quarters of the population was centrally-located (Robert and Jones 1999 p. 262). Between 1865 and 1900, several planning projects promoted and even designed by King Leopold II himself, transformed definitely Brussels into a modern 'capital city' with long avenues connecting the centre to the decentralised eastern rich 'green' municipalities. In particular, Louise Avenue was 'a magnificent road that leads to the Bois de la Cambre where the Art Nouveau flourished at the end of the century ...' (Robert and Jones 1999 p. 22). It is interesting to note that many large houses – including art nouveau masterpieces – that were built around 1900, look today as if they will last indefinitely.

This suburbanisation has in fact continued until fairly recently – thus for more than one century – and was even reinforced by several political decisions or passive attitudes regarding the housing market. First, as pointed out by Donner (2000): 'The First Housing Law of 1889 ... tried to stabilise the political situation and improve sanitary conditions by developing an anti-urban vision of owner-occupied housing for workers and government support to reach this ideal'.

More recently, in the 1960s and 1970s, the development of an automobile-based transportation system, extremely dense and efficient around Brussels, combined to a favourable tax treatment of owner-occupied housing (and even of car ownership!) have accelerated the decentralisation of residents. Moreover, a generous zoning approach caused probably an excessive decentralisation of residents. Finally, real low gasoline and energy costs has also probably induced some inefficient home (and job) locational decisions but of course this is common to all developed countries (see Mills and Hamilton 1994 p. 415). Still, according to Goossens et al. (1999) p. 276: '... Belgium has 'led' suburbanisation to the extreme form of this phenomenon'.

2.2.1 Housing Stock by Urban Area and Tenure: 1981 and 1991

Table 2.2 gives the stock of occupied dwellings at two moments: the 1981 and 1991 Censuses. The Brussels housing market is obviously spatially segmented. The central city (BCR) is characterised by a high proportion of flats (77.4 per cent) and a majority of renters (62 per cent) whereas in the suburbs dwellings are generally owner-occupied single-family houses or villas.

In 1991, 42 per cent of the housing stock in BCR was built before 1945 which is 10 percentage points above the EU average but is lower than the Belgian average equal to about 50 per cent (Donner 2000 p. 536).

In BCR, it is impossible to know precisely whether the number of dwellings increased or decreased between 1981 and 1991 because of a high number of 'non-responses' in 1991. Following Goossens et al. (1999), we have made our analysis on available data, thus assuming implicitly a uniform distribution of 'non-responses' in the population. About 30,000 dwellings were not occupied in BCR at that time (not in the table). Since then, due to the lack of precise statistics, it is difficult to assess how many of these dwellings have been demolished.

Table 2.2 also indicates that the rate of homeowners in the central city has grown between 1981 and 1991, from 31 to 38 per cent. NIS has published recently some preliminary results of the General Socio-Economic Survey (2001) showing that the home ownership rate would be around 43 per cent nowadays. According to the last Regional Development Plan (PRD)[1] preliminary report, this movement is due to several reasons: '– purchases by young households that settle in central Brussels; – purchases by foreigners (immigration and international civil servants); – the 'noodaankoop' phenomenon – i.e., necessary purchase for lack of finding, on the rental market, a dwelling suited to both financial situation and needs' (PRD Preliminary Report 2001 Sect. 7.2). The latter observation may indicate the existence of discriminatory practices (see Sect. 2.3).

Table 2.2. Occupied housing stock by area, tenure and size

	BCR		Suburbs (FB + WB)		Total	
	1981	1991	1981	1991	1981	1991
Total, thereof:	453.8	460.1	430.0[a]	493.4	883.8[a]	953.3
– unfilled forms (1000)	0.015	65.5	–	18.3	–	83.8
– available data (1000)[b]	453.7	394.5	428.2	475.1	881.9	869.5
% owner-occupied	31	38	70	72	50	57
% built before 1919	24	17	21	16	22	17
% built 1919–45	31	25	21	15	26	19
% built in 1971–81	11	13	23	22	17	18
% built after 1981	–	2.8	–	12	–	7.7
% transformed 1971–81	5.3	5.6	8.5	–	6.9	–
% transformed 1981–91	–	5.3	–	7.5	–	6.5
% of flats	81	77	18	17	50	45
% < 55 sqm	39	38	16	18	28	27
sqm per dwelling	71	74	87	91	78	83

[a]Own estimate.
[b]Analysis made from these dwellings.
Sources: own calculations made on data from NIS, Population and Housing Census 1981 (Tome 2: Recensement des logements 1986) and 1991 Census (Tome 2B, Recensement des logements par commune 1993).

2.2.2 Intraregional Housing Rent and Price Structure

In Belgium, the rental price of housing services is decided freely between the tenant and the owner (generally) in a three-year contract. During the lease, the rent is fixed but the landlord may index it each year under some weak conditions (a letter to the tenant is normally sufficient). The rent can be changed by the owner each

[1] Plan Régional de Dévelopement. The second regional development plan project was approved on July 19, 2001 by the Brussels region.

time he signs a new contract so that rental prices at any moment are closed to market prices (see also Donner 2000 p. 136).

The standard theory of urban residential location predicts that in a monocentric urban (free) economy, the price per unit of housing and land rent decline with distance to the central business district (CBD) in order to compensate suburban residents for higher commuting costs (bid rent theory). At the border of the metropolitan area, urban land rent falls to the value of agricultural land. As a corollary, dwelling (households) density and the capital-to-land ratio – i.e., the height of buildings – also decrease with distance since higher land costs near the CBD cause a substitution of capital for land. If central areas have not a strong amenity advantage on suburbs it is likely, although far from certain, that richer households will prefer to locate at more distant sites where they consume more square metres of floor, more land (mainly backyards) and possibly better environmental amenities (see Brueckner et al. 1999). However, the pattern will be reversed if high-income households have a high opportunity cost of commuting time and (or) if the city centre has superior amenities, historical, environmental or cultural – as in Paris, for example (see Brueckner et al. 1999).

All these predictions have been tested in the empirical urban economic literature (see e.g. Mills and Hamilton 1994, Chap. 6). The bid rent theory is generally verified. However, the tendency for high-income households to live in the outer outskirts is less pronounced in European cities where historical centres are often more pleasant to live in (at least compared to American downtowns). In Brussels, even though the average income of residents increases actually with distance, many EU high-income civil servants have chosen to live near the 'Cinquantenaire Park', i.e., in the vicinity of the 'European' CBD (70,000 employees working there in 1991). Using the hedonic-price econometric method we could also check that in Brussels, the average rental price of flats declines with distance to the European CBD as shown by Fig. 2.2.

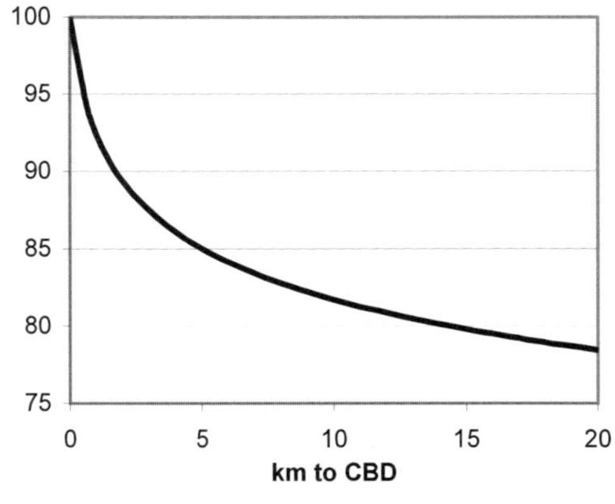

Fig. 2.2. Rental price for flats in Brussels 1991, CBD = 100 (Source: Baudewyns 1998 p. 63)

At 5 kilometres from the CBD, rents are 15 per cent lower than in the CBD. In the suburbs (i.e., beyond 15 kilometres), the rent function becomes relatively flat.[2]

There is no index of property values per unit of housing for the whole metropolitan area (for an index of quality-adjusted house price in BCR, see below). For want of anything better, researchers in Belgium use data from the National Institute of Statistics yearly publication on real estate sales which gives both the number and the total value of dwellings sold in each municipality. We can hence easily derive the average price of properties sold but we do not have any information on dwelling sizes or other structure variables. These data will be used later to analyse the evolution of the housing market in recent years but we can already attempt to check the standard urban location theory from these data. Indeed Fig. 2.3 gives for each suburban district the ratio of average house price to house price in BCR.

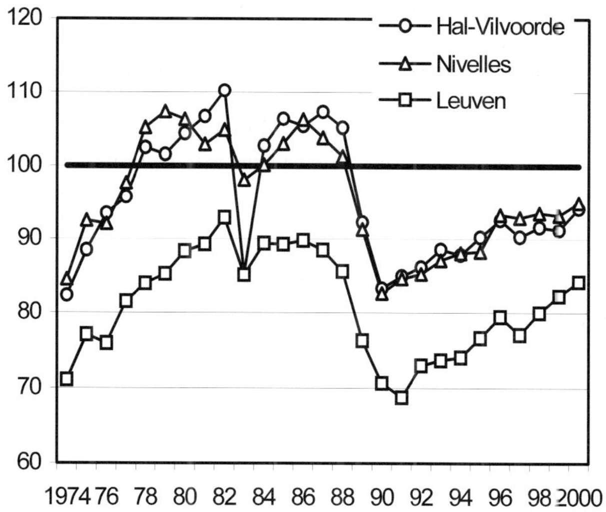

Fig. 2.3. Relative prices of suburban family-houses, central-city = 100 (Source: NIS: Statistiques financières, 'Ventes de biens immobiliers')

Clearly, property values are lower in Leuven, i.e., at the more distant outskirts. Since the average square metres of floor space per dwelling and housing quality are similar in both Leuven and Hal-Vilvoorde (89 and 90 square metres per dwelling, respectively), we conclude that the higher the distance from BCR, the lower

2 Notice however that the rental price in the municipality of Zaventem was in 1991 significantly higher than the average rent in the suburbs (+ 60 per cent): this is not surprising since this municipality hosts the Brussels Airport and is the second business district of the metropolitan region in terms of employment (27 thousands workers at the time of the estimation above). There is thus a 'secondary business district' effect and competition for land translates in higher rents (with the exception of the immediate neighbourhood of the airport where noise pollution reduces property values at about 69 per cent of the suburbs average).

the price of a single-family house (per square metre of floor space). Note that prices in the suburbs have recently been converging to the BCR level after the dramatic drop in relative prices between 1988 and 1992. This drop is in fact a trivial mathematical (reverse) expression of the dramatic increase of real estate values in the central-city during that period, as will be explained later.

This spatial rent structure is confirmed in the next table: the price of a flat located in BCR was, in 2000, equal to €1,200 per square metre on average whereas it was €956 in the suburbs. Also observe that land rent is significantly lower in the suburbs as predicted by the standard theory. Moreover, higher income households tend to live in more suburban locations. The city-suburb income ratio is equal to 0.82 which is close to the same ratio computed for the south and the west of the US in the beginning of the nineties (see Hamilton and Mills 1994 p. 417). As in US cities, despite longer commutes, higher income households actually prefer more distant sites where they can consume more land and, in their eyes, superior environmental amenities.

The Walloon municipalities in the immediate suburbs of Brussels are the richest of Wallonia and in 1998, the average taxable income (per statement) in the Nivelles district was equal exactly to the one in Hal-Vilvoorde: €27,437 (Leuven: €26,187). We will come back later on the recent evolution of incomes and its implication for the central city.

Table 2.3. Comparison of city-suburb real estate rent and income

	Average amounts in 2000 [€]	
	Central-city (BCR)	Suburbs
Single-family house (value)	113,400	103,200
Family-house: price/sqm	1,400 [a]	1,080
Flat (value)	77,400	71,800
Flat: price/sqm	1,200	956[b]
Land rent/acre (1999)	6,540	5,170
Per-statement taxable income (1999)	22,300	27,000

[a]CEPI, cited by Confederation Construction Bruxelles-Capitale, annual report 2000 p. 65.
[b]The average size of flats built in 1998 outside BCR is used in the calculation: 75 m^2 (NIS)
Source: own analysis made on data from NIS, Ventes de biens immobiliers, 2001; NIS Population and Housing Censuses, 1981 and 1991 plus assumptions on the evolution of the size of dwellings – unless otherwise stated.

2.2.3 Cost of Capital and Taxation

As is true for any other commodity, the demand for housing depends on price and income. The price that is relevant for the demand for housing is the rent per unit of housing. The relationship between property price and rent is one of the most important notions in housing economics. It is in principle straightforward. Neglecting taxation for the moment and assuming that the rental market is competitive, the annual rent *R* will cover annual cost as follows:

$$R = (i + c - g)V \tag{2.1}$$

where i is the interest rate, V is the value of the house, cV operating costs (maintenance, repair, utilities, insurance) and gV the expected capital gain net of depreciation.[3]

Now, the cost of renting tends to be higher than the cost of owner-occupied dwelling for the simple reason that many homeowners use work on the house as a hobby and better maintain their capital (O'Sullivan 1996 p. 382). Moreover, in Belgium as in many other developed countries, the above relationship is further complicated by the existence of taxation. Rental housing and owner-occupied housing are treated differently by the fiscal authority (see below). The taxes levied on real estate have been regionalised with the main exception of the VAT levied on construction costs (see below). Mortgage interests are income-tax deductible up to certain amount as will be made clear below. Belgium's position in this respect is intermediate between Australia, Canada, Britain where interest deductibility was eliminated, and Spain where tax relief is full and imputed rents have been suppressed in 1998 (see The Economist March 28, 2002).

Registered rent

In Belgium, any dwelling is considered as an asset producing housing services and yielding revenues. Consequently, an imputed rent called 'cadastral' revenue is calculated by the tax authority. This registered revenue serves as a base to a 'real estate advance payment' which is de facto a property tax since it is no more reimbursed by the tax department. It is income taxable and defined, on a given land lot, as 60 per cent of the rent normally obtained from a house built on that lot during the last year of reference which is 1975 (!).[4]

Cadastral revenues are indexed only since 1991. As a result, imputed rents are far below market rents. For example, in 2001, the value of a one-bedroom 100 square metres flat in Ixelles (a middle-class residential municipality in BCR) is about €190,000: the cadastral revenue after indexation is equal to 1.2857 × 1,859 = €2,390 per year, while the rental price of such a flat is around €8,000 per year. The total property tax (regional tax plus additional taxes paid to the municipality of Ixelles) for 2001 is equal to 36 per cent × 2,390 = 860 Euros or about 10 per cent of the market rent (0.45 per cent of the asset value in this example).

The effective total 'property tax'rate (regional tax rate of 8.6 per cent plus local additional tax rate) may vary significantly from one municipality to another. The average for the 19 central municipalities is 40 per cent. The property taxes paid by suburban residents are generally below the BCR's average amount for two reasons. First, cadastral revenues have been estimated at a time when land rents were declining even more strongly than today with distance from the CBD. Secondly, local additional property tax rates are lower in the immediate suburbs, Flemish or

[3] To simplify, these costs and gain are assumed to be proportional to value.

[4] If such a rent cannot be estimated for the land lot in question, it is established by comparison to other neighbouring houses.

Walloon (by about 8 percentage points).

Since incomes are lower in the central areas, local additional 'land' taxes are perceived as a source of inequity. Moreover, the whole system of real estate taxation – being based on 1975 land values – is not fair since it has not taken into account yet the gradual downward shift of the rent curve (rent as a function of distance) in those relatively poor central areas.

Ordinary and complementary deductibility

In principle, mortgage interests deductibility is straightforward: interests on loans taken out for purchasing or retaining a house is deductible from the imputed rent. This is called 'ordinary deductibility'. However, in practice, the taxation of real estate is so complex in Belgium that advice from an expert and even computer simulations are often needed to know exactly what will be the tax saving from itemising mortgage interests.

Let us consider here the simplest case: owner-occupied housing. Any homeowner may choose not to itemise mortgage interest deductibility in order to benefit from for the lump sum deduction for unique occupied dwelling (up to the cadastral revenue). The last deduction is equal to €3,953 and does not depend on the existence of a mortgage. It is generally greater than the cadastral revenue so that housing taxation does not occur.

However, for a loan incurred for the building or the renovation of a main home, the owner will be well-advised to itemise both ordinary deductibility and the so-called complementary deductibility of mortgage interests.

First, itemising the ordinary mortgage-interest deduction allows the repayment of 12.5 per cent × cadastral revenue – which is a net advantage over the above lump sum deduction.[5]

Second, the balance of interests after ordinary deductibility (i.e., the difference between mortgage interest payment and registered revenue)[6] is used to calculate a complementary deductible amount. For example, if the cadastral revenue is equal to €1,000 and the mortgage interest payment is €6,000 then €5,000 will be taken into account for complementary deductibility. This amount must be reduced because of the existence of loan ceilings. For example, in 2001, for a tax payer without children (one child), the share of the loan taken into account is equal to about €58,000 (respectively €59,000). In our previous example, for a €100,000 loan, the amount of interest that can be deducted is simply: (5,000 x 58,000)/100,000 = 2,900 Euros. During the five first years of the mortgage, the latter amount is again reduced by 20 per cent. Hence, 0.8 x 2,900 = €2,320 will be deducted from the taxable income. After these five years, the latter amount is reduced by 10 per cent each year so that after 12 years no more complementary deduction is possible.

5 We assume that the cadastral revenue is lower than €3,953, which is generally the case for single-family houses. We also suppose that mortgage interest payments are greater than the cadastral revenue.

6 Mortgage interests must be greater than the registered revenue in order to benefit from a complementary deduction.

Under the same conditions (main home, same loan ceilings), capital repayments can be additionally deducted from taxable income.

For rental housing, the system of ordinary deductibility of interests (from imputed rent)[7] is the same with the crucial exception that complementary deductibility for main home is impossible. This means that the cost of capital is generally higher for rental housing. Since the rent paid by the tenant must cover the costs incurred by his landlord, we conclude that income taxation is more favourable to homeowners than to renters.

Some rationale for the Belgian taxation system

First, the main rationale for encouraging homeownership is the so-called renter externality: 'Because the renter has no long-term stake in the dwelling, he has little incentive to participate in everyday maintenance' (O'Sullivan 1996 p. 382).

Second, the existence of ceilings on mortgage-interest deductions is justified by the fact that it decreases the subsidy to the wealthiest households. Should tax relief on mortgage payments be full, an even larger amount of capital would be diverted to residential consumption. This would in turn create a larger gap between the marginal social benefit and the marginal social opportunity cost of housing.

Transaction costs

Yet the benefits owner-occupiers obtained from the deductibility of mortgage interests are partially offset by the existence of high transaction costs when purchasing their dwelling. For example, the purchase of a €150,000 house implies the following charges:

- Notary fees (mandatory registration of the purchase): €1,872
- Other 'mortgage' charges: €595
- Regional registration tax: 12.5 per cent × purchase price = €18,750

Total registration costs = €21,217, or 14 per cent of the market value in our example. The registration tax rate is reduced to 1.5 per cent for sales from the social housing stock and to 6 per cent for dwellings with 'cadastral revenue' lower than €745, which is typically the case of 1–3 bedroom flats in Brussels and small houses (but not typically for single family-houses or villas).[8] On January 16, 2002 the region of Flanders has reduced the registration rate to 10 per cent (and from 6 per cent to 5 per cent for low cadastral revenues). Of course, these new rates apply only to houses or land lots bought in the Flemish suburbs of Brussels.

---

[7] If the rental house contains commercial premises than the total imputed rent is equal to the registered rent plus 60 per cent of the rents really received from these premises.

[8] Notice however that since May 15, 2001 the buyer of such a flat or small house does not benefit automatically from the low registration tax rate: he must now wait until the visit of a tax inspector who will update the 'cadastral' revenue (to take into account any upgrading, extension, …). This decision has been criticised by local activists who are in charge of housing the poor in central areas of Brussels.

Moreover: '... mortgage contracts involve fees ranging between 2.1% and 4.0% of capital. Total transaction costs usually amount to 15–20% of the purchase price' (Donner 2000 p. 134). Compared to other European countries, these transactions costs are indeed very high – the highest in the European Union as a matter of fact[9] – and it is admitted that they reduce residential mobility in Belgium (see also Donner (2000 p. 145) and The Economist (March 28, 2002)). Notice however that 60 per cent of the registration taxes can be recouped if the house is resold within two years.

When building a new house or villa, the purchased land lot is also subject to registration fees while building costs paid to the construction firm is subject to the VAT levied by the federal government (21 per cent).

This complex regional and federal taxation system gives some incentives to do-it-yourself building in the suburbs. Indeed, in more distant sites, the registration outlay will be calculated on a relatively low land value while a substantial part of the VAT will be saved if the homeowner achieves the construction or renovation works himself. It is actually a well-known fact that self-building is very widespread in Belgium as pointed out by Donner (2000 p. 137).

Finally, capital gains are taxed at a 16.5 per cent rate if the house is resold within five years following the purchase (speculation tax). It can be easily shown by properly modifying Eq. 2.1 that nominal interest partial deductibility combined to the absence of capital gain taxation makes inflation the homeowner's friend – which is a widespread view. Should however the inflationary component of capital gain be taxed (as in case of speculation) then the positive effect of inflation would be substantially reduced.[10]

To sum up, compared to other types of assets, houses and apartments receive a favourable tax treatment in Belgium. Stable owner-occupancy is strongly encouraged by the system of interest deductibility and the existence of a speculation tax. All this may explain why Belgians widely consider the payment of rents to a landlord as a waste of money. They also value the greater control over one's life when being a homeowner (avoidance of disputes over lease terms, for example). The greater flexibility of 'moving at one's wish' is however dampened by the existence of high transaction costs.

2.2.4 Timely Data: Housing Prices, Population, Average Income and Housing Starts

Housing prices

Since the housing market is clearly spatially-segmented, let us analyse the evolution of house prices in BCR and in the suburbs separately.

[9] Registration costs average 3.5 per cent of market vales in other EU countries (own calculation made on 1996 figures cited by Confederation Construction 2001 p. 61).

[10] By 16.5 per cent × μ × V, where μ is inflation. On request, the author can provide the modified Eq. 2.1 that is the cost of capital for a main home with ordinary and complementary interest deductibility.

We have first used the above-mentioned NIS data on 'real estate sales' from 1974 to 2000. All real estate properties sold are divided into three types: single-family houses, large houses/villas and flats. The following chart shows the evolution of housing prices for the three types of housing since 1974.

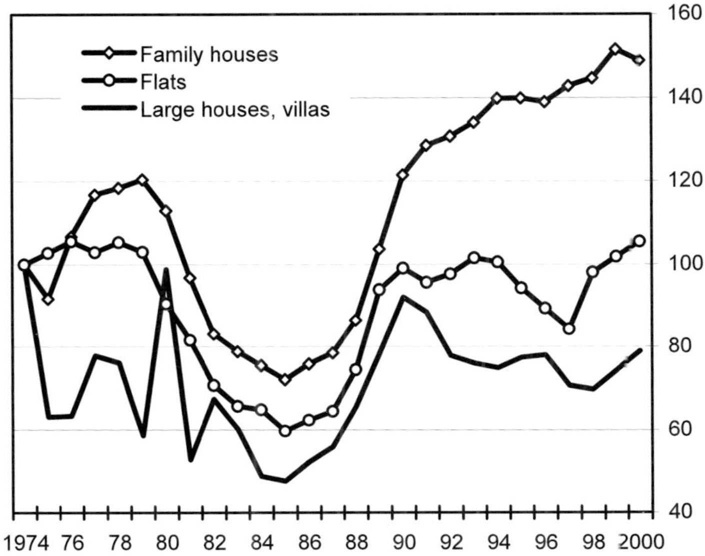

Fig. 2.4. Real average values of housing sold in BCR, 1974 = 100 (Source: Own calculations on NIS data: Statistiques financières, 'Ventes de biens immobiliers')

Note first that the exodus of high income and middle class households has translated into a sharp decline in the average value of large houses ('Maisons de Maître') and villas from the mid-seventies to the mid-eighties: in 1985 the average real price of large house was half the 1974 level. After this period of depression, real estate prices raised faster in Brussels than in other Belgian cities. This was common to many capital cities in the world but this price movement was amplified in Brussels from 1987 on by rumours on the coming of the European Parliament. In fact, the building to host the latter institution started in 1989 – i.e., well before the 'Edinburgh decision' (1992). Not only more and more large houses were gradually sold (see Fig. 2.13, in the Appendix) and converted into offices near the CBD at that period but also some real estate properties were demolished and replaced by high-rise buildings. Using the hedonic-price method, Ginsburgh and Walebroeck (1998) found indeed strong evidence of a real estate rent due to EC between 1988 and 1992.

After 1991, during the slowdown that followed the Gulf War, housing price indices fell in almost all OECD countries because central banks raised real interest rates to squeeze inflation. Since 1998, interest rates have decreased and inflation has been remaining low so that housing prices have been rising again in Spain, Britain and other countries (The Economist March 28, 2002). The picture is in fact the same in Brussels for large houses, villas and flats but not, seemingly, for single-family housing prices that have continued to rise from 1991 to 2000 (see Fig. 2.4). This is however misleading because recall that the family-house index obtained from data on real estate sales is not corrected for housing quality (not even dwelling size). Has the average quality-adjusted price of single-family houses continuously increased since 1991 unlike the other developed countries? The answer is no. Indeed, observe Fig. 2.5.

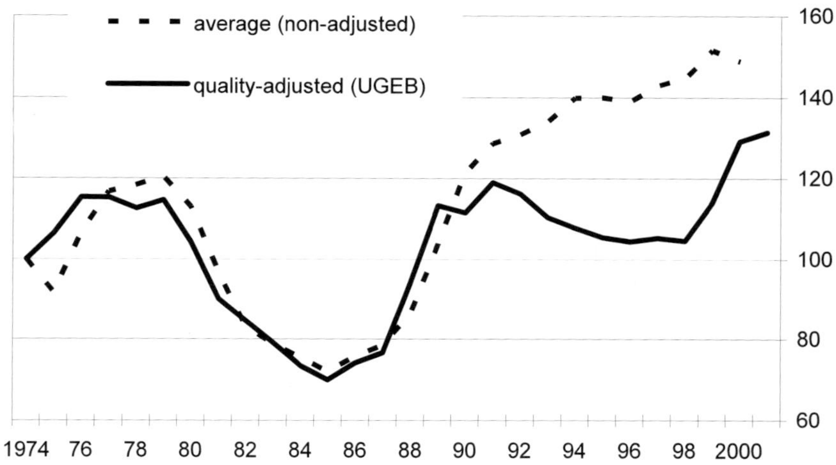

Fig. 2.5. Single-family house prices in BCR 1974–2001, real, 1974 = 100 (Sources: NIS and UGEB, mutual agreements index and own calculations; CPI: NBB 2002)

It plots the index established each year by the union of 'geometers-experts' of Brussels (UGEB) (we have corrected this index for consumer price inflation). Geometers-experts (or surveyors) transform the prices of properties sold in BCR (flats or single-family houses) into a coefficient which takes into account location, total floor space, use (commercial or residential), age, maintenance, depreciation, land lot, fittings. In short, the UGEB coefficient for single-family houses is a true quality-adjusted price index. We used the index of prices from mutual agreements solely – not public sales – since these agreements account for more than 90 per cent of total sales of both houses and estate properties. We see that real quality-adjusted prices they estimated fell after 1991 in Brussels as in many other cities or countries. From 1998 on, the real price index has continuously risen and is now well above its 1991 peak. In 2001, single-family prices actually rose 1.7 per cent in real terms after two years of sharp increases (successively +8.9 per cent in 1999 and +13.4 per cent in 2000 – in real terms).

The UGEB real price index for flats is exhibited on Fig 2.6 (mutual agreements). In 2001, the average quality-adjusted price of apartments was at its 1991 peak but still below the 1978 level – contrary to single-family houses. Actually, the sub-market for apartments has been more strongly depressed by the decentralisation of middle and upper-income households over the last 25 years simply because of the higher proportion of flats in central areas (recall Table 2.2 and see also below the section on renters). In recent years, the number of apartments sold has been about three times the number of single-family houses put on the market – which reflects the housing stock.

According to NIS, between 1975 and 1998 the size of flats built in Belgium have increased by 30 square metres on average. In 1998, the average size of a new flat in BCR (respectively in Flanders and in Wallonia) was equal to 73 square metres (respectively 83 and 68 sqm). The observed increasing gap between average values of properties sold – the dashed line in Fig. 2.6 – and the quality-adjusted price is thus not surprising.

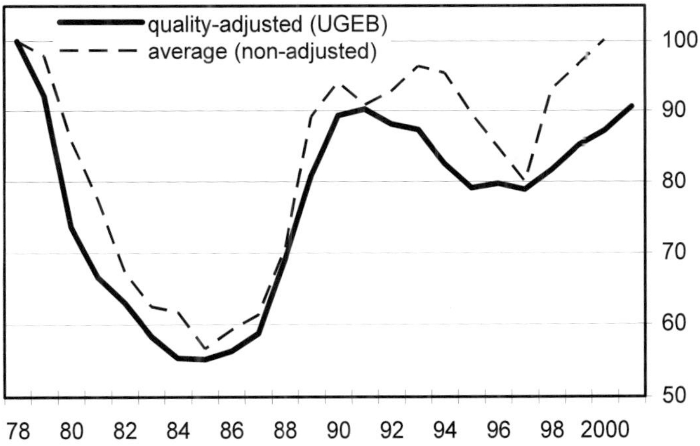

Fig. 2.6. Real prices of flats in BCR 1978–2001, 1978 = 100 (Source: Own calculations on data from NIS and UGEB, mutual agreements index, CPI from NBB 2002)

Suburbs: As far as we know, there is no index similar to the UGEB coefficient for FB + WB that would allow us to analyse the evolution of quality-adjusted property values. Still, from NIS data we have calculated, for each year of the period 1974–2000, the average price of real estate properties sold in the suburbs of Brussels (Fig. 2.14 in the Appendix). The picture is similar to the one for BCR: after the boom of 1986–91, prices of flats and villas have stagnated during six years before being pushed up again by relatively low real interest rates and a steady economic growth (GDP growth from 1995 to 1999 in greater Brussels: 3.4 per cent per year, see Table 2.1). As in the central-city, real prices of single-family houses (not adjusted for quality) have been rising almost continuously for the past ten years, with the exception of 1996–97 when house prices raised at the same pace than general inflation.

Taxable income and disposable income

Still, in contrast to BCR, we cannot reject the hypothesis of positive increases in prices per unit of housing in the suburbs during the period 1992–97. Indeed, average household incomes in suburban municipalities have grown more rapidly than in Brussels over that period. In 1995, the BCR's average real taxable income was equal to its 1991 level whereas suburban incomes rose 7 per cent over 1991–95 (Fig. 2.15 in the Appendix). The latter increase was due to two facts. First, economic growth was faster in the periphery – which employs 57 per cent of its residents.[11] Second, and more importantly, the decentralisation of high income residents was especially pronounced: from 1990 to 1995, around 18,000 people moved each year from BCR to the suburbs. In-migration from the suburbs was about 10,000 per year (BRES, Iris, Indicateurs statistiques bruxellois, Tableaux, 1994 and 2000, Tableau I.3). Interestingly enough, more and more EU-foreigners have decided to live in 'green' municipalities near the Soignes Forest, such as Waterloo, Overijse or Wezembeek. Those areas are not only highly-accessible from the city centre by car (15–20 minutes in off-peak periods) but they have also excellent public recreation and sport facilities, schools for foreigners (for example Scandinavian School and American school in Waterloo, British School Brussels in Tervuren, B. American School in Sterrebeek, Deutsche Schule Brüssel in Wezembeek-Oppem).

Clearly, the demand for housing in the suburbs has been less affected by the downturn and the convergence plan to meet the Maastricht criteria (e.g. additional 'crisis' tax of 3 per cent applied to income taxes from 1994 onwards). Actually, the number of single family houses sold in the immediate suburbs (Hal and Nivelles) increased continuously from 1990 to 1995 whereas in the central city the reversed trend was observed (see also the construction activity in the next section). As a result, land cost increased by about 32 per cent in Hal and 42 per cent in Nivelles over 1990–95 while in the same period the cost of acres sold in the central city decreased by 10 per cent. All this tends to show that the price per unit of housing probably increased between 1990 and 1997 in the suburbs in contrast to the central city.

Now coming back to incomes, Fig. 2.7 indicates that BCR has become poorer and poorer relatively to the rest of Belgium since 1979 whereas the average income in WB + FB has increased continuously. In some central municipalities of Brussels, the current average taxable income is half the national average whereas in the 1970s these areas were well above this average. Two recent surveys made by NIS show that after deducing income taxes and adding net social transfers to households, the picture is not quite different: the net disposable income of the sample-average household living in BCR in 2000 (in 1999) is equal to 92.5 per cent (89 per cent) of the national average.[12] We will come back later on the conse-

[11] In 1991–97, the real growth rate of the value added in WB + FB was 3 per cent per year on average whereas it was only 0.66 per cent in BCR (1.6 per cent for Belgium, own calculations).

[12] The average disposable income in the 2000 sample was about €302,000 for households located in BCR while it is €345,000 for households residing in Flanders. It is likely that

quences of the relative impoverishment of the central city.

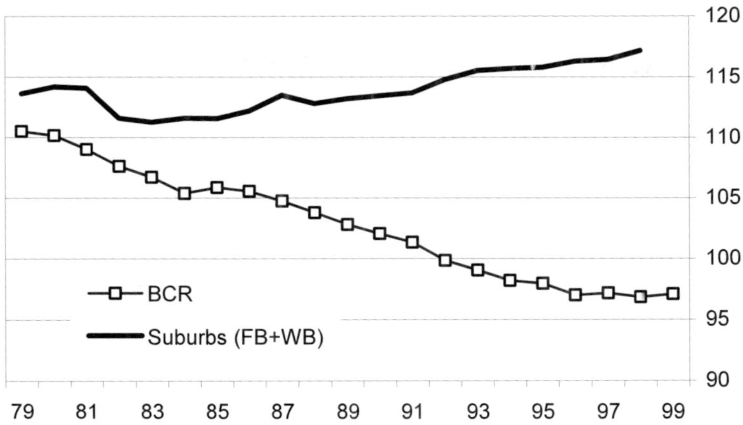

Fig. 2.7. Relative taxable income in greater Brussels, Belgium = 100 (Source: NIS, Annuaires de statistiques régionales)

Tobin's q and construction activity

In the short run, the housing stock is relatively fixed and the price of houses is determined by demand. In the long run, property prices are determined by construction and land costs. If the short-run price of housing exceeds the development costs then land developers build houses. In the opposite case, the construction activity slows down. This is verified in Fig. 2.8, which depicts the evolution of the Tobin's q index, i.e., the ratio of housing prices to construction cost. The cost index used here is the official ABEX index which is used by insurance companies, real estate experts, lawyers, etc. This index takes into account changes in VAT.

Recall the following: 'Developers try to anticipate demand one year or more in advance, so they can have enough houses available to match the demand. To the extent that anticipations are accurate, supply can increase to match an increase in demand with almost no increase in prices above the long-run equilibrium level.' (Hamilton and Mills 1994 p. 211).

The reverse works also as shown in Fig. 2.8: housing starts dropped 60 per cent from their peak in 1976 (about 6,600 units) to 1981 (2,400 units) whereas prices for houses rose only a little bit faster that the cost index. It seems that developers anticipated correctly the dramatic drop in housing demand that occurred in 1980–82. In recent years, the activity in the residential building industry has remained low in the central city; about 30 per cent of the 1974 level. Since 1999 about 2000 dwellings have been added each year in BCR, i.e. 0.5 per cent of the stock or so.

---

the latter figure is close to the average income in the suburbs and the rich Walloon municipalities of greater Brussels.

In the periphery, the level of activity over the recent years is also at about 30 per cent of the 1974 level (see Fig. 2.16 in the Appendix). Note however that the decline in the construction activity in suburban sites started in 1994, i.e. two years later in comparison with the central city because of a higher level of demand as explained earlier. From 1990 to 1994 about 7,000 dwellings were added to the housing stock each year (in total 7.2 per cent of the 1991 stock) before the construction activity dramatically dropped. Of course, from the greater land availability more houses and apartments are generally built in the periphery. In 1998, only 3,700 dwellings were built in WB + FB. On the other hand, between 1995 and 1998, the demand for single-family houses grew in the suburbs as already mentioned. Thus again it appears that developers would have anticipated correctly the surge in housing demand from 1995 on by building more houses and apartment blocks in the first half of the 1990s.

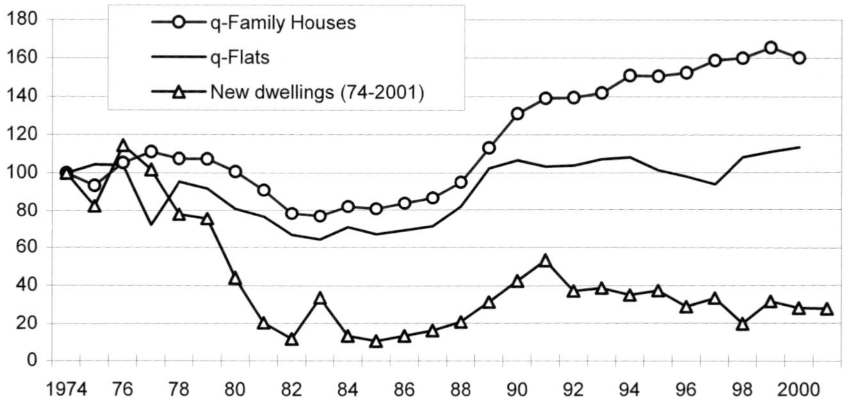

Fig. 2.8. Tobin's q and residential construction activity, BCR (Source: Own calculations on data from NIS, ABEX and NBB 2002)

Demography

From 1990 onwards, housing demand in the whole area has been partly driven by a faster population growth and a continuous reduction of the average size of households.

The average size of households in BCR has decreased continuously in the last 30 years from 2.37 in 1970 to 2.01 in 2000. Between 1991 and 2000, the number of households in BCR has increased by about 9,000 units (+1.9 per cent) but the number of families has fallen: +19,000 singles (+3.5 per cent) and –10,000 families.[13]

The population of greater Brussels grew by 3.6 per cent between 1990 and

[13] An estimated population growth equal to 2 per cent from 1995 to 2010 would cause a 14 per cent increase in the number of households: see Donner (2000) p. 138.

2000 (see Table 2.1). After a long period of decreasing population (peak in 1967), the population of the city-centre has been growing again since 1995 – still at a lower rate than the rest of the metropolitan area (Table 2.1). The recent population growth in BCR must be decomposed in three parts:

- a lower migration out of BCR to the rest of Belgium: from a balance equal to about –13,000 in 1990 to –6,000 in 1998,[14]
- a constant high level of immigration (from outside Belgium) which relates to the internationalisation of BCR (balance of about +10,000 per year in the 1990s),
- and a positive natural balance in the foreign population of BCR.

Affordability: bubble in the housing market?

There have been some concerns recently about the possible existence of some house-price bubbles in some countries that could result in sudden busts in the near future (see The Economist March 28, 2002). In those countries, the ratio of house prices to average disposable income, a measure of affordability, is actually above the late 1980s peak – i.e., the peak that was followed by a dramatic plunge of housing indices (see, for example, in Fig. 2.6, the decrease in the prices of flats in Brussels between 1991 and 1997).[15] Fig. 2.17 in the Appendix gives the ratio of housing prices to taxable income for single-family houses and apartments. Those prices are not quality-adjusted. If we assume that disposable income has evolved in the same way than taxable income then this ratio measures the evolution of housing affordability.

Is there any house-price bubble in Brussels? Observe first that in 1999, the ratio for houses is about five while it is just above three for flats, that is, well below the EU average 'global' index (flats + houses) computed by Urban Audit: 5.8.[16] This is in line with the general idea that real estate is much cheaper in Brussels than in many other capital cities in Europe. Then, if we compute the affordability index from the UGEB index, we obtain Fig. 2.9. Clearly, the price-to-income ratio has reached a new high in 2000. Single-family house prices have increased by about one per cent in real terms in 2001, so that pessimists would conclude that the Brussels real estate market is today over-evaluated. However, a sudden bust in the near future is not expected because interest rates should not rise sharply as in the early 1990s.

The optimists claim that the recent surge in house prices would be entirely justified by the anticipated EU enlargement. Actually, the European Commission has

---

[14] Thereof, the balance of migration between the central city and FB + WB: –9,000 in 1990 and –6,000 in 1998.

[15] Commenting on the recent surge in the price-to-income ratios, The Economist March 28, 2002: 'In Ireland and the Netherlands, (…) warning sirens should have been blaring as the ratio has hit new highs.'

[16] Urban Audit, European Commission 2000: the global index for Brussels (3.8) is consistent with our findings.

announced in April 2002 that it would hire about 3,900 additional employees in the coming years to 2008 – of course, mainly people coming from the 10 'new member countries' (European Commission, press release, April 30, 2002). This would boost housing demand in the near future in the central city.

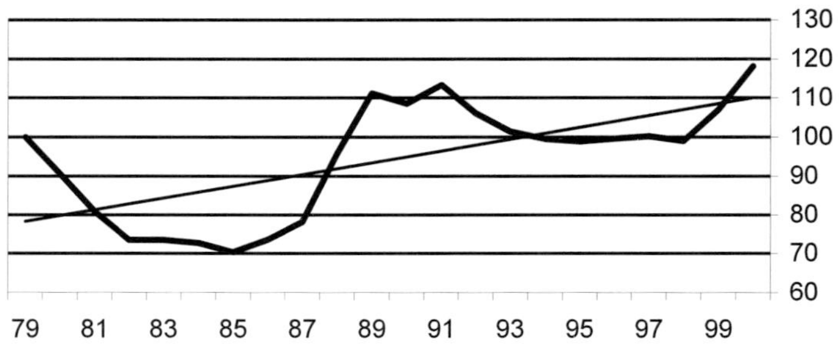

Fig. 2.9. Ratio of single-family house prices to taxable income, BCR 1979 = 100 (Source: NIS, UGEB and own calculations

Renters

Real rental prices have slightly increased from 1981 to 1997 (+3.7 per cent) as shown in Fig. 2.10. From 1992 on, the hedonic index follows more or less the evolution of the real interest rate.[17] From 1987 to 1991, the evolution of rental prices could seem less consistent with the evolution of real estate values and Eq. 2.1. This would be misleading for two main reasons. First, the pure land rent due to the EC would have not affected a large segment of the rental housing market. As already indicated, an important share of houses near the CBD was actually converted into offices during the period 1987–92. Moreover, Ginsburgh and Waelbreock (1998) actually showed that between the sub-periods 1980–87 and 1988–92, real estate prices rose 64 per cent within a radius of 1 km around the CBD but only 5 per cent at a distance 4–7 km from the CBD; the EC effect was even zero beyond 7 km. In other words, a large urban area was not affected by the EC effect.[18] We conclude that the housing-price index established from transactions observed between 1987 and 1992 overestimated average values of rental houses.

Secondly, in the section on demography, we have seen that out-migration to the rest of Belgium was especially pronounced until 1995. Rental housing – i.e., three fourths of the housing stock in BCR – was of course the main market segment to be hit by this exodus.

[17] Recall indeed the simplified Eq. 2.1: if the price value of the house rises 10 per cent but the interest rate falls 10 per cent then the rental price remains unchanged.

[18] Let us say that the central-city is approximately a disk with a radius of 13 km.

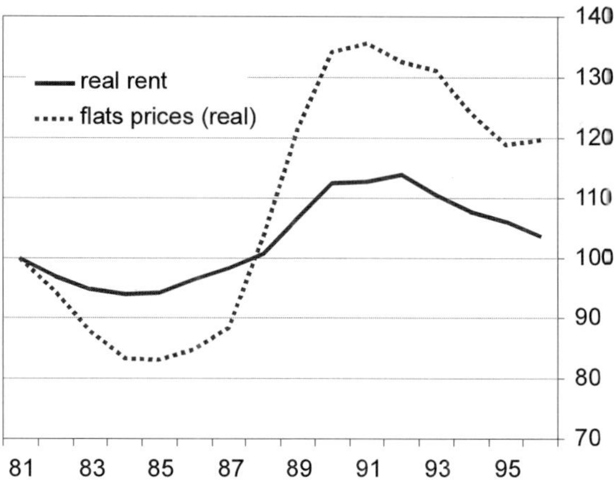

Fig. 2.10. Hedonic rental prices and asset values of flats in BCR 1981 = 100 (Source: Data on rent from Observatoire des Loyers, 1998 cited in: Confederation Construction Brussels 2001 Report p. 20)

2.3 Housing Problems

2.3.1 Moving Income Distributions and Decaying Housing Stock

In an economy with rising incomes and durable houses, it is normal to observe an excess supply of low-quality houses and an excess demand of high-quality housing. Indeed, the quality of houses built in the 1930s or 1940s was probably in line with housing demand at that time but does not satisfy today's demands simply because we live in a richer society. In Brussels, there has been painful adjustments of that chronic 'disequilibrium' both spatially (suburbanisation) and between market segments (filtering down).

Consider first the two following charts. The first one (Fig. 2.11) exhibits the distribution of real taxable incomes in BCR for two different years: 1978 and 1999 (in thousands 1999 Euros). Clearly, there are today fewer very poor people (€0–5,148), which is good news, and more people with a relatively low income (€5,148–12,869). However, in total, the number of residents with a real income below €12,869 is about the same as in 1978. On the other hand, the number of middle-income households (€12,869–25,739) has increased by 15 per cent. The number of income statements above €36,000 has decreased between 1978 and 1999, not because thousands of people would have moved from the higher class to a lower one but because there has been an exodus of the rich as already mentioned. As a result, the average real income (per statement) in BCR has decreased by 7.3 per cent in real terms between 1978 and 1999.

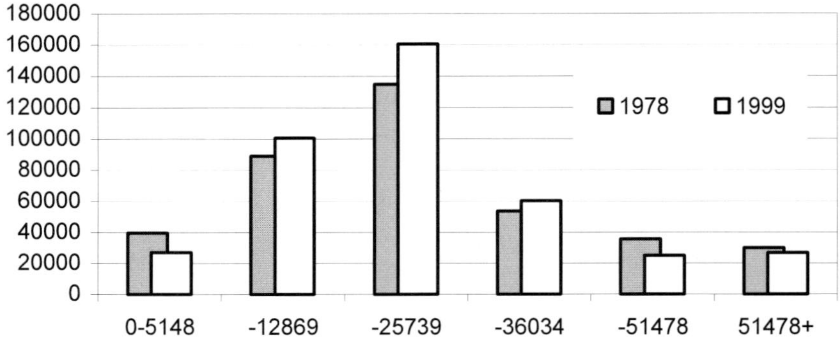

Fig. 2.11. Distribution of real income in BCR, thousand Euros in 1999 prices (Source: NIS and own calculations)

Fig. 2.12 exhibits the evolution of real incomes in the immediate periphery (Hal-Vilvoorde). In these municipalities, there are also fewer low-income people today than before but there has been a dramatic increase of people with a very high income, clearly those who left the city-centre plus new EU and other international immigrant employees. In particular, the number of residents with a very high real income (i.e., above €514,000 in 1999) has more than doubled!

From 1960 to 1975, those dwellings left by the middle class have been gradually filled by the immigrant workers (filtering). Their efforts to upgrade their dwellings have been limited by the lack of means and the relatively high cost of 'gut-rehab' (see Mills and Hamilton 1994 p. 245). As already mentioned, the excess of high-quality large houses (Hôtels de Maître) has probably been absorbed by the growing demand for offices and the EC effect between 1987 and 1992. On the other hand, in the absence of adequate renovation-subsidy programmes (certainly until the early 1990s), we are left today with an excess supply of very low quality dwellings – and to a lesser extent, with an excess demand of middle-quality dwellings.

There is indeed strong evidence that the housing stock has substantially aged in BCR during the last 20 years. In 1991, the stock of dwellings built before 1945 in the central city was especially high: 42 per cent (see Table 2.2). We also infer from Table 2.2 that about 80 thousands houses built before 1919 were still occupied in 1991 whereas the (quasi-exhaustive) 1981 Housing Census reports 93 thousands of such occupied dwellings.

Moreover, there has been a dramatic depression in the construction industry after the boom of the 1970s. This phenomenon is common to all Belgian regions but BCR was the most affected (Fig. 2.8): while during the 1970s, about 40,000 dwellings were added to the stock (i.e., 11 per cent of the 1981 stock), only 15,000 dwellings have been built during the following decade (1981–90). When adding the number of housing units renovated between 1981 and 1991 to the stock of new dwellings built during that period, we obtain 8.5 per cent of the 1991 stock that has been built or upgraded, that is less than 1 per cent per year. This rate is very low and probably below the long run depreciation rate of houses in Brussels. The 20,000 units built during the period 1991–2001 (NBB 2002) was neither sufficient to replace properly the decaying housing stock in the central city.

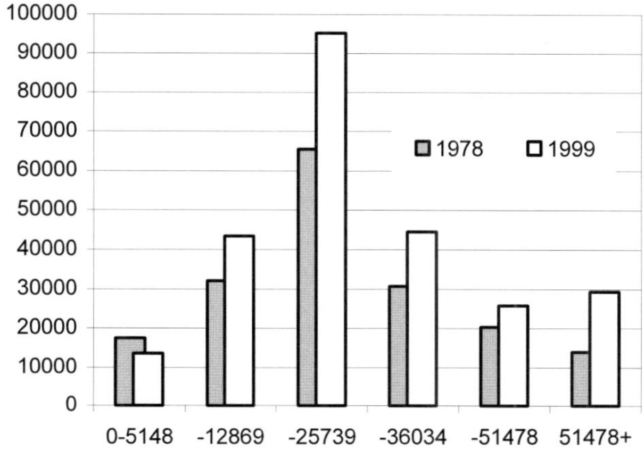

Fig. 2.12. Distribution of real income, immediate suburbs, thousand Euros in 1999 prices (Source: NIS and own calculations)

In fact, according to the survey 'urban diversities'[19] achieved in 1998, the overall quality of houses would have not significantly improved in BCR since 1991 (4,096 households surveyed). An index of 'housing salubrity' has actually been established as in Table 2.4. From an optimistic point of view, 'improvable' might describe some dwellings that require simply a maintenance but the second item means that 10 per cent should be upgraded and the third one that 2 per cent must be renovated or retired. The last PRD Preliminary Report published by the BCR's government comments on these results as follows: 'Despite renovation effort carried out in the last two decades by public and private agents, the Brussels housing stock suffers from a qualitative deficit' (PRD Report 2001 Sect. 7).

Table 2.4. Index of 'housing salubrity'

The dwelling …	Per cent dwellings
… is improvable	34
… is in an unsatisfactory condition	10
… is in bad condition	2

Source: PRD Preliminary Report 2001.

[19] Cited by the PRD Preliminary Report 2001.

2.3.2 Level of Comfort and Housing Segregation

The level of comfort has improved between 1981 and 1991. While in 1981, 26 per cent of the dwellings were without minimal comfort (i.e., no bathroom and no private WC) there were 16 per cent of such low-standard dwellings in 1991. However, according to the survey mentioned before, the situation would have got worse in the 1990s as a result of the decaying stock: 19 per cent of the households surveyed in 1998 were without minimal (acceptable) comfort.

Problems are worse for immigrants and the poor living in Brussels that often face discriminatory attitudes.[20] This observation is unfortunately confirmed by Table 2.5 that gives the level of housing comfort and the ownership rate for three countries of origin.

Table 2.5. Some dwellings indicators (%) by occupier's country of origin

	Owner-occupied		Uncomfortable		Few rooms	
	1981	1991	1981	1991	1981	1991
Belgians	34	43	25	16	2	3
Maghreb	13	32	60	38	42	41
Turks	7	35	69	40	45	46

Source: Goossens et al. (1999) p. 123.

In particular, the rate of owners in the Turkish community was multiplied by 5 while in the same time the level of 'discomfort' decreased mainly thanks to their upgrading efforts. As a matter of fact, for the three nationalities, the relative number of uncomfortable dwellings was divided by 1.6–1.7 between 1981 and 1991.

Still, compared to Belgians there are 2.5 times more uncomfortable dwellings in the housing stock occupied by immigrants. Of course, the high rate of occupancy (few rooms) is related to household's size, which is, in 1991, 2.5 for Belgians and about 4.4 for Moroccans and Turks.

2.3.3 Impoverishment of BCR

Not only average incomes have dramatically decreased in the centralised municipalities as a result of the exodus of high income people over the last 30 years, the rate of unemployment has also sharply increased more recently from 11.1 per cent in 2000 to about 18 per cent in March 2002.[21] According to the last PRD Preliminary Report, this would be due to the inadequacy between an excess supply of low-skilled (manufacturing) workers and a high demand for skilled workers in the business services. This phenomenon is common to all developed countries but in

[20] See Donner (2000) p. 135. The situation is similar in the main Belgian city-port: Antwerp.

[21] Last figure: Ministry of Labour, April 2002. The sources of the two figures are different but the trend is clear.

Brussels it took on considerable proportions in the 1990s (see the PRD Preliminary Report 2001 Sect. 3). Moreover, the number of Brussels residents entitled to earn the state-guaranteed minimum income (called minimex) has increased from 6,890 to 14,718. The number of individuals depending on the Belgian minimum allowance is in fact higher since we must add old people (11,400) and other groups receiving an equivalent amount from the social security system. As a matter of fact, 4.6 per cent of the BCR's population would depend directly or indirectly on the minimex amount (PRD Preliminary Report 2001).

Consequences for the financing of the autonomous region of Brussels-capital

In Belgian urban areas, the problem of redistribution is theoretically less important than, for example, in US inner-cities. Indeed, the national tax system is one of the most progressive in the world and the social security system is generous and (still) national. Moreover, education and culture are subsidised by the French Community.[22]

However, BCR – which is responsible for the housing policy on its territory – is financed mainly by a share of the income tax levied by the federal government (9 per cent in 2000) and to a lesser degree by the so-called regional taxes (e.g. the additional tax on real estate advance payment). The bases of these additional taxes are decided by the federal government so that the fiscal power of BCR is de facto quite limited.

The dramatic plunge of the average taxable income in the last 10 years is thus bad news for the region, not much for financing reason (at least in the short run) but for political reason. Indeed, since 1997 BCR benefits from the so-called national solidarity mechanism by which a region with proceeds from income tax below the national average receives a monetary compensation from other regions.[23] Thanks to this compensation, the budget of BCR has actually not decreased since 1997. However, in the context of the devolution of the Belgium State, BCR has become more dependent on other federated entities, especially Flanders, the region which has currently the 'economic power' in Belgium – and probably so the bargaining power each time a constitutional reform is negotiated between federated entities.

2.3.4 Filtering Down and Housing Abandonment

The phenomenon of filtering down in the housing market is the fact that most poor people live in hand-me-down housing (Mills and Hamilton 1994 p. 251). Abandonment can be viewed as the end product of the filtering-down process. An

[22] This is the political institution common to all French-speaking Belgians (living in BCR + Wallonia), in charge of education and culture. The adjective French is abusive.

[23] The compensation is proportionate to the number of inhabitants in the region (see Bayenet and DeBruycker 2003).

owner would like to abandon its property title if the present value of the sequence of future rental incomes from the property (plus the expected value of the cleared land) cannot cover all future costs (including the demolition cost). To avoid the property tax, he may then decide to abandon his or her real estate property (see Mills and Hamilton 1994 p. 249).

We have seen that about 30,000 dwellings were vacant in 1991 (6 per cent of the housing stock).[24] Casual observation suggests that things have not progressed much despite a few recent apartment blocks developments in centralised areas.

This is harmful not only for the safety but also the appearance of central neighbourhood areas containing abandoned houses. As a result, property values are depressed in these locations. This classical negative externality[25] justifies market interventions by the government of the region. However, the special tax on abandoned housing that has been introduced (in the three Belgian regions) has got little effects so far because the decision of abandoning the house still remains economically rationale (despite the monetary punishment). Since 1993, any municipality may requisition any vacant building in order to provide accommodation to homeless people (Onkelinx Law). According to the memorandum published by the Brussels Union for the Right of Housing (RBDH 2001, Memorandum Sect. I.3.3), no one single Brussels municipality has used this legal instrument yet.[26]

2.4 Housing Policies in BCR: Housing the Poor Versus Return-to-City Movement?

Because housing problems in greater Brussels are mainly concentrated in the central city, let us analyse briefly the different housing policies implemented by the Brussels region.[27] Since it got its autonomy in 1989, the successive governments of the region of Brussels-capital have put forward two different priorities which are sometimes contradictory:

1. the so-called 'protection' of the housing function against land speculation in central areas and
2. the stopping of the decentralisation of middle and upper class residents.

To reach these goals a more global revitalising approach has been adopted

[24] The scale of this problem has been confirmed by a study carried out by the Foundation Roi Baudouin: in 1990, about 5.8 per cent of the land lots in centralised areas were totally abandoned while an additional 7.7 per cent was partially occupied.

[25] Individuals do not perceive the non-price negative impact of their decision on the total welfare of the neighbourhood.

[26] See also Donner (2000) p. 135, for the municipalities' fear of rising costs when registering homeless people.

[27] The forms of market intervention in the suburbs (by the Flemish region in FB and the Walloon region in WB) are of the same fashion since the regional institutions in charge of housing are the results of the split of a past common national authority. For a study of the policies applied in Flanders and Wallonia, see Donner (2000).

since the first PRD.[28] The results are quite mitigated. On the one hand, the quality of life is today clearly better in those central areas. On the other hand the social indicators have not much improved until now. Of course, some positive effects should be felt in the long-run.

Regarding housing policies more specifically, the government of BCR has focused on two types of policy action since the beginning of the 1990s:

1. the building and the maintenance of a social housing stock which is rented to targeted low-income groups,
2. monetary transfers to low and middle income households direct (capital grants) or indirect (low-interest loans), in order to acquire or renovate a main home.

In the last decade, the region has contributed directly, or indirectly through grants, to the renovation of about 7,000 dwellings per year – i.e., 1,800 units more than the target value set in the first Development Region Plan (PRD Preliminary Report 2001 Sect. 7.2.3). Direct grants to individuals and (more rarely) associations would have accounted for 90 per cent or so of regional government subsidies for housing renovation (own calculation made from Zimmer 2002, Table 9).

The regional budget for housing in 2000 was equal to 76.25 millions Euros, i.e., 4.3 per cent of the total government budget (or 0.1 per cent of the GDP of the metropolitan area). About 40 millions Euros were spent on land use programmes in 2000. Recall however from Sect. 2.2.3 that in the three Belgian regions: 'the most important items of housing policy expenditure are foregone tax revenue caused by mortgage interest tax relief and the loss of rental income caused by the income-independent rent system in the social rent sector' (Donner 2000 p. 134).

2.4.1 The Social Housing Sector in BCR

The main actors

There are three main actors in the Brussels social housing system (in addition to the Brussels State Secretary for Housing): the Brussels Regional Housing Company (SLRB)[29], the approved social housing companies (the SISPs)[30] and the Brussels Housing Fund.[31] The government of BCR provides loans from the re-

[28] Donner (2000) p. 129: 'Since 1993, ... the Brussels regional government has signed 18 neighbourhood contracts for a revitalisation of selected areas with multiple problems, embarking on an integrated approach to urban renewal.'

[29] Société du Logement de la Région Bruxelloise.

[30] Sociétés Immobilières de Service Public.

[31] The AISs are social agencies created by local activists in Brussels. They manage about 600 dwellings in BCR (source: PRD 2001). As pointed out by Donner (2000) p. 133: 'Their relative importance, however is still very small. The Brussels AISs were legally recognised in 1998, but their function will be somewhat different from that of Flemish SVKs, as they are to sub-let dwellings belonging to both approved housing companies and private landlords.'

gional budget to the 34 SISPs that offer rental housing to low income households in their municipality. These loans carry no interest rate and are redeemable over 20 or 33 years (regional decree of October 29, 1998). The loans are channelled through the SLRB that is in charge of: (1) helping the SISP in their day-to-day management, (2) exerting the administrative supervision of the SISPs, (3) promoting the relationship between the SISPs and their renters, (4) advising the regional government, and (5) participating in real estate development projects. The SLRB may also build, renovate and rent its own housing stock.

The Brussels Housing Fund is a distinct organisation also financed by the region in a similar way. Its main mission is to offer low-interest rate to low-income families for homeownership. It also helps low-income tenants by:

- providing loans for the payment of the rental security to the owner,
- purchasing and renovating dwellings that are rented to low-income families (maximum 12 per cent of the Housing Funds' budget): 'As a speciality of the Brussels region, should be mentioned: dwellings of the Brussels Housing Fund are offered to accessible rent, combined with a letter of intent by the tenant to buy after five years. The tenant has to follow a savings plan as well' (Donner 2000 p. 131).

However, according to the RBDH, the latter rent-buy scheme would not be applied anymore because households could not afford the financing of housing capital expenditure during the lease period.

In the 1990s, about 5,500 units have been be added to the supply of rental dwellings thanks to the renovation activity undertaken by the main actors: +1,900 dwellings added by the SISPs, +1,920 units by the SLRB itself and the rest by the Housing Fund (PRD Preliminary Report 2001 Sect. 7.2.3).

Decaying social housing stock and growing demand

There are about 38,000 social dwellings today in BCR, i.e., 8 per cent of the Brussels housing stock (or 13.1 per cent of the total rental housing stock). The net increase in the social housing stock itself was actually weak in the recent years: +1,953 units between 1990 and 1998, a mere +5 per cent (report of the SLRB 1999). After the financial crisis of the entire (past national) social housing system at the end of the 1970s, the building activity in the social sector has been indeed very low in the last two decades (some hundreds units built in the 1990s in BCR, and even less in the 1980s). This low level of replacement is bad news given the recent surge of poverty in the region. Today, there would be about 15,000–20,000 people registered on what Donner (2000) called 'infamous waiting lists'.

More serious, the efforts above have not been even sufficient to maintain many bad-quality apartment blocks that were built in the 1960s and the 1970s. According to the last PRD Preliminary Report: '… many of these [dwellings] are without minimal comfort (heating, bathroom, warm water,…) and/or in bad conditions' (PRD Preliminary Report 2001 Sect. 7.2.2).

Rental social housing

To be eligible for a social rental dwelling, incomes must be below the following limits: €16,430 for singles, €18,260 for a one-income household, €20,870 for a household with two revenues.[32] During the selection process, some situations are favoured: handicapped persons, single women with children, victims of some social or natural calamity.

Rents are determined according to income and revised every two years.[33] In any case, the rent must not exceed 22 per cent of the household's income. The approved housing company can put an end to the lease if the renter refuses an alternate dwelling which is not more expensive in terms of price per unit of quality (price increase $\leq$ 15 per cent for a more comfortable dwelling).

2.4.2 Acquisition Grants and Other Subsidies

Housing funds

Until the end of the 1990s, the Family Housing Funds provided subsidised low-interest loans for the acquisition of dwellings by families with children exclusively. Following the demands expressed by some associations such as the RBDH, since January 2002 households without children may now also apply for a loan. The income ceiling is €33,000 for a couple plus €3,750 per child (reference: 1999 tax statement). The amount of the loan may not exceed the asset value of the house (estimated after renovation works if the case arises). The effective interest rate paid by the household is a proportion of a reference interest: the lower income (or the more children are), the lower the interest actually paid by the household.[34] From 1995 to 2000 the Housing Funds provided 1,767 loans in total, i.e., about 300 per year.

Acquisition and renovation grants

For homebuilding or the purchase of an existing dwelling (with a floor space surface > 35 square metres), the BCR's government awards to the owner-occupier a once-for-all grant equal to 10 per cent of the purchase price (€6 197 for a new construction). The purchase price of the dwelling must be below €99,157. The in-

---

[32] About €1,500 must be added to the last limits for each additional person (SLRB 2002).

[33] The rent is calculated as the multiplication of a basic rent by an income coefficient: RENT PAID2001 = 'BASIC' RENT x (INDEXED YH1998 / YREF2001), where YH is the household's income three years before the rent comes into effect, YREF is the reference income indexed each year (€14,233 in 2001). For example, for a €50,000 flat, the basic rent is 5 per cent x 50,000 = €2,500 / year divided by 12 = €208 / month. For YH = €10,500, the rent paid is thus: 208 x (10,500 x 1.0379 / 14,233) = €159 / month (source: SLRB 2002).

[34] For a household (with ages less than 35) with 2 children and income = €28,500, the loan carries an interest rate equal to (28,500 / 33,000) x 6.75 per cent – 1 per cent (< 35 years old) – 1 per cent (2 children) = 3.83 per cent.

come ceiling is €6,250 (+ €2,748 per additional person). The remaining conditions are quite restrictive: the dwelling must be occupied for the ten years following the acquisition, be located in one 'neighbourhood contract' area or a zone backed by the Brussels Regional Development Company (13 centralised municipalities) and not be rented. According to the last PRD Preliminary Report, 1,850 acquisition grants were awarded in the 1990s to middle and low income households.

Renovation grants are also awarded to owners or renters of an 'insalubrious but improvable' dwelling. The amount of the grant is equal to 50 per cent (respectively 40 per cent) of the costs of accepted works if the taxable income is lower than €19,930 (respectively €24,790).[35]

2.4.3 Some Evaluation

Quantitatively, the most important housing policy instruments are decided at the federal level: the favourable tax treatment of owner-occupancy, VAT, rent regulation (if any). At the regional level, Flanders has recently decreased the registration tax rate by 2 percentage points, a decision that reinforces the attractiveness of homeownership in the Flemish suburbs of Brussels.

The RBDH is favourable to lower income ceilings for all types of policy action in order to tackle the true problem: housing the poor. Instead, the Brussels Minister of Housing has increased the household income limit for renovation works and relaxed the conditions of eligibility for a loan from the Housing Funds. For the renovation of a dwelling located in one of the targeted central areas, there is no income ceiling anymore. The government explained that the goal of the last decision was to favour the forming of a better 'social mix' in central depressed areas.

Donner (2000) is rather sceptical about this system of acquisition/renovation: 'the effectiveness of this kind of housing policy seems low since it seems unlikely that subsidies of the size granted actually determine individual investment decisions. In view poor social targeting, these grants could be characterised as subsidisation by large-scale sprinkling of funds' (Donner 2000 p. 489).

Concerning the building and the maintenance of a social housing stock, it is generally admitted in the economic literature that such a supply-side programme is more costly than demand-side programmes. Indeed, the costs a government incurs by producing itself subsidised dwellings are (generally) greater than the costs of acquiring equivalent housing units on the private market.[36] This is also true in Belgium where in 1995, the average production cost of a social dwelling has been estimated at €82,500 compared to €57,500 for an average dwelling on the private market (Donner 2000 p. 140–41). Moreover we must add other social costs. Indeed, since in Brussels there is an excess of low-quality dwellings, subsidising social dwellings adversely depresses the low end segment of the private market and even hastens housing retirement in some neighbourhoods.

[35] Add 10 per cent to those percentages for dwellings located in the targeted centralised areas just mentioned before.

[36] See Mills and Hamilton (1994) p. 269 for some empirical estimates for the United States.

It is also a well-known fact in Brussels that many households living in a social dwelling have currently an income above the ceiling set by the government. It is possible, although far from certain, that they could improve their living standards (e.g. find a job) thanks to their social housing conditions.

One could argue that one of the objectives of social housing is to improve the quality of housing for low-income people. The today's state of decay of the social housing stock and the 15 or 20 thousands people registered on waiting lists show that this policy has failed in Brussels. In line with this observation, the RBDH has proposed the introduction of a general housing allowance with eligibility contingent on the satisfaction of housing quality standards. This does not exist in Belgium and is similar to Sect. 8 of the US Housing Act 1974 (see Mills and Hamilton 1994 pp. 267–68). However, this kind of demand-side policy would not necessarily solve the housing problems in Brussels. Indeed, in view of the decaying housing stock in the low end of the rental market, not all the recipients of a voucher – i.e., the poorest population of Brussels – would necessarily find a dwelling meeting the quality standards. More importantly, it is almost certain that such a policy would generate significant rent increases. Susin (2002), for example, has found the following for the US housing vouchers programme between 1974 and 1993 (see also Laferrère and Le Blanc (2004) for the impact of housing allowances on rents in France):

> In the 90 biggest metropolitan areas, vouchers have raised rents by 16 percent on average, a large effect consistent with a low supply elasticity in the low quality rental housing market. Considered as a transfer programme, this result implies that vouchers have caused a $8.2 billion increase in the total rent paid by low-income non-recipients, while only providing a subsidy of $5.8 billion to recipients, resulting in a net loss of $2.4 billion to low-income households (Susin 2002 p. 109).

2.5 Conclusion

The standard housing problems facing many old central cities in developed countries, i.e. the decentralisation of people – and thus of housing investment – and the filtering down process in poor centralised areas, have been worsened in Brussels by a national attitude towards housing that can be summarised as follows (see also Donner 2000 p. 489):

- an anti-urban and individualistic vision of the residential market since the end of the 19th century,
- near absence of planning (at least until the 1990s) and a generous zoning approach that translated into an unchecked suburbanisation,
- a priority given to the subsidisation of stable owner-occupied housing,
- partial tax relief on mortgage-interest payments (the most important housing programme),
- weak legal protection of tenants,
- high transaction costs that limit speculation.

In fact, regarding the housing policy per se: '... the state considers the promotion of ownership as its main housing policy task' (Donner 2000 p. 487).

As a result of all these facts, BCR has suffered from an exodus of middle and high income people for the past 40 years. Moreover, Brussels has been the victim of both a 'constitutional uncertainty' (certainly until the end of the 1980s) and the relative lack of solidarity from the federal state towards its impoverished capital. Facing these problems, the government of BCR has given a priority – especially in the last Regional Development Plan 2001 – to the development of the attractiveness of the central city. That is why two types of actions have received – and would probably continue to receive – more attention:

- an integrated urban 'revitalisation' approach in central areas, and
- small grants awarded to young middle-class households that decide to acquire or renovate their main home in the central-city.

Until now the results of those programmes have been mitigated. Yet, one has observed more young households purchasing a home in need of renovation, investing a lot of energy and time in what is called 'sweat equity' (Mills and Hamilton 1994 p. 421). However, in view of the small amounts granted and the increasing 'fiscal' competition with Flanders and Wallonia, it is doubtful that any steady return-to-the-city movement will be observed in the near future. The last increase in population size could actually appear to be mainly a demographic phenomenon.

Meanwhile, 'housing the poor' has become a secondary aim. The proposition of the RBDH on a general housing allowance has been debated recently but the regional government has finally opted for a supply-side policy, more precisely, the renovation of the existing social housing stock and the building of 5,000 new units in the coming years. Despite a relatively high cost, this public housing project should lead to some price decreases in the low end of the private market and also encourage landlords to stop the filtering down process alongside the different segments of the market (Baudewyns et al. 2004).

References

Baudewyns D (1998) Economie Urbaine et Localisation: Essais sur les Interactions Stratégiques et Spatiales des Agents Economiques. PhD thesis, Université Libre de Bruxelles

Baudewyns D, Gangji A, Plasman R (2004) Impact des Politiques d'offre de Logements sur le Marché Résidentiel: Le Cas de Bruxelles. mimeo DULBEA, december

Bayenet B, de Bruycker P (2003) Belgium: A Unique Evolving Federalism. World Bank Institute, Washington

Brueckner J, Thisse JF, Zenou Y (1999) Why is Central Paris Rich and Downtown Detroit Poor? An Amenity-based Theory. European Economic Review 43: 91–107

Carton L, de Keersmaecker ML (1992) Action Publique et Droit au Logement. Fondation Travail-Université, Bruxelles

Donner C (2000) Housing Policies in the European Union. Donner, Vienna

Ginsburgh Y, Waelbroeck P (1998) The EC and Real Estate Rents in Brussels. Regional Science and Urban Economics 28: 497–511

Gofette-Nagot F, Thomas I, Zenou Y (1998) Localisation Résidentielle et Revenu des Ménages: Paris-Bruxelles. Congrès des Économistes Belges de Langue Française Commission 2, rapport préparatoire, pp 175–206

Goossens L, Thomas I, Vanneste D (1999) Le Logement: Réalités Socio-économiques et Géographiques 1981–1991. Monographie no 10, INS Brussels

Laferrère A, le Blanc D (2004) How do Housing Allowances Affect Rents? An Empirical Analysis of the French Case. Journal of Housing Economics 13: 36–67

Mills ES, Hamilton BW (1994) Urban Economics. 5th edn. Harper Collins, New York

Noël F (1998) La Ville Rapiécée. Les Stratégies de la Réhabilitation. Editions de l'Université de Bruxelles, Brussels

O'Sullivan A (1996) Urban Economics. 3rd edn. Irwin, Chicago

PRD Preliminary Report (2001). Government of BCR, Brussels

Robert-Jones P (1999) Bruxelles Fin de Siècle. Benedikt Taschen, Köln

Susin S (2000) Rent Vouchers and the Price of Low Income Housing. Journal of Public Economics 83: 109–52

Zimmer P (2002) La Politique de l'habitat de la Région de Bruxelles-Capitale. Courrier hebdomadaire du CRISP, no 1746–47

Appendix

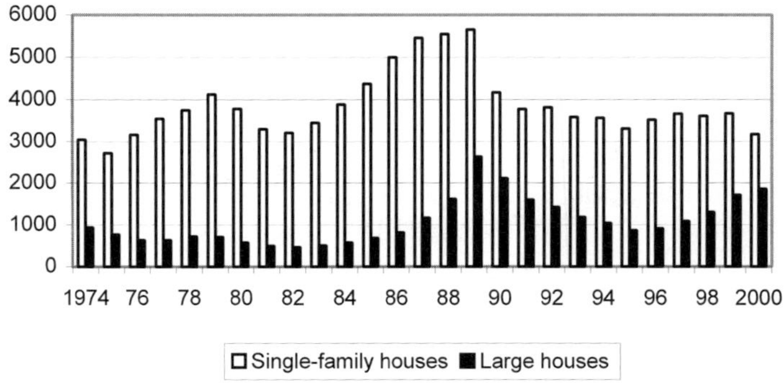

Fig. 2.13. Number of properties sold in BCR (Source: NIS, Statistiques financières – Ventes de biens immobiliers)

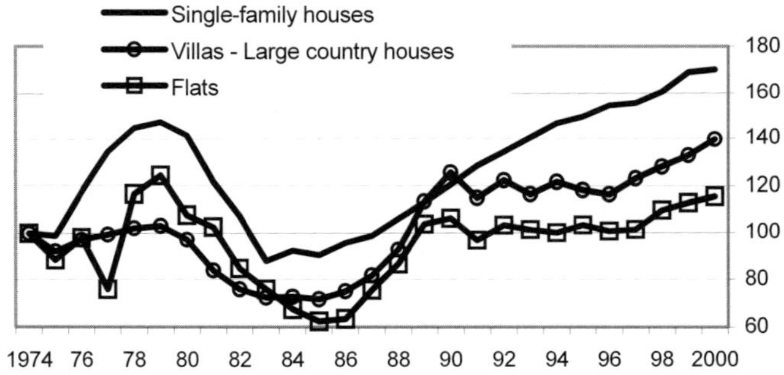

Fig. 2.14. Average values of properties sold in the suburbs of Brussels real. Not quality-adjusted 1974 = 100 (Source: NIS and own calculations)

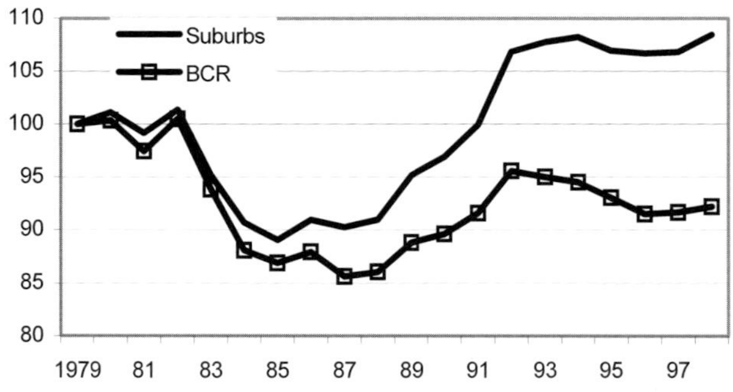

Fig. 2.15. Real taxable income 1979 = 100 (Source: NIS and own calculations)

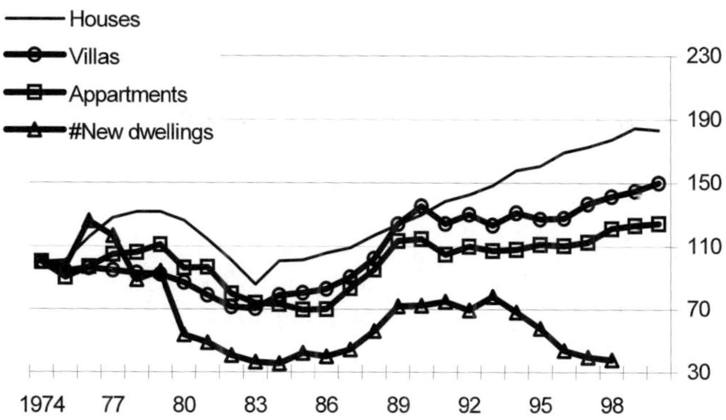

Fig. 2.16. Tobin's q and housing starts in suburbs 1974 = 100 (Source: NIS and own calculations, Statistiques régionales et Construction et Logements)

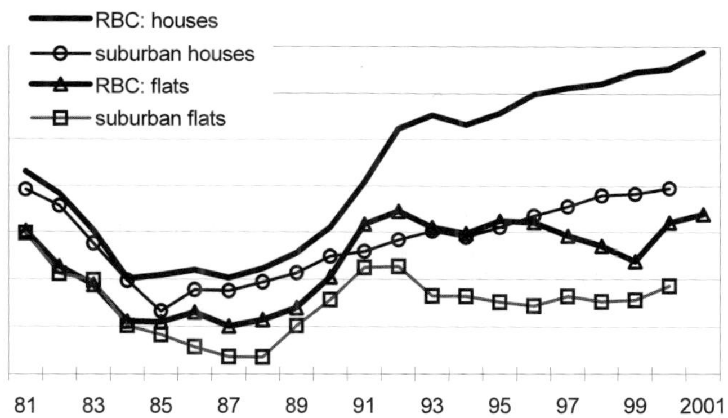

Fig. 2.17. Ratio of housing prices to taxable income (Source: Own calculations on NIS data)

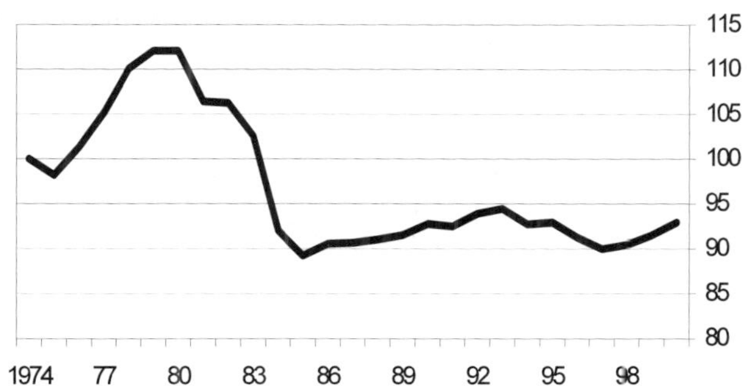

Fig. 2.18. Real construction cost 1974 = 100 (Source: ABEX)

3 Metropolitan Housing Markets – The Case of Helsinki

Heikki A. Loikkanen[1] and Henrik Lönnqvist[2]

[1]University of Helsinki, Helsinki
[2]City of Helsinki, Helsinki

3.1 Introduction

The purpose of this chapter is to analyse housing in the Helsinki metropolitan area (HMA) in the context of national economic developments and policies in Finland since mid-1980s. At the beginning of this period the old institutional framework including fixed exchange rate policy, capital import controls, and interest rate regulation was still in operation. Regional policies at large aimed at even development throughout the country. Urban growth problems were not emphasised although Finland was internationally lagging behind in the rate of urbanisation relative to its GDP per capita. Increase in mobility to urban centres, when economic growth accelerated, always seemed to come as a surprise. Immigration from abroad to Finland was marginal. As for housing policies, rent regulation policies applied to private rental housing throughout the nation. For owner occupiers, lack of specialised institutions and credit rationing characterised private housing finance. State housing finance with subsidised interest rates (ARAVA loans) was available for municipal and non-profit investors in rental housing, and also for buyers of new ARAVA owner-occupied housing. Alongside regulated financial markets, extensive tax deductibility of interest expenses of all housing loans applied.

This chapter describes how this institutional framework changed in Finland with financial liberalisation, the collapse of fixed exchange rate policies, a period of floating currency, EU membership and participation in EMU. These changes as well as tax reforms and the abolition of rent regulation affected the functioning of housing markets. Besides institutional changes, the period since mid-1980s is also unique in economic history of Finland due to its volatility. A boom was followed by an economic disaster in early 1990s. In mid-1995 a new, to great extent ICT industry based growth phase started reshaping the economy and its regional structure. This chapter first describes how the Finnish economy came 'down from the heavens and up from the ashes' (cf. Kalela et al. 2001 for an extensive analysis). In relation to this we also discuss deregulation of housing markets. In Sect. 3.3 we present basic facts about housing in the Helsinki metropolitan area (HMA) and in Finland. These include demography, income, housing expenditure, tenure structure, housing stock and spaciousness. In Sect. 3.4, we concentrate on housing production and housing prices in the HMA. Sect. 3.5 offers some conclusions.

3.2 Institutional Changes and Macroeconomic Instability Since Mid-1980s

3.2.1 Recent Macroeconomic Developments in the Operating Environment of Housing Markets

As for long-term income level, Finland has been catching-up EU average from below. Real GDP per capita has doubled during the last thirty years and reached e.g. the level of Sweden for the first time at the turn of the millennium. Although economic growth has been fast on average, it has by no means been steady. On the contrary, Finland has been a rather volatile country in a West European perspective. Macroeconomic stability problems and their repercussions on housing markets became especially acute since latter half of 1980s.

In the end of 1980s favourable international economic developments and financial deregulation led to a boom where GDP growth was exceptionally high and asset prices, especially prices of owner-occupied housing sky rocketed relative to normal times (Figs. 3.1 and 3.2). Abolishment of capital import controls ended extensive credit rationing and this led to a credit expansion much of which was channelled to housing markets, where supply by no means could expand respectively despite a construction boom. Also, the restrictive reaction from interest rate hikes, made possible by abolishment of interest rate regulation in 1987, was delayed, and did not constrain borrowing in the first phase.

The turn from a boom to a bust in early 1990s was also unprecedented in Finland, more severe than the depression in the 1930s. The declared policy of sticking to a fixed exchange rate lost credibility, when current account deficits cumulated fast. Export demand in western markets decreased, and also barter trade with the former Soviet Union, an important trade partner, collapsed. The consequent currency and bank crises, together with pursued economic policies lead to a cumulative decline of GDP of more than 10 per cent in 1991–93. Unemployment rate, which had been 3.2 per cent in 1990, reached 16.6 per cent in 1994. The bust increased public expenditure at the same time as tax revenues decreased. Public sector deficits led public debt to increase from about 15 per cent of GDP in 1990 to more than 60 per cent level in mid-1990s. The share of public expenditure in GDP reached 62 per cent in mid-1990s. It has recently declined below 50 per cent.

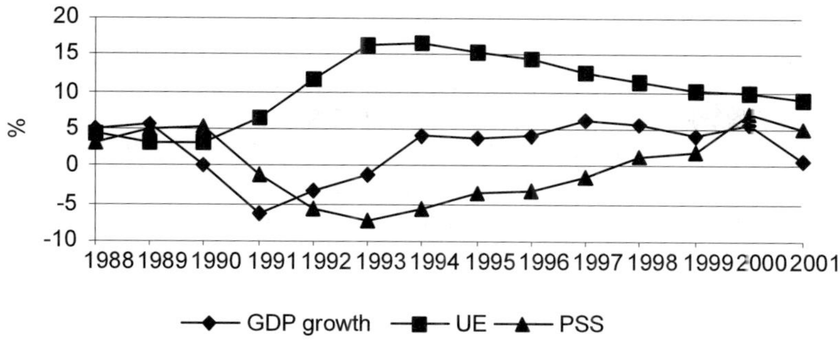

Fig. 3.1. GDP growth rate, unemployment rate (UE) and public sector surplus (or deficit) as per cent of GDP (PSS) in Finland 1988 (Source: Statistics Finland)

The period under consideration included a number of institutional changes, which are relevant for understanding housing market developments both nationally and in the HMA. When the boom turned to a depression in 1991 the fixed exchange rate policy lost credibility. After unsuccessful defence with high interest rates, the Finnish Markka was devalued by 12 per cent in November 1991 and in September 1992 the Markka was floated. In 1995 Finland became an EU member, in October 1996 Finland joined ERM, and in 1999 EMU.

The credit expansion of late 1980s, financed to a great extent by foreign borrowing, lead to a banking crisis when interest rates increased, the Markka was devalued and asset prices collapsed. Prices of owner-occupied dwellings decreased almost to half of their top level (Fig. 3.2).

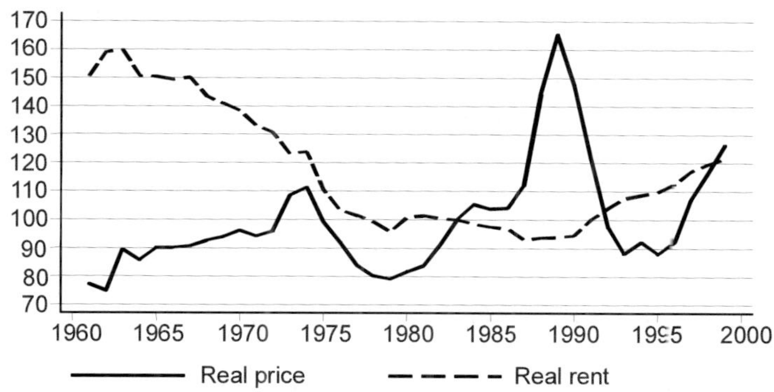

Fig. 3.2. Real housing prices and rents in Finland 1960–99, 1983 = 100 (Source: Laakso 2002)

The economic crisis resulted in banks with non-performing loans and missing collateral values and construction companies with unsold dwellings. A record high number of households suffered from unemployment or no income growth. Quite a few of them were unable to manage with their housing expenses, especially if the dwelling was bought with credit in the boom with high price, which soon collapsed. Despite cuts in welfare programs, the transfers of the welfare state softened the loss of incomes. In the income basket of households, the percentage of income transfers grew from one-fifth to one-third in mid-1990s. This kept e.g. inequality in the distribution of households' disposable income surprisingly unchanged especially in the early years of the bust. During this stage also regional income disparities remained much the same as before. As for banks, some went bankrupt, others merged with domestic or foreign banks and heavy state subsidies were used to bail out the banking sector. Bankruptcies and mergers also occurred in the construction sector. No major bank or construction company survived the turmoil of 1990s without some form of restructuring, something that reflects in the almost complete disappearance of previously familiar company names and entry of new ones, including some foreign ones.

From 1995 and onwards economic growth has been exceptionally high until the last downturn of the economy in 2001. During this phase the structure of the economy has changed as IT industries have been the fastest growing sectors. Despite recent favourable developments unemployment has remained at high level. Also regionally recent growth has been less evenly distributed than earlier. Concentration of economic activity and migration to urban centres during economic booms has been a stylised fact for long, but now the process has been more selective than earlier and especially based on the growth of ICT industries. Only half a dozen urban areas (HMA, Tampere, Turku, Jyväskylä, Oulu and Salo regions) have been attracting new investment and gained from net migration. Earlier almost all urban centres increased their population in booms, although the capital city region benefited most even in earlier times. After the collapse of housing prices, they stayed at the same level for some years. When fast economic growth started in 1995, it also led to an increase of housing prices as the supply side, as usual, was sluggish in its reaction (Fig. 3.2 above).

Although housing is durable capital and slow to change, our description of the HMA housing market and respective national situation below must be looked at remembering the described macroeconomic and institutional changes, which took place after mid-1980s.

3.2.2 Deregulation and the Housing Markets

Still in mid-1980s the Finnish financial markets were undeveloped because of the central role of banks and lack of specialised financial institutions. Incurring bank loans rather than issuing shares was the most important source of external finance for business firms and there were no specialised private institutions for funding housing. Private commercial, savings and cooperative banks carried out funding as part of their normal business activity. Until early 1980s this happened, however, in thoroughly regulated financial markets. Highly politicised decision making kept interest rates below equilibrium level and led to credit rationing. Thus, availability of credit instead of its price caused fluctuations in prices of unregulated owner-occupied dwellings.

For households, the combination of regulation and the tax deductibility of interest payments resulted in negative real rates of interest (Fig. 3.3). Under these circumstances most people attempted to take out the largest housing loans they could. The banks, however, also placed in-advance savings requirements to prospective homeowners as a precondition for getting loans. They were of the order of one-third or even half of housing value still in early 1980s. Furthermore, the average maturity of loans was less than ten years.

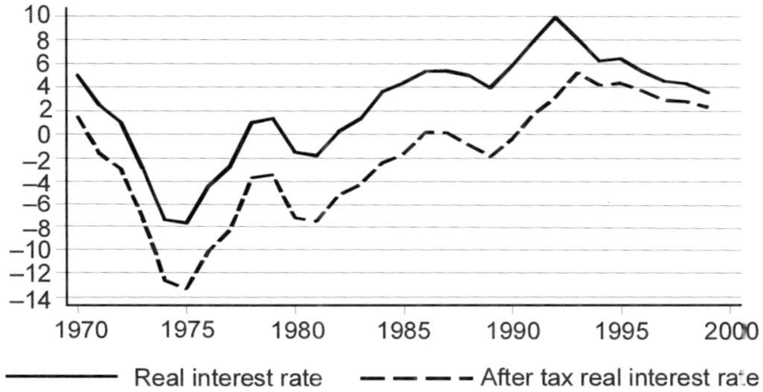

Fig. 3.3. Real interest rate and real after tax interest rate (per cent) in Finland 1970–99 (Source: Laakso 2000)

As for rental housing in mid-1980s, the private market was rent regulated since 1967. Real rents had declined and the supply of private rental housing declined over time as institutional investors were leaving the market gradually. Partially state-financed so-called ARAVA rental housing offered another alternative, but access was based on means testing and family size criteria, which also limited the size of dwelling. The owners of ARAVA rental real estate companies were typically municipalities, non-profit organisations or business firms offering rental housing for employees. Previously also ARAVA loans for owner-occupiers were available, but also here access was means tested, though much looser than in the rental case. For both tenure forms, ARAVA loans were more benevolent in terms than private funding: their interest rates were lower and their maturities were considerably longer than in private loans. Not surprisingly, there was also excess demand for state loans, especially in urban growth centres, where quotas based on regional policy limited their availability. The second hand markets for owner-occupied ARAVA dwellings were also regulated. As long as state loan had not been completely paid, the price was restricted to initial construction costs plus (regulated) land price corrected by national construction cost index (CCI). The obvious aim of all this was to prevent capital gains.

Alongside the ARAVA system, in Helsinki an additional system with similar aims was adopted in 1970. This so called HITAS system means that the City of Helsinki, as the biggest land owner, leases land for housing purposes, also for owner-occupied housing, with subsidised (and indexed) rents, but the resale prices of housing units are controlled with an index which originally was national CPI (consumer price index), but later was a weighted average of CCI and housing price index. Prices of HITAS units remain regulated without time limit. On the other hand, the rules of the system have changed over time to some extent, and are subject to continuous debate because the gap between regulated and market prices varies over time. National legislation makes it also possible for all other municipalities to adopt the HITAS system, but they have not.

Under the described circumstances all segments of the housing market were regulated in one form or another. A typical household living in the HMA faced either credit rationing or housing consumption rationing in the owner-occupied segments and rental markets were characterised by excess demand or a queue system with means testing. These measures clearly aimed at protecting the households from interest or housing price changes in the name of income distribution targets, and they also aimed at affecting the distribution of housing space. Means tested housing allowances supplemented the system. A more extensive summary of the old Finnish housing system and related policies can be found in Bengs and Loikkanen (1991).[1]

Because of the complexity of the regulatory system, it is hard to predict its consequences in detail. However, it obviously affected life cycle housing consumption patterns, since due to credit rationing and other constraints dwellings of newcomers to the housing market are typically small. Then through a moving cycle households upgrade their housing consumption towards more spacious ones. This is verified by Kuismanen et al. (1999), who estimate the demographic demand for housing in the HMA in 1988. The demand by age class of household head increases almost linearly throughout the life cycle, whereas similar exercise in the United States and Sweden has an inverse U-shape pattern implying that housing consumption is relatively high already in early stages of the life-cycle, and then it increases and turns down when the household head is 40–50 years old. Besides different life-cycle pattern, one also expects average housing consumption to be on a low level the more rationed the financial and rental markets are.

The institutional description of housing markets and housing finance makes it obvious that there was a lot of excess demand constrained by regulation. Thus, when the most important steps in financial liberalisation took place in 1987 in an already otherwise booming economy, the demand for housing finance was massive and lead to an unprecedented housing price and construction boom. For the first time since an episode in early 1970s (price hikes in Fig. 3.2) banks offered housing finance to households, who tried to close the gap between their housing demand and current housing consumption. This process was halted by the bust and related turmoil in early 1990s. The next opportunity to adjust housing consumption to correspond to more normal long-term income prospects came when the economy recovered and grew fast. This new adjustment process, which still continues, takes place in new circumstances. The fruits of financial liberalisation with

[1] See also Aarma et al. (1993), which compares housing in Finland and Estonia since the end of 1930s.

new instruments are finally showing their positive aspects. Credit rationing has eased and EMU membership has kept interest rates at reasonable levels, although the tax reform in 1993 limited essentially the deductibility of interest payments of housing loans in taxation, narrowing the gap between real interest rate and after tax interest rate significantly (cf. Fig. 3.3). On the other hand, taxation of imputed income from owner-occupied housing and so-called street charges and the like were abolished, and property taxation was introduced as a part of the tax reform in 1993. Despite increased monetary stability, it is surprising how many Finnish households still prefer housing loans with short maturity and choose annually revised (so called one year Euribor) interest rates instead of longer or fixed interest rates to shelter themselves from interest risks.

There were also institutional changes in public funding of housing. The National Housing Board was closed down by the end of 1980s, and a new governmental agency The Housing Fund of Finland (ARA) was established in 1993. Its main task is to provide financing for ARAVA (state-subsidised) rental housing production, allocate interest subsidies and grants (for housing repairs) and guarantees on loans for owner-occupied housing. During the bust of 1990s, housing production was predominantly based on financing from ARA. Later, privately financed housing production began to increase. In recent years ARA has raised funds through securitisation in order to be competitive alongside private housing finance with low interest rates and long maturities (Tulla 1999).

Also the private rental market has changed. Rent control was lifted from new contracts in 1993, and it was abolished completely in 1995. During the economic crisis years unsold newly constructed housing and parts from old dwelling stock were rented and rents stayed first at their previous levels. With the improving economy rents began to increase, especially in the HMA. The supply and the share of rental housing in housing stock has increased as, in addition to supply of public housing, household owned dwellings (flats in housing companies) have been increasingly rented. However, private institutional investors have not increased their investments in rental housing. This may reflect old fears of rent control and on the other hand, the high returns available from the stock market before their last turn down in 2001.

3.3 Basic Facts About Housing in Helsinki Metropolitan Area and in Finland

3.3.1 Institutional Aspects of HMA and Housing

Helsinki is the capital city of Finland, a country with 5.2 million inhabitants. The Helsinki metropolitan area (HMA), as defined here, consists of Helsinki and eleven surrounding municipalities with about 1.2 million people. We shall call Helsinki and the three nearest surrounding municipalities Espoo, Kauniainen and Vantaa (cf. Fig. 3.5) the capital city municipalities (CCM), which has a population of one million people. Fig. 3.5 displays the geography of CCM. Finland is a unitary (non-federal) country. Unlike in Scandinavian countries, there are only two tiers of government with their own revenue sources: the central government and 448 (in 2000) municipalities. At the regional level there are, however, 19 regional councils who are responsible for regional planning and development and as such key actors in carrying out regional policies with national and EU finance and local sources. To compensate for the missing regional tier, municipalities co-operate in the provision of public services, especially social and health services, in the form of joint municipal authorities (226 in 2000).

HMA belongs to Uusimaa regional council, but the four CCM municipalities also form a unique voluntary Helsinki metropolitan council, which deals with traffic and solid waste management. Concerning planning in the area, its role is mainly that of research and planning co-operation, which is not binding. Members to both types of councils are elected by municipal councils, not by the electorate directly. The central government is represented at regional level by provinces and some other regional units of the state apparatus. HMA belongs to Uusimaa province.

Municipalities are responsible for master planning and detailed planning, and hold so-called planning monopoly under which they have the right to plan and make zoning decisions affecting all land, including that in private ownership. No dense development can take place without detailed plans drawn by the municipality. Ratified town plans are legally binding in the sense that they confirm the right to build, but they do not require it. Previously ministry level ratified plans made at local level but a reform in 1992 abolished the confirmation requirement of town plans and increased local power.

In the Finnish system landowners have the basic right to build, a general principle which can be restricted by zoning and site-specific development plans of municipalities. An implication of this freedom is that often the landowner gets compensation when the right to build is restricted by planning. On the other hand, most land-use projects are initiated and carried out by landowners, who in this role have considerable influence on planning. They must also be heard at various stages of the planning process and their interests are safeguarded by an appeal procedure. The new building code since the year 2000 also increases residents' participation in the planning process.

In order to have elastic supply of housing (and small price reactions) in growing urban areas, all parts of the supply chain, including land market and urban planning must function well. In Helsinki, the city is the biggest landowner (approximately two-thirds of land area) and its land management policies are thus essential. The state owns 14 per cent and 22 per cent is in private hands (Laakso and Keinänen 1995). The city does not sell land, it only leases land and has in this role more influence on developers decisions and timing of projects. On the other hand, for instance insurance companies do not invest in rental housing unless they also own the land on which houses are built. Contrary to Helsinki, in the rest of HMA most land is privately owned, municipalities owning less than a quarter of land.

The geographical structure of HMA, where the centre of Helsinki is on a coastal peninsula, makes land scarce relative to a circular metropolis, but there are also other problems. Most of already planned and well-located land with unutilised building right consists of single-family house plots, where only part of the building right has been utilised. Existing carrots and sticks are not sufficient to get this potential built. This is one reason why HMA, since 1960s, first spread to remote 'forest suburbs' where construction companies could buy raw land and develop it on the basis of so called site development contracts. Municipalities within HMA zoned remote areas for the firms and in exchange the firms did not face competition on their site and were allowed to pass costs of infrastructure to prospective buyers of dwellings. This practice, which ended with the last site development contracts, was contrary to the obligation of the municipality to finance infrastructure in urban planned areas.

On the other hand, there are still no development charges. This means that urban expansion (infrastructure) is financed by all local taxpayers. Local public finance, is predominantly based on local income tax, state grants and to less extent on user charges. Each municipality can freely set a flat tax rate, but on the top of that comes progressive state income tax. The local property tax introduced in 1993, could give an incentive to develop and build planned lots in good locations, but it has been and still is minor in importance. Its rate is determined at municipal level, but must fall within a band of allowed rates by type of building. Since 1993 the municipalities have also received a share (initially 44 per cent) of corporate income tax revenue, channelled from state to municipalities on the basis of the location of firms' employees.

Hedonic price regressions by Laakso (1991) indicate that income tax rate differences between Helsinki, Espoo, Kauniainen and Vantaa capitalise into prices of owner-occupied dwellings after controlling for a number of internal, external and distance characteristics of dwellings. The differences in the structure of housing stock within HMA also have consequences on local public finance. Namely in Helsinki, most dwellings are small, whereas Espoo, Vantaa and the affluent Kauniainen (inside Espoo) mainly consist of more spacious single family houses, detached houses and row houses. They zone and provide less of social housing (ARAVA etc.) than Helsinki. Under these circumstances, affluent families with children have increasingly moved out of Helsinki and eroded its income tax base. Only quite recently, the decision makers in Helsinki have acknowledged that they also need more affluent tax payers to be able to finance their increasing expenditure.

The financial situation has become especially acute since 2001, when economic growth and especially corporate income decreased substantially. The revenue from municipalities' share of corporate income tax receipts after its introduction in 1993 was initially minor in bust, grew in importance with the boom since mid 1990s, and has recently declined considerably, as one could expect of this rather unorthodox volatile local revenue source (cf. Musgrave 1959). Later, the state has decreased the share the municipalities get from corporate tax revenues first from 44.8 per cent to 40 per cent in 1998 and to 37.25 per cent in 2001. Lowering of municipalities' share has been partly compensated by abolishing a system of transfers from municipalities to state, which was related to value-added taxation of municipal services. These reforms and the fall in corporate income tax revenues affected negatively HMA, and especially Helsinki and Espoo, where ICT industry firms, which had boomed since mid-1990s, have their main concentration in Finland.

3.3.2 Population and Income Development in the HMA

In Finland urbanisation, as a large scale phenomenon, began after World War II. It was even then delayed by the relocation of the Karelian population (almost half a million) from areas lost in the war mainly to the countryside. The main reasons for urban growth were changes in the agricultural sector and rapid expansion of the industrial sector in cities. The first phase of urbanisation in 1950s and 1960s was characterised by the growth of a large number of cities, and, of course, also HMA grew rapidly. This development caused heavy pressures on the housing sector. In large cities, lack of both planned and well-located land, and financing infrastructure became major obstacles to housing production. The solution was site development contracts, which eased the financial burden. Large housing estates were built far from the city centre. At the same time, in the late 1950s and early 1960s, construction technology was switched to pre-cast concrete blocks. Multi-storey blocks became the dominant form of building in most suburban areas in the larger cities. This first phase on urbanisation increased the number of inhabitants in Helsinki from 368,519 in 1950 to 523,677 in 1970. For the same period the population of HMA grew from 496,517 to 827,400.

Table 3.1. Population development 1970–2000

	1970	1980	1990	2000
Helsinki	523,677	483,675	490,691	555,474
Espoo	92,655	133,835	169,833	213,271
Vantaa	72,215	129,918	152,263	178,471
HMA	827,400	930,368	1 033,796	1 200,568
Finland	4 705,961	4 771,292	4 974,563	5 181,115

Source: City of Helsinki: Regional data.

The aspiration to restrain mobility to Southern Finland and to largest cities had only minor success. Regional policy measures undertaken were of various types: new factories were established to areas suffering from the lack of job opportunities, new universities were established around the country and some governmental agencies were relocated away from the capital region. Also expansion of the welfare state in public service sectors (especially health and education) supported local employment and living conditions in remote areas. ARAVA-loans were given especially to those areas were unemployment problem was most severe. In 1980s also a special investment tax was collected in Helsinki in order to curb concentration of firms and job opportunities. Population growth in Helsinki was negative in late 1970s and only modestly positive in 1980s. On the other hand, Espoo and Vantaa grew steadily all the time. This suburban growth is a phenomenon that has been going on also during the second phase of urbanisation, which began in 1990s. In HMA population grew by roughly 167,000 in the period 1990–2000, that is about 16 per cent. As such it is one of the fastest growing areas in Europe. At the same time, and this is new compared to earlier developments, the number of growing areas outside HMA has been very limited, only half a dozen urban areas.

Alongside urbanisation, another stylised fact applying to most countries in the long run has been convergence of regional per capita income levels, usually measured by regional GDP per capita. In Fig. 3.4, we present results based on the use of household surveys (1971, 1976, 1981 and 1985) and income distribution data (1991–99), to show that there has been convergence in disposable income per equivalent consumption unit since early 1970s. In 1971 Helsinki was about 50 per cent and the rest of CCM (Espoo, Vantaa and Kauniainen) about 45 per cent above national average. In 1999, Helsinki was about 30 per cent and the rest of CCM about 20 per cent above national average. These results are based on incomes, which have not been corrected by regional (non-existing) price indices, where the biggest regional difference is in housing component.

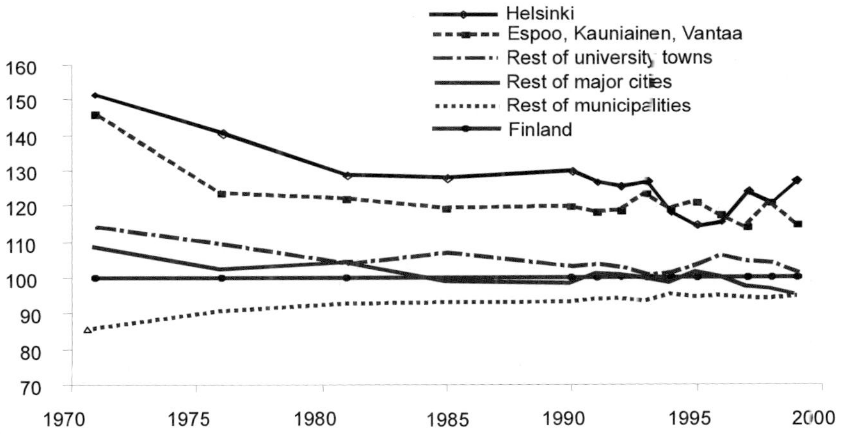

Fig. 3.4. Relative disposable income per capita differences in 1970–99 Finland = 100 (Source: Laakso and Loikkanen 2004)

As for intra-urban disparities, what is new is the increase of income differentials inside HMA. During the economic boom in the latter half of 1990s, the highest decile has really been taking off and inequality of disposable income within HMA has grown. This development is mainly due to increased capital income (option arrangements etc.) of ICT-firms' shareowners, quite a few of which live in HMA. This phenomenon has also implications on HMA's spatial socio-economic structure. Earlier low-income areas were quite evenly distributed in the core municipalities of HMA (Helsinki, Espoo and Vantaa). During the 1990s, to some extent as a result of recession but mainly as a result of economic boom after recession, a new kind of development has emerged. Clear east-west divide is apparent

(Fig. 3.5). Districts with a concentration of relatively low-income inhabitants are emerging. Western part of Helsinki, Espoo almost as a whole, and some other municipalities in HMA, receive on the average more affluent and more educated new residents. Eastern part of Helsinki, with the exception of small house dominated affluent coastal districts, and areas along railroad lines, fall behind. Still, we must keep in mind that in most of these areas, the absolute income level is not declining.

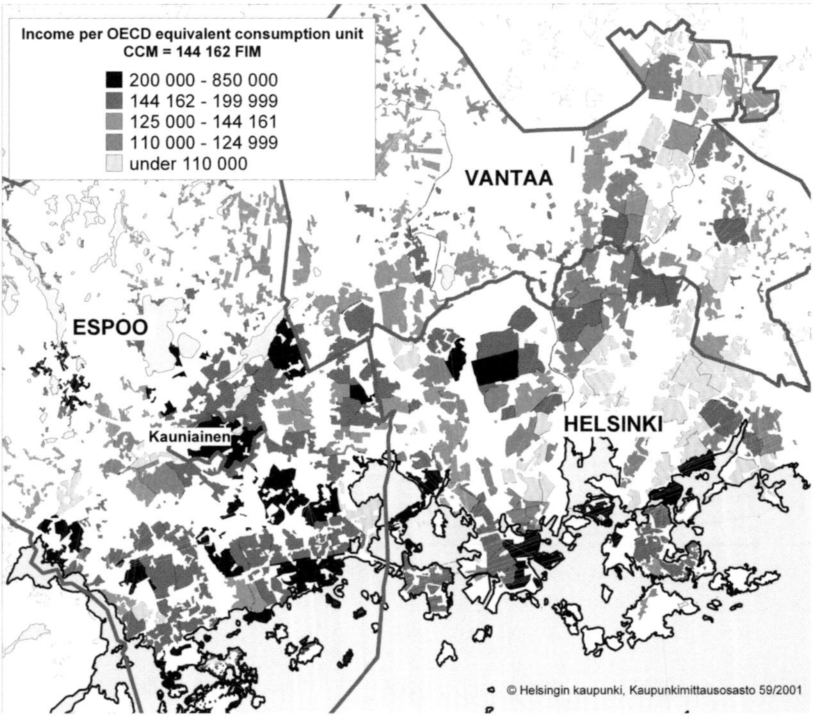

Fig. 3.5. Income per OECD equivalent consumption unit in 2001 in CCM (Source: City of Helsinki: Pekka Vuori)

3.3.3 Tenure Structure

In Finland, two types of tenure, owning and renting dominate (Table 3.2). Other tenure forms (housing co-operatives) are of minor role. From 1950 to early 1990s, owner-occupancy gained its position as the major tenure form. Since then, rental (living in rented apartment etc.) has increased its share. HMA differs noticeably from the national average. In 2000 rental dwellings accounted for almost 47 per cent of the housing stock in Helsinki and about 42 per cent in HMA. Nationally rental-dwellings represent only 31 per cent of the housing stock. There are in all 680,000 rental dwellings in Finland of which government-subsidised (ARAVA) dwellings account for little over half. Owner occupancy is still the major tenure form in HMA, but it has lost some of its dominance over the last ten years.

Table 3.2. Housing stock broken down by tenure type[2] (per cent)

	1990 Owner-occupied	Rental	Other	2000 Owner-occupied	Rental	Other
Helsinki	54.4	30.5	15.1	43.3	46.8	9.9
Espoo	67.0	20.5	12.5	53.6	35.2	11.2
Vantaa	66.2	23.5	10.3	53.8	36.6	9.6
HMA	60.9	25.5	13.6	47.8	42.2	10.0
Finland	66.7	20.2	13.1	58.1	30.8	11.1

Source: City of Helsinki: Regional data.

Right-of-occupancy dwellings (a kind of limited ownership) are a new phenomenon in Finnish housing markets; the system was established in 1990. In 2001, there were 26,299 right-of-occupancy dwellings in Finland. From that stock, about 51 per cent is located in HMA. Rental dwellings fall into two major categories: private rental and municipality or non-profit organisation owned rental dwellings. The latter group is mainly financed by ARAVA loans which are currently managed by the Housing Fund of Finland. Distribution of these dwellings is subject to income level qualifications. During the recession years in early 1990s, housing production consisted to a great extent of ARAVA-rental dwellings. As a result, the share of ARAVA-rental dwellings grew in all HMA's three large municipalities (i.e. except Kauniainen): in Helsinki from 12.5 per cent (1990) to 15.2 per cent (1998), in Espoo from 8.1 per cent (1990) to 12.1 per cent (1998) and in Vantaa from 6.9 per cent (1990) to 10.3 per cent (1998). Out of all rental dwellings, the share of municipality-owned units increased during 1990–98 in Espoo from 32.4 per cent to 35.4 per cent and in Vantaa from 25.3 per cent to 29.1 per cent. In Helsinki, it decreased slightly from 33.9 per cent to 32.7 per cent.

Private rental dwelling stock has declined from 1960s. Due to the production of municipality-owned rental dwellings, total rental dwelling stock in Helsinki declined only slightly in the period 1975–90. During the 1990s, the number of private rental dwellings has increased. There are mixed reasons for this. The depression in early 1990s left quite a few owner-occupied dwellings unsold and they were rented. On the other hand, rent control was lifted from new in 1993 and in 1995 also from old rental units as well. Furthermore, there were changes in taxation, which made rental income subject to capital income tax rate (currently 29 per cent) as dual income taxation (DIT) was adopted. These changes made renting more profitable. On the other hand, new profitability requirements in insurance sector have diminished the interest of institutional sector to rental dwellings.

[2] When interpreting Table 3.2, we must keep in mind that column *other* consist of four types of dwellings; company-owned dwellings, co-operative dwellings, tenure type unknown and dwellings that are not permanently-occupied. So the tenure forms *owner-occupied* and *rental* are very tightly defined.

3.3.4 Housing Stock and Spaciousness

In 1990, there were 487,607 dwelling units in HMA. Over half of that stock, 259,033 dwellings, was located in Helsinki. The average size of dwelling in Helsinki has been, and still is, well below the regional and national level (Table 3.3). It is also worth mentioning that new dwellings are also quite small – in Helsinki the average size of dwelling has increased one square metre in eight years although over 30,000 new dwellings have been constructed. The development is similar also in Espoo and Vantaa, although the average size of dwelling in 1990 was higher.

The average floor area per person in Finland was 29 square metres in 1985 and it increased to 35 square metres by 1998. In this respect HMA and the whole country do not differ significantly, and also inside HMA, the municipalities are at similar level, all having 32–33 square metres per person (Table 3.3).

As for housing consumption profiles over the life-cycle, at national level in 1996 spaciousness still starts low; around 30 square metres or less per person for younger people, reaches the average (about 35 sqm/person) in the age category 45–49 and the maximum (46 sqm/person) at the age of 60–64 and remains at that level for oldest people (Housing indicators 1999).

As for tenure type, owner-occupied dwellings (36 sqm/person) are less crowded than private (28.6 sqm/person) or social rental (28.1 sqm/person) dwellings. Similar life cycle profiles and tenure form differences apply roughly speaking for HMA, too.

The number of homeless people in Finland was about 10,000 (0.2 per cent of the population) in 1998 and 5,300 (0.6 per cent) of them were in the HMA. The number of queuing households per vacancy in social rental housing was about three in the whole country and five in the HMA.

Table 3.3. Number of dwellings, average size of dwelling and average floor area per person in Helsinki, Espoo, Vantaa, HMA and Finland, 1990 and 1998

	1990 Number of dwellings	Average size of dwelling [sqm]	Average floor area per person [sqm]	1998 Number of dwellings	Average size of dwelling [sqm]	Average floor area per person [sqm]
Helsinki	259,033	60.3	30.6	290,128	61.3	32.2
Espoo	72,369	77.0	31.2	88,640	78.1	32.9
Vantaa	65,334	71.3	29.3	77,597	72.1	31.7
HMA	487,607	68.0	30.7	561,269	69.5	32.6
Finland	2 209,556	74.4	31.4	2 449,115	76.0	34.5

Source: City of Helsinki: Regional data.

Dwellings also differ considerably in size, when we break down the housing stock by building type and tenure form. By building type, detached dwellings (104 sqm) and semidetached and row-house type dwellings (96 sqm) are bigger than apartments (56 sqm) in blocks of dwellings. On average rental units are smaller

(53 sqm) than owner-occupied dwellings (72 sqm).

With regard to building type, municipalities in HMA differ significantly (Table 3.4). Helsinki is clearly a city dominated by blocks of dwellings in multi-storey buildings. Over 85 per cent of dwellings represent this type. In Espoo the share of blocks was 55.7 per cent and in Vantaa it was 61.6 per cent. These shares were quite stable over the period 1990–2000. Municipalities also differ when housing stock is broken down according to number of rooms (in dwellings).

In Helsinki the largest portion, over 60 per cent, of stock consists of dwellings with one or two rooms and a kitchen or kitchenette (Table 3.5). This is a distinctive feature of the housing stock in Helsinki. In Espoo, the respective share is less than 40 per cent (below national average) and in Vantaa it is about 45 per cent (about national average). Relative share of large dwellings, five rooms or more is in Espoo almost threefold relative to Helsinki.

Table 3.4. Housing stock broken down by building type in 1990 and 2000 (per cent)

	1990			2000		
	Blocks of flats	Detached, semi-detached and row-houses	Other or unknown	Blocks of flats	Detached, semi-detached and row-houses	Other or unknown
Helsinki	85.1	12.7	2.2	85.6	12.7	1.7
Espoo	56.5	41.1	2.4	55.7	42.8	1.5
Vantaa	61.6	36.9	1.5	61.7	37.5	0.8
HMA	68.9	28.9	2.2	68.4	30.0	1.6
Finland	42.5	54.2	3.3	43.5	53.8	2.7

Source: City of Helsinki: Regional data

Table 3.5. Structure of housing stock in 2000 by number of rooms[a] in dwellings (per cent)

	1 room	2 rooms	3 rooms	4 rooms	5 rooms or more
Helsinki	24.2	36.6	21.4	11.4	5.7
Espoo	10.9	27.9	25.8	20.5	14.0
Vantaa	11.9	33.3	27.3	18.4	8.7
Kauniainen	9.3	19.2	15.9	18.5	35.0
Rest of HMA	11.5	28.4	23.4	20.2	15.4
Finland	15.6	30.8	22.5	18.0	12.1

[a]Number of rooms in addition to kitchen or kitchenette.
Source: City of Helsinki: Regional data.

After World War II, the Helsinki metropolitan area has experienced a rapid growth. During the first decade, in 1950s, the growth was concentrated to Helsinki. After that, growth extended also to the municipalities surrounding Helsinki. Thus, it is quite natural that Helsinki as a regional centre also has the oldest housing stock in HMA. A bit more than 60 per cent of housing stock in Helsinki is built after 1960, whereas in Espoo 90 per cent and in Vantaa over 93 per cent of housing stock is built after 1960.

Table 3.6. Age of housing stock

	Construction period –1939	1940–59	1960–79	1980–2000
Helsinki	21.5	16.4	34.7	27.2
Espoo	1.5	7.5	40.9	49.1
Vantaa	1.3	5.5	47.7	45.4
Kauniainen	5.6	3.6	56.3	33.7
Rest of HMA	4.9	11.5	37.5	44.9

Source: City of Helsinki: Regional data.

3.3.5 Housing Expenditure

During the 1990s, the share of households' housing expenditure[3] out of disposable income has grown significantly. It grew from 22.6 per cent in 1990 to 28.1 per cent in 1998 at national level. In CCM the respective shares were 20.7 per cent in 1990 and 25.8 per cent in 1998.

When we eliminate non-monetary components from housing expenditure, we find a clear division between tenure forms. Rents have increased especially during latter part of 1990s whereas income growth of typical renter households, which was negative during the bust, has also later been modest. Thus the burden of housing expenditure has increased for renters. For them the share of housing expenditure relative to disposable income was 16.4 per cent in 1990 and reached the peak level of 25.5 per cent in 1996. As for owner-occupiers, households without housing loan found their housing expenditure position quite stable during 1990s. On the contrary, quite a few of those who bought dwellings in the boom of late 1980s got into serious problems during the following bust. As the economy collapsed incomes of many owner-occupiers dropped. Also increased interest rates raised the share of housing expenditure relative to income. For all those who had housing loan, this share was 26.5 per cent in 1990 and 29.3 per cent in 1996 (Siikanen et al. 1999).

3.4 Housing Production and Housing Prices in the Helsinki Metropolitan Area

In early 1990s, when Finland experienced the deep economic recession, housing production, which had peaked in 1990 (over 65,000 dwellings), fell drastically (Fig. 3.6). In 1996 less than 21,000 dwellings was produced. Also in HMA housing production fell sharply – in 1996 less than 6 000 dwellings were completed.

[3] Housing expenditure is calculated using the gross rent method. As such it also includes some imputed components like the return to residents' investment in owner-occupied housing (calculated by using market rents) and appreciation or depreciation of housing value.

Since then production has recovered, but it still lags behind the increase in demand for housing, which stems from both rapid population and income increase in HMA. As a result of this, housing prices and rents have increased.

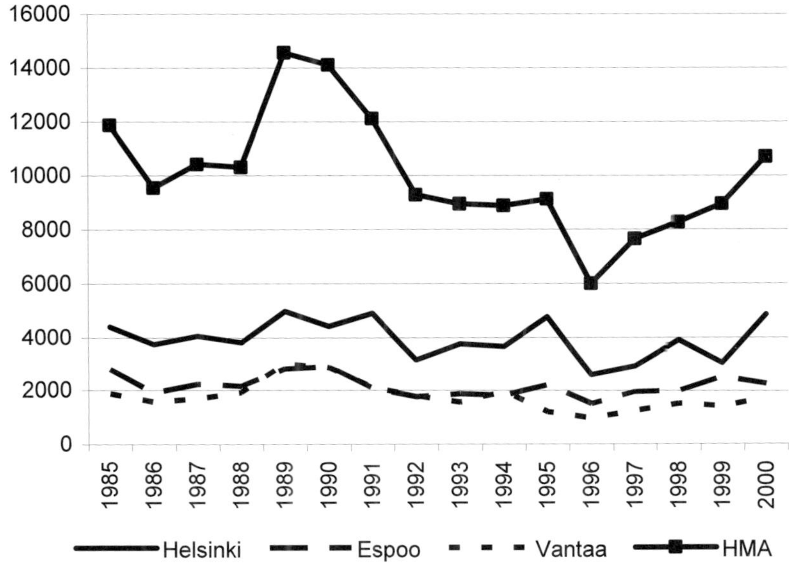

Fig. 3.6. Housing production in HMA 1985–2000 (Source: City of Helsinki: Regional data)

During the period 1991–2000 housing production in Helsinki, but to some extent also in other HMA municipalities, concentrated on municipality-owned rental dwellings. Only 30 per cent of production in that period was owner-occupied dwellings, and HITAS-dwellings represented a substantial portion inside this share. In some new areas, there are practically no unregulated owner-occupied dwellings at all. This development can partly be explained by the recession. There is also bias inside the rental sector – production of privately financed rental dwellings has not really started at all despite abolishment of rent control and tax reforms. In Helsinki one reason for this is the fact that institutional investors want to own both the land and the buildings, whereas the city as the biggest landowner only leases land.

During the 1990s real rents in private rental units increased substantially in HMA and especially in Helsinki (Fig. 3.7). One basic reason for this is the underlying limited supply due to longstanding rent control. Its abolishment in 1993 and 1995 lead to rent increases once the bust was over and the economy began to grow fast, and mobility to HMA increased. In 1985 the rent level of private rental dwellings in the core municipalities of HMA was 8–13 per cent above national average. In 2001 the respective rent level in Helsinki was nearly 40 per cent and in both Espoo and Vantaa about 20 per cent above national average. In new contracts the difference in rent level between Helsinki and the national average is substantially larger. Behind this development is of course rapid increase in population and housing demand, to which it is difficult to get response from the inelastic supply of rental housing.

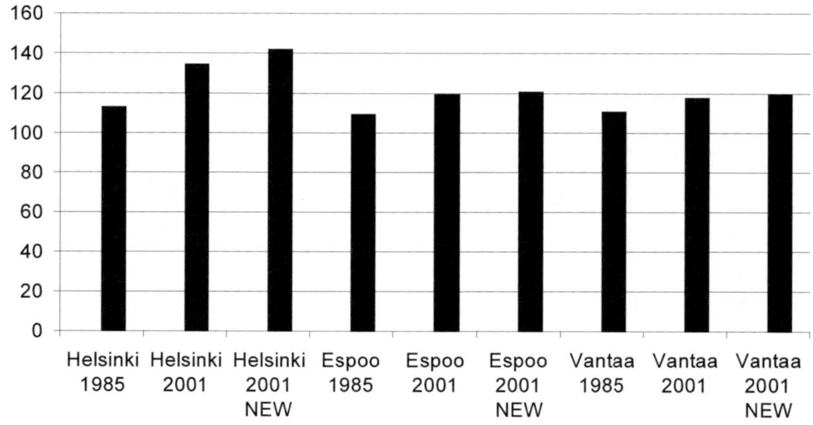

Fig. 3.7. Relative rent level in private rental dwellings in Helsinki, Espoo (including Kauniainen) and Vantaa 1985 and 2001, Finland = 100, NEW = new contracts (Source: Statistics Finland: Rents 2001 and Rents 1987)

In publicly financed ARAVA rental dwellings rents are determined on the basis of a formula which is applied to each rental housing company consisting of one or a few multi-storey building. Annual rent levels are based on running costs plus subsidised interest rate and down payment of housing loans. As such they are tied to historical construction costs, which cause rent dispersion in the rental stock according to age and location. To avoid some of this, pooling of municipal rental stock has taken place in quite a few municipalities, but not in Helsinki. As for average rent level in ARAVA rentals, in 1990 in CCM it was 19 per cent and in Finland 10 per cent lower than unregulated rents. In 2001 the difference in CCM was 27 per cent and in Finland 17 per cent.

During the last 15 years, house prices have been very volatile. In 1989 real house price index of Helsinki broke the line of 200 (1970 = 100) and only a few years later it decreased well below 100. In 2000/2001 the index was at the level of 160 (Fig. 3.8). This reveals the fact that although nominal prices are now at the same level as they were in 1989, in real terms the current situation, although problematic in many ways, is far from the overheated situation in late 1980s. On the other hand, current demand pressures are evident as housing production lags behind. The cyclical turns and movements in the house price index for CCM and for Finland are identical and simultaneous although Helsinki seems to react more strongly than other CCM municipalities and the whole country.

The relative differences between housing price levels (per square metres) in CCM core municipalities, Helsinki and Espoo, and Finland are now larger than they were in 1985 (Fig. 3.9). In Helsinki, the average price level is currently over 60 per cent and in Espoo almost 40 per cent above the national level. In Vantaa the housing price level exceeds the national average only by a few percentage points in 1985 and the relative difference has increased only slightly by 2001.

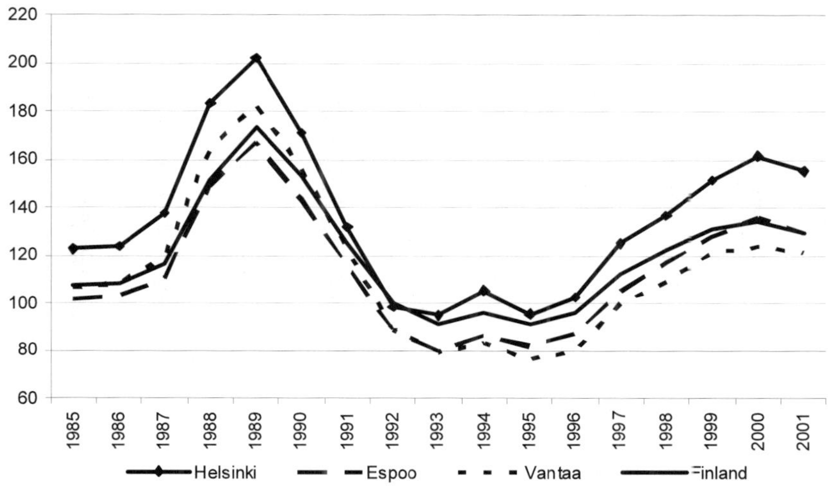

Fig. 3.8. Real house price index 1985–2001, 1970 = 100, apartment houses (Source: Statistics Finland: House prices 2001)

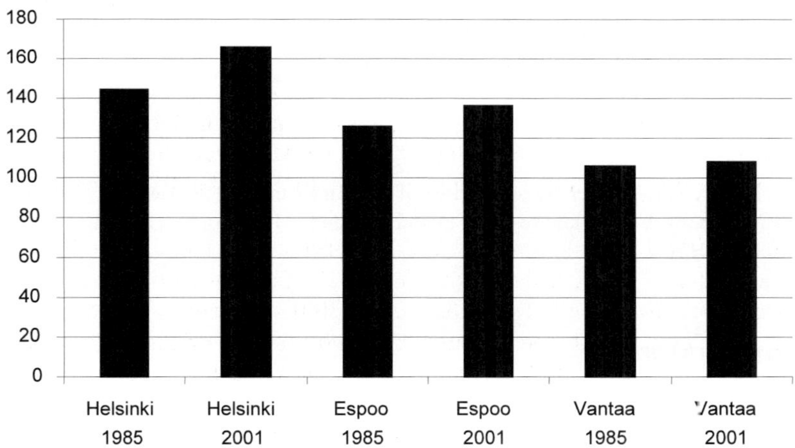

Fig. 3.9. Relative house prices (per m^2) in Helsinki, Espoo (including Kauniainen) and Vantaa 1985 and 2001, Finland = 100 (Sources: Statistics Finland: House prices 2001 and House prices 1987)

In order to take a closer look at intra-city housing price differences, we divide Helsinki into four parts by location and income level. Helsinki 1 is the southern part of city centre. There are only apartments in block of dwellings in that area. Helsinki 2 includes districts, which are located in western part of Helsinki plus some single family and row house dominated coastal districts from the east, and also two areas from the north belong to this category. It consists of both blocks and single family and row houses. All districts in Helsinki 1 and 2 are, by income statistics, well above city average. Helsinki 3 and Helsinki 4 are northern and eastern Helsinki, respectively. They have also small houses, but blocks dominate in these areas. Their income level is near the city average or clearly below it.

With this classification of Helsinki, it turns out that the housing price level in Helsinki 1 is more than twice the national average. On the other hand, it is almost threefold relative to the average of the rest of Finland outside CCM (Fig. 3.10). Even Helsinki 4 has a price level which is 1.5 times higher than in the rest of Finland.

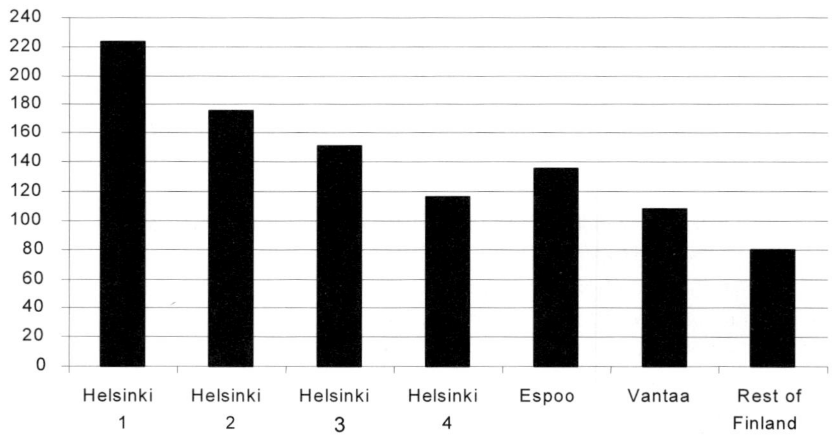

Fig. 3.10. Relative prices (per square metre) of dwellings in 2001 in Helsinki, Espoo (including Kauniainen), Vantaa and rest of Finland, Finland = 100 (Source: Statistics Finland: House prices 2001)

3.5 Conclusions

Urbanisation has come as a surprise in Finland despite the fact that this trend has been prevailing internationally. The share of urban population in Finland was only 64 per cent in 1998, a rather low figure relative to countries with similar GNP per capita level. This means that urbanisation is likely to continue and problems in urban areas and especially in the HMA will not fade away in the future. In addition to domestic factors, also immigration can increase population in HMA. In the year

2000 there were only 90,000 foreigners living in Finland, of which 40,000 live in HMA. In Helsinki the share of foreigners was 5 per cent. The challenges of urban growth for housing in the HMA can be expected to continue.

In 1960, Finland and the Helsinki metropolitan area were lagging behind West European countries both in income level and housing conditions. Subsequently, there has been progress in both respects. During the next 20 years, economic growth in Finland exceeded the average of OECD-Europe. As for housing, the number of rooms (counting kitchen over 7 sqm as one room) per person increased from 0.76 to 1.28 in Finland (and from 0.85 to 1.32 in HMA). Despite this progress, in absolute terms, housing consumption gap relative to other countries did not decrease. Among Nordic countries, for instance Sweden the number of rooms in 1960 was 1.21 and it grew to 1.76 in 1980, and the respective figures for Norway were 1.26/1.84 and Denmark 1.40/1.98. Finland has reached the Swedish GNP per capita level at the turn of the millennium, but spaciousness still clearly lags behind the Swedish level in 1980 (1.76), as in 1998 there were 1.6 rooms per person (1.59 for HMA). As for the current (1997) situation in Nordic capitals, Helsinki is clearly lagging behind the other ones. The number of square metres per inhabitant was in Copenhagen 46, in Oslo 43, in Stockholm 38, and in Helsinki only 33.

These figures suggest that the Finnish housing markets are still undergoing a structural adjustment to the new institutional framework described in this chapter. Underdeveloped housing finance is no longer an obstacle to increasing real housing consumption (especially spaciousness) to internationally comparable level relative to income. After the first stage of turmoil, financial deregulation, as well as Finland's membership in EU and EMU have increased macroeconomic stability, improved access to housing finance and lowered interest rates, thus increasing housing demand throughout the household sector. The structural adjustment problem is nowadays predominantly related to the limited ability of the supply side to respond to increased housing demand. Supply side problems have to do with the working of land markets, urban planning and the construction industry. They have led to an outcome during the last few years, where housing production and real housing consumption have increased less and housing prices and rents have risen more than in case of more elastic supply. This is especially true for the whole capital city area where the share of housing expenditure in disposable income increased from 20.7 per cent in 1990 by about 5 percentage points by the year 1998.

References

Aarma H, Laakso S, Loikkanen HA (1993) Housing in Estonia and Finland. In: Lugus O, Vartia P (eds) Estonia and Finland. A Retrospective Socioeconomic Comparison. The Research Institute of the Finnish Economy (ETLA) series B 86, Helsinki, pp 333–80

Bengs C, Loikkanen HA (1991) The Finnish Housing Market: Structure, Institutions and Policy Issues. In: Hårsman B, Quigley JM (eds) Housing Market and Hhousing Institutions: An International Comparison. Kluwer Academic Publishers, Boston

Kalela J, Kiander J, Kivikuru U, Loikkanen HA, Simpura J (eds) (2001) Down from the Heavens, up from the Ashes. The Economic Crisis in Finland. Government Institute for Economic Research and the Academy of Finland, Helsinki

Kuismanen M, Laakso S, Loikkanen HA (1999) Demographic Factors and the Demand for Housing in the Helsinki Metropolitan Area. Government Institute for Economic Research, Discussion Papers 191, Helsinki

Laakso S (1997) Urban Housing Prices and the Demand for Housing Characteristics. A Study on Housing Prices and the Willingness to Pay for Housing Characteristics and Local Public Goods in the Helsinki Metropolitan Area. The Research Institute of the Finnish Economy (ETLA) series A 27, Helsinki

Laakso S (2000) Regional Housing Markets in Boom and Bust: the Experience of Finland. Pellervo Economic Research Institute Reports 169, Helsinki

Laakso S Keinänen O (1995) Helsinki. In: Berry J, McGreal S (eds) European Cities, Planning Systems and Property Markets. E&FN Spon, London, pp 121–37

Laakso S, Loikkanen HA (1995) Finnish Homes – Through Passages or Traps? Real Estate Economics 23: 475–95

Laakso S, Loikkanen HA (2004) Kaupunkitalous [Urban Economics]. Gaudeamus, Helsinki

Musgrave RA (1959) The Theory of Public Finance. McGraw-Hill, New York

Siikanen A, Säylä M, Tahvanainen M (1999) Suomalaisten Asumismenot [Housing Expenditure of Finns]. Suomen ympäristö 330. Ympäristöministeriö, Helsinki

Statistical Yearbook of the City of Helsinki (2001)

Statistics Finland, Asuntojen Hinnat 1987 [House Prices 1987]. 3th quarter. Statistics Finland, Helsinki

Statistics Finland, Vuokrat 1987 [Rents 1987]. Statistics Finland, Helsinki

Statistics Finland, Housing Indicators 1999. Statistics Finland, Helsinki

Statistics Finland, Asuntojen Hinnat 2001 [House Prices 2001]. 4th quarter. Statistics Finland, Helsinki

Statistics Finland, Statistical Yearbook 2001. Statistics Finland, Helsinki

Statistics Finland, Vuokrat 2001 [Rents 2001]. Statistics Finland, Helsinki

Tulla S (1999) Securitisation and Finance for Social Housing in Finland. Urban Studies 36: 647–56

4 Housing Markets and Policies in the Munich Metropolitan Area

Peter Friedrich[1] and Christian Piesch[2]

[1]Bundeswehr University Munich, Neubiberg
[2]City of Munich, Munich

4.1 Introduction

Housing markets in the Munich metropolitan area are undergoing new developments and are facing new challenges because of changes in the determinants of the supply of and demand for housing as well as changes in housing policies and urban planning. Some of those developments concern:

- the suburbanisation and city to hinterland migration,
- the evolution of the population,
- economic growth,
- development projects in the surrounding communities like around the new airport,
- city and development planning,
- changes in social housing policies,
- growing financial strain and narrowing limits to the fiscal resources of municipalities, the Free State of Bavaria and the Federal Republic of Germany.

In the following we will present information on these factors influencing the metropolitan housing markets. Therefore we shall

- define the region under analysis,
- describe the housing markets,
- describe housing policies, and
- formulate policy recommendations.

In particular, the following questions will be addressed:

- How to characterise the Munich metropolitan area (MMA) and to define the metropolitan area to be analysed? Which regional housing market conditions prevail in the MMA compared to other metropolitan areas in Germany?
- Which are the general features of the housing markets of Munich and its hinterland?
- How will the supply of and the demand for housing evolve?
- Which are the housing policies and their results?
- Which are the future perspectives of the Munich housing market?

The first question will be dealt with in the next section which focuses on basic assumptions, the region and its delineation, and general features of the Munich metropolitan housing situation compared to other German metropolitan areas. A third section is devoted to the third and fourth questions whereas housing policies are intensively discussed in the fourth section. The fifth section offers results, future perspectives, and recommendations concerning housing policies.

4.2 The Munich Metropolitan Area

4.2.1 Basic Assumptions

The metropolitan housing markets will be analysed with the help of data available mostly up to 2000 or even 2001. Regarding past developments, data from 1987 or 1980 are used and presented. The time horizon for the projections is 2015.

Economic developments underlying these data are considered. With respect to future oriented data some assumptions are stated explicitly, others are used implicitly. In line with other analysts we assume that recent trends will continue; they may, however, get more accentuated by 2015.[1]

Housing comprises all buildings used for housing purposes. Sometimes buildings for commercial and industrial usage are also considered if they can be adapted for housing purposes and vice versa.

The methods used will be of an informative nature in the sense that no sophisticated econometric modelling is offered. The latter is not available for the Munich housing market. Therefore, we shall embark on an interpretation of existing materials which, in part, will be presented in a systematic manner for the first time. We shall concentrate on insights that are gained from reports of the City of Munich, the Assoc. of Regional Development of Outer Munich, the Chamber of Commerce of Munich and Upper Bavaria, from housing companies and investment firms and from statistical offices. The form of analysis chosen is economic reasoning.

[1] Mostly we follow the arguments employed by the City of Munich in their projections and reports, but also those of the Free State of Bavaria in their regional development plan (Bayerische Staatsregierung 2001), and expert studies on development of German metropolitan areas as well as housing markets.

As there is lot of commuting between Munich and its hinterland and some households choose housing inside the city of Munich while others prefer its hinterland, the housing market of Munich is closely interrelated with that of surrounding towns and counties. Moreover, there is a tendency toward suburbanisation as more and more people settle in the Munich hinterland. Therefore the regional dimension of the housing market of the Munich metropolitan area has to be specified.

4.2.2 Delineation of the Regional Dimension of the Munich Metropolitan Housing Market

Munich is situated in Bavaria, in Southern Germany. It is located at the banks of the river Isar in upper Bavaria between the river Danube and the Bavarian Alps (see Fig. 4.1). As the capital of Bavaria it is well connected by highways to other cities like Stuttgart, Nuremberg, Berlin, Salzburg, Vienna, Innsbruck, Milan and Prague. Railway connections are adequate, and it possesses the second busiest airport of Germany. The nearest agglomerations are at Stuttgart, Nuremberg and Zurich.

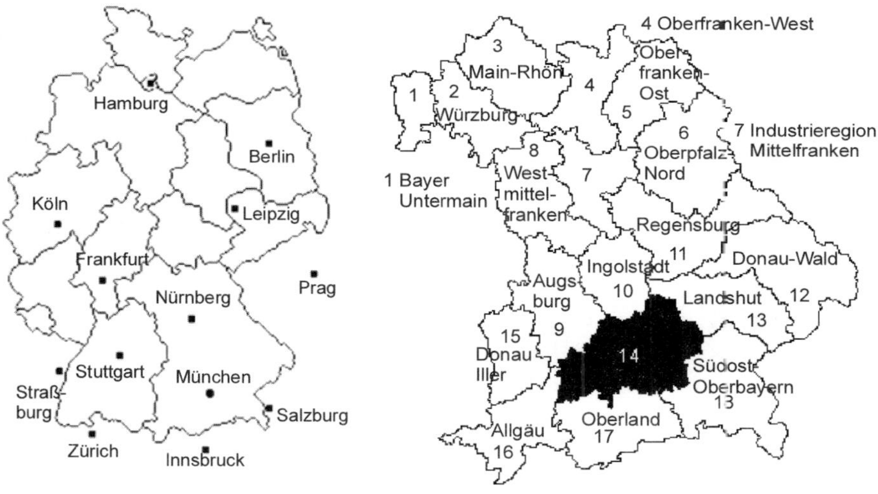

Fig. 4.1. Location of the Munich agglomeration

The Munich metropolitan area covers approximately. 5,500 km^2 and is the second largest of the 18 Bavarian planning regions. With its 2.4 million inhabitants (of which 1.2 million live in Munich, see Fig. 4.2), it is one of the most populated regions of southern Germany and neighbouring countries. The size of the Munich metropolitan area is comparable to the metropolitan area of Hamburg.

The city of Munich is divided into 25 districts, which are not identical to the 23 intra-urban housing market areas (see Fig. 4.12). At 5.2 per cent, Munich has the lowest unemployment rate of the bigger Germany cities (Fig. 4.2 and Table 4.1).

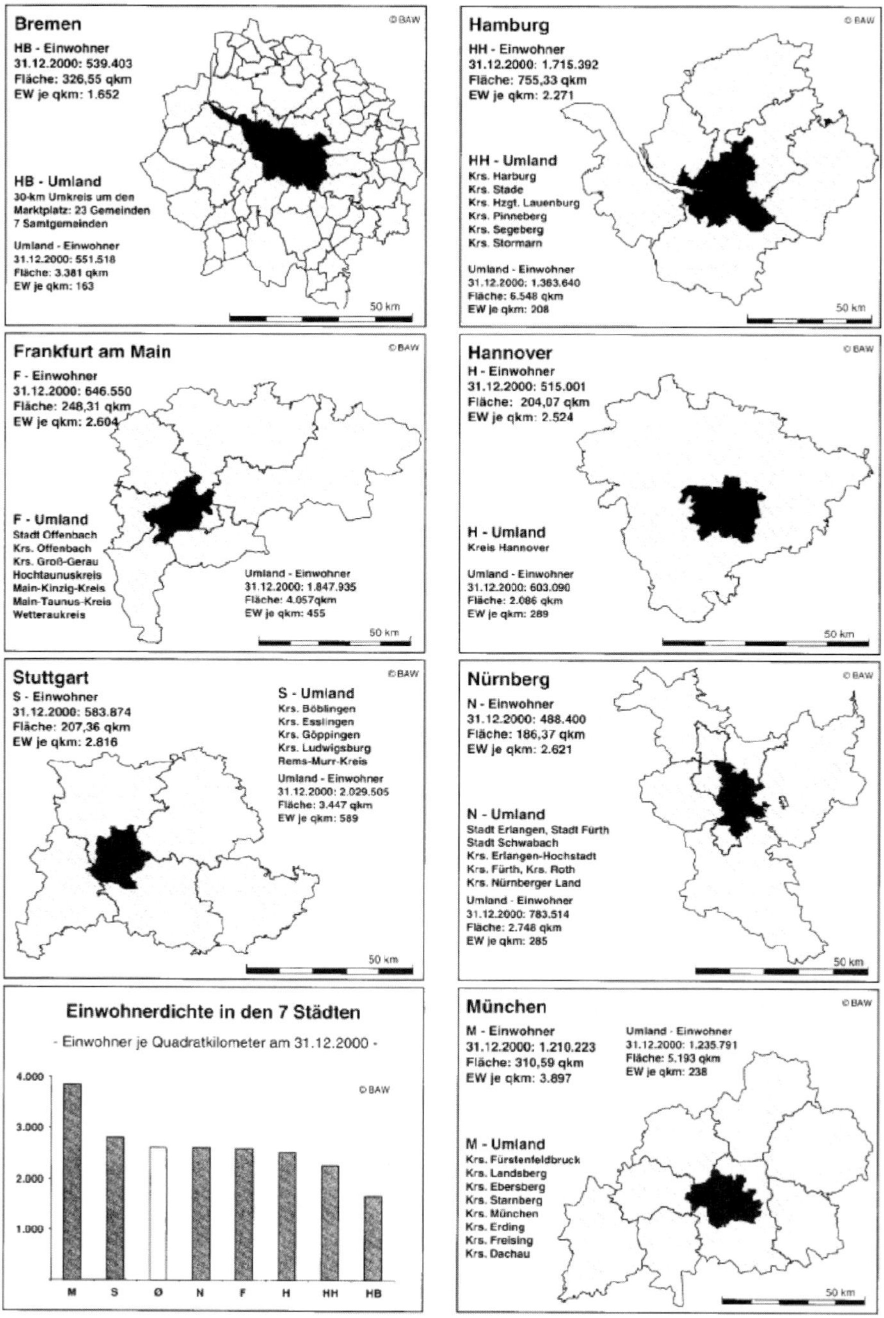

Fig. 4.2. German monocentric agglomerations and their hinterland (Source: Schönert 2002 p. 3)

Table 4.1. Comparison of housing market indicators

City	Area 2000 [km^2]	Population (first residence) 2001 [Million]	Net out-migration to hinterland per 100,000 inhabitants 1981–99	Unemployment rate related to all civilian employees 2000 [%]	Price of land multi family dwellings, good location 2001 [€/m^2]	New constructions (housing units) 1998–2000	In per cent of housing stock 2000	Flat price (good standard) 2001 [€/sqm]	Rent newly constructed 2001 [€/sqm]
Berlin	862	3.382		17.60	511	39382	2.16	1738	6.60
Bremen	327	0.539	481	12.60	345	5150	1.86	1326	6.50
Dortmund	280	0.585		14.80	358	6121	2.09	1768	7.20
Duisburg	232	0.514		14.50	261	4216	1.67	1585	7.20
Düsseldorf	217	0.596		9.50	716	6583	2.12	2352	11.80
Essen	210	0.596	587	12.40	435	2705	0.87	1892	7.70
Frankfort	248	0.651	398	6.90	818	7757	2.35	2301	9.20
Hamburg	755	1.715	400	10.10	511	21181	2.52	2045	9.50
Hannover	204	0.506		11.70	496	3688	1.33	1380	6.90
Cologne	405	0.969	574	12.20	343	14484	2.96	2301	9.20
Munich	310	1.248	483	5.20	946	16364	2.38	2659	13.00
Stuttgart	207	0.552		6.50	690	5962	2.10	1790	9.50

Sources: Statistical Yearbook Munich 2001; Referat für Stadtplanung und Bauordnung der Landeshauptstadt München 2002; Schönert 2002.

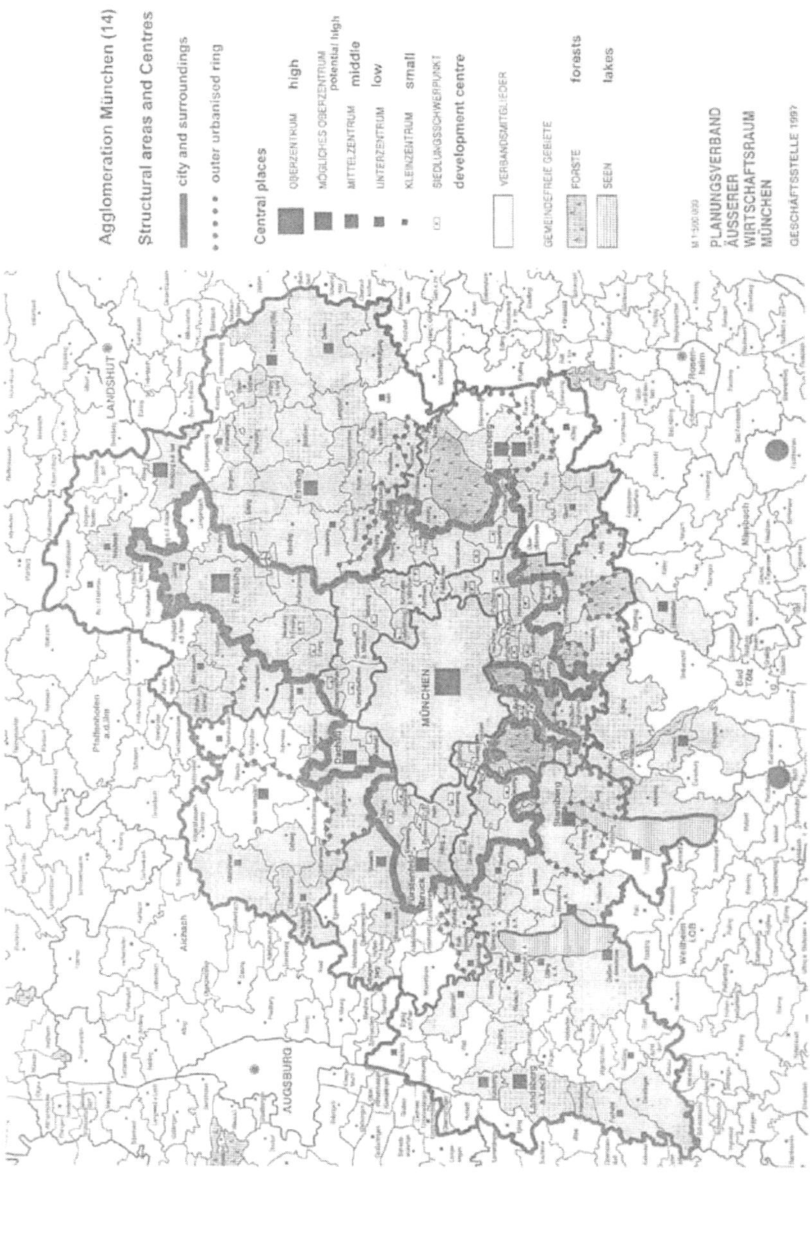

Fig. 4.3. German monocentric agglomerations and their hinterland (Source: Planungsverband äußerer Wirtschaftsraum München 2001)

The structure of the economy of Munich is rather diversified. This is shown in Table 4.2 which presents structural data concerning the city of Munich and its hinterland, consisting of the neighbouring counties, Bavaria and Germany. Although the ratio between service industries and production industries does not deviate much from the general German situation, many firms in the service sector belong to high-tech industries, e.g. media and cultural industries, and the IT sector.

The production sector comprises advanced industries like automobiles, transportation, aerospace, computers, and mechanical engineering. The great variety of industries gives stability to the economy of Munich and provides chances of further development in the direction of high-tech industries but also modern crafts and services.

Great efforts are made to raise the skill level of labour, to improve the soft and hard location factors, to extend private-public-partnerships, to utilise the advantages offered by three universities, many colleges and other institutions of higher learning and professional training (Referat für Stadtplanung und Bauordnung der Landeshauptstadt München 2000). Munich is aware of regional competition and hence enforces city marketing, the improvement of the infrastructure such as the extension of the airport, mass transport systems such as regional trains (S-Bahn), underground and perhaps even magnetic trains.[2]

During the past ten years, the population of the city of Munich has been rather stable, income increased as did disposable income and employment (see Tables 4.1 and 4.2). In the counties around Munich, including the county of Landsberg on Lech, similar developments have prevailed. Population, income and employment have been growing (Planungsverband äußerer Wirtschaftsraum 2001 p. 4)

Although the city of Munich is well defined by its administrative borders, it is a difficult task to determine the extent of the metropolitan housing market. As shown in Fig. 4.3, there are several ways in which the regional housing market may be defined, because there are various options of how to delineate the hinterland. Functional areas like labour market areas could be used. These functional areas seem appropriate to some extent, but the data relevant for housing markets fit such a delineation of the hinterland only partly. Moreover, data are gathered mostly on the county level.

There are four common definitions of the Munich hinterland:

- One definition comprises contiguous municipalities and the city of Freising.[3] The advantage of this definition is that it stresses the industrial and housing developments caused by the new airport. This hinterland is becoming more densely populated and more integrated with the city of Munich. It does not

[2] It supports investments in highways and the improvement of railway passenger and freight traffic, the enlargement of fair and exhibition companies and their capacities. It supports the improvement of universities and research institutions, sports arenas, projects in the fields of communication, and efforts to keep the high standards of opera, museums and the many cultural and historical monuments. Munich preserves the traditional shape and city panorama however, with adaptations to modern architecture.

[3] This hinterland definition includes Dachau and Füstenfeldbruck.

comprise the whole housing market area (676,374 inhabitants: Planungsverband äußerer Wirtschaftsraum 2001 p. 3).

- Another definition excludes Freising and its neighbouring towns. Both definitions cover the Munich agglomeration. The so-defined hinterland is too small to cover the entire housing supply and demand. Many employees working in Munich choose flats and houses outside this region (617,804 inhabitants: Planungsverband äußerer Wirtschaftsraum 2001 p. 3).
- A third definition adds to the first one an outer urbanised ring of municipalities. It considers several additional towns in the south, south east and in the north west. It reflects more adequately the agglomerative areas existing directly in the vicinity of Munich. However, not all towns that are connected by S-Bahn to Munich (see Fig. 4.8) or can easily be reached by highway are captured. Not all necessary statistical data are available for this definition (820,430 inhabitants: Planungsverband äußerer Wirtschaftsraum 2001 p. 3)
- The hinterland definition comprising the NUTS[4] counties of Dachau and the county of Munich is also too small and does not coincide regionally with the housing markets.

Some indications on the size of the hinterland housing market areas are given by the advertisements for houses and flats in the local sections of newspapers such as 'Süddeutsche Zeitung' (see Sect. III, 4a). The area referred to in the advertisements coincides better with the official regional planning area 14 (see Fig. 4.4). For this area relevant statistical data are available, and hinterland regional development goals of the Free State of Bavaria have been defined in the 'Landesentwicklungsprogramm' (Bavarian state development programme).

Therefore, we shall define the Munich hinterland as the counties of Dachau, Ebersberg, Erding, Freising, Fürstenfeldbruck, Landsberg on Lech and the county of Munich. This hinterland comprises 1.2 million inhabitants and that of the whole metropolitan area including the city of Munich 2.4 million (Planungsverband äußerer Wirtschaftsraum 2001 p. 3).

4.2.3 Suburbanisation in Munich Compared to Other Metropolitan Housing Markets in Germany

There is considerable migration to and from Munich, partly due to movements from Munich to the hinterland. This kind of movement, which takes place in most German metropolitan regions, causes losses of inhabitants in the central cities. The main reason for this centre-to-periphery movement is the wish to improve one's individual housing condition.

Recently a study was conducted to discern the volume, the reasons and consequences of such movements related to the housing markets of the metropolitan ar-

[4] NUTS are the assistance areas of the European Union. NUTS I areas are in Germany the states (Kreis).

eas (Schönert 2002). For the period 1981–1999 seven German metropolitan regions were chosen that have a core city over 400,000 inhabitants and a hinterland based on the planning regions[5] (Munich region 14). The polycentric metropolitan Rhein–Ruhr region was excluded because of the many links among cities such as Cologne, Essen, Dortmund, Düsseldorf, Duisburg, and Bochum. For metropolitan regions in East Germany such as Berlin, Leipzig and Dresden statistical data for a period of twenty years are not available; therefore the survey was made for Bremen, Hamburg, Frankfurt on Main, Hanover, Stuttgart, Nuremberg and Munich.

Number of inhabitants, area and population density are presented in Fig. 4.2. Munich has the highest density of inhabitants per km^2, but occupies rank four with respect to hinterland density. Five core cities experienced an increase in population during the past ten years, whereas Bremen and Munich shrank slightly until 1999 (Schönert 2002 p. 1). All seven cities experienced an average loss of inhabitants to their hinterland. Frankfurt showed the highest net-migration to its hinterland, followed by Munich. Hamburg and Nuremberg had smaller losses.

The main reasons for the city-hinterland migration were found to be the following: young one-person households tend to migrate into the centres. They tend to have low or middle incomes. These households plan to stay temporarily in the centre, relatively close to their jobs or to educational institutions. They like the proximity to cultural events, leisure industry and friends.

Those leaving the centre are mostly multiple-person households like couples with children. They are of middle age and have middle or higher incomes. They want to improve their housing situation and environment and try to combine better living conditions with access to the infrastructure of the centre. These households are willing to bear the disadvantages of distance.

Table 4.1 stresses that on average Munich and Hamburg had the highest housing construction of all the metropolitan areas, followed by Stuttgart and Nuremberg. The Munich hinterland averages the highest housing construction. The ratio of construction in the hinterland to construction in the city of Munich turns out to be satisfactory. There was high construction activity in the city and in the hinterland. A similar good situation is true of Hamburg.[6]

The ratio of construction of one- and two-family houses in the city to that in the hinterland is generally about five to one. Bremen and Hamburg show high construction activity in the hinterland. In Munich, however, the volume of construction of small houses in the centre is relatively low, whereas it is relatively high in the hinterland.[7]

Recently a survey (IMU 2002) of city-hinterland migration in the Munich agglomeration was conducted by the Munich Planning Department and Statistical

[5] For Bremen municipalities located within a distance of 30 km from the central market place of the city were chosen.

[6] Especially Bremen leaves the supply of dwellings to the surrounding region.

[7] The share of small houses in Munich and Frankfurt is relatively low (approximately 13 per cent). Bremen (45 per cent), Hamburg and Nürnberg show higher percentages (approximately 30 per cent) (c.f. Schönert 2002).

Office in co-operation with the IMU-Institute. 10,000 households, which moved from Munich to the hinterland between 1998 and 2000 were questioned by mail. 2,700 questionnaires were returned. The most important results are the following:

- City-hinterland migration is strongly influenced by the tight Munich housing market. The type and location of newly chosen housing units reveal the following motives of decision making: individual preferences, the general and local price level and the economic situation of the households.
- The city of Munich has no problem of being accepted as a residential location.
- The experts recommend focusing urban housing policies on the segment of larger rental apartments in buildings with two to six housing units. Policies to increase ownership-rates in the central city might be appropriate, but will not be able to reduce significantly the trend of city-hinterland migration.

These studies show that the trend of out-migration is partly due to the relatively greater attractiveness of the hinterland not only in terms of price, but also because of a more 'problem-free' environment (Stadt Karlsruhe 1998; Stadt Dortmund 1998; Brake Dangschat and Herfert 2001). Other investigations show that inhabitants would prefer to stay in town if the social environment was improved and reasonable prices for land and dwellings were available. It seems that the development of city-specific quality housing could help to keep inhabitants in town.

4.3 Characteristics of the Munich Metropolitan Housing Market

4.3.1 Housing Demand

There are several factors of the demand for housing referring to the existing housing stock and to newly constructed houses. Demand may be for owner-occupied housing or for rentals. The economic agents on the demand side consist primarily of households.

Therefore demand is related to the number of households, their structure and their economic and social situation. The number of households is linked to population growth (Table 4.2). From 1993 to 1998 the number of inhabitants of the city of Munich declined by about 2 per cent. Since then it has increased again.

The 'nominal' increase of 105,000 inhabitants between 1998 and 2001 (Table 4.3) is partly due to the shift from the so-called MIDAS to the new ZIMAS system by the statistical office of the city of Munich. The 'real' increase amounted to about 55,000 persons. The main reason for the population growth was an increased labour-market induced immigration to the city and its hinterland from other parts of Germany. This situation was different from the early 1990s, when the population experienced an influx of foreigners. The proportion of foreigners raised from 17 per cent in 1990 to 21 per cent in 2001. But compared to other German cities, segregation is not such a problem in Munich.

Table 4.2. Structure of Munich

Criteria	Dimension	Criteria value
Inhabitants Munich		1 210,223
Inhabitants hinterland		1 235,791
Size Munich	km^2	310.59
Size hinterland	km^2	5,931
Income per capita in Munich	'000 DM	38.68
Sales wholesale in Munich	mill. DM	16,584
Sales retail in Munich	mill. DM	7,765
Sales services in Munich	mill. DM	29,750
Sales manufacturing in Munich	mill. DM	99,116
Sales construction in Munich	mill. DM	12,038
Sales transportation and communication in Munich	mill. DM	15,874
Unemployment rate in Munich	per cent	4.1
Centrality of Munich	rank	1
Real interest rate of money and capital market, Munich	per cent	4.0
Pupils in Munich	'000	139.984
Population of Bavaria	mill. person	12.117
Population of FR Germany	mill. person	82.087
Migration potential from abroad (% of vacant jobs)	per cent	80
Size Bavaria	km^2	70,546
Size Germany	km^2	356,978
Sales wholesale Bavaria	mill. DM	178,397
Sales retail trade Bavaria	mill. DM	152,905
Sales services Bavaria	mill. DM	262,591
Sales manufacturing Bavaria	mill. DM	463,723
Sales construction Bavaria	mill. DM	87,455
Sales transportation and communication Bavaria	mill. DM	30,734
Sales wholesale Germany	mill. DM	1 240,576
Sales retail trade Germany	mill. DM	1 100,803
Sales services Germany	mill. DM	1 087,285
Sales manufacturing Germany	mill. DM	2 895,084
Sales construction Germany	mill. DM	454,230
Sales transportation and communication Germany	mill. DM	287,727
Unemployment rate in Bavaria	per cent	4.8
Unemployment rate in other German states	per cent	9.0
Employment regions with high unemployment, Bavaria	district	1
Employment regions with high unemployment in other states	district	78
Employment regions in Germany	district	181
Price index of real estate in Munich	index	732
Price index of real estate in Bavaria	index	165
Price index of real estate in other states	index	87
Price index of real estate in Germany	index	87
Interest rate savings deposits	per cent	2.5
Interest rate savings deposits in Munich	graph	2.5

Source: Friedrich, Feng, Kosinski and Wonnemann (2004) p. 62

Table 4.3. Population development – city of Munich

Year[a]	Population	German		Foreign nationals	
		Absolute	Per cent	Absolute	Per cent
1990	1 277 576	1 063 991	83.3	213 585	16.7
1991	1 303 593	1 062 815	81.5	240 778	18.5
1992	1 320 634	1 056 027	80.0	264 607	20.0
1993	1 326 306	1 050 829	79.2	275 477	20.0
1994	1 323 624	1 043 082	78.8	280 542	21.2
1995	1 324 208	1 038 186	78.4	286 022	21.6
1996	1 321 557	1 035 470	78.4	286 087	21.6
1997	1 307 609	1 034 553	79.1	273 056	20.9
1998	1 298 537	1 036 987	79.9	261 550	20.1
1999	1 315 254	1 045 601	79.5	269 653	20.5
2000	1 387 455	1 098 428	79.2	289 027	20.8
2001	1 404 158	1 109 984	79.0	294 174	21.0

[a]Inhabitants with first and second residence (December 31).
Source: Statistical Office, City of Munich; up to 1999 MIDAS from 2000 ZIMAS.

Table 4.4. Migration (persons) – city of Munich

Year	Intra-urban migration	Per cent	In-migration	Out-migration	Net migration
1990	105 494	8.3	111 240	100 626	10 614
1991	101 184	7.8	121 137	93 794	27 343
1992	115 863	8.8	141 596	123 265	18 331
1993	126 088	9.5	109 920	105 339	4 581
1994	129 779	9.8	92 112	96 100	–3 988
1995	125 705	9.5	92 150	92 490	–340
1996	127 625	9.7	93 347	97 299	–3 952
1997	121 471	9.3	95 818	111 638	–15 820
1998	125 312	9.7	103 476	114 303	–10 827
1999	119 580	9.1	107 991	93 374	14 617
2000	110 135	7.9	107 453	87 603	19 850
2001	103 015	7.3	111 008	94 152	16 856

Source: Statistical Office, City of Munich; 1990–1999 MIDAS, 2000–2001 ZIMAS.

How migration of Germans and foreigners has caused varying population and housing demand is shown in Table 4.4, showing the movement of persons into and out of Munich. Negative net-migration was one of the reasons for a weaker demand for housing in the mid-nineties.

In more centrally located areas of the city of Munich the average time of residence is short because there is a concentration of students and foreigners. These are also areas of high mobility as shown in Fig. 4.4.

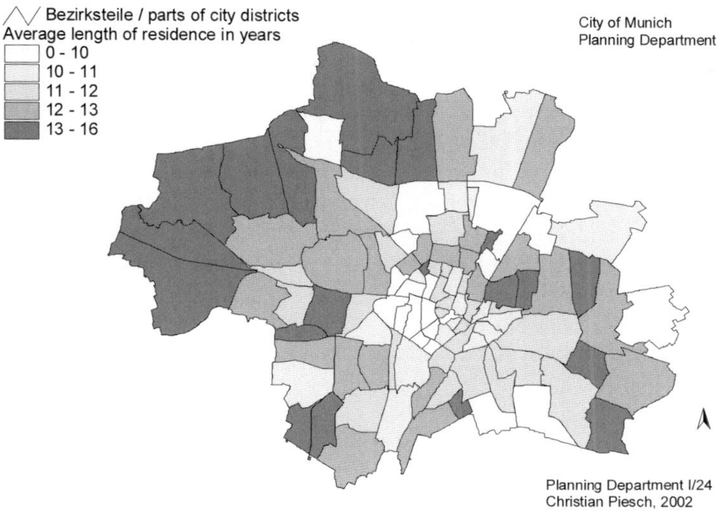

Fig. 4.4. Average length of residence in Munich 2000 (Source: Munich Planning Department)

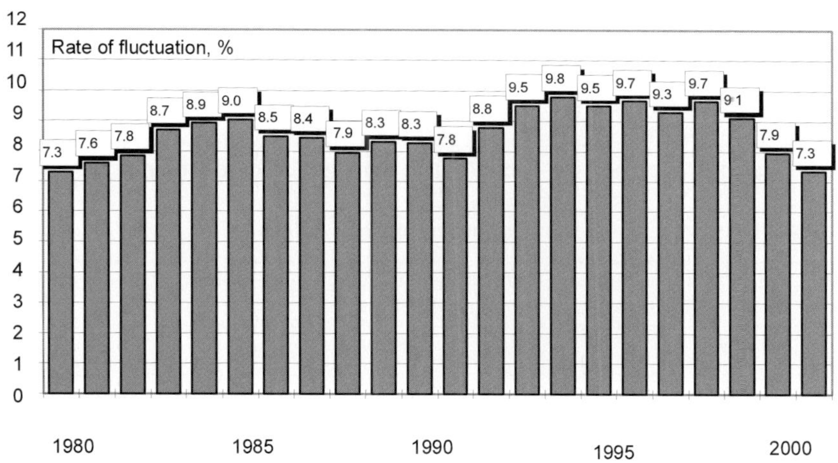

Fig. 4.5. Share of internal migration as percentage of the total population of Munich (Source: Statistisches Amt)

With increasing net in-migration since 1999, the housing market has become tight again. The interdependence of internal migration and the housing market cycle is shown in Fig. 4.5.

The number of households has increased as a result of developments such as the increasing number of single-person households, divorces, children leaving a family household, change from a three or two generation family to a one generation family. The number of households has risen from approximately 590,000 in 1970 to approximately 760,000 in 2001 (see Table 4.5). Whereas the number of households comprising several persons was stable, the number of single households has risen considerably (see Table 4.5). As a result of the increasing number of households, the demand for housing has increased, and since 1999 more sharply. Families with younger children shift their demand to the hinterland and try to move there. This concerns especially families with children less than five years of age and their parents or other adults in the age-group of 30 to 40 years.

Table 4.5. Private households in the city of Munich

	1970	1987	2000	2001
Inhabitants	1 293 590	1 242 818	1 387 455	1 404 158
in private	1 236 051	1 201 007		
in single person households	246 511	327 972	398 000	413 112
in two and more person households	989 540	873 035		
Number of private households	591 432	652 904	741 000	761 938
Single person households	246 511	327 972	398 000	413 112
Multiple person households	344 921	324 955	343 000	348 826

Source: Statistical Office, City of Munich: up to 1999 MIDAS from 2000 ZIMAS.

Household size influences demand as mentioned. Another component is the development of household income to which housing demand is positively related. The real increase in income was smaller than the nominal increase. Disposable income per capita increased rose steadily during the past ten years in nominal terms. In most years, with the exception of 1993 and 1997, the increase in real disposable income was positive, too (see Table 4.6). A demand increase took place.

Table 4.6. Development of disposable income and cost of living

Year	Disposable income in €/inhabitant	Annual rate of change nominal [%]	Living costs [%]	Real [%]
1991	11,964			
1992	12,782	6.8	4.1	2.7
1993	13,140	2.8	3.7	–0.9
1994	13,549	3.1	2.8	0.3
1995	13,958	3.0	1.6	1.4
1996	14,418	3.3	1.3	2.0
1997	14,521	0.7	1.8	–1.0
1998	14,930	2.8	0.9	1.9
1999	15,236	2.1	0.7	1.4
2000	15,799	3.7	2.4	1.3
2001	16,310	3.2	2.4	0.8

Source: Federal statistical office.

The income structure also affects the housing demand as do changes in income distribution. Between 1993 and 1998 the distribution of households of different income groups in Munich has changed. If four income groups (Statistisches Amt der Landeshauptstadt München, München 2001 p. 43–5)[8] are considered, the following changes took place:

- The share of the highest income class has increased.
- The share of the lowest income group slightly increased, but was nearly stable.
- The proportion of low-income households decreased.
- The proportion of the middle income group remained constant.

In the hinterland the share of higher income recipients turns out to have been higher and that of low income households smaller. This is partly due to the movement of higher income recipients and middle income groups with children to the hinterland. The share of low income households decreased in the hinterland. Consequences for housing demand are a higher demand for higher quality housing and for special small income housing.

Another determinant of demand is the increasing size of housing space per capita as a result of the growing number of single and wealthier households (see Fig. 4.6).

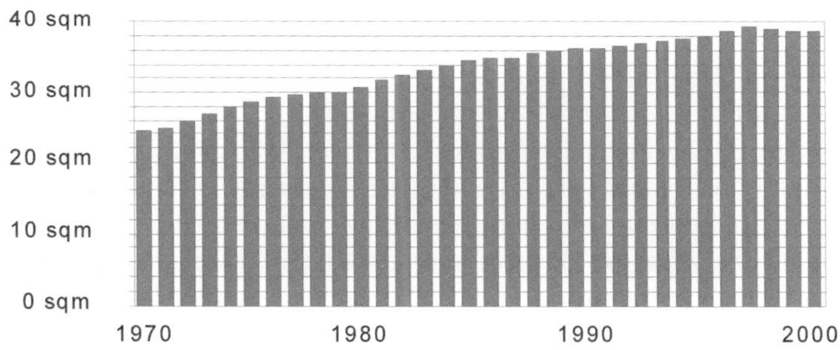

Fig. 4.6. Increasing size of housing space per capita (Source: VZ/GWZ 68/70 – 87, WS 93 + 98 und Schätzung PLAN HAI/24)

Other important factors for demand and supply are rental and real estate prices (owner occupied housing). In Germany, three kinds of rent definitions are used. The basic rent ('Nettokaltmiete') which comprises no additional costs. A gross rent ('Bruttokaltmiete') contains additional cost with exception of heating and energy, whereas an all-inclusive rent ('Warmmiete') comprises additionally energy and heating costs (Referat für Stadtplanung und Bauordnung der Stadt München 2000 p. 25). The so-called second rent, comprising additional costs of lodging,

[8] With less than 1,000 DM, DM 1,000 to 2,500, DM 2,500 to 5,000 and above DM 5,000 net income.

must be added.[9]

Table 4.7 indicates that in Munich average basic rents have risen from €5.11 in 1987 to €8.74 in 2001. The level of rents in Munich is approximately 50 per cent higher than in the rest of Germany. Gross rents (including auxiliary costs) for new dwellings fluctuate more than rents for homes of tenants living in older houses. The relationship between gross rent and households' net income amounts to approximately 30 per cent in Munich.

Additional factors which influence the demand-side include the growing diversity of lifestyles, changing needs because of different phases of the life cycle, e.g. longer life expectations, variation in the age structure, a healthier old-age population, tendencies towards work at home, extended leisure time at home. These factors increase the need for more housing space. Therefore demand is increasingly oriented towards (Gewos 2000 p. 21):

- cheap lodging,
- big flats (rentals: 55 to 90 sqm, owner-occupied flats: 65 to 95 sqm),
- high quality dwellings,
- row houses (110 to 130 sqm).

4.3.2 Housing Supply

Supply consists of the existing housing stock and of new houses. The stock of housing units in Munich amounted to approximately 715,000 in 2001 (Referat für Stadtplanung und Bauordnung der Landeshauptstadt München 2002 p. 22). Suppliers of existing housing units are private owners, housing co-operatives, municipal housing firms and other public housing firms or public owners such as the federal government, the State of Bavaria and the City of Munich. Main investors providing new housing are private investors, housing co-operatives, municipal housing firms and other public housing investors (Herde 1993; Referat für Stadtplanung und Bauordnung der Landeshauptstadt München 2000 p. 53; Gewos 2000 p. 2).

The share of owner-occupied flats is 11 per cent and that of owner-occupied houses comes to 8 per cent. Owner-occupation concentrates on unit sizes of over 120 sqm (up to 50 per cent); the average size of an owner-occupied flat is higher than that used by tenants and the share is increasing with age and income. The share of owner occupation as a determinant of supply emphasises that in this sector construction is oriented towards bigger flats and houses.

Fig. 4.7 depicts the periodical relationship between the housing cycle expressed

[9] The so-called second rent comprises additional costs which increased with exception of garbage collection, heating, warm water provision that decreased (Referat für Stadtplanung und Bauordnung der Landeshauptstadt München 2001 Table 9). Rents increased but because of rising disposable income the demand was not reduced seriously, however, the migration to surrounding areas was intensified.

by the rents of first occupation and the reaction of investors reflected by building permits and construction completion:

- The cycle of rents of first occupation peaked in 1992. Then the housing market was less tight until 1996. Since 1997 rents of first occupation have risen again; their increase has accelerated since 1999.
- Due to long planning and project realisation periods, the reaction of building permits to these market signals lags two to three years and that of the completion of construction lags four years.
- It is likely that 2001 may be the trough of construction completion in the construction cycle of housing in Munich, as building permits, the leading indicator, signal an upward trend.

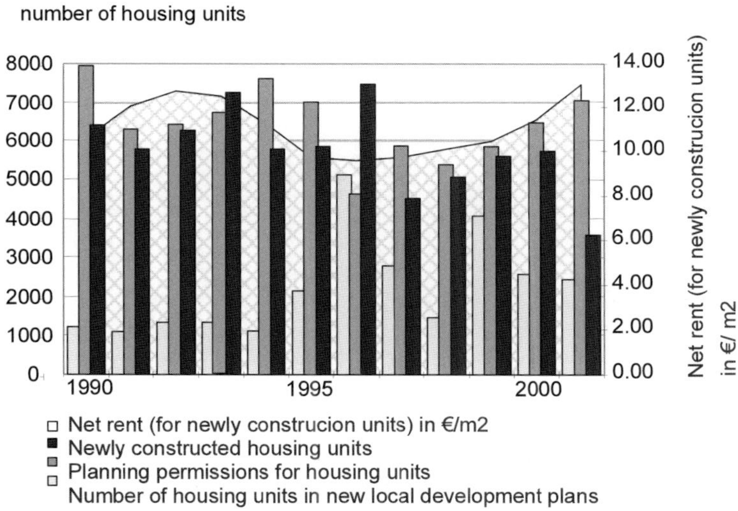

Fig. 4.7. Munich housing market: planning, new construction and rents 1990–2001 (Sources: Munich Planning Department; Munich Statistical Office; RDM)

The number of finished units declined to 3,563 units in Munich in 2001. This reduction, in contrast to 5,720 units constructed in 2000, is not easy to explain in view of the growing number of building permits.

The proportion of social housing construction amounted to between 20 and 25 per cent during this period. The housing programme 'Housing in Munich III' (Wohnen in München III) from July 7, 2001[10] wants to achieve the construction of 7,000 dwellings by 2005, including 1,800 social housing units (see Sect. 4.4.2).

Between 1980 and 2000 approximately 140,000 housing units were completed in Munich. The annual average was approximately 6,600 new units constructed which comes close to the 7,000 units planned. Zoning was realised for 60,000 new

[10] See http://www.muenchen.de/mhb/index_w.html

units. Between 1980 and 2000 approximately 45 per cent of housing construction took place in areas with new local development plans. These numbers reflect the active Munich housing policies. The housing programmes of the 1980s and 1990s primarily tried to activate reserves of small vacant areas within the existing settlement structure as shown in Fig. 4.8.

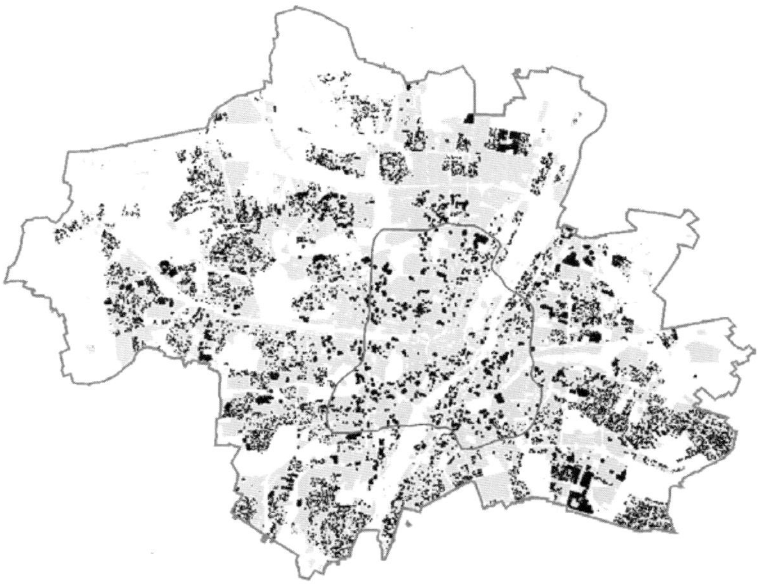

Note: Newly constructed dwellings with over 50 per cent housing use; all housing construction activity in areas with local development plans (§30 BauGB) and without local development plans (§34 BauGB)

Fig. 4.8. Location of new housing construction in Munich 1980–2000 (Source: Munich Planning Department I/12, Lechner 08.05.2002)

For tenant housing there is a certain shift from low-price housing to higher quality housing. The existing housing stock changes because of demolition, change of use, and the abolition of rent ceilings in former social housing units. The share of low-price housing in Munich was reduced from 41 per cent in 1993 to 28 per cent in 1998 (Referat für Stadtplanung und Bauordnung der Landeshauptstadt München 2000 p. 24). This reduction of low-price housing units presents a serious problem for the urban housing policy since lower income groups are restricted to this sub-market.

Housing construction in Munich and its hinterland amounted to between 12,000 and 18,000 units during the last two decades. The ups and downs are reflecting the housing-market cycle. The share of the central city is steadily decreasing due to the suburbanisation trend.

Expected rents as a determinant of supply decisions were discussed above. Higher basic rents (see footnote 7) lead to higher turnover calculations and higher returns on investment and therefore to a larger supply. Again supply is directed toward homes for wealthier people.

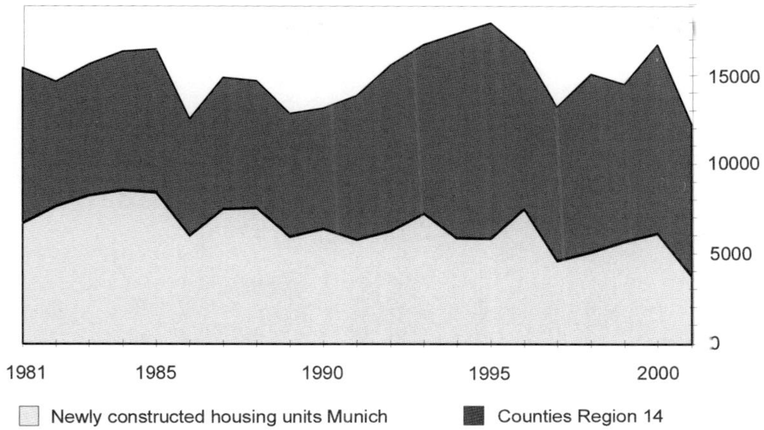

Fig. 4.9. Construction in Munich and its hinterland 1981–2001 (Source: Statistical Office of Bavaria)

Investors reduced the construction of flats for tenants as a reaction to changes in tax rates and depreciation periods (see the section on housing policy).

Supply is also a function of tenants moving (see Table 4.4) making available new offers of flats out of the existing housing stock. The potential supply refers to approximately 560,000 rental units (1998). 103,015 people moved within Munich, while 94,152 persons left Munich in 2001. On the other hand, rising factor prices led to reduced supply. Real estate prices have risen recently (see Fig. 4.11) and will do so in a longer-term perspective.

Construction activity in the Munich hinterland was relatively stronger than in the central city in the last decade. There was a concentration around the development axis to the new airport (Fig. 4.10). In contrast to the goals and expectations of regional planners, the outer hinterland that is not accessible by 'S-Bahn' also experienced a relatively high construction activity due to land price differentials.

The proportion of subsidised housing units became smaller as financial assistance from the federal government and the Free State of Bavaria decreased. This leads to a reduced supply of subsidised homes. The city of Munich has reacted with a special five-year programme to increase the supply of social housing (see Sect. 4.4 about housing policy).

The number of building permits as a prerequisite of for future supply rose to over 7,000 units in 2001 (Fig. 4.7). Urban planning also influences the supply side via a large number of development projects and plans for new housing areas.[11]

[11] An overview of projects is presented in the exhibition 'Zukunft findet Stadt', see http://www.zukunft-findet-stadt.de/

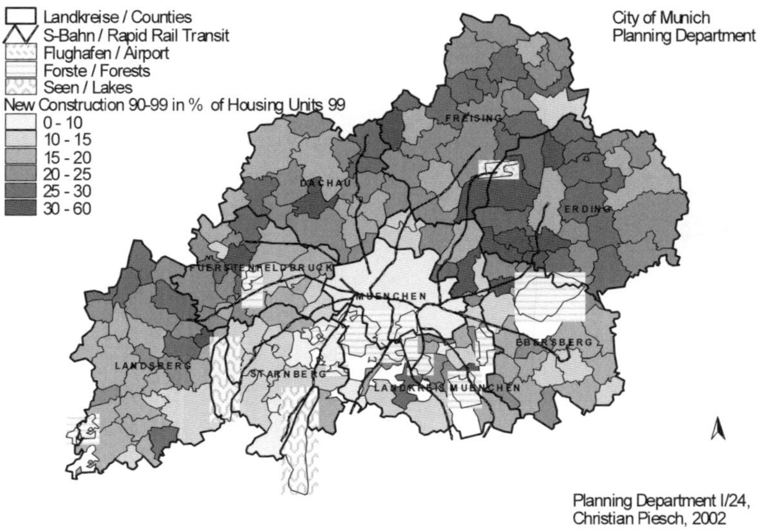

Fig. 4.10. Location of construction in Munich and its hinterland (Source: Survey of newspaper ads, Süddeutsche Zeitung)

4.3.3 General Tendencies of the Metropolitan Housing Market

Several problems characterise the Munich housing market:

- high real estate prices,
- high level of rents,
- difficulties rental situation especially for families with children,
- great need of subsidisation of lower-income households.

Expected developments include:

- an ongoing increase in rents,
- reduced federal and state-funding of social housing,
- difficulties to balance demand and supply especially in the sub-market of low-price housing,
- the trend of new construction towards the owner-occupied sector,
- continuous pressure towards suburbanisation because of the migration of families to the hinterland (see Sect. 4.1.2).

The resulting increase of rents and real-estate prices has been shown in Fig. 4.11 and Table 4.7. Especially in the sectors of high-quality and row houses prices increased considerably as shown in Fig. 4.11. The tendencies discussed above differ between the housing market areas of Munich as shown in the next section.

These developments are influenced by federal, state and municipal housing policies through appropriate goals and the realisation of adequate housing policies.

Table 4.7. Development of average rents by housing age groups

Age group	Munich average LHM	Age of stock –1948	1949–1978	1979–
May '87 (GWZ)	5.11	4.09	5.32	6.90
Dec '89	5.68	4.55	5.93	7.67
Dec '91	6.39	5.11	6.65	8.59
Sept '93 (GWS)	7.16	5.78	7.21	8.85
Dec '95	7.52	6.29	7.62	9.00
Dec '97	7.87	6.85	7.93	9.15
Dec '98 (GWS)	8.08	7.11	8.23	9.20
Dec '00	8.48	7.46	8.64	9.66
Dec '01	8.74	7.69	8.91	9.96
Comparison: Germany (without new states)				
1998	5.62	5.01	5.78	6.70
2000	5.83	5.27	6.03	6.60

Source: Munich statistical office Germany SOEP – Sozioökonomisches Panel

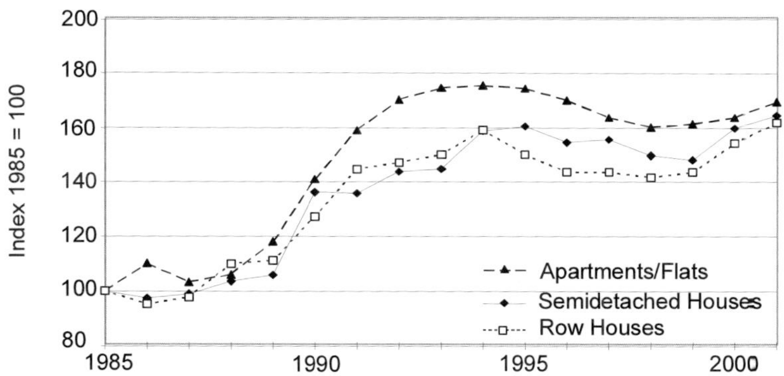

Fig. 4.11. Development of housing prices in Munich 1985–2001 (Source: City of Munich)

4.3.4 Intra-urban Munich Housing Markets, Regional Price Levels

Rents

The city of Munich can be divided into 24 housing-market areas as depicted in Fig. 4.12. These housing-market areas in Munich do not coincide with the administrative district borders. In the hinterland the housing market areas do coincide with administrative borders of single or groups of municipalities (see Fig. 4.15).

Neighbourhoods and residential areas exist where similar market and locational conditions prevail. The 24 urban housing-market areas were identified by a survey of newspaper advertisements undertaken by the Munich Planning Department in the beginning of 2001. Approximately 8,000 housing advertisements were gathered from the Internet. The results were carefully checked. Each advertisement contained information about the location of the housing unit offered for sale or rent. That information was assigned to housing-market areas and to hinterland municipalities, respectively.

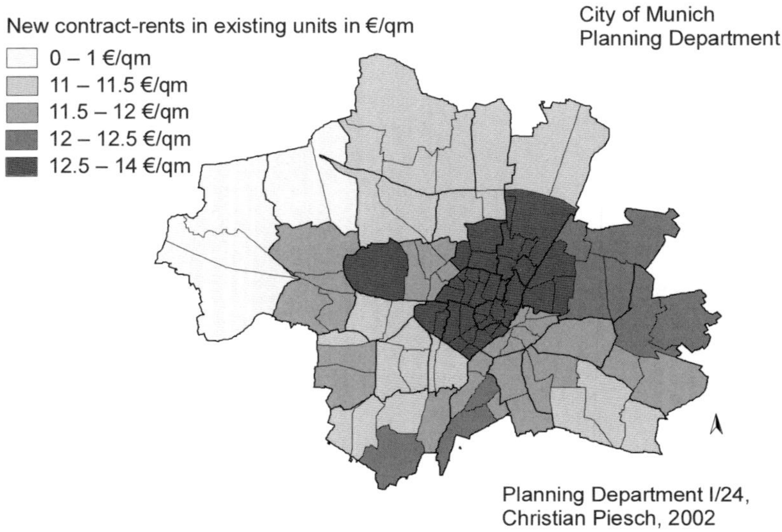

Fig. 4.12. Rents for new lease contracts in existing flats in the Munich housing market areas in 2001 (Source: Survey of newspaper ads, Süddeutsche Zeitung)

Munich rents for new lease contracts of existing housing units vary widely. The most expensive residential areas (rents are above 12.50 €/sqm) are the three central areas Zentrum, Schwabing and Bogenhausen and the area around the Nymphenburg palace.

The second category of housing areas is dominated by lower density housing and row houses. They are situated near the southern and eastern city limits and offer a higher degree of environmental amenities (rents are between 12.00 and 12.50 €/sqm).

The third category of housing areas comprises middle class neighbourhoods. The housing stock was built primarily after World War II (new tenants have to pay between 11.50 and 12.00 €/sqm).

Lower price areas are in the north and the south-east, where there are large social housing estates (rents are less than 11.50 €/sqm).

As an indicator for the hinterland rent situation we use the classification of rent allowances. Each German municipality is classified into one of six categories according to the local rent level.

As depicted in Fig. 4.13, the city of Munich and some nearby municipalities belong to the highest category six (e.g. Grafelfing, Germering, Gauting, Pullach, Grünwald). Rents are similar to those in the city. Municipalities belonging to the next category five are situated primarily in the eastern and north-eastern agglomerative fringe of Munich such as Ismaning, Freising. The housing market areas at the periphery of region 14 show the lowest price levels, especially the county of Landsberg on Lech. In these municipalities rents turn out to be lower.[12]

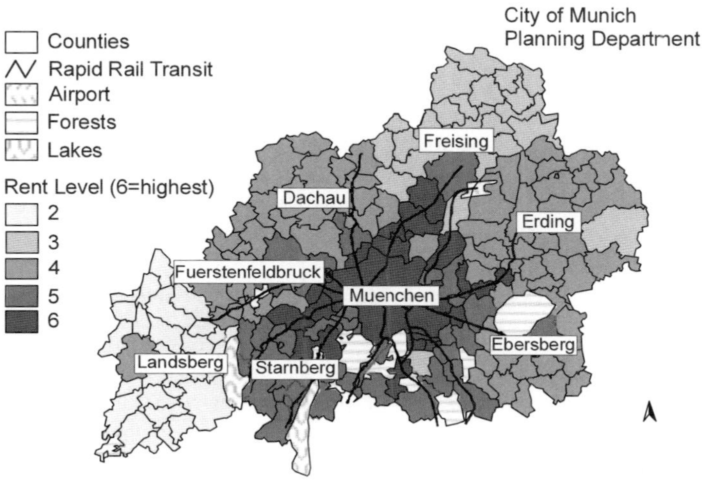

Fig. 4.13. Hinterland municipalities and their assignment to rent allowance categories (Source: Survey of newspaper ads, Süddeutsche Zeitung)

Real estate prices

The highest flat prices, both for newly constructed as well as for already existing units in the hinterland have to be paid in the county of Starnberg, the county of Munich and the city of Munich. The price level for newly constructed flats amounted to around 3,300 €/sqm and for already existing units to around 2,900 €/sqm. The county of Starnberg reflects a special situation. Even though Starnberg is located at the outer fringe of the Munich region, it is considered to be very attractive because of the Starnberg lake and its proximity to the Alps. Therefore, the level of housing prices is among the highest in the Munich hinterland (Fig. 4.15).

Real estate prices in Fürstenfeldbruck, Dachau and Ebersberg are only 10 per cent to 20 per cent lower than those in the city of Munich. These three counties are in close commuting distance to the central city. The 'inner' part of these counties is relatively urbanised as there are very good regional transit connections ('S-

[12] On average, rents are a little lower than in Munich. In 2000 the average rent in the hinterland was €4.85 in social housing and €7.88 when financed privately (Gewos, München, Wohnungsmarktentwicklung im Expertenbild, Hamburg, Berlin 2000 p. 6).

Bahn') to the three towns (Fig. 4.15). There older flats cost approximately 2,400 €/sqm, newly constructed flats range from approximately 2,700 to 2,900 €/sqm.

In the hinterland counties and within the city of Munich considerable price differentials prevail. The prices of existing flats in very good residential areas of Munich (such as Obermenzing, Trudering, Harlaching, Schwabing, Nymphenburg and Solln) are higher than 3,000 €/sqm (Fig. 4.14). Even higher prices are paid in very good hinterland locations (such as Starnberg, Krailling, Grünwald and Pullach). In these housing areas the prices of existing flats range around 3,200 €/sqm.

Relatively modest flat prices in the hinterland were found in the three counties of Landsberg, Erding and Freising with prices of existing flats around 2,100 €/sqm (Fig. 4.15).

Lower priced housing market areas in Munich are Giesing, Perlach, Moosach and Laim where existing flats cost around 2,500 €/sqm (see Fig. 4.14).

Real estate prices of newly constructed units correspond to the price situation of already existing flats in the above mentioned housing markets. However, their price level is approximately 15 per cent higher (see Table 4.8).

Table 4.8. Prices of new and existing flats in Munich and its hinterland

Area	Existing flats [€/sqm]			New construction [€/sqm]		
City/counties	Cases	Mean	% of Munich	Cases	Mean	% of Munich
Dachau	51	2 400	83	34	2 700	79
Ebersberg	85	2 500	86	10	–	–
Erding	28	2 200	76	5	–	–
Freising	36	2 200	76	14	2 800	82
Fürstenfeldbruck	340	2 400	83	147	3 000	88
Landsberg	32	2 100	72	8	–	–
City of Munich	1861	2 900	100	579	3 400	100
München Land	339	2 900	100	133	3 200	94
Starnberg	274	2 900	100	168	3 300	97

Source: Referat für Stadtplanung und Bauordnung der Landeshauptstadt München 2001a.

The spatial pattern of housing price differentiation in the city and its hinterland shows a more sectoral than concentric pattern. The higher priced residential areas are found in the centre and the south-west of the city and the hinterland due to the relative attractiveness of the Munich inner city and the beautiful countryside around the lakes (Lake Starnberg, Ammersee).

The structure of housing prices and the population-structure of the housing market areas are closely related. Fig. 4.16 shows the percentage of households receiving housing benefits in the various neighbourhoods of Munich in 2000. The income structure is reflected by this indicator. Fig. 4.12 and 4.14 show that only few poorer households can afford to live in neighbourhoods with high levels of rent and housing prices. Housing market conditions and price differentials lead to residential and social segregation. In comparison to other German cities the segregation in Munich is relatively moderate.

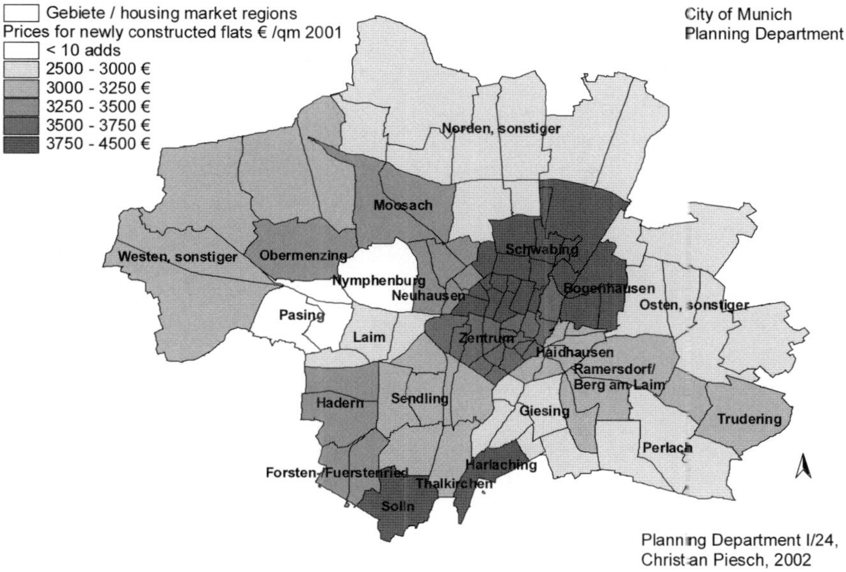

Fig. 4.14. Prices for newly constructed flats in the Munich housing areas in 2001 (Source: Survey of newspaper ads, Süddeutsche Zeitung).

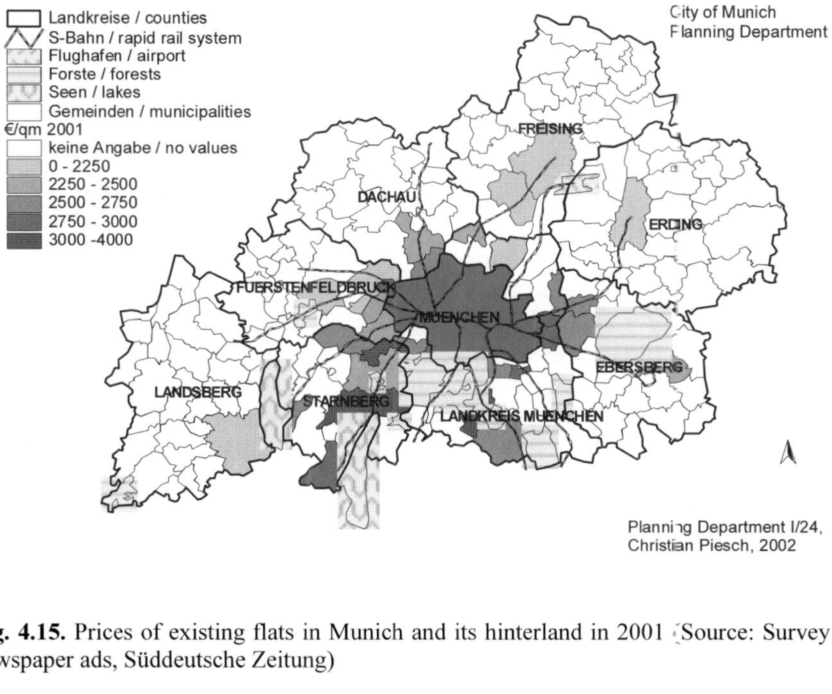

Fig. 4.15. Prices of existing flats in Munich and its hinterland in 2001 (Source: Survey of newspaper ads, Süddeutsche Zeitung)

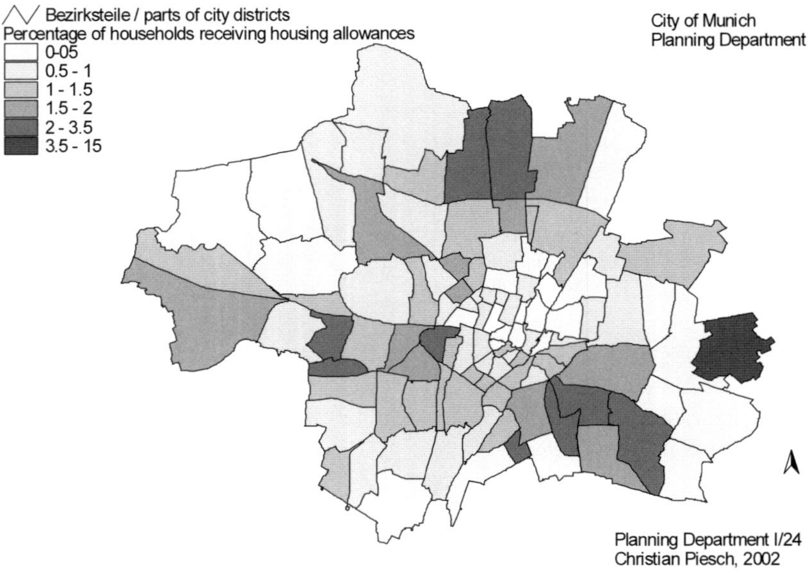

Fig. 4.16. Percentage of households receiving housing benefits in the Munich housing areas in 2000 (Source: Munich Planning Department)

4.4 Housing Policy

4.4.1 Federal and State Levels

Housing policy in Germany has always been an important field of social and economic policies. From post World War II until the 1970s the main focus was on new constructions. In the 1980s and 1990s housing market recoveries occurred in the beginning and recessions in the middle of the decades. The intensity of political debate and subsequent market interventions varied according to the housing market-situation.

German housing policy was very pro-cyclical. Since it was always relatively market-oriented, policy reacted especially by means of changes in tax rules (e.g. rules of tax depreciation for housing investors).

Besides taxation other instruments to influence housing production were also applied:

- Rules concerning land (zoning, land taxation).
- Housing finance.
- Social housing.
- Policy instruments regarding the existing housing stock.
- Rent laws.

Housing policy in Germany is a joint responsibility of the federal government, the states and the municipalities. The federal government is responsible for the framework of housing policy (laws concerning tenant-owner relationships, tax laws, general land use laws and social housing law).

The new housing law of 2002 (Söfker, Burger, Otte and Gerstinger 2001) requires the states to ensure an appropriate housing supply for households in need. Therefore, there is general housing support for lower and middle income classes. The states are responsible for the implementation of this general framework. Loans and grants are provided at favourable conditions. In return, the investors have to accept tenants with a nomination right by the municipalities.[13]

At present the subsidisation is geared to the tenants' household income ('Einkommensorientierte Förderung'). After fulfillment of his obligations, e.g. after paying back the received loan, the owner is free of any social housing restrictions.

Other programmes are intended to promote private housing ownership. Moreover, there are housing benefits, subsidies for owner-occupants (to support the formation of housing capital), income-tax incentives for new construction and programmes to improve the existing housing stock. Modernisation activity resulted in the conversion of low-cost housing into middle or higher cost housing. This added to the shortage of supply of cheap housing in Munich.

Federal and state co-financing of social housing dominated, such as the programmes mentioned and the so-called social city programme. As the federal government has reduced funding, social housing must be funded by the state and some bigger cities (like the City of Munich).

Rent regulation was common in Germany after World War II. At present the regulations are no longer very strict. Investors or owners are relatively free in setting the rents of newly constructed housing units or existing units whose tenants change. Rent regulation is dominant in the sector of social housing where rents are under review of rent control.

The only major restriction is the so-called 'Kappungsgrenze', a ceiling on the allowed rent increase. It means that for existing lease contracts the rent increase is limited to 20 per cent within three years. This rule has only a limited effect on the overall rise of the market price, however. As Munich has a long history of a tight housing market, the 'Kappungsgrenze' is considered an instrument to protect long-term tenants from sudden rent hikes.[14]

In general, the increased rent has to be in line with rents for a comparable dwelling, the reference rent. An official representative list of typical rents for

---

[13] The so-called first way of support social housing formed the main Munich social housing programme until 2001, following similar principles. It is still effective as far as the old social housing stock is concerned. The second way of support was abolished in 1997; it showed raised revenue limits for the tenants and reduced repayment periods. Thus a shorter period of controlled rent-levels and nomination rights resulted. The third way of housing support is also object-bound and comprises interest free credits or subsidies with a low debt service burden. (Referat für Stadtplanung und Bauordnung der Landeshauptstadt München 2001 p. 24).

[14] For example when the owner of larger housing estates changes.

housing units in certain locations with different standards is compiled every two years by the city of Munich for the purpose of rent comparison.[15]

Whereas in the decades after World War II the German housing situation and housing policies were relatively coherent, today different regional sub-markets vary greatly. Therefore, federal and state policies must be adjustable to the situation of the local housing markets.

4.4.2 City Level

Although the population of Munich was nearly stable from 1970 to 2001, the housing stock increased by approximately 240,000 units. Housing space per capita grew from 24 sqm to 38 sqm. The average increase of housing space consumption 0.5 sum per capita; for the future a yearly increase of approximately 0.2 sqm is expected (Referat für Stadtplanung und Bauordnung der Landeshauptstadt München 2001 p. 42).

To keep up with the growing demand for housing in Munich, an average volume of 6,000 housing units was built every year. Since 1995 the city has planned the construction of 7,000 units a year.

Although sufficient housing projects were assigned in local development plans, investors refrained from housing construction for various reasons. Thus other capital investments seemed more profitable and the unfavourable framework set by the federal government made residential construction less attractive.

The share of newly constructed rental housing units in Munich decreased. A survey of residential construction firms and investors by the Planning Department yielded a sharp increase of owner-occupant units from approximately 30 per cent in 1996 to more than 60 per cent of newly constructed units in 2000. Even though Munich is still dominated by the rental sub-market, only one third of the new housing development is for rent today.

The 'owner ratio' in Munich is approximately 20 per cent, i.e. still approximately 80 per cent of all existing housing units are for rent. The reasons for the decrease of the new construction activity in the rental sub-market are the following:

- Tax laws (digressive depreciation of housing investments, tax reforms resulting in lower tax bases and therefore less depreciation potential, increased taxes on real estate transactions, an extended 'speculation period' for housing investments from formerly one to ten years now).
- Unfavourable experiences of many small investors in eastern Germany.
- The high price level in Munich, but only a moderate net yield of rental housing investment (compared to attractive middle-sized cities with moderate price levels, but also compared to alternative investments).

In spite of these shortages the city tries to focus its urban housing policies on

[15] http://www.mietspiegel.muenchen.de/

the goals that have been formulated on the basis of the guidelines of city development,[16] housing programme 2001 (Referat für Stadtplanung und Bauordnung der Landeshauptstadt München 2001 p. 24) and a report on the housing situation in Munich 2000 and 2001 (Referat für Stadtplanung und Bauordnung der Landeshauptstadt München 2002). These goals are:

- adequate housing for low-income and middle-income households,
- a balanced settlement structure,
- avoidance of segregation,
- the promotion of housing property formation,
- affordability of city housing for families with children,
- balancing the growing housing demand and ecological aspects according to the principles of the urban development plan,
- maintenance of ecological principles of sustainable development and economic allocation of resources, energy saving and flexible adaptation to changing live styles or cycles.

Munich housing policy concentrates on (1) new housing construction and (2) on the existing housing stock.

(1) New housing construction: One bundle of measures is to activate land for housing. There is a construction potential for approximately 60,000 units up to 2005 on land assigned for housing in land use plans and local development plans. This potential volume of housing construction will be realised primarily in:

- Larger intra-urban centres of development and city quarter development areas (approximately 21,000 units).
- Conversion of former military barracks (approximately 7,500 to 8,000 units).
- Intra-urban restructuring such as areas formerly used by the federal railways (approximately 8,300 units).
- Another 12,000 housing units are already included in local development plans.

As a result of these policies, the release of land for housing development has increased considerably. Whereas local development plans for approximately 1,400 housing units per year were produced by the City of Munich between 1990 and 1994, annual output grew to 3,100 units during the period of 1996 to 2001. Housing development is realised in some larger projects (e.g. Messestadt Riem,[17] 'Panzerwiese') and a lot of smaller projects.

As a consequence of the cyclical increase in demand for housing, the number of building permits has increased in Munich and the surrounding region since 1998. In Munich like in Bavaria as a whole and in all parts of Germany construction de-

---

[16] http://www.muenchen.de/plan/leitlin/leitlin-4.htm

[17] See www.messestadt-riem.com. The further main projects are: Neusserstraße, Theresienhöhe, Ackermannbogen, former container station of the Federal railways. Housing development plans consider approximately 27,500 units.

creased dramatically in 2001. This decline does not reflect special conditions in Munich, but the general unfavourable conditions for residential construction in Germany.

To rekindle investors' interest in housing construction and to help households find affordable homes, a special municipal programme called 'Housing in Munich III' (Wohnen in München III, Referat für Stadtplanung und Bauordnung der Landeshauptstadt München 2001) was initiated in 2001. It comprises a concept for municipal housing policy setting out goals, measures and framework conditions for the period to 2005.

The most important housing policy goals and measures are:

- Increasing the target construction rate of new housing units to 7,000 per year and providing legal prerequisites via zoning and urban development planning.
- Augmentation municipal funding of social housing by approximately €50 million per year to achieve a construction rate of 1,800 subsidised units per year.
- Activating the programme 'München Modell' to extend the construction of rental housing especially for families with several children.

Lord Mayor Ude has reactivated the successful 'Munich movement to support housing construction' (Münchner Bündnis für Wohnungsbau) established for the first time, in 1997, a co-operative effort of private investors and the City of Munich.

The Munich city council had introduced, on February 14 1996, the 'München-Modell'. The 'München-Modell' was extended by the above mentioned 'Housing in Munich' (Wohnen in München III). The programme schedules the sale at subsidised prices of municipal real estates to investors renting flats, self-occupiers or owners who rent their flats to tenants, and housing co-operatives.[18] Until the end of 2001 builders of nearly 1,300 units were sponsored under the 'München-Modell'. To date the main focus (up to 90 per cent) has been on owner-occupiers. In future more rental housing will be provided under the 'München-Modell'.

Lower priced housing market areas in Munich are Giesing, Perlach, Moosach and Laim with existing flats costing around 2,500 €/sqm (see Fig. 4.14). Real estate prices of newly constructed units correspond to the price situation of already existing flats in the above mentioned housing markets. However, their price level is approximately 15 per cent higher (see Table 4.8).

Past and present measures to extend new social housing include:

- Regulations concerning social housing quotas in local development plans (Bindungsverträge).
- The subsidized sale of municipal land for the 'München-Modell' and income based housing support (EOF).
- Increased co-financing of social housing by the City of Munich and demands for additional funding by the state and federal governments.

[18] Details of the 'München-Modell' can be found in the Internet http://www.muenchen.de/plan/rundgang/haiii/index.html

- A special fee to be paid by higher income households living in social housing which has been one of the sources for financing social housing.
- Measures to build rental or owner-occupied housing under the 'München-Modell'.
- Construction of dwellings for homeless persons. 1,500 dwellings are to be built within 10 years.
- Construction of houses by the three municipal housing companies. Although the municipal housing companies have done a good job their capacities are limited and they are highly engaged in modernisation activities. As far as they build on land provided by the city they use the support programmes mentioned.
- Construction of houses by housing co-operatives that buy municipal land and receive support from social housing programmes and the München. The problem is that not all members of the co-operatives meet the requirements of the social housing programmes.
- Additional measures such as construction of social housing in redevelopment areas, municipal regulations that guarantee that property owners who benefit from land use plans contribute to the costs of the infrastructure (Referat für Stadtplanung und Bauordnung und Kommunalreferat der Landeshauptstadt München 2000), legal requirements to protect the character of garden city districts and the quality of their housing environment (Ausschuß für Stadtplanung und Bauordnung 2000).

Measures to extend the construction activities of investors in general include:

- Leaseholds of land (Referat für Stadtplanung und Bauordnung der Landeshauptstadt München 2001 p. 62) for residential construction that reduces the financing problems of certain investors.
- Increase the density of low-density housing blocks to allow for higher returns on investment. This instrument is difficult to apply as tenants fear a loss of quality of already existing housing. 1,800 dwellings are expected to be established that way, however.
- There are again measures for owner-occupants under the 'München-Modell'.

The general framework for housing investment is primarily a responsibility of the federal government and the State of Bavaria. There have been subsidy cuts and a shift towards more unfavourable taxation for housing investors.

(2) Existing housing stock: Other measures of housing policy are related to the existing housing stock:

- Construction of new housing but also modernisation of existing housing occurs in several areas of urban renewal under the responsibility of the Munich Town Renewal Company (Münchner Gesellschaft für Stadterneuerung mbH). There is a special programme to finance modernisation and to assist tenants who have to move to other dwellings during the period of modernisation.[19] These measures increase the supply and the quality of housing.

- There is a reserve of 65,000 social housing units, and 27,000 other units owned by the city housing companies. The city housing office allocates housing according to social need to a mix of tenants, and according to the economic needs of the housing companies. There are special municipal rules for the allocation of social housing and municipal housing.
- Another measure is the organised change of residence within the municipal housing companies.
- A typical measure of the Munich housing policy is the so-called 'preservation regulation' (Erhaltungssatzung). In certain residential areas abolishment, conversion and modernisation has to be permitted by the city housing office. 23 areas with 130,000 housing units fall under this regulation. In these areas the city has the option of purchasing the real estate that an owner wants to sell. Exercising this option can be avoided by the vendor's declaration not to do a luxury modernisation or to convert housing into individual ownership units.
- Another instrument is a regulation to prevent a change from residential to commercial purposes.[20]
- A potential instrument is the purchase of dwellings by the city housing companies[21]. This policy needs to be funded in order to increase the capitalisation of the municipal housing companies.
- Prolongation of social housing agreements could be achieved by the purchase of nomination rights. To date there have been only a few cases.
- There is a special programme to assist homeless persons. These include citizens of Munich who lost their housing, as well as immigrants of German ancestry, asylum seekers, and refugees.
- More than 30,000 households receive rent support. Although not financed by the city of Munich, it influences the demand side of the housing markets. Fig. 4.16 shows the city districts in which the recipients of rent support live.

Munich housing policy thus applies many instruments to influence the demand for housing and to extend the supply with the intention to increase the welfare of the Munich citizens.

[19] Moreover, there is additional promotion of modernisation out of the areas of town renewal. A Bavarian modernisation programme backs modernisation of housing too. Another modernisation programme refers to the dwellings which belong to the City of Munich, and their is an additional subsidisation of the city in favour energy saving in housing.

[20] Zweckentfremdungsverordnung: Abolishment of dwellings can be restricted or if this gets allowed requirements can be formulated to construct new dwellings. The city has the right to control the rental conditions ensure healthy housing conditions.

[21] This can happen with respect to dwellings belonging to the Federation, e.g. former army dwellings, or dwellings formerly occupied by NATO soldiers who retreated in the course of disarmament.

4.5 Outlook

The actual situation of the German housing market is not as good as some experts believe (HypoVereinsbank 2002 p. 12). In 2001, the rate of German housing construction was less than 340,000 units and thus fell short of the expected average volume of 376,000 units projected by the Federal Agency for Urban and Regional Planning (Bundesamt für Städtebau und Raumordnung). Compared to 1997 there was a reduction of approximately 40 per cent. This concerned particularly the construction of multi-storey buildings and recently also the construction of owner-occupied homes. Responsible for this development are the demographic factors mentioned above and the change in household incomes. As these situations differ from region to region, the housing markets also show different developments:

- In prosperous agglomerations of West Germany like Munich, Hamburg, Frankfurt, housing demand is still high and rising. The number of households will grow as will the demand for housing space. A shortage of reasonably priced homes and owner-occupied houses for families with children can be expected. Rents and land prices continue to rise.
- Housing markets in distressed areas of West Germany that have high unemployment and are in economic decline are unsatisfactory. Rents and real estate prices are stagnating.
- East Germany suffers from high unemployment and out-migration. Many housing markets are characterised by high vacancy rates. East German housing prices are consolidating on a low level.

At rates of return of 4.25 per cent to 5.5 per cent, investment in new housing is not very profitable. Moreover, certain rent restrictions and high administrative costs impair residential investment.

As far as the housing stock is concerned, the supply of used dwellings will increase because of inheritances, bankruptcies, privatisation of municipal houses and flats, and the sale of houses by enterprises, insurance companies, pension funds, et cetera.

Munich, however offers a more favourable environment for investors than other German cities. It is assumed that this development will also prevail in the next decade (Strubelt 2001). According to the forecast for the city of Munich and its hinterland, the population living in private households will increase moderately. The percentage of small households is growing, and the average household size is declining (see Table 4.9). The movement of people from the city of Munich to the hinterland is expected to continue.

This forecast of market developments in Munich and its hinterland seems optimistic. The housing market will grow in terms of housing units, rising prices and profits in certain market segments. The city of Munich, however, will face stagnating financial resources for housing, a tight real estate market and varying submarket developments. Therefore, the following goals must be discussed:

Table 4.9. Housing forecast for Munich and its hinterland

Region 14	1998	2000	2005	2010	2015
Demographic development					
Population in private households in 1000	2440.4	2448.5	2483.0	2516.5	2551.4
Total private households in 1 000	1227.0	1234.1	1265.3	1295.8	1323.5
Share of one and two persons households %	75.4	75.8	77.1	78.1	78.9
Average household size (persons/household)	1.99	1.98	1.96	1.94	1.93
Characteristics of demand					
Share of owners in %	32.2	32.8	34.0	35.4	36.3
Average housing space in sqm /person	41.0	41.6	42.9	44.3	45.4
Average housing space owners in sqm/person	48.6	49.0	50.3	51.5	52.3
Average housing space tenants in sqm /person	36.6	37.0	38.0	39.0	39.0
Development of demand					
Demand of housing space in 1000 sqm	89648	91316	96107	100908	104634
Share of one and two family houses in %	43.7	43.9	44.5	45.0	45.1
Change in demand for one and two family houses index values 1998 = 100	100.0	102.5	109.1	115.9	120.4
Change in demand for multiple houses index values 1998 = 100	100.0	101.4	105.7	110.0	113.8
Construction					
Construction of flats in new buildings in 1000 per year		12.0	13.4	12.5	10.3
Construction of flats in one and two family houses in 1000 per year		4.5	4.8	4.6	2.7
Construction of flats in multiple family houses in 1000 per year		7.4	8.6	7.9	7.6
Construction of dwellings per 1000 inhabitants		4.9	5.4	5.0	4.0

Source: Strubelt 2001 p. 111

- Reduction of land consumption, infrastructure and construction costs by appropriate densities.
- Redefinition of standards like building regulations.
- Reduction of unjustified profits – e.g. when municipalities enact local development plans which increase the property values of private investors.
- Reduction of long-term financing costs.
- Redefinition of social housing policies.
- Policy measures for more owner-oriented housing in the city core of Munich (Thalgott and Piesch 2000).

The city of Munich must focus on measures of city development and land use planning to promote construction and to reduce construction costs. City social housing policies may be redefined in favour of families with children according to housing sub-markets as far as the city has the competence to do so. The limited financial means should be used to increase the construction activities of the municipal housing companies, using them as instruments of social housing and construction in general. They may be reoriented as profitable developers, thus enlarging their financing scope. Standards of construction could be redefined in terms of building style, density, environmental conditions and access to infrastructure. Another measure could be the introduction of planning and development fees. The sale of municipal land should be further linked to urban development criteria. Furthermore, the instrument of the purchase of nomination rights could be extended.

Modernisation should also be related to owner-occupied housing. City and hinterland municipalities should try to practice joint land use planning (Bayerisches Staatsregierung 2001 Änderungsbegründung p, 35) to react to different demands in the city and the hinterland and to share the financial burden of housing development. This may not be successful due to regional competition and lagging regional financial compensation possibilities among municipalities.

There is also a need for more favourable general regulations for housing in prosperous agglomerations like Munich.

References

Ausschuss für Stadtplanung und Bauordnung der Landeshauptstadt München, Gartenstadtsatzung vom 12.07.2000

Bayerische Staatsregierung (2001) Landesentwicklungsprogramm Bayern. Gesamtfortschreibung, Entwurf 24.07.2001, München

Brake K, Dangschat J, Herfert G (eds) (2001) Suburbanisierung in Deutschland – Aktuelle Tendenzen. Opladen

Friedrich P, Feng X, Kosinski J, Wonnemann G (2004) Gutachten über die Effekte des Neuen Fußballstadions München. Diskussionspapier Nr. 46, Lehrstuhl für Finanzwissenschaft, Universität der Bundeswehr München

GEWOS München, Wohnungsmarktentwicklung im Expertenbild 2000. Endbericht, Hamburg, Berlin

Herde Ch (1993) Wohnen in München. Darmstadt

HVB Expertise (2002) Immobilienmarktanalyse Wohnungsmarkt Deutschland. München, http://www.hvbexpertise.de/HVBExpertise/Markttendenzen/Wohnungsmarkt/Deutschland.htm

IMU–Institut für Medienforschung und Urbanistik (2002) Raus aus der Stadt? München, January 2002 (see http://www.muenchen.de/plan/aktuelles/index-wmu.html)

Planungsverband äußerer Wirtschaftsraum München (2001) Datenspiegel 2001. München

Referat für Stadtplanung und Bauordnung der Landeshauptstadt München (2000) Bericht zur Wohnungssituation in München 1998–1999, München

Referat für Stadtplanung und Bauordnung der Landeshauptstadt München (2001) Wohnen in München III, Wohnungspolitisches Handlungsprogramm 2001–2005. München

Referat für Stadtplanung und Bauordnung der Landeshauptstadt München (2001a) Immobilienpreise in der Region 14. Unpublished, München

Referat für Stadtplanung und Bauordnung der Landeshauptstadt München (2002) Bericht zur Wohnungssituation in München 2000–2001. München

Referat für Stadtplanung und Bauordnung der Landeshauptstadt München (2002) Perspektive München, leitlinien für eine zukünftige Stadtentwicklung vom 28.1. 2000. http://www.muenchen.de/plan/leitlin/leitlin-4.htm, April 2002, München

Referat für Stadtplanung und Bauordnung und Kommunalreferat der Landeshauptstadt München (2000) Die Sozialgerechte Bodennutzung. Der Müncher Weg. München

Schönert M (2002) Stadt-Umland-Wanderung der Bevölkerung. BAW, Institut für Wirtschaftsforschung, Monatsbericht, Heft 12, Dezember 2001, Bremen

Söfker W, Burger P, Eggert O, Gerstinger W (2001) Das Gesetz zur Reform des Wohnungsbaurechts. In Bundesbaublatt 8/2001, Bonn, p 10–21

Stadt Dortmund (ed) (1998) Bilanzen. Wohnwechsel und Beweggründe, Dortmunder Statistik, Dortmund

Stadt Karlsruhe (ed) (1998) Motive der Stadt–Umland Wanderung in der Region Karlsruhe 1997. Beiträge zur Stadtentwicklung Nr. 6, Karlsruhe

Statistisches Amt der Landeshauptstadt München (2001) Privathaushalte nach ihren Nettoeinkommen in München und im Umland. Ergebnisse des Mikrozensus 1993–1998. Statistische Blätter, München, p 43–5.

Strubelt W (2001) Bundesamt für Bauwesen und Raumordnung. Wohnungsprognose 2015, Bonn

Thalgott Ch, Piesch Ch (2000) München setzt auf differenzierte Eigentumsstrategien. In: vhw Forum Wohneigentum. Bonn, Heft 1, pp 14–6

5 Recovery and Change: Glasgow's Housing 1991–2001

Duncan Maclennan

Glasgow University, Glasgow

5.1 Long Decline, Grand Design

Glasgow is the UK's fourth largest city and is home to 650,000 (12.5 per cent) of Scotland's people and is the largest Scottish employment centre, generating 16 per cent of Scotland's GDP. It sits at the heart of a city-region, Scotland's only conurbation, of 2.2 million people. Glasgow's importance as a centre of wealth creation, innovation, retailing and culture is inarguable; however it is also beset with social problems associated with high concentrations of severe deprivation and population decline.

By European city and city-region standards, it has modest scale, quality and low growth, but given the experience of the last half century these parameters are in themselves remarkable. In 1951, after a century of early, fast growth of a heavy industrial economic base and dense residential environments, Glasgow had a population almost double the present level and some 350,000 manufacturing jobs, ten times the present number, were locate within the city. Hardly had the city begun to cope with the socio-economic and physical issues of being a protracted 'boom in space' when rapid decentralisation and then de-industrialisation set in train a protracted downward spiral in the economic and population base of the city.

But it was not just exogenous or economic change that produced a dramatic backcloth for the evolution of the city. Politics, governance and policy played a major, and not always beneficial, role in the process. At least four major phases of housing and city policy, each layered upon each other, shaped the present landscape.[1]

[1] See Maclennan, Meen and Gibb (1997) and Maclennan (2002) for more detailed discussion of the long term policy changes and their consequences.

After 1915, UK rent controls, partly a response to tenant rent strikes in Glasgow, remained deep and in place well into the 1970s. Combined with the growing significance of home-owner tax breaks after 1950, housing market policy had a strong anti-city/pro-suburb emphasis. Welfare state expansion (after 1950) and then urban slum clearance (after 1960) were proportionately more significant than in any other UK city. Throughout the post war period until 1980 there was not a single year when more than 200 units were built for the market sector, yet the public sector constructed more than 100,000 homes in the same period.

Both these phases were also decentralising. Much of the older city was demolished by 1974; 80,000 city residents (often more skilled workers) were moved to new and over-spill towns away from the city. And close to 100,000 poorer people were moved to large scale municipal housing estates lying on the edge of the city. This triumph of social commitment and hope over careful choice of sustainable housing system is more evident in Glasgow than in any other West European city.

The decentralising thrust of housing policies contributed to neighbourhood decline and dereliction in core areas, and some 10 per cent of the city still comprises vacant and derelict brown-field land and reinforced market shifts away from the city. However, since 1974 and the start of what are now globally known regeneration programmes, housing policies have increasingly re-favoured city locations and there have been neighbourhoods in renaissance in Glasgow for more than 20 years.

In effect, early concentration of public renovation grants in the hands of not for profit, community-led housing associations created regeneration growth poles. As they improved areas for the less affluent, more residential developers initiated construction for the market and over time this investment has moved up the relative price distribution. In contrast to the period to 1980, the subsequent decades have seen an average of more than 1,000 new market dwellings each year since then. And grant-aided upgrading by home owners increased sharply until it was curtailed by local authority funding decisions.

However as Glasgow's older neighbourhoods began to show signs of policy-led recovery the rising unemployment of 1980s Britain, and associated deep cuts in public spending programmes, exacerbated the already incipient difficulties of the municipal sector. Tenants in the municipal sector were ageing. Unskilled manual workers, a key client group in peripheral council housing, had major job search and commuting problems, and many were trapped into benefit dependency as steeply means tested benefits came to replace bricks and mortar subsidies. In extensive parts of the city male unemployment rates exceeded 20 per cent and by 1990 only one in three households in the council sector had anyone in the labour market. And this was a housing sector (see Table 5.1) supplying half the homes of Glaswegians.

Within the sector property quality was low and falling; low rents had always been a political priority ahead of adequate maintenance; local state planning of housing had, after the 1950s, built homes fast and without community involvement and with little regard to consumer preferences. In Glasgow vacant council housing has been a problem since the 1970s; in 1978 there were 8,000 vacant dwellings. By 2005 it is likely that close to 30,000 municipal homes, most built since 1950 and still with outstanding loan debts, will have been demolished since 1980. There is a major, distinctive process of restructuring social housing, with sector decay and decline masked by demolition, in Britain's cities and nowhere has this process run deeper than in Glasgow.

So Glasgow entered the last decade as social deprivation and structural change in social housing became more apparent and as the housing market was simultaneously showing signs of sustained recovery. It is important to stress that the term recovery, in Glasgow's case relates to long term investment levels. A number of studies have shown that the city, like the other Scottish cities, has a significantly more stable market sector than English cities and that housing market boom-bust and disproportionate equity withdrawal have not been major features of the market (Maclennan et al. 2000). Clearly dual housing sectors were operating within the city and the development and resolution of this duality has been the recurrent theme of change over the last decade.

The final decade of the last millennium was not, then, a quiet period in a policy noisy city. For the first time since the 1960s, growing home-ownership meant that the market sector (renting plus owning) provided more than half of the stock of homes in the city. And much thought is being given to how to sustain that expansion and to adapt planning processes to facilitate growth. In the social sector the issues have been not just about demolition but about where and how to renew poorer neighbourhoods. The acute need for property improvement in the social sector has prompted not just major efforts to expand community involvement but to seek new routes to major private funding which, in the UK context, also requires shifts from municipal to community ownership.

But these market changes and the prospect for public action, not least through the new Scottish Parliament after 1999, have been much shaped by changes in the city economy over the last decade and these have become increasingly positive. The rest of this chapter aims to describe and explain recent developments in the city, and the wider city-region, by indicating the broad structure of the housing system (Sect. 5.2), establishing the major economic and demographic changes over both the last decade and the next (Sect. 5.3), identifying how these changes have impacted the market and social rental sector (Sect.5. 4).

Table 5.1. Housing tenure in Glasgow (per cent)

	1981	1991
Public sector	63	50
Private renting	9	7
Housing associations	4	8
Owner occupation	24	36

In 1999, the occupied housing stock was estimated at 273,900, comprising 46 per cent owner occupied (increased from 32 per cent in 1989), 5 per cent private rented, 34 per cent LA (52 per cent in 1989), 2 per cent Scottish Homes and 13 per cent Housing Association. Between 1989 and 1999 the stock increased by 331 houses, as private and housing association new builds offset demolitions.

5.2 Housing System Structure: Which Market, Where?

Spatially distributed markets, for housing and labour, do not have sharp boundaries, nor do functional limits or contours generally coincide with administrative boundaries. Much effort has been made, by academics and planning bodies in and around Glasgow to identify 'the structure' of the housing market. Although there is no single definitive answer, and the results depend on purpose, method data and time period these exercises help understand how the housing market functions and changes.

Studies revolve around the extent to which markets in the city overlap into a wider regional system and, in more fine grain the extent to which markets can be de-composed into different product groups and sub-markets. Since housing is heterogeneous, with every unit different in some way, it is reasonable for analysis to try to identify more aggregate groups of housing stock; some may simply identify spatial aggregations, or neighbourhoods and ignore product variety, others may try to group houses into product groups and, combining both approaches, market structure can be identified by mapping product groups in space. All this tells us is that the local housing system is differentiated and that differentiation is spatially expressed.

It is not valid to move from disaggregation to the identification of sub-markets. Sub-markets, properly defined, exist when then are persistent differences in commodity prices, and in the housing context this requires either hedonic standardisation over time or repeat sales or quasi repeat sales to identify sub-markets. Mobility studies are essential in understanding the functional structure of the housing market but the anatomy of flows identifies structure or areas and not, per se, sub-markets.

The Register of Sasines (the Land Register of Scotland), although not including key housing characteristics, provides a complete record of housing sales with dates, prices and origin of sellers (usually). Researchers have used this data to identify migration flows and degrees of local area closure within the market. The approach adopted was migration based and involved examining the pattern of purchaser moves from city areas to surrounding locations.

In 1996, the Glasgow and Clyde Valley Structure Plan Joint Committee (GCVSPJC) looked at HMAs for the conurbation, largely on the basis of a 65 per cent local mover closure criteria for 60 settlements across the conurbation and identified different structural tiers within the broad structure identifies in Fig. 5.1. The city lies within areas 1, 3 and 5. Jones (2002), builds up housing market areas using a finer settlement base (over 160 settlements were identified) and lower containment level (of 50 per cent local moves) and identifies 11 different areas.

Whichever closure criterion is adopted two general conclusions stand out. First, the Glasgow city-region housing market does not fit comfortably with the current administrative boundaries, e.g. The Clyde Valley Structure Plan. Second, the city boundaries are not well matched to the local housing market and the limits excludes many of the city's more affluent functional suburbs. There is a sense in which Glasgow city's poverty is exaggerated by the functional structure of the housing market, not least because municipal housing policy pushed home buyers out beyond the city limits for thirty years. But it is also clear that there is significant variety within the city and the important issue is whether there are any signs that particular sub-markets are under pressure and need to be expanded.

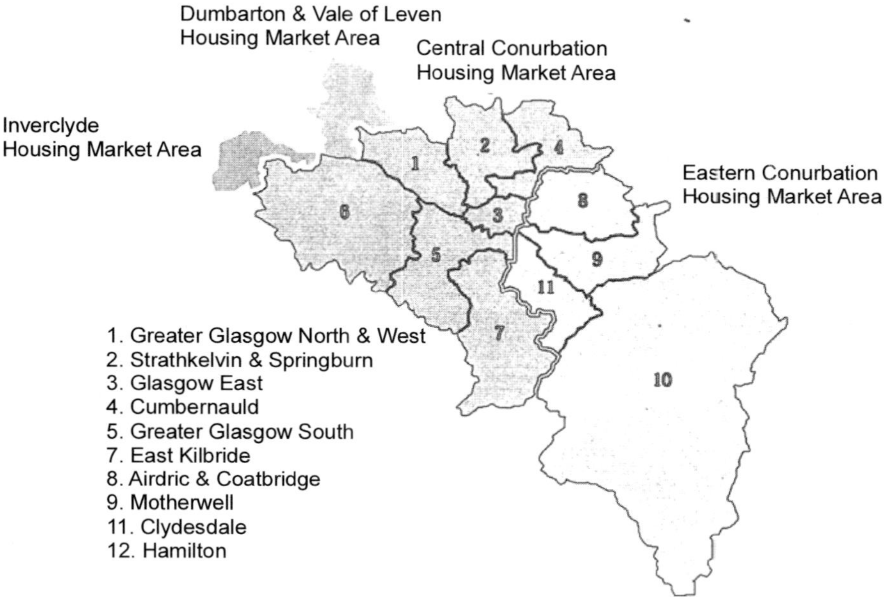

Fig. 5.1. GCVSPJC defined Glasgow conurbation HMAs (Source: CVSPJC Technical Report 5 2000)

An early study looked at the product group and sub-market structures of Glasgow between 1975 and 1977, just at the period when these markets were set to stop declining (Maclennan et al. 1987). This study, based on hedonic price adjustment of detailed housing data, identified 5 main product groups, spread across the city which formed 6 linked sub-markets (areas with significant differences in hedonically adjusted house prices). This sub-market structure had persisted over 3 years of available data but the data suggested that the significant area improvement programme in the city was beginning to coalesce middle quality and central area sub-markets.

The work was replicated for 1990 data (Maclennan 1994), suggesting both diversity and convergence. But that work was rapidly superseded by a later and larger study (O'Sullivan and Lee-Bourke 1997) which used 1991 Census data to define product groups. The study area for this work was the city-region, the Glasgow metropolitan area. A total of 7 product groups were defined for owner occupied housing in Glasgow for 1991. The 1991 product groups have recognisable antecedents in the earlier work reported, but are not identical (Table 5.2). They show considerable agreement with the Maclennan et al. (1987) product group geography (O'Sullivan and Lee-Bourke 1997).

Table 5.2. Glasgow metropolitan area 'product groups': Conceptual relationship between different studies (Source: O'Sullivan and Lee-Bourke 1997)

Maclennan, Wood and Munro (1987)	Maclennan (1990)	O'Sullivan and Lee-Bourke
1. Low status inner city tenements	1. Smaller flats in poorer neighbourhoods	1. Low status tenement housing
2. Middle to high status tenements and terraced housing	2. Smaller post-war semi-detached and terraced homes	2. Middle status terrace housing
		3. Middle status semi-detached housing
3. Medium quality inner city tenements	3. Larger flats in better neighbourhoods	4. Middle status tenement housing
4. Medium to high quality semi-detached, terraced and semi-detached block housing	4. Older larger semi-detached and terraced homes built between 1900 and 1940	5. High status terraced housing
		6. High status semi-detached housing
5. Middle to high status areas of detached, semi-detached and terraced housing	5. Larger detached and semi-detached homes built between 1800 and 1920 and in prestigious neighbourhoods	7. Very high status housing

More recent evidence on the internal structure of the Glasgow housing market comes from a series of papers by Jones and colleagues (Jones et al. 2000, 2001a, 2001b) looking into the migration structure of the market (and are not sub-markets nor product groups in the sense defined above). Using data covering all open market transactions for financial year 1991/92 in Glasgow, Jones et al. (2000a) begin with an a priori set of six potential sub-markets identified through a prior study (Watkins 1998).

The authors then go on to examine household flows between these migration areas. They found that in excess of 50 per cent of all house purchasers relocate within the same sub-market, with the exception of the city centre sub-market. No more than 11 per cent of movers into any one sub-market do so from another sub-market. In a separate study, Jones et al. (2000) then tested whether for the period 1984–1997 altered the sub-market structure identified. And this is closer to a real identification of true sub-markets as they did this by testing for 'co-integration' between pairs of repeat sales area price indices over the study period.

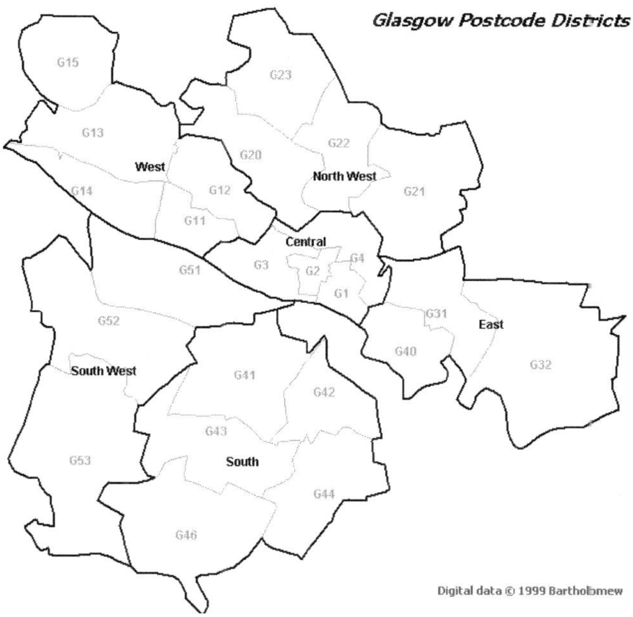

Fig. 5.2. Glasgow sub-market (Source: Jones et al. 2001a)

The study concluded that over this period the 'central' and 'west' sub-markets showed evidence of collapsing into one, as did the 'east' and 'north-west' sub-markets, but that on balance despite considerable change in stock, sub-markets have persisted. The authors conclude 'these [sub-markets] have remained stable in their geographical dimensions for over a decade' (Jones et al. 2001b) and they are indicated in Fig. 5.2. This provides a modern, plausible basis for practical disaggregation of the Glasgow market for broad spatial purposes.

The volume of work on the internal structure of the greater Glasgow HMA is, at least compared to other cities, considerable and complex. In broad terms, academic studies show some consistency on the product group and sub-market structures within the Glasgow housing market. Moreover, while subject to change, these geographies show considerable stability over time. Additionally there appears to be considerable consistency in intra market price trends, and what they signify. At this juncture it is important to look at the social and economic factors which have driven change of and within these structures over the last decade.

5.3 Driving Change: Economics and Demographics

In contrast to the housing market, there is much less detailed analysis of the economic geography of the city and city-region. Again the economy of the city sits at the core of a larger, partly connected system. In 2000 the city generated 16 per cent of Scotland's gross domestic product (GDP), and the remainder of the city region (approximate to the broad housing market region described above) a slightly larger share of 20 per cent.

But the city remains the concentrated powerhouse for the regional economy, not least because significant proportions of jobs within the city are held by commuters from the rest of the city region, and this proportion has increased over time. In the early 1970s just under three-quarters of jobs in Glasgow were held by Glaswegians. This had fallen to 58 per cent in 1991. The latest figures indicate that there are some there are 222,000 workers who live in Glasgow, but 338,000 employee jobs located in the city. Most of the remaining jobs are taken by people living in the immediately surrounding areas. The city economy is a key shaper of prosperity and jobs in the adjacent municipalities, providing half the jobs for residents in East Dunbartonshire and East Renfrewshire and a quarter in North Lanarkshire, Renfrewshire, South Lanarkshire, and West Dunbartonshire.

The economic history of the city region, let alone the city, has been an adverse one. Over the last 30 years employment has fallen by almost a quarter. The major factor underlying this fall in employment has been de-industrialisation and the loss of traditional heavy industries not only in Glasgow, but also in other city-region centres of employment.

There has been a faster rate of decline in employment in the city itself than in its hinterland largely as a result of the decline in manufacturing. The number of manufacturing jobs in Glasgow, which had already fallen spectacularly through the 1950s, 1960s and 1970s, fell further from 73,200 in 1981 to just 31,300 in 1999, with the majority of these shed in the 1980s. New manufacturing, such as electronics and other light industries have typically located in the new towns of East Kilbride and Cumbernauld as well as former green field areas. Despite the overall decline in employment in greater Glasgow, selected areas such as these have been able to increase employment in recent years, including manual jobs.

However a number of end of millennium studies have shown that the rate of decline in employment has slowed significantly in recent years. Bailey et al. (1999) calculate that the rate of decline in employment fell from 1.4 per cent per annum in the 1970s to 0.3 per cent in the 1990s. Indeed, when the 1990s are divided into pre and post 1995 there may now be signs that the long slow demise of the old economic base, which is now proportionately so much less significant, is now being outweighed by growth in newer city-loving sectors. This requires closer examination.

5.3.1 Recent Performance and Prospects

Recently available GDP per capita figures suggest that since the early 1990s Glasgow has grown faster than the rest of the region and that both have expanded at rates above the UK average (see Table 5.3). More recent work suggest that Glasgow has been growing at an annual rate close to 3 per cent between 1999 and 2002, above the Scottish and UK rates.

Table 5.3. GDP[a] per capita in Glasgow, West of Scotland and Scotland

	1993	1994	1995	1996	1997	1998
Glasgow	11 700	12 500	13 500	14 100	15 200	16 500
West of Scotland[b]	8 800	9 400	10 200	10 400	10 700	11 500
UK	9 700	10 200	10 600	11 200	11 900	12 500

[a]Figures adjusted for current prices.
[b]Excludes Argyll and Bute, Arran and the Cumbraes.

These improving output figures are also reflected in employment indices and in greater Glasgow and Glasgow city. For the wider region total employment increased from 793,384 in 1995 to 811,639 in 2000 (BSL 2001), although this was attributable to employment growth within the city as the total number of jobs in Glasgow increased from 332,100 (1995) to 352,000 (2000).

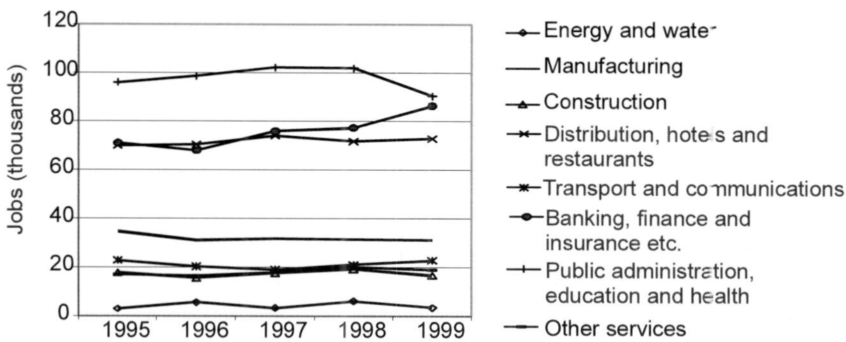

Fig. 5.3. Jobs in Glasgow (Source: NOMIS)

Table 5.4 shows that, over the 1990s, the number of jobs in Glasgow increased by 5 per cent, compared to little change for Scotland as a whole and identifies the sectoral pattern of change.

During the 1990s, service sector jobs grew by around 1 per cent per annum in greater Glasgow, as service sector jobs in banking, finance and insurance, as well as distribution, hotels and catering were attracted into the region. Many of these jobs have located in Glasgow city itself, where now almost 80 per cent of jobs are in the service sector, up from 49 per cent in 1971. Of the 340,000 or so jobs in Glasgow, around half are based in the city centre. These are typically in finance/business, the public sector, as well as hotel, restaurant, and retail. Glasgow is the largest concentration of retailing outside of the West End of London. After London and Edinburgh it has by far the highest visitor numbers for any British city. After London and Oxbridge it is the largest agglomeration of higher and further education in Britain and the second largest locus of academic research.

Table 5.4. Change in employee jobs 1991–98

Industrial Sector	Scotland No. [1000s]	Per cent	Glasgow No. [1000s]	Per cent
All industries	1.2	0	15.4	5
Agriculture, forestry, fishing	–14.8	–	–	–
Production & construction				
Total	–56.4	–11	–16.0	–23
Mining & energy	–1.3	–3	2.9	91
Manufacturing	–38.4	–11	–11.6	–27
Construction	–16.7	–13	–7.4	–31
Services				
Total	72.4	5	31.7	13
Retail and hotels	22.7	5	4.5	7
Transport & communications	–11.6	–10	–1.8	–8
Finance & business	32.2	12	15.5	26
Public sector and other	29.1	5	13.5	12

Sources: 1998 Annual Employment Survey; 1991 Census of Employment.

Incomes as well as employment rates reflect economic wellbeing. Average net household incomes lie below the Scottish average, both for the city-region, by 4 per cent, and in Glasgow city, by 11 per cent. However, by UK standards (at least outside of the pressured south east of Britain) the incomes of home-buyers both in the city and the suburbs are not significantly different from other metropolitan housing markets. In Glasgow, indeed the region as a whole, there is the social rental sector with a share significantly above metropolitan area averages. In consequence that sector absorbs the unemployed, the poor and the unemployment prone to a greater extent that other UK cities and research has shown (Maclennan et al. 1995, 1998) that this has both reduced risks and instability in the owner occupied market and led to more pronounced income separation between owned and social sectors. Another consequence is that rising prosperity in Glasgow is more likely to induce further significant increases in the home-ownership share than in cities with already ownership rates.

It would therefore appear that the historical decline in Glasgow city's employment opportunities has now and begun to reverse. Sustaining and expanding this new economic base is a key challenge for the city and as it does so it has to address the persisting problems from the decades of decline.

5.3.2 Persisting Problems

Historically, as the number of jobs within the region fell in Glasgow, the total number of Glaswegians who work in Glasgow has fallen even more dramatically, as this pattern continued until the second half of the 1990s. But the city still shows the consequences of high, accumulated stocks of unemployed population, even as recovery proceeds.

The best indicator of the poor past performance of the Glasgow economy is the employment rate (most of these commuting areas outside Glasgow city have residence based employment rates at or above the Scotland average). Fig. 5.4 shows that between 1993 and 1998, the employment rate in Glasgow was between 11 and 16 per cent below that of Scotland as a whole, though recent improvement has narrowed the gap and now the rate in Glasgow is 9 per cent below that of Scotland.

The 'stock' nature of Glasgow's problem means that employment rates for younger working age groups, up to the age of 40, are much closer to Scottish and UK averages. Coupled with rising employment and the propensity for households to have well defined owning or social renting careers from an early age, means that the housing market is driven by this younger margin of change whereas the social sector is left to deal with obsolescent human capital.

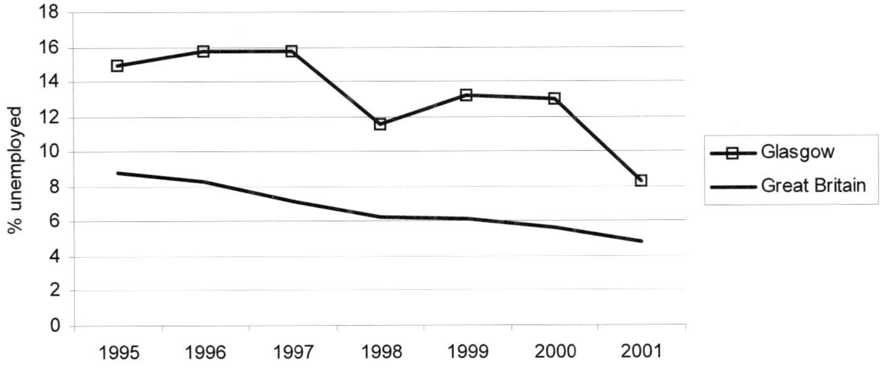

Fig. 5.4. ILO unemployment

One consequence of falling employment opportunities has been a high, sustained unemployment, much of which has been disguised as higher rates of economic inactivity. Within Glasgow city itself, opportunities for blue-collar workers to find alternative employment have not been helped by the fact that much employment growth has been in professional and managerial occupations. Indeed, junior non-manual jobs in the service sector and other industries also contracted alongside manufacturing.

Unemployment in Glasgow is high. Under the ILO measure (for which rates of unemployment are based on resident populations rather than the workforce), the unemployment rate in Glasgow in autumn 2000 was 8.5 per cent, compared to 6.2 per cent in the rest of Scotland. Despite a dramatic fall in ILO unemployment between 2000 and 2001, the Glasgow ILO rate is still double the Great Britain average (Fig. 5.4).

However, ILO unemployment is only a small part of worklessness in the city. Beatty et al. (1997) produced estimates of 'real' unemployment for each Local Authority Area in Britain. This count of unemployment included a proportion of people on sickness benefit, government schemes and in early retirement. They concluded that in January 1997, over 30 per cent of Glasgow city's working aged population could be termed 'real' unemployed. There are currently 23,000 ILO unemployed people in Glasgow, but a further 104,000 people inactive in the labour market, only a quarter of whom want to work.

And this may reflect the effects of housing benefit and other 'traps'. In mid 2000, 116,000 working aged people in Glasgow were claiming at least one key DSS benefit.[2] This is 30 per cent of the working aged population: easily the highest in Scotland, with only three areas of the UK higher. The main reason for this high figure is the 71,000 Glasgow residents claiming sickness/disability benefits.

Around two-thirds of Glaswegians who are not working have either been out of work for more than five years, or have never worked. This is significantly higher than the rest of Scotland (55 per cent). In addition, of those Glaswegians not in work, 42 per cent have no qualifications, compared to 30 per cent in the rest of Scotland. This confirms the large segment of the working age population in Glasgow detached from the labour market, most of whom live in the social rental sector (Maclennan et al. 1992), and the cumulative tyrannies of unemployment, ill-health, social housing segregation.

The 1998 Deprivation Index, which is based on a number of indicators of disadvantage, concluded that 57.7 per cent of the worst 10 per cent of enumeration districts in Scotland are in Glasgow, and the city contains the three poorest parliamentary constituencies in Britain. Given these figures, it is hardly surprising that the city is a dual system with a thriving market sector, in both jobs and housing, co-located with a social sector dominated by poor housing and neighbourhood decline and multiple deprivation.

[2] Key benefits are defined as at least one of: job seekers allowance, income support, incapacity benefit, severe disablement allowance, or disability living allowance

5.3.3 A Better Future

There is much concern in the UK at present regarding the future of employment and incomes in the cities. City recovery, as in Glasgow's case has coincided with the long expansion of overall employment in the UK since 1992 and especially since 1997. But there are also signs of structural change, noted above, which highlight the emergence of newer economic bases for the cities. Estimates for the future of the Glasgow economy have been positive in recent years, suggesting that the absolute and even relative recovery of the city will continue; and this may have cumulative benefits as the 'deprivation stock problem' is worked through.

The Fraser of Allander Institute predicts that employment in greater Glasgow is likely to rise over the decade from 2001, with the main employment growth occurring in the service sector. Of the 16,000 anticipated extra jobs, 10,000 are expected to be in Glasgow city alone. As a result they expect ILO unemployment to fall to 9.49 per cent by 2010. However whether these extra jobs are taken up by residents of Glasgow city or lead to further increases in commuting remains an open question.

The Strathclyde Labour Market Intelligence and Monitoring Service (SLIMS) produced similar, but more optimistic forecasts for the period 2000–2008, forecasting 21,000 additional jobs, an increase of 6 per cent for the city. This is above the rate of growth for surrounding areas, but is for jobs in the city, rather than jobs for Glasgow residents. SLIMS predict that part time jobs will grow by 36,000, replacing 23,000 full time jobs. Self employment is seen to increase by around 8,000.

Forecasts suggest that over the next seven years, the banking, finance and insurance sector will be the fastest growing, and this sector, along with retail, hotels, and restaurants will more than make up for the predicted loss of manufacturing jobs. The number of management and professional jobs is predicted to increase, along with sales occupation (mainly call centre type jobs). The types of manufacturing jobs which may be lost are those skilled trades, particularly the non-electronic specialists.

5.3.4 Demographic Change

Whilst there are better prospects for an improving economy to drive the city and regional housing market the demographics, at least at first sight, seem more daunting. The population of Glasgow is however in long term decline, and predicted to continue falling, albeit at a much slower rate. Between 1979 and 1999, Glasgow lost a quarter of its population largely as a result of out-migration. It is predicted that the population will decline by a further three per cent in the next 15 years, compared to a projected one per cent loss in Scotland. All bar one of Glasgow's neighbouring authorities are expected to experience population loss in the next 15 years (Fig. 5.5).

Population stagnation for Scotland and decline for the city and the region, as the centre of gravity of Scottish population is dragged east by the expansion of Edinburgh and its hinterland, is a major policy challenge. However it does not mean a declining demand for housing in the city. First, the official forecasts are extrapolations and do not fully allow for policy, or even economy, induced shifts and there is a greater prospect now that they are likely to underestimate the future population share of the cities. Second, unlike the former argument which relies on the city gaining at the cost of the remainder of the region, the continuing reduction in household size means that household numbers are rising in both city-region and city, and the figures for Glasgow are indicated in Table 5.5. Third, and again this reflects a potential increase in city versus region competitiveness, most of the growth in households numbers is due to single person increases, both young and elderly (Table sets out a 1996 prediction to 2005).

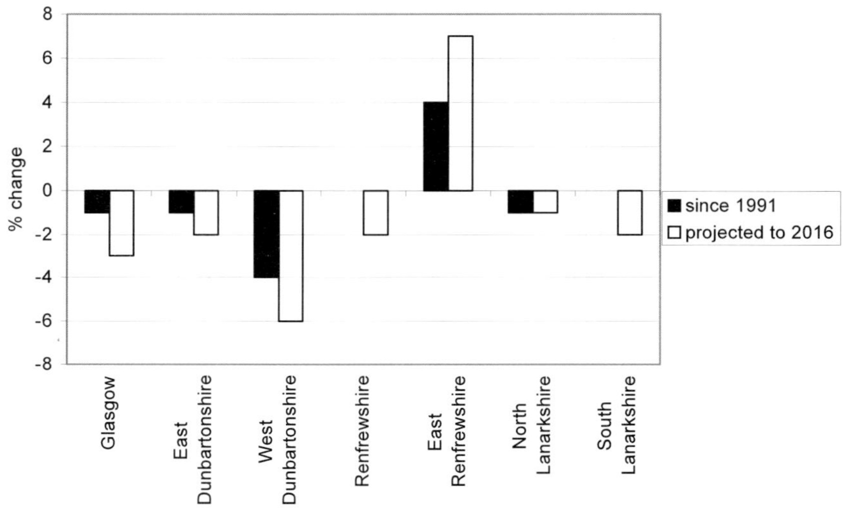

Fig. 5.5. Population change in Glasgow and neighbouring authorities (Source: GRO)

Table 5.5. Projected household types in Glasgow (post 1995 boundaries, 1000s)

Household type	1991	2005
One adult, non-pensioner	51	80
Single parent families	25	26
Two parent families	48	37
Single elderly	48	42
Two plus adults	103	96
Total	272	281

Smaller, more easily maintained homes with ready access to amenities will increasingly be in fashion and rising fuel costs and suburban to city traffic congestion may resurrect the traditional Scottish preference for higher density, high accessibility homes. However the table also indicates what research has recognised as a well developed pattern and issue for more than a decade but which policy has been painfully slow to address. Households with families, and even newly formed two adult households, leave the city. This is unsurprising as households may wish more space or suburban settings in which to raise children.

However, research also makes clear that there is a part of this outward flow (estimated at close to 1,000 households per annum) which comprises households who work in the city centre and who would ideally like to have their housing aspirations met within the city. But they are not, for three reasons. There is only a small stock of family housing in the city, and little choice. Parents are concerned by the poor performance of schools in the city. Many households, with and without children, are concerned about their security. With large tracts of social housing in the city being demolished, let alone 10 per cent of the city already comprising unused brown field land, there is the potential to rebuild up to 20,000 low rise homes in the city. But this will require vision, planning and service provision to be integrated and to date they have not been.

Table 5.6. Households in Glasgow

1996	271 900
1999	275 900
2009 (projected)	285 400

Source: GRO.

Despite falling total population, the number of people of working age increased between 1991 and 2001 by one per cent to 392,000, and is predicted to increase by a further two per cent by 2016, against a backdrop of a predicted three per cent decline for the rest of the city-region (and for Scotland as a whole, Table 5.7). Also, the age profile of the Glasgow population differs from other parts of Scotland: there is a significantly higher proportion of people aged under 35 living in Glasgow and this partly reflects the significance of the city as a centre of higher and further education and the rapid growth of these sectors since the start of the 1990s.

Table 5.7. Changes in population 1991–2001 and to 2016 (per cent)

	since 1991	to 2016	since 1991	to 2016
Total population	0	–1	–3	–3
Below working age	–3	–12	–2	–14
Of working age	1	–3	0	2
Above working age	2	18	–15	–10

The growth in working age numbers, allied to the predicted improvement in the demand for labour, will probably mean an increase in the city-region demand for home-owner units (starter homes) but the education sector expansion will pressure the small private rental sector. In order to attract students and then retain them, a strategy now regarded as crucial for economic competitiveness, young single person housing and neighbourhoods will have to be given a greater priority in policy thinking.

5.3.5 Demand Forecasts

The sections above have examined past trends in key housing demand factors and also touched upon sectoral extrapolations and forecasts. However, at the end of the 1990s housing decision takers for the city had become so concerned with some of the problems and lost potential of housing in the city that, after 80 years of intensive policy action, they would commission some formal demand estimates for housing, tenure and broad location for a decade ahead. The details of that model are set out in Meen et al. (2001) and their baseline conclusions are reported below.

The estimates from the model have played a major role in informing discussion about the future of the social sector in the city but their salience for the market and the future of the city are also recognised. The baseline estimates of the model, incorporating key economic and demographic trends imply a net increase in housing demand in both the city and the remainder of the city region, by 4 and 11 per cent respectively. However, there are marked changes in the tenure demand patterns (and actual events to 2002 give the estimates real credence to date). Owner-occupation in the city and the rest of the area will both increase by about 30 per cent. However social housing demand will fall in Glasgow by 18.1 per cent and by 19.1 per cent in the rest of the area.

Table 5.8. Base housing demand change 1996–2009

Tenure and location	Absolute change (number of households)	Percentage change in households
Glasgow owning	+34 681	+30.2
Glasgow social renting	–25 667	–18.1
Outwith owning	+81 104	+30.9
Outwith social renting	–32 135	–19.1

The research team also undertook scenario simulations of policy levers and other factors which could change to assess implications for sectors and areas. For instance, improving neighbourhood quality (reducing multiple deprivation scores) would lead to a large shift into home-ownership in Glasgow owner-occupation both by Glasgow renters and suburban owners and rising incomes and employment would both raise home-ownership rates. At present the model cannot be used to make more localised or more detailed sectoral predictions, and this is in no way to detract from its present usefulness. Understandings of more detailed change impacts have had to come from less formal, often cross sectional assessments.

5.4 Market and Social Sectors: Change, Policy and Impacts

5.4.1 Market Policies and Prices

The decade under study in this chapter started with the then conservative government committed to their longstanding goal of maximising the scale of the owner occupied sector. The policy framework supporting this objective has changed over the decade and, of course, political change and devolution meant that the core aim of policy had changed by 2000. The Scottish Executive recognise strong consumer preferences for home ownership but have no sector scale targets as they see scale being determined by rising income and employment and, instead, have evinced market quality and stability as the core aims of housing market policy.

There has been both change and continuity in the set of policy instruments used. At the start of the decade tax relief on mortgage interest payments had been of apparent significance, especially to higher rate tax payers; but by 1996 the conservatives had already started to reduce it and by 2000 it was removed entirely. The removal of this fiscal support for housing has had none of the adverse effects argued by the mortgage and building industries, and indeed Mrs. Thatcher's governments; the sector has continued to grow and so have prices. Low interest rates and asset gain expectations allied to the poor quality of social housing have sustained the shift to ownership without this regressive tax relief (Maclennan 1995, 1998).

Almost half of the growth of home ownership in the UK, and indeed Glasgow, since the start of the 1980s has been the purchase of individual municipal homes by their tenants using the provisions of the Right to Buy. In Glasgow just under 30 per cent of the 1980 stock has been sold, mostly in better council neighbourhoods and in areas of low rise housing. Recent estimates suggest that the average subsidy involved in such sales (based on discounts related to length of residents and type of dwelling) was around 52 per cent of the value of the dwelling, this was a massive redistribution of assets from the state to households.

In the 2001 Housing Act, the Scottish Parliament voted to modernise the Right to Buy. The measure was in fact extended to all social sectors, including previously exempted housing associations (as part of an integration of the rights and organisation of the different fragments of the social rental sector), but then significantly reduced in value. In the long term the average value of RTB subsidies will fall to around half their present rate, and with RTB to be suspended in areas of identified housing shortage this will mean a reduced rate of RTB in the future.

The ex post subsidy rate now to be available to RTB purchasers has been set at a rate and value broadly compatible with a range of other measures to promote low cost home-ownership in Scotland, either provided by housing associations as part of mixed tenure projects or as a capital grant, called GRO-grant, to private developers investing in specified regeneration areas. The policy rationale of these grants was to diversify tenures within regeneration communities and to overcome market failures in the provision of such mixes.

The effective subsidy on these diverse schemes is in the range 20 to 35 per cent and since 1990 some 2,000 association low cost ownership units have been developed and close to 7,000 GRO grants used in the city. By way of contrast, the provision of improvement and repair grants to private owners to upgrade their properties (for particular kinds of work in particular kinds of area) has fallen sharply since the mid-90s. The reason is simple. Prior to 1996 the grant aid was earmarked by central government and thereafter it was included as part of general central government permissions to local authorities to borrow for capital investment. In general the municipality have been incapable of grasping the consequences of squeezing upgrading in the poorer private sector as they have in their own rental stock.

These measures, combined with the economic and demographic changes set out above have produced a generally positive change period for Glasgow's market sector. Analyses of second hand sale prices for Glasgow city indicate that nominal house prices increased by almost a half over the period 1991 to 2001 and by 40 to 45 per cent in the surrounding municipalities. This rate for the city was less than Edinburgh (68 per cent) and Aberdeen (58 per cent) and was a little below the UK average but not markedly so. Scottish and Glasgow house price cycles are not simultaneous to southern Britain, and tend to follow southern peaks so Glasgow prices may yet return to their long term relativity (over the period 1971 to 1996 Glasgow house prices inflated at the UK average rate). But this is not a certainty.

Within the city and city-region the small area pattern of price inflation rates was affected both by regeneration programmes and by different demand supply imbalances across different product groups.

Towards the end of the 1980s, Glasgow was the most intensively rehabilitated city in Western Europe (OECD 1987). Major residential rehabilitation programmes, with a cumulative current investment value in excess of £2 billion were implemented between 1974 and 1990 (Maclennan 1993). Since 1990 a further £billion of expenditure has occurred. For the most part, as noted in the introduction, this expenditure has been delivered through housing associations operating in specific areas of the city. Research undertaken at Glasgow University in 1977, 1982 and 1987 identified major house price effects from these initiatives. These sorts of rehabilitation programme and associated spillovers, in combination with broader economic and social change, have driven change in the underlying structure of the Glasgow housing market. There is a much flatter price gradient for homes, of a given size, now than two decades ago, when prices with distance away from the city centre towards the city limits. And the potential convergence in sub-markets was noted above.

O'Sullivan and Lee-Bourke, see above, examine price trends across their seven product groups using second hand house price sales data for Glasgow for 1989–96. The data showed considerable variation in the price paths for individual product groups, with limited transmission of price pressure between groups. Low status tenement property prices grew strongly to the mid point of the period before tailing off; middle status tenement property prices exhibited moderate sustained pressure over the period, as did middle status and high status semi-detached properties. Middle status terraced housing performed consistently but unspectacularly over the study period, with the greatest growth in prices occurring in the high status areas. Overall, the Glasgow house price distribution looks to have been widening over this period, with demand relatively greatest at the upper end of the distribution. Their analysis is consistent with both purchaser studies and of area price trends post 1996.

In conclusion, Glasgow's starter home market expands but so does relevant supply. But frustrated families, with few choices, either buy in pressured markets or leave for the suburbs. There is a clear opportunity for the city to capture that interest and potential tax base. Re-balancing tenure continues as an issue for the city but the emerging issues for the future are to re-use space and place to make Glasgow a competitive, stable, quality housing market to attract and retain higher income households.

5.4.2 Remaking the Social Sector

Clearly Glasgow's housing market faced new and interesting challenges at the outset of the millennium. The social sector, or more particularly the council owned stock of 90,000 homes, simply faced a crisis. The broad, adverse evolution of the sector was described in the introduction but the policy setting for the sector became more adverse in the 1990s. A number of key factors were at play.

In Scotland, like the rest of the UK, municipal housing is financed by councils borrowing and that borrowing is scored as part of overall controlled public expenditure and the debt as public debt. Loans for new construction are repaid over 60 years and for major modernisation over 30. The current account for all of the housing schemes operated by the municipality, a pooled account, is called the housing revenue account (HRA). Prior to the mid-80s (in Scotland, English approaches were different), local tax revenues provided 10 to 15 per cent of the revenue stream and a central government subsidy to defray interest costs, called housing support grant (HSG) provided 20 to 30 per cent and rents the remainder.

By the 1990s local tax subventions to the HRA been abolished and HSG was sharply reduced. This reflected a central government policy, which lasted up until 1997, to induce rent increases above inflation and to protect poorer households by housing benefits. At present some 80 per cent of the council's tenants are now in receipt of housing benefit. In Glasgow, over the decade, rents rose at more than 5 per cent per annum above the RPI to amongst the highest rents in the UK.

But at the same time the services provided in exchange for these rents were being, sometimes literally, eroded. The amount that the municipality was being allowed to borrow to improve homes (the RTB had effectively ended council new construction) was more than halved between 1991 and 2001.

The decline of the council sector stood in marked contrast to the fortunes of the not-for-profit sector. As, after 1974, they renewed the older, city centre housing stock housing associations (which in Glasgow have typically been small, neighbourhood based organisations with 500 to 2,000 units) developed a reputation for community engagement and empowerment, imaginative leadership and good service delivery. Housing associations, unlike councils, are subsidised by the ex ante payment of grants, not loans, for renovation and new construction. After 1989, changes in legislation meant that the non-grant element of their financing was, unlike council investment, treated as private spending and lay outside of the public budget. Given the existing low incomes and poor property quality in Glasgow grants per property have been high, now averaging 70 per cent in the city but often involving schemes with grant rates of up to 90 per cent. Throughout the 1990s the role of associations in the city has continued to expand; the support budget over the decade was close to £1billion, the sector owned 40,000 homes by 2000 and areas of operation had spread from older areas into parcels of property transferred from the City council to 'community ownership' associations.

As the association sector there was another lethal dynamic reducing physical and financial viability of the council sector. When councils sold homes under the RTB they received a net receipt (now averaging about £13,000 per home). In Scotland, unlike England, there was, until 1996 no requirement for the council to repay out standing loans of homes they sold. Often they retained and spent the receipt, as their borrowing permission was reduced. In consequence outstanding debt per remaining tenant began to rise. Where they rose more than rents this meant the cancellation of maintenance and slower service delivery. As the 1990s progressed with more jobs in the city, and even more outside, tenants who could be owners voted with their feet as rents rose and their homes deteriorated or as new sector applicants were offered poorer and poorer quality homes. And of course, as existing tenants moved out and list applicants refused poor homes more and more houses were demolished. And demolition, of homes with outstanding loans, simply again increased debt per remaining tenant. During the 1990s the council demolished some 15,000 of their homes, most with non-redeemed debt outstanding.

By 2001 these non-sustainable trends meant that; real rents could not be increased further; debt servicing principle payments were taking 52 per cent of rental income and £2billion was needed for reinvestment in the stock, or double the present rate; a further 12,000 to 15,000 houses would have to be demolished (see demand estimates in the previous section). Clearly this dynamic had to be stopped as it meant worse housing for Glasgow's poor and the possibility of financial damage for the city or significantly increasing the Scottish housing budget. An innovative solution has been found and is in the infancy of implementation.

When the Labour government succeeded the conservatives they did not rush to rescue failing council sectors and, particularly in Scotland, embraced the promotion of community ownership, both by giving new investment resources to associations rather than councils and by encouraging the latter to transfer all of their stock to associations. This policy recognises both the merits of association style empowerment and management and the reality that part of additional investment costs will be financed by the private sector. Indeed, where councils are transferring stock to associations the transfer price will reflect the poor condition of the stock and that all of the upgrading work will be paid for by private funds supported by the rental income stream. The policy is clear in aim and principle and, in reality a major implementation challenge, not least because it is tenants who decide in a ballot whether transfer takes place or not.

It has taken four years to move from the policy decision, by the council, to investigate transfer possibilities to the reality of ballot. But this is hardly surprising. Glasgow City was once the largest municipal landlord in Western Europe, with more than 140,000 houses and the idea of public housing has lain close to the soul of politics in the City. And the technical problems involved in assessing quality, repair costs, future demands and financial possibilities, as well as the organisational issues of informing tenants and advising them have been considerable.

However, in April 2002 tenants voted (in a 60/40 split) to transfer all of the city's municipal homes to a new not for profit association, the GHA, which will commence with 60 local management vehicles which may, in time, become local owners of the stock (indeed it is likely that a third of the homes moving to the GHA will move on quickly to existing local housing associations). The GHAs business plan valued the Glasgow stock at £25 million; the billions spent of public housing in the post-war period have little real value now. Unfortunately in Glasgow's case the outstanding loans for municipal housing were £980 million. At the same time the resource requirement to upgrade properties to an adequate standard was estimated at £1.6 billion over the next decade.

The contraction of the sector, local and national political concerns all meant that raising rents was not the route to redeeming debts and raising standards. Indeed tenants have now been given a guarantee that rents will not rise by more than the RPI for the next six pears and by no more than RPI plus 1 per cent for the subsequent two. At first the Scottish Executive proposed to pay for the cost of servicing the residual debt, essentially by using the funds that it had previously given to the council for investment, over a twenty year period. However the UK Treasury had allowed English transfer authorities to have overhanging housing debt written off after transfer and this measure was extended to Scotland and Wales in 2001. For Glasgow this was a massive redistributive measure with the Chancellor lifting the burden of past housing debt from the city's poorest households (or an annual debt cost of close to £85 millions) and allowing the new headroom in rents to pay for new housing. The Executive have now, for a period of ten years ahead, committed their £50 millions per annum to providing a doubled rate of new association investment to replace some of the worst municipal housing with new homes.

The next decade will see the physical and organisational remaking of the social rental sector in the city. Investment rates are set to double and remain higher for at least a decade. GHA are aware that they have to deliver refashioned neighbourhoods and stronger communities as well as better homes and as they do so this will unwind Glasgow's past 'stock' problem both faster and at a higher quality of life for all. That can only be to the long term benefit of the city economy, even leaving aside the favourable impacts of an additional 3,000 construction sector jobs to deliver the new programme.

5.5 Better Prospects

In retrospect the 1990s were a far from quiet or unimportant decade in Glasgow's evolution and the second half of the decade, especially after 1997, saw some marked changes with the past. The city began to show signs that it had survived four decades of economic contraction and was finally showing real signs of growth in employment and in household numbers. Both the economics and the demographics have turned to re-favour the core city and it may be that the real future difficulties will lie in the smaller declining towns at the edge of the city-region. But Glasgow is flourishing, in parts again and the housing market is set to expand.

The disconnected segment of this near dual city remains a serious difficulty. Training and education programmes have major roles to play in raising skills and aspirations but as they do so there is at least now a major vehicle for community engagement and substantial physical improvement of homes and neighbourhoods. The too self-evident lesson of Glasgow's history is that well intentioned but housing dominated solutions do not work to provide sustained change. But equally the housing conditions that GHA are set to change have damaged not just the health of citizens but the vitality of communities and the economy. Glasgow and the city region will be better places in 2012 than they are now.

References

Bailey N (1999) Deregulated Private Renting: A Decade of Change in Scotland. Netherlands Journal of Housing and the Built Environment 14: 363–384

Bailey N, Turok I (1999) Adjustment to Job Loss in Britain's Cities. Regional Studies 34(7): 631–653.

Bailey N, Turok I, Docherty I (1999) Edinburgh and Glasgow: Contrasts in Competitiveness and Cohesion. Department of Urban Studies, University of Glasgow

Beatty, C, Fothergill S, Gore T, Herrington A (1997) The Real Level of Unemployment. Centre for Regional Economic and Social Research, Sheffield Hallam University

BSL (2001) Submission to the Commonwealth Advisory Committee on Homelessness Response to National Homelessness Strategy Paper. Affordable Housing National Research Consortium 2001 in demand for housing assistance in Victoria (Housing Justice Roundtable 2001), Australia

GCVSPJC Technical Report No. 5 (2000) www.gcvcore.gov.uk/GCV2005/technical_ reports

GRO www.gro-scotland.gov.uk

Jones C (2002) The Definition of Housing Market Areas and Strategic Planning. Urban Studies 39(3): 549–564

Jones C, More A, O'Sullivan T, Young G (1998) Local Housing Systems Analysis: Best Practice Guide. Scottish Homes, Edinburgh

Jones C, Leishman C, Fraser WD (2000) The Influence of Uncertainty on House Builder Behaviour and Residential Land Values. Journal of Property Research 17(2): 147–168

Jones C, Leishman C (2001a) The Extent, Spatial Pattern and Causes of Homelessness. In: Jones C, Robson P (eds) Health of Scottish Housing. Ashgate

Jones C, Leishman C, Watkins C (2001b) Housing Market Processes, Urban Housing Submarkets and Planning Policy. Paper presented to RICS Cutting Edge Conference, University of Oxford

Jones C, Dunse N (2002) The Existence of Office Submarkets in Cities. Journal of Property Research (19)2: 159-182

Maclennan D, Meen G, Gibb K (1997) Fixed Commitments, Uncertain Incomes: Sustainable Owner-occupation and the Economy. Joseph Rowntree Foundation, London

Maclennan D, O'Sullivan A, MacIntyre C (2000) Evolving the Right to Buy: Evidence for Scotland. Scottish Executive, Edinburgh

Maclennan D, Brown J (2002) The Establishment of Markets for Owner Occupation within Public Sector Communities. European Journal of Housing Policy (2)3: 265–292

Maclennan D, Dunse N (2002) Rental Depreciation, Obsolescence and Location: The Case of Industrial Properties. Paper presented to the annual European Real Estate Society Conference, Glasgow, June, 2002

Meen G (2001) Social Interactions in Local Housing Markets: A Research Programme for Quantitative Analysis. Centre for Spatial and Real Estate Economics, University of Reading

NOMIS, Official Labour Market Statistics, www.nomisweb.co.uk/

Official Labour Market Statistics (1991) 1991 Census of Employment. National Statistics, UK, http://www.nomisweb.co.uk/home/catalogue.asp

Official Labour Market Statistics (1998) 1998 Census of Employment. 1998 Annual Employment Survey, National Statistics, UK, http://www.nomisweb.co.uk/home/catalogue.asp.

Watkins C (1998) Are New Entrants to Residential Property Markets Informationally Disadvantaged?. Journal of Property Research 15(1): 57–70

Watkins C (1998) Examining Spatial Patterns in the Pace of Housing Commodification. Scottish Geographical Magazine

Watkins C (1998) The Position and Role of Former Public Sector Homes in the Owner occupied Sector: New Evidence from the Scottish Housing Market. Journal of Economic and Social Geography

6 The Housing Market in Zurich's Urban Agglomeration

Angelo A. Rossi

The University of Applied Sciences of Southern Switzerland, Manno

6.1 Introduction

The urban agglomeration of Zurich is the most important urban region of Switzerland in demographic and economic terms. At the onset of the 1100th century it accounts for almost one million inhabitants and nearly 600,000 jobs, the largest share of them in the service sector. The position of the Zurich agglomeration inside Switzerland is dominant regarding international activities and research, as well as transfer and development activities (Rossi and Steiger 1995; Bretschger et al. 1995). Thus the Zurich region is very dynamic in economic terms. It is also a very attractive region as far as immigration of population is concerned. In Swiss terms the Zurich agglomeration knows higher-than-average rates of GDP and population growth (Schuler 2002).

As shown by Table 6.1, the population increase is in fact attributable to the increase of the population in the suburban ring communities. This, in turn, is due to the demographic dynamics of the existing rings as well as to the development of new suburban rings continuously enlarging the urban agglomeration radius (compare footnote 1). In Table 6.2 we analyse the sources of demographic growth in recent years. We observe that in the city both the natural and the migratory component are negative. But in the city, the population decreases mostly because of the negative balance of the natural component. Conversely, in the suburban ring communities the natural component is the one that contributes most to demographic growth. The positive suburban migration balance is larger than the negative migration balance of the city. This means that the suburban communities attract households from the rest of the country and from abroad as well. We finally notice that the largest demographic growth is probably taking place just beyond the current border of the urban agglomeration, in local jurisdictions which by the most recent definition did not belong to Zurich's urban agglomeration. Because the city centre of Zurich still loses inhabitants the prevailing demographic trend, as far as the internal development of the agglomeration is concerned, is characterised by suburbanisation.[1]

Table 6.1. Zurich's urban agglomeration population development 1980–99

	1980	1990	1999	Variation 1980–90 [%]	Variation 1990–99 [%]
Zurich	369,522	365,043	333,486	–1.2	–8.6
I Ring	136,787	135,777	134,566	–0.7	–0.9
II Ring	140,088	154,226	163,815	10.0	6.2
III Ring	59,823	67,567	71,799	12.9	6.2
IV Ring	132,144	145,165	154,613	9.8	6.5
V Ring[a]		72,402	80,752		11.5
Total 5 Rings	838,364	940,180	939,031	12.1	–0.1
Total 4 Rings	838,364	867,778	858,279	3.5	–1.1
Total 5 Rings without Zurich	468,842	575,137	605,545	22.7	5.3
Total 4 Rings without Zurich	468,842	502,735	524,793	7.2	4.4

[a]The fifth ring did not exist before 1990.
Source: Statistical yearbook of the city of Zurich.

Table 6.2. Population variation and sources of demographic growth in Zurich's urban agglomeration in the period 1.1.1994 to 31.12.1998

Sources of changes	Zurich city	Suburban ring communities	Urban agglomeration's total
Natural increase	–5,627	13,178	7,551
Net migration	–597	8,553	7,956
Total change	–6,224	21,731	15,507

Source: Statistiques des villes suisses, different years.

The yearly list of the best world cities drawn up by the Personal Consultant Company Mercer in London puts Zurich at the top in the year 2002 (Tages An-

[1] Definition of Zurich's urban area as used in this Chap.: Agglomeration is the term used by the Swiss statistical office to define the functional area around an important urban centre. The main criterion to trace the perimeter of an urban agglomeration is the volume of commuters flowing from the suburban local communities to the main hub. As these flows evolve, the agglomeration perimeter is checked and changed every ten years, when the results of the federal population census are published. In this chapter we have used the definition of the 1990 population census because the results of the 2000 population census have not yet been completely worked out (Schuler and Joye 1994). In order to have more information on the working of the housing market, we also used another definition of Zurich's urban area, namely the perimeter of the Canton of Zurich. The two spatial units are different and they overlap only in part. Finally we observe that today's functional urban region of Zurich ranges beyond the border of the agglomeration of the 1990 census. In order to take account of this reality the Swiss statisticians have defined so-called metropolitan areas, which are even larger than the agglomeration. We did not refer in to the metropolitan area of Zurich simply because official statistics do not publish relevant housing data for this kind of spatial unit.

zeiger 2002). Zurich's population agrees with this judgement. Zurich's inhabitants like to live in town. As the results of the last year survey about the population's feelings have revealed, 91 per cent of the respondents said they enjoy life in Zurich. Asked about the city's most bothersome problems, they put traffic problems on top of the list. Housing conditions, on the other hand, ranked only sixth among their concerns, trailing the problems related to alien residents, drugs addicts, criminality, and waste and graffiti (Fachstelle 2001).

Housing construction in the urban agglomeration of Zurich accounts for more than 10 per cent of all housing construction in Switzerland. Zurich's housing market is therefore the country's largest. Zurich is home to the most important real property companies, the largest building cooperatives, Switzerland's top-ranking mortgage bank as well as the leading consultant firms and associations in the housing sector.

Since the end of World War II, the dominant feature of this housing market is excess demand. But this has not caused the public sector to intervene as an important investor in the market. The public-sector share of new housing construction in the agglomeration is consistently below 10 per cent. Instead, the building cooperative plays a more substantial role in providing new housing, at least inside the city (Koch, Somandin, Süsstrunk 1989). Notwithstanding the role of the building cooperative, the major share of residential properties is in the hand of profit-seeking private investors.[2]

As we will see further on in the chapter, the development of housing construction in Zurich's urban agglomeration has over the last twenty years known a different time pattern than the one experienced by the national market. The content in this chapter is an attempt to explain this difference. Sect. 6.2 contains an outline of the development of housing production at the national level and in the Zurich agglomeration over the last twenty years, whereas Sect. 6.3 will analyse the influence of demographic and financial factors on the housing construction cycle inside the Zurich urban agglomeration. Sect. 6.4, finally, will cast some light on the im-

---

[2] Private and public sector housing. In 1999 this was the breakdown of Zurich's citywide housing stock among the different categories of landlords.

Table 6.3. Housing stock of the city of Zurich by categories of landlords in 1999

Landlord categories	Percentage share in the housing stock
Individuals	49.5
Companies	14.9
Building cooperatives	19.1
Pension funds	5.5
Public sector (city, canton, central government)	7.5
Non-profit organisations	3.5

Source: Statistical Yearboook of the city of Zurich.

We note that the share of landlords who are individuals is still half of the total. On the other hand the building cooperatives own nearly 20 per cent of the stock. Finally we note that the public sector holds less than 10 per cent of the housing stock. The most important landlord in this category is the city with 6.6 per cent of the stock.

pact of political measures already implemented or currently under discussion with a view to improving the efficiency of this housing market.

6.2 Recent Development of the Housing Market in Zurich's Urban Agglomeration

The long-term development of Switzerland's housing market, measured by an indicator of the relative yearly variation in the housing stock, shows a downward trend. As Fig. 6.1 indicates, in the last century the yearly variation has decreased from 1.6 per cent in the early 1980s to 1 per cent at the end of the century. In absolute terms the yearly production has shrunk from around 40,000 units at the beginning of the 1980s to 33,000 units in the year 1999. These figures are a far cry from the production records achieved in the early 1970s, when Switzerland's construction industry was producing more than 50,000 units of housing every year. This long-term trend can be attributed to the significant decrease in the rate of demographic growth witnessed from the middle of the seventies onward.

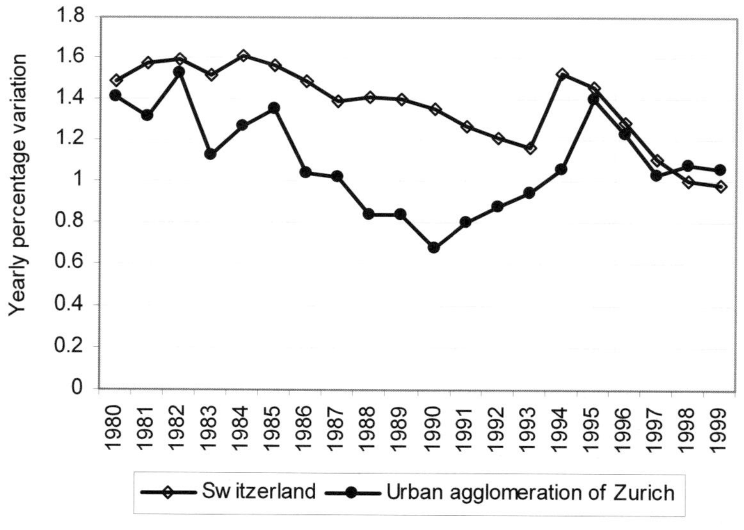

Fig. 6.1. The business cycle in the housing market of Switzerland and in the urban agglomeration of Zurich measured by the yearly growth rate of the housing stock (Sources: Statistical yearbook of Switzerland, statistical yearbook of the city of Zurich from 1980 to 1999)

The long-term development of housing production in the Zurich agglomeration market has been different from the national trend, as the former has been marked by a more significant recession through the 1980s and in the first part of the nineties. The average yearly net increase of the housing stock in the analysed period is

4,300 units. Over the whole period, however, the net increase varied between a minimum of 2,688 in 1990 and a maximum of 6,188 units in 1995. The housing production of the urban agglomeration of Zurich thus accounts for more than 10 per cent of the Swiss total, a proportion equivalent to the size of its population vs. the total population of Switzerland.

Owing to the characteristics of the spatial distribution of population growth, it is interesting to divide the analysis of the recent business cycle in housing construction into two parts, namely:

- the business cycle in the suburban ring communities,
- and the one in the city.

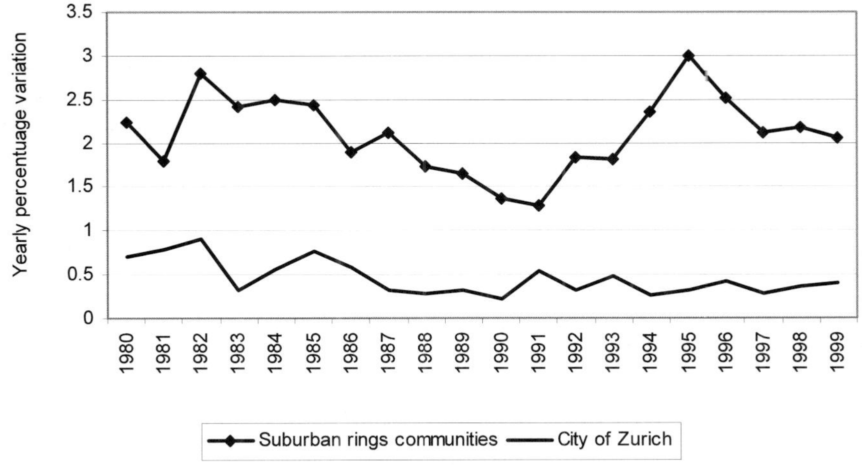

Fig. 6.2. The housing market cycle inside the urban agglomeration of Zurich from 1980 to 1999 (Source: Statistical yearbook of the city of Zurich, author's estimates)

The time pattern of the index for net housing construction in the suburban ring communities of Zurich's urban agglomeration is very different from both the national and the urban one. Its values are greater than the national ones and it shows a long-term cycle, decreasing from 1982 to the beginning of the 1990s to increase afterwards until 1995. After 1995, there is again a downward trend. In other words, the overall urban agglomeration cycle, which we represented in Fig. 6.1, has been determined by the development of housing construction in the suburban ring communities.

Owing to the different pattern of long-term development it is possible that the factors governing housing construction in the suburban communities have been markedly different from those that governed the long-term development of net housing construction in the city as well as nationwide. It is therefore interesting to deepen the analysis of the determinants of the net housing construction within the agglomeration.

6.3 Demographic and Financial Determinants of the Housing Construction Cycle in the Urban Agglomeration of Zurich

Housing demand and supply in the urban agglomeration of Zurich are influenced by at least three sets of different factors:

- Market factors determine the market situation (excess demand measured through the number of empty housing units) and thus have an impact on rents and prices.
- Financial and demographic factors affect the development of the number of households as well as the internal migration of these household within the agglomeration.
- Political measures such as controls and checks, city development policy and marketing, differences in local taxation, fiscal zoning or investment in the agglomeration's transport infrastructure can affect internal migration as well as housing demand and supply.

In the context of this section we will deal with the demographic and financial determinants. In the next one, on the other hand, we will look at the factors deriving from public-sector initiatives.

6.3.1 Households

As in other countries, in Switzerland the demand for housing is generated both by new households and households who would like to change their house or flat. Figures on the development of households are obtained every ten years from the federal population census. As the new figures for the 2000 census have not yet been published, we had to estimate the household figures for 1999. Our hypothesis for the estimates was that household size has decreased in both the city and the suburban ring communities, but to a lesser extent than during the 1980–90 intercensus period.

The information available on household development shows a noticeable decline of the growth trends in the last of the two examined periods. This probably means that the agglomeration has grown beyond the demarcation line of the 1990 population census, so that the trend toward a suburbanisation of the population, as it seems to be confirmed by the first results of the federal population census of the year 2000, is now especially visible at and beyond the edge of the agglomeration (Schuler 2002).

If we compare the percentage change in the number of households over the two periods with the corresponding percentage change in the housing stocks of the city and of the suburban ring communities, we notice that in the city, the change in the housing stock is positive whereas the change in the number of household is negative. In time, the change in the housing stock tends to grow positively while the change in the number of households tends to grow negatively. In other words, it seems probable that in the city the demand for housing is nurtured by factors other than the simple increase in the number of resident households. Of these, one of the most important is certainly the number of households looking for a new residential location.

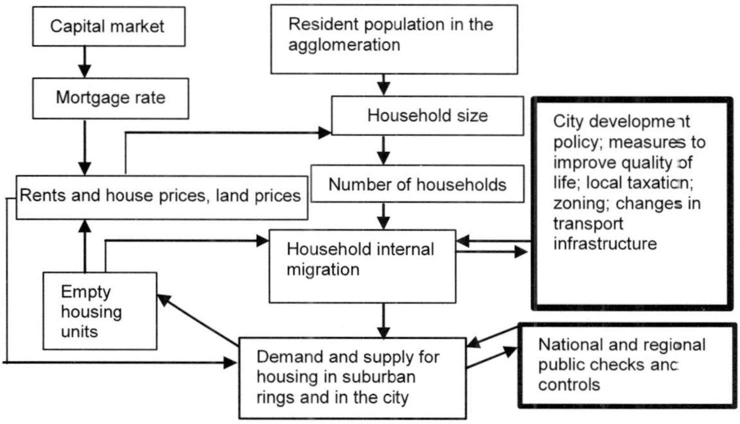

Fig. 6.3. A simple graphical representation of the factors affecting housing demand and supply in an urban agglomeration like that of Zurich

Less than 15 per cent of the city households move yearly, changing their housing units within the city. According to Troxler (1996), the number of moving families is influenced by the number of empty housing units available. As we will further see, in the first half of the 1990s the number of empty housing units tended to grow. With it, the number of families moving inside the city also grew.

When we compare the number of households moving inside the city with the net increase of the housing stock, we notice that this increase represents only a small fraction of the supply of housing in the city. The vast share of moving households relocates into existing flats and houses which become available because their occupants have left the city, moved into collective households (homes for the aged) or died. Some of these are displaced people, who were forced to leave their house because it was torn down. Over the long term the share of housing units that are replaced yearly represents 20 per cent of the annual net increase of the housing stock in the city (vs. 2.5 per cent in the suburban ring communities). But compared with the total number of moving households, the number of displaced households is insignificant. Households migrate within the city of Zurich for reasons other than displacement. As shown by the results of a recent survey of the reasons for migrating, which dealt mainly with moves within the city, the most important reasons for moving are not related to housing unit location or quality. It seems instead that the life cycle largely influences these changes (Fachstelle 1999). For older people (especially those over 60 years) internal migration has been determined by changes in their work situation. For younger households (people under 30 years), on the other hand, changes in the family situation have been at least as important as changes in the job situation.

Table 6.4. Household development in Zurich's urban agglomeration 1980–99

	1980	1990	1999[a]	1980–90 change in %	1990–99 change in %
Zurich					
Households	182,482	190,127	190,563	4.3	0.2
Average size	2.0	1.9	1.7	–5.0	–7.9
Suburban rings					
Households	202,396	240,797	302,772	19.0	25.7
Average size	2.3	2.1	2.0	–8.6	–5.0
Agglomeration					
Households	384,877	430,924	453,843	11.9	5.3
Average size	2.2	2.2	2.1	–4.5	–4.8

[a]Author's estimate.
Source: Statistisches Amt der Stadt Zürich, various Statistical Yearbooks.

Table 6.5. Internal migration in the city of Zurich

	1991	1995
Number of internal migrants	33958	39953
Share of people migrating within the same city neighbourhood [%]	23.4	26.4
Number of households migrating within the city	26806	29650
Household size of the internal migrant households	1.3	1.3

Source: Troxler (1996).

We recall further that part of the demand in the city is also determined by the needs of people (businessmen, people from the academic, cultural, media, air transport and entertainment sectors) who need a 'pied-à-terre' in town but reside with their families outside of Zurich, often in rural Switzerland. Unfortunately, we do not have any recent information on this aspect. According to data gathered in the 1980 population census, there were then 3,514 secondary housing units in the city of Zurich. Most of them were small flats in central locations, used by people having professional or business activities in town. They represented something less than 2 per cent, i.e. an insignificant share, of the housing stock. It is also possible – but again we have no data on this – that household occupy more than one housing unit in town (separated couples, grown-up children at study and so on).

In the suburban ring communities the situation is different: the overall rate of increase of the housing stock as well as of households from 1980 to 1999 has been about the same, namely 49.7 per cent for the housing stock and 49.5 per cent for households. We can therefore assert that in the suburban communities the long-term growth of the housing stock is closely related to the growing number of households. At this juncture it is important to point out that the growth of the number of households in the suburban ring communities depends on three kinds of events, namely:

- the net creation of households within the ring communities,
- the net immigration of households from the rest of the world,
- the net immigration of households from the city of Zurich.

The city component of this growth ranges between 10 and 20 per cent of the total growth. As the results of a recent survey confirm, households moving out of town are looking for better housing. A large share of them leave rented flats in the city to become resident owners of a house or flat situated in suburban ring communities immediately adjacent to the city (Landert 1999).

We notice, however, that the growth of the two stocks has followed different trends. In the 1980s the housing stock was growing more rapidly than the stock of households. The contrary happened in the 1990s. It is therefore possible that in the 1980s more housing units were built in the suburban rings than needed, the excess supply having then been reduced during the 1990s. To test for this possibility, it is useful to observe the behaviour of the empty housing unit index.

6.3.2 Empty Housing Unit Index (or Vacancy Index)

The empty housing unit index is an indicator of the housing market situation. It gives the number of vacant housing units at a certain date. In recent times, census day was set at the beginning of July. Also, until 1982 the participation in the census was voluntary. According to international criteria, a 'normal' housing market should show at least 2 per cent of empty housing units. But this figure is contested by the representatives of the landlords association, who think that the Zurich housing market can work efficiently even if the percentage of empty housing units is very low (Hegetschweiler 2002). Fig. 6.4 illustrates the development over time of the empty housing unit index of the city and of the agglomeration's ring communities.

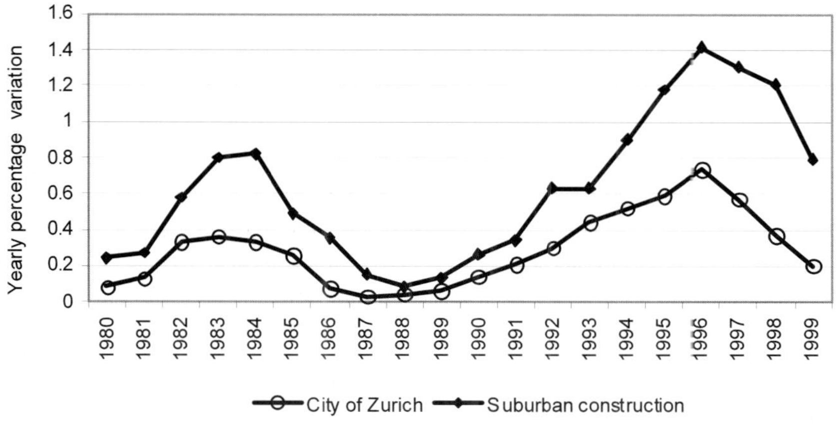

Fig. 6.4. Development of the empty housing unit index of the city of Zurich and of the suburban ring communities 1980–99 (Source: Statistical Yearbook of the city of Zurich)

The empty housing unit indices for the city as well as for the agglomeration's ring communities have followed the same time pattern over the examined period. They increased at the beginning of the 1980s to decrease afterwards until 1987/1988. From the end of the 1980s until 1996 they again increased, eventually giving way to a downward trend in the late 1990s.

These patterns are correlated with the pattern of development of the net construction of housing in the agglomeration. However, the indices for empty housing reach their peaks after the index for net housing construction. On the contrary, the net housing construction index reaches its bottom value a couple of years after the indices for empty housing. This means that when the number of empty housing units increases, in a significant way, the investors reduce their engagement in the housing market. But owing to the period of construction, this change in decision behaviour, on the side of the investors, can not avoid that the number of empty housing units continues to increase for a time, because a certain number of housing projects are already in the construction phase. The same lag, due to the construction period, will be found at the bottom of the cycle. In this case the empty housing units will stop to decrease before the redevelopment of the net housing construction. We observe that the correlation between the development of the empty housing unit index and the index of net housing construction does not work for the city. The city index for empty housing units is, as a matter of fact, correlated with the net housing construction in the agglomeration, more precisely with the net housing construction in the suburban rings communities. We think that this correlation reveals an influence of the housing market situation in the suburban rings on the migration flows from the city to the suburban rings.

The increase of the supply of housing in the agglomeration's ring communities is a pull factor that favours the emigration of households from the city to the agglomeration's ring communities, thus having a direct impact on the index of empty housing units in the city. In other words, it seems that the time development of the city index for empty housing units is influenced by the housing market conditions prevailing in the agglomeration, rather than by the development of the housing market supply in the city. A filtering-up phenomenon coupled with migration to the suburbs seems to be at work. This is also confirmed by the fact that the empty housing units in the city are to a large extent small and generally less expensive flats. As the data for the period 1971–95 show, if we divide the population of the city of Zurich in two groups, namely singles on one hand and families on the other hand, we notice that the migration behaviour of the two groups is very different. While net migration is positive for singles, it is largely negative for families (Troxler 1997). In the period 1991–95 approximately 33,000 people annually left the city. 30 per cent of the emigrants found a new residence in the suburban communities of the Zurich urban agglomeration. In the same period, nearly 36,000 persons migrated yearly into the city of Zurich. 24.5 per cent of them were coming from the suburban communities. For the suburban communities, the migration balance with the city of Zurich was therefore slightly positive in this period. Since people coming to Zurich from the agglomeration are young and single while people leaving Zurich for the agglomeration are older and married, it is fair to say that a significant share of the households leaving Zurich for the agglomeration are going to occupy new housing. It follows that for the suburban housing market migration from the city is an important demand factor.

6.3.3 Costs and Prices

If the housing market was working in an efficient way, the empty housing unit index should reflect the conditions prevailing in the market and affect the development of prices and rents. We should in particular observe, in situations of endemic excess demand like the one we found in the urban agglomeration of Zurich, that a decrease in the vacancy index should be reflected in an increase of both house prices and flat rents. This is also the meaning of the arrow between the empty housing units box and the rents and prices box in Fig. 6.3. There is no doubt that the demand/supply conditions prevailing in the housing market of the urban agglomeration have an influence on prices and rents in the medium and long term. We do think, however, that market conditions do not represent the most important determinant of prices and rents. This is so, because in Switzerland's housing market, since 1972 for urban agglomerations and since 1990 for the country as a whole, a system of 'second-generation rent control' prevails under which the most important factor for determining rents is the mortgage rate (Werczberger 1997). With the term 'second-generation rent control' one designates a system under which a part of the rental housing stock – in the case of Switzerland new construction or units vacated by their tenants – is typically exempt from controls. The Swiss rent-control system is defined in the federal decree of June 1972 against abuses in rented housing as a series of principles aimed at limiting the possibilities of rent increases or decreases. If the rented house or flat has not been built with public financial help and if the lease does not foresee an automatic adjustment to the increase in the consumers' price index, rent can generally be increased only in three cases:

- when the mortgage rate increases,
- when the other housing costs increase,
- and (partially at least) when the consumers' price index increases.

The landlord can also try to increase the rent in order to adjust it to the rent level prevailing in the community or in the city neighbourhood where the rented property lies. According to new jurisprudence he can even plead insufficient earnings as an argument to justify his request for a rent increase. But, with the exception of the rent prevailing 'in the community or in the urban neighbourhood', he cannot adjust the rent in any case because the demand for housing is high. The consequence of this rent-control system is that in Switzerland – and hence in Zurich's urban agglomeration as well – housing rents move parallel to the behaviour of housing costs. One can consequently show that the change in the rent index for the city of Zurich is very much correlated with the development over time of the mortgage rate. Through the provisions of the rent control system, the development of prices in the housing market for the Zurich agglomeration is thus very much determined by the development of the capital market and in particular by the development of the supply of mortgage capital. That this is the case can be shown conclusively by recalling the trend of net housing construction in the suburban communities. As we noted above, over the long term in the suburban ring communities the increase in new housing units equalled the increase in the number of households. During the 1980s, however, the increase in construction was larger than the increase in the number of households, whereas during the 1990s the opposite happened. This was probably due to the fact that investment in housing in the suburban communities was determined more by the conditions prevailing in the long-term capital market than by the potential development of housing demand.

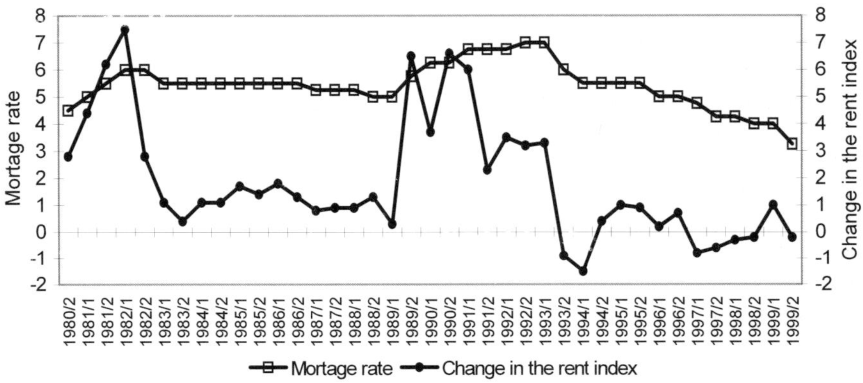

Fig. 6.5. Mortage rate development and rent index development in the city of Zurich 1980–99, semi-annual data (Source: Pelli 1997, updated by the author for the period 1997–99)

Table 6.6. The development of the land price in housing zones 1980–99 of the canton Zurich (average yearly price in Swiss francs per square metre of land)

Time periods	City of Zurich average price	Variation with respect to the previous period [%]	Rest of the canton average price	Variation with respect to the previous period [%]
1980/84			219.5	
1985/89	1083.2		383.2	74.5
1990/94	1544.0	42.5	664.0	73.2
1995/99	1128.4	–26.9	595.6	–10.3

Source: Cantonal Statistical Office, various Yearbooks.

When the mortgage rate increases, the demand for new mortgages decreases. With a lag, which can be longer than one year owing to the time needed to build the house, net housing construction also decreases (Sore, Schips, Jaeger 1993).

During the second half of the 1980s and the first half of the 1990s, the abundance of long-term capital supply engendered a speculative bubble in the land and housing markets, especially in those of Switzerland's larger urban agglomerations.

The supply of longer-term capital was significantly enhanced by the extension to all firms – starting in 1983 – of the obligation to set up pension funds for their employees.

Owing to the provisions of the federal law instituting this obligation, the financial wealth available to pension funds had to be invested largely in the real-property markets. As the figures in Table 6.6 show, this situation originated a rapid increase in the prices of land for housing construction, especially in the sub-urban communities.

One can therefore argue that owing to the rapid increase in land prices during the period of the speculative bubble, the potential movers inside the urban agglomeration households postponed their decision to move to a new residential location. Conversely, the decrease in land prices which set in after 1994 had a positive influence on internal mobility.

Next to the favourable development of land prices, internal residential mobility was also very much helped in the 1990s by the opening in 1990 of the S-Bahn, a suburban railway network which greatly improved the communication links of the suburban ring communities with the city as well as with one another (Hilber 1998). This leads us to consider the impact that government policies and measures have had on the recent development of demand and supply in the housing market of the Zurich urban agglomeration.

6.4 The Influence of Public-Sector Policies and Measures

In the previous section we dealt with the impact of the demographic and financial factors on the development of the housing market in the Zurich urban agglomeration. One can assert that this impact is mostly of an exogenous nature. Public-sector policies and measures, on the other hand, both determine and are determined by the housing market situation, even inside a relatively small geographical area such as the urban agglomeration of Zurich. As a matter of fact, the public sector agencies step in when a housing market problem arises in order to correct it. Their actions are therefore determined by the market situation. But then, if their actions are effective they will influence future housing market development in the manner hoped for. In Fig. 6.3, where we have tried to represent graphically the workings of the housing market in the Zurich urban agglomeration, we highlighted this double causality link by drawing two arrows, pointing in opposite directions, for each group of policies and measures of the public sector.

The break-down of public-sector policies and measures into two groups has more a didactic than a scientific meaning. In the first group of measures we included checks and controls which are largely under the jurisdiction of the national or cantonal governments and have limited application in time. In the second group of measures we included instead the measures by which the public sector, in this case mostly the local authorities, try for different policy reasons to promote housing demand and supply through changes in the agglomeration's internal migration flows. These measures are generally longer-term.

6.4.1 Checks and Controls

The most effective public instrument to control the development of the housing market is zoning. But we will not deal with zoning in this subsection, for zoning, like rent control – which we already have dealt with – is a tool for public intervention with long-lasting effects. We will instead focus on two groups of measures which have been used over a certain span of the analysed period in the urban agglomeration of Zurich.

The first group consisted of cantonal and local measures, applied practically only inside the city, by which the local authorities tried to keep the supply of housing floor space at a certain level. They were enacted at the beginning of the seventies when it was noticed that the built housing space was being increasingly transformed to make room for other uses (Schläpfer 1978). They included:

- the prohibition to demolish flats and replace them with buildings devoted to commercial or other uses,
- the prohibition, applied to certain residential areas of the city, to use flats for commercial or productive activities,
- a city planning measure which imposed fixed housing shares in certain residential areas.

While the third measure is still applied in ever more flexible ways, the first two measures were repealed during the 1980s because it was felt they were no longer necessary. The annual number of torn-down housing units has been significantly reduced and the practice of redirecting houses and flats in residential areas to some other use has also gone back in the 1980s. The implementation of these measures, on the other hand, was relatively cumbersome and generated considerable loss of time for the investors.

The second group of measures revisited here are the three federal urgent decrees introduced in October 1989 in an effort to eliminate the speculative bubbles which were developing in the real estate market in all urban agglomerations of Switzerland by cutting the development of demand. (Bignasca et al. 1996). The first of these measures compelled investors to keep any land they had purchased in construction zones for at least five years without reselling it. This limitation lasted from October 1989 to 1992. The second decree forced an investor to finance at least 1/5 of the investment with his own capital. This decree was replaced in time by similar recommendations adopted by the banks operating in the mortgage market. The third decree, also repealed in 1992, set a mandatory cap of 30 per cent on insurance companies' and pension funds' investments in the real estate markets. The impact of these three decrees on the short-term development of housing construction and housing demand is difficult to assess. While 1990 was a recession year for both the nationwide and the agglomeration's housing market, 1991 and 1992 saw a revival of housing construction, at least in the agglomeration of Zurich. More explicit about the impact on housing demand are the empty housing unit indices, which for both the city and the suburban ring communities show a significant increase from 1989 till 1996. As good judges of the situation prevailing in the housing market of the urban agglomeration in those times, we reckon that the demand for housing was very low both in the city and in the suburban ring communities during the first four years of the 1990s. The three federal urgent decrees of October 1989 have had a negative impact on the development of demand. But the increase in mortgage rates between the second half of 1989 and the first half of 1993 (compare Fig, 6.5) probably contributed more to the slowdown of housing investment and housing demand than the three federal decrees.

6.4.2 Influencing Internal Migration

From the point of view of this objective, we can distinguish between measures that sought to keep the population in the city and measures which instead led the population of the city to suburbanise.

Keeping the population in the city

Among these measures we must of course cite the measures to protect the residential function, which we referred to earlier. But next to these it is useful to cite the city's development policy, as well as the measures that the city has adopted to improve its quality of life. Over the last twenty years local development policy in Zurich has experienced a significant change. Throughout the 1970s and at the beginning of the 1980s it was dominated by the city's attempt to fight against the suburbanisation of the population (Rossi 1983). The visions of the future saw that Zurich was, through the 1980s, going to experience a significant phase of re-urbanisation mainly through mass transit measures (the construction of a subway) and the stabilisation of the number of jobs. In order to favour the attainment of this objective the city council in the 1980s adopted a restrictive traffic policy and proposed a new master plan which was relatively hostile to the further growth of the number of jobs. This caused a number of service companies to leave the city for the contiguous area situated between the north of Zurich and the airport. Other companies left the city to resettle in neighbouring cantons, which were more attractive in terms of taxes. At the same time a tendency to restructuration in the industrial sector began, which led to the closing of numerous industrial firms in the city's two main industrial areas, namely Zurich-North and Zurich-West. The problem now was no longer reining in the too-rapid development of jobs, but promoting economic activities in the city, which were declining as a result of both the suburbanisation of part of the service firms and the restructuring of the industrial firms. Large industrial areas like the ABB-Oerlikon site in the north of the city and the Escher-Wyss-Sulzer site in the west were in the process of being abandoned. During the 1990s these two areas have become Zurich's two major development areas. Thanks to agreements between the city council and the private realty owners it became possible to devote the surface that had become available to mixed multi-use development in which housing, too, in particular quality flats, had an important place. Housing in the city has therefore benefited under the new flexibility with which the city's authorities now tackle the problems of the redevelopment of abandoned industrial areas.

The local authorities of the city have become very active in the field of the quality of life as well. Over the last twenty years Zurich has become the leading city in Europe in keeping a strong check on the development of the flow of cars. The city promoted public transport with new investments as well as with appealing rates, but also with a very restrictive car parking policy. The objective is to cut down the number of commuters who drive their own car into the city. The city has also invested significant amounts of money in the building of noise-dampers along major city roads. The whole complex of measures to reduce car traffic inside the city has of course raised much opposition from car drivers, both living in and commuting to the city. At the same time it seems that in certain areas of the city traffic-related nuisances are still resented by the resident population as excessive. These are probably the reasons why today the inhabitants of Zurich still indicate – in the annual survey on their problems – that traffic is still the major problem.

Finally we mention that the city has tried, in the analysed period, to improve the structure of the housing stock, especially with a policy authorising the building cooperative to build housing on public land. The main objective of this policy was to increase the share of larger housing units in the city's housing stock. As the far-right column of Table 6.7 shows, some positive results have been achieved by the recommendation to build larger housing units in town, though in absolute terms these changes are not very significant.

Table 6.7. Development of the city housing stock according to the size of the housing units 1980–99

Size of housing units by number of rooms	Percentage in the 1980 housing stock	Percentage in the 1999 housing stock	Variation of the share 1980–99 [%]
1 room	10.7	10.1	–5.6
2 rooms	21.3	22.1	3.7
3 rooms	41.0	39.3	–4.1
4 rooms	20.4	20.7	1.5
5 rooms	4.5	4.5	0.0
6 rooms	2.0	2.8	40.0

Source: Statistisches Jahrbuch der Stadt Zurich, various years.

Measures that induce suburbanisation

Local taxation is an important, but probably not decisive, inducement for average and higher-income households to leave the city for the suburban ring communities. As is known, in Switzerland the main source of revenue at the local level is the taxation of household income. The local bodies (communes) have the right to set the amount of their tax base, generally within a set of minimum and maximum levels which vary from canton to canton. While the income tax coefficient for the city of Zurich lies above the cantonal average, that of most suburban ring communities is lower than average. In many cases, the difference between the income tax coefficient in the city and that of a local township in the suburban rings can be larger than 25–30 per cent which, of course, makes for a very attractive source of savings, especially for wealthy households. Rich taxpayers are therefore attracted to suburban ring communities where income tax rates are lower.

This phenomenon can become cumulative (at least so long as the local authority has enough land for residential construction) if the local councils adopt a fiscal planning approach in defining their zoning plans, i.e. limiting the construction densities in residential quarters. In order to break this vicious circle, causing rich taxpayers to leave the city, various measures have been introduced. For more than ten years now, the canton has been paying financial compensation to the city of Zurich to alleviate its financial burden. The city of Zurich has also tried to force suburban communities to pay for services that they use but which are thus far being financed mainly by the city. All these measures have not been very effective. The income tax differentials between the city and most of the suburban ring communities have not decreased in any substantial way.

Finally, we would like to again call to mind, in this paragraph, the effect of the S-Bahn network. The S-Bahn became operative at the beginning of the 1990s. Owing to the advantages that it offers to Zurich's commuters it has probably very much influenced the development of housing demand in the suburban ring communities throughout the 1990s.[3]

6.5 Summary and Conclusions

The housing market of the urban agglomeration of Zurich is the most important one in Switzerland representing more than 10 per cent of the supply and demand. Over the last three to four years it has also become the most dynamic regional housing market. While the development of net housing construction in the Swiss market over the last twenty years was influenced mostly by demographic factors, i.e. by the tendency of the population to become older, the agglomeration market was influenced by the evolution of costs and prices as well. This could suggest that in the urban context, the market laws in the housing market work better than at the national level. As we point out, however, the main impact on the develop-

[3] The S-Bahn suburban railway system: The S-Bahn system was built during the 1980s after the city's electorate had turned down the first project of a city-underground-railway. The S-Bahn is a mass transit transport system of around 25 railway lines serving all of the urban agglomeration of Zurich and part of the contiguous areas (see Fig 6.6 in the Appendix). For the residents of the suburban ring communities the S-Bahn system has three big advantages, namely:

- it moves people very rapidly between the suburban ring communities and the city proper,
- its time-table is co-ordinated with that of the bus lines serving even very isolated villages in the rural parts of the agglomeration,
- bus and S-Bahn, the lake ships as well as the city's streetcar network are now part of one single community-wide rate structure. This means that passengers do not have to purchase separate tickets when they switch from one means of transport to another'

ment of the supply of housing in the Zurich's urban agglomeration should be attributed to the development of the mortgage rate on one hand, and to the impact of the short-term measures adopted by the federal government to cut demand in the real estate markets at the end of 1989. The importance of the mortgage rate's influence is further to be attributed to the system of rent control which has been applied, in the urban agglomerations of Switzerland, throughout the analysed period. Owing to this system, rents are probably growing slower than they would have if they were determined by market conditions. This introduces an element of inefficiency in the market, above all in the city housing market. On the other hand, the soft rent control system applied in Switzerland favours the building of a consumer rent for the tenants who keep the same flat for a long time. This again can have positive effects on the conservation of the housing inventory in the city if the investors, as could be the case with pension funds, are not so much interested in the maximisation of their revenue. It is also possible that rent control cut down potential suburbanisation, reducing to an insignificant percentage the share of city households who might have become displaced because their houses were going to be torn down. Finally, as the frequent surveys on the ratio between rent and household incomes show, in the city the share of household income needed to pay a flat's rent is relatively low despite the high standards of the houses built (Baur and Konrad 1996).

Given this situation, it is therefore not surprising that the forces currently pushing for a liberalisation of the housing market have not been really listened to in the national parliament. The proposals put forward by the government point to a weakening of the rent control system, but the solution which seems to be coming out of the parliamentary debate will not be akin to a complete liberalisation of the market. On the other hand, the recent reform of the federal law on financial help toward the construction of social housing and to encourage home ownership by private citizens is probably going to further weaken the government's already small part in housing investment. In any case, we think that the reforms already implemented and those still under discussion at the federal level are probably not going to significantly change the way in which the housing market of Zurich's urban agglomeration works.

References

Baur R, Konrad C (1996) Wohnverhältnisse der Bevölkerung in der Schweiz. In: Wohnen in der Schweiz. Bundesamt für Statistik, Bern

Bretschger L et al. (1995) Wirtschaftsstandort Zürich. Regierungsrat des Kantons Zürich, Zürcher Kantonalbank, Zürich

Fachstelle für Stadtentwicklung (1999) Gründe der Weg- und Zuzugsverhaltens der Privaten Haushalte

Fachstelle für Stadtentwicklung (2001) Befragung der Einwohnerinnen und Einwohner der Stadt Zürich 2001

Hegetschweiler R (2002) Der Wohnungsmarkt Funktioniert. In: Hauseigentümer, 84(1): p 2

Hilber Ch (1998) Auswirkungen Staatlicher Massnahmen auf die Bodenpreise: Eine Theoretische und Empirische Analyse der Kapitalisierung. Chur

Koch M, Somandin M, Süsstrunk C (1989) Kommunaler und Genossenschaftlicher Wohnungabau in Zürich. Finanzamt und Bauamt II der Stadt Zürich, Zurich

Landert Ch (1999) Gründe des Weg- und Zuzugsverhaltens der Privaten Haushalte. Fachstelle für Stadtentwicklung der Stadt Zürich, Zurich

Pelli C (1997) Entwicklung des Hypothekarzinssatzes und der Mietpreise bis Herbst 1996. Zürcher Statistische Nachrichten, Bericht 1

Rossi A, Steiger Ch (1995) Die Attraktivität des Zürcher Wirtschaftsraums. Orl-Institut der ETH Zürich, Zürich

Rossi A (1983) La Décentralisation Urbaine en Suisse. Collection 'Villes, Régions et Sociétés', Presses Polytechniques Romandes, Lausanne

Rossi A (1995) Concurrence Territoriale et Réseaux Urbains. L'armature Urbaine de la Suisse en Transition', vdf, Programme National de Recherche 'Ville et Transport', Zürich

Schläpfer K (1978) Die Erhaltung von Wohnraum in Zürich, Zürich

Schips B, Bignasca F, Kruck R, Maggi R, Schellenbauer P (1996) Immobilienmarkt Zürich: Immobilienpreise und Bauinvestitionen unter der Lupe. Züricher Kantonalbank

Schuler M, Joye D (1994) Les Niveaux Géographiques de la Suisse. Recensement Fédéral de la Population de 1990. Office Fédéral de la Statistique, Bern

Schuler M (2002) Die Räumliche Bevölkerungsdynamik der 90-er Jahre. Federal Statistical Office, press release, Neuchâtel

Sohre P, Schips B, Jaeger F (1993) Hypothekarkreditmarkt. Verlag Rüegger, Chur/Zürich

Tages Anzeiger (2002) Obacht Zürich. Tages Anzeiger, March 16, 2002, p. 2

Troxler J (1996) Räumliche Bevölkerungsmobilität in der Stadt Zürich. Teil 1, Zürcher Statistische Nachrichten, Bericht 8

Troxler J (1997) Räumliche Bevölkerungsmobilität in der Stadt Zürich. Teil 2, Zürcher Statistische Nachrichten, Bericht 9

Werczberger E (1997) Home Ownership and Rent Control in Switzerland. Housing Studies 12(3): 337–53

Appendix

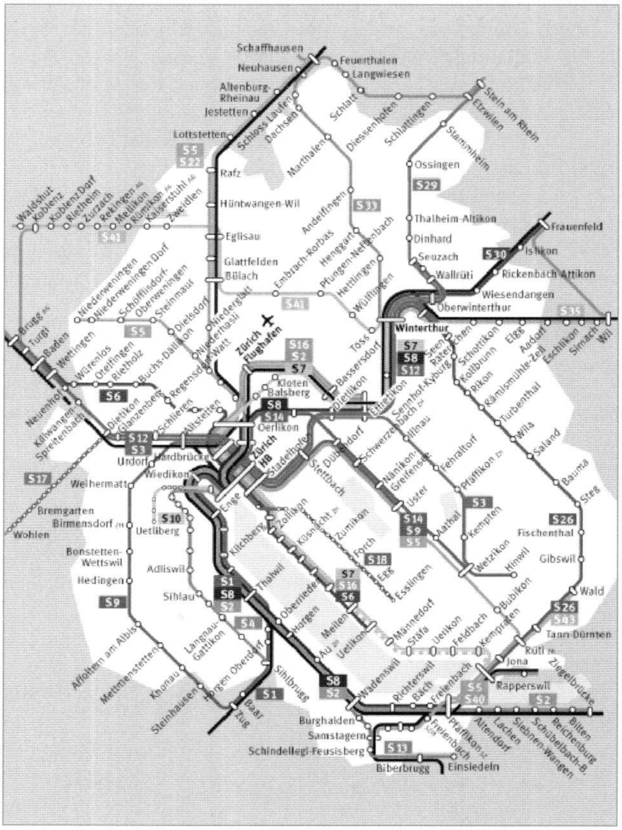

Fig. 6.6. S-Bahn suburban railway system

7 The Amsterdam Metropolitan Housing Market: How a Prosperous Metropolitan Area Co-exists with a Central City Dominated by Social Rental Housing for the Poor

Arno J. van der Vlist[1] and Piet Rietveld[2]

[1]Wageningen University, Wageningen
[2]Free University, Amsterdam

7.1 Introduction

Most European countries have experienced a fundamental change in the residential function of metropolitan areas. Till the beginning of the 19th century the structure of cities was organised around their centres where the residence was typically located close to the place of work. The introduction of fast and affordable transportation enormously expanded the area of possible residential locations around a job location. In the meantime, changes in the structure of the economy from handcraft toward large-scale manufacturing and services altered the structure downtown. From an early outset, the development of cities and the functioning of its housing market have been intimately related to long run economic developments.

This chapter aims to describe Amsterdam metropolitan housing market. More specifically, it aims to relate the functioning of the housing market to these (long run) contextual factors, describing its past developments and possible course in the future.

The outline of this chapter is as follows. In Sect. 7.2 we give a historical overview of Amsterdam and its metropolitan housing market. Based on this, we consider in Sect. 7.3 the development of the urban structure in relation to developments in housing stock and population. Here, the influence of the planning system on urban sprawl and housing market developments is described. Housing demand, housing careers and housing allocation-issues are subsequently addressed in Sect. 7.4. In Sect. 7.5 we conclude with a discussion of future prospects for Amsterdam metropolitan housing market.

7.2 History of Amsterdam

Going back into the history of Amsterdam one observes a city in which turmoil time periods are alternated with relatively quiet time periods. The associated evolution of the housing stock cannot be fully understood without referring to these economic, social and institutional changes that took place during these periods. In this section we give an overview of the development of Amsterdam and of the Amsterdam metropolitan area (AMA).

The history of Amsterdam goes back to the 12th century, around the time period at which a dam in the river Amstel was constructed where people settled. From an early phase Amsterdam's inhabitants specialised in trade and finance. The import-tax on beer from Hamburg around 1320 made Amsterdam a prosperous city, with Amsterdam becoming one of the main trade centres and financial markets of Europe for the 16th to 18th century. The economic hausse in the late 16th century resulted, due to the political instability in other parts of Europe, in a large inflow of immigrants who settled in downtown Amsterdam. During the 'golden age' the population raised from 30,000 inhabitants in 1578 to 206,000 inhabitants in 1675. Fig. 7.1 shows the population dynamics of Amsterdam.

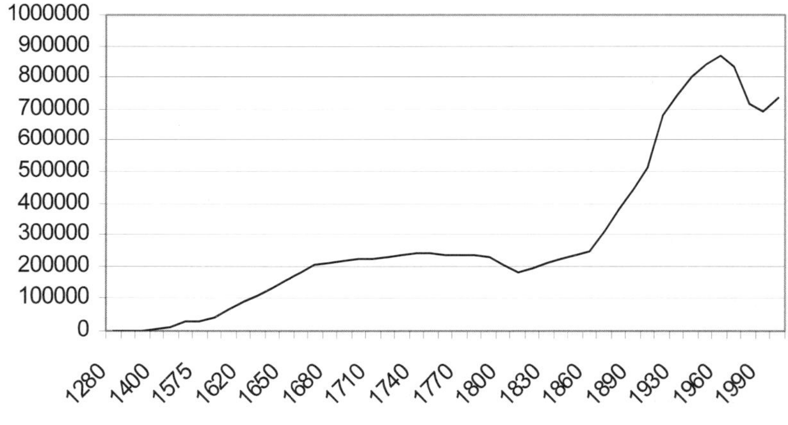

Fig. 7.1. Population development of Amsterdam 1280–2000 (Source: CBS)

This sharp increase in population led to the first large suburb of Amsterdam, resulting in the canal-area to the west of Amsterdam that still exists today. During the golden age an almost continuous expansion took place around the inner city of Amsterdam; sometimes considered as one of the first metropolitan area of the world. The wars with England in 1652–54 and 1665–67 and afterwards with France in 1672 marked the end of a prosperous period characterised by a sharp rise in the population and housing stock.

The period of 1672–1795 was less fortunate, characterised by financial crises, internal political tension and wars with France and England. This made that Amsterdam became a stagnant city (see Fig. 7.1) and lost its central role on the world trade market, entering a period with extreme poverty for large parts of the population. The period of 1795–1813 is one of economic downturn where one observes a decrease in population; from 210,000 in 1795 to 180,000 in 1810. Yet, by 1800 Amsterdam was still the fifth largest city in Europe (Dieleman and Musterd 1992). Migration out of Amsterdam during these years resulted in a large number of vacant dwellings, hardly any new construction and a dramatic filtering down of some neighbourhood areas.

The 19th century is characterised by a general increase in economic activity. The industrialisation in the late 19th century changed the economic and spatial structure of Amsterdam, separating residential areas and working areas. The restructuring of the previously manufacturing-based urban labour market resulted in a decentralisation of employment no longer located downtown. In the second part of the century, a process of urbanisation also took place where people moved from rural to urban areas. This led to a rise in population and an increasing pressure on the housing market. The rise in population during 1815–1900 can be clearly seen in Fig. 7.1. In consequence, thousands of new houses were built in the '19th century neighbourhoods' in these years. The uncontrolled urbanisation and the construction of many low-quality housing led the government to introduce the National Housing Act (1901). This act, together with a general increase in economic activity, has led to large volumes of new construction during 1900–1945 of a much higher quality than those built in the 19th century.

The provision of affordable social housing together with the large inflow of immigrants resulted initially in a rise in the population after World War II. The period thereafter, however, showed a sharp decline in the population marking the structural change in the development of Amsterdam. After the 1960s, Amsterdam changed because of demographic and cultural changes, and the specific new construction and urban renewal policy (Jobse and Musterd 1992). This together with the increasingly negative imago of Amsterdam resulted in selective residential mobility patterns not observed before (cf. SCP 2001). The period after 1960s is characterised by a mass outflow of middle-class families with children to the suburbs (in the 1970s) or to growth cities (in the 1980s). Despite the large inflow of immigrants, Amsterdam lost a substantial part of its population in the period 1960–1985. Particularly after the oil crises and the economic downturn in the 1970s a large influx of migrants took place (SCP 2001). This resulted in a population in Amsterdam no longer representative for the Dutch society rather over representing unemployed, one-person households, single-parents families, poor elderly and ethnic groups (Jobse and Musterd 1992; SCP 2001). These years were rather turbulent, resulting in conflicts among population groups, residential segregation, and increasing trends of separation in education (Dieleman and Musterd 1992). In these years large renewal projects took place in order to revitalise slum areas. It is in these years that local government became aware of the fact that the decreased spending power of the population seriously affected the economic activity in neighbourhoods, the social stability and economic viability of cities also threatening the provision of both commercial and non-profit services and facilities.

As from 1985 the socio-economic level of the population in downtown Amsterdam started to improve significantly, diminishing the sharp contrast with the socio-economic position of the population in the suburbs. Particularly the neighbourhoods located in the outer part of downtown Amsterdam showed signs of gentrification, with more recent gentrification processes also occurring in the adjoining 19th century neighbourhoods (see also Musterd and van de Ven 1991). In the mid-1980s, a period in which the economy began to recover, most neighbourhoods experienced a rise in population due to the growing individualism, the decrease in average household size and the continuous inflow of immigrants (Jobse and Musterd 1992). Yet, despite gentrification in downtown Amsterdam, revitalisation in surrounding neighbourhoods had not brought social improvements despite large urban renewal programmes. The early urban renewal programmes generally maintained the improved neighbourhoods for lower-income groups only, preventing higher-income households to enter the neighbourhood. Later urban renewal programmes and construction initiatives during the 1990s therefore included the construction of new, more expensive housing as well, with an increasing share of owner-occupier units.

7.3 Urban Structure, Housing Stock and Population Developments

7.3.1 Urban Structure and Physical Planning

As already mentioned, the uncontrolled urbanisation and the construction of many low-quality housing in the late 19th century, led to the National Housing Act. This National Housing Act, which still exists today, has enabled government to intervene in the housing market. This law intended to prevent construction of low-quality housing and dramatic filtering down of neighbourhoods in periods of economic downturns. From then on, government has actively intervened with construction codes, enforced maintenance of housing, and subsidised new construction initiatives for social housing in designated areas. Particularly after World War II, however, government started controlling the development of large parts of the housing market. It was only in the 1980s when government started discussing changes in housing policy as part of a broader discussion regarding the welfare state, subsequently carried out in the 1990s. Yet the institutional set-up of the current system of government intervention originates in the post-World War II reconstruction period.

Post-war reconstruction

One of the obvious reasons for the intense government intervention just after World War II was the enormous housing shortage at that time. This led the national government to set (relatively low) rents, introduce a system of housing allocation based on waiting lists, and initiate strictly planned, large-scale construction of subsidised housing. This system of rent control, together with a long period of inflation and a strong increase in construction costs discouraged private investment in the commercial rented sector. All this has led to a rapid expansion of social rented housing in the Netherlands, and Amsterdam in particular (from about one per cent in 1900 to 56 per cent in 2000). In these years considerable suburbanisation took place (cf. Feddes 1985; van der Schaar 1986).

Growth cities

The rapid growth in population combined with the uncontrolled urbanisation in the 1960s led to a shift in planning policy, to concentrated deconcentration in order to limit urban sprawl, expressing the general belief that the big cities had reached their limits of expansion (cf. Fokkema et al. 1996). As from the mid-1970s, central government policy was aimed at concentrating those who wish to live in suburbs in a number of designated so-called growth cities, preventing most existing settlements to grow fast. These growth cities, the cornerstone of Dutch Physical Planning until the mid-1980s, refer to a number of strictly planned, large-scale new construction areas where central government highly subsidised land, new construction, infrastructure and welfare facilities (Faludi and van der Valk 1994).

Housing in growth cities like Lelystad and Almere was cheap, with large units on relatively large sites compared with Amsterdam. Together with the social problems in large parts of Amsterdam this led to a large outflow of households with children in the 1970s and 1980s.

In Table 7.1 the numbers of inhabitants are given by municipality for the period 1960–2000. The population dynamics clearly reveal the changes in residential function of Amsterdam, as well as the impact of physical planning viz. growth cities. The five growth cities of Amsterdam were all located at relatively long distances (30–70 km) from Amsterdam, leading to large commuting flows between the growth cities and Amsterdam.

Table 7.1. Population dynamics of growth cities versus Amsterdam 1960–2000

	1960	1965	1970	1975	1980	1985	1990	1995	2000
Alkmaar	43.2	47.5	52.1	64.4	71.2	85.4	89.6	93.0	92.8
Almere	0.0	0.0	0.0	0.0	11.0	40.3	71.1	104.5	142.8
Hoorn	16.1	16.7	18.6	23.1	39.3	51.8	57.4	61.4	64.6
Lelystad	0.0	0.0	4.5	19.0	43.3	57.9	58.1	60.7	64.7
Purmerend	10.0	14.4	23.3	31.2	32.6	48.6	58.7	65.0	70.3
Amsterdam	869.6	866.3	831.5	757.9	716.9	675.6	695.2	722.2	731.3

Source: CBS.

Also, Table 7.2 shows a steady decline in Amsterdam's share in AMAs population; from 75 per cent in 1960 to 51 per cent in 2000. This is in contrast to the suburban areas and other municipalities around Amsterdam which have grown over the last decades. The decline in Amsterdam's population together with the concentration of low-income housing in Amsterdam, led to increasing pressure on the economic viability of commercial centres and welfare facilities in large parts of the city in the 1980s. The initial support by the big cities for this process of concentrated deconcentration in the growth cities diminished for these reasons in later years.

Table 7.2. Population dynamics AMA by region and Noord-Holland 1960–2000

	1960	1965	1970	1975	1980	1985	1990	1995	2000
AMA	1152.8	1196.4	1219.8	1197.8	1202.8	1200.1	1282.3	1376.1	1448.0
Waterland	60.4	70.3	85.1	102.0	111.9	125.7	138.0	147.7	155.4
Zaanstreek	99.7	109.4	120.9	130.5	135.4	135.1	137.4	141.7	144.7
Amsterdam	869.6	866.3	831.5	757.9	716.9	675.6	695.2	722.2	731.3
Amstel-Meerlanden	123.1	150.5	182.3	207.3	216.5	223.4	240.6	259.9	273.9
Almere	0.0	0.0	0.0	0.0	11.1	40.3	71.1	104.5	142.8
Noord-Holland	2054.5	2163.2	2244.4	2284.8	2307.6	2311.5	2376.0	2463.6	2518.4

Source: CBS.

The economic downturn in the early 1980s led to a dramatic decline in housing demand, especially affecting the owner-occupier housing market segment in growth cities. Fig. 7.2 indicates the sharp decline in selling price in the early 1980s. It is in these years that new constructed dwellings in growth cities remained vacant immediately after completion, also threatening the social stability in these just constructed areas. Some growth cities even slipped into a similar position as the least-favoured neighbourhoods in the large cities in these years (Jobse and Musterd 1992).

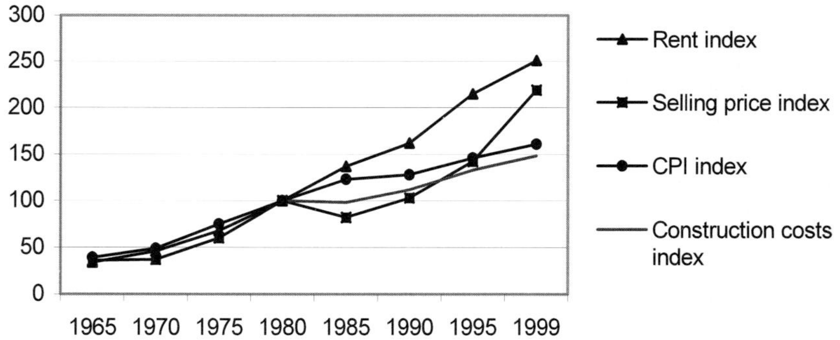

Fig. 7.2. Price indices for the Netherlands 1965–99, 1980 = 100 (Source: VROM/CBS)

Compact cities

In the mid-1980s one can observe a shift in planning policy, so-called compact city policy, promoting the central cities. The compact city policy aimed at decreasing the automobile usage, locating commercial services, employment centres and welfare facilities within or nearby residential zones (cf. Minvrom 2001). Also, within the compact city design housing units on relatively small sites were constructed, increasing the economic viability of those neighbourhoods. Two types exist (Dieleman 1999): *brown sites* referring to revitalisation of former residential or employment zones in urban cities, and *greenfield sites* referring to new construction outside the cities.

Unlike the previous planning period, however, changes in the welfare state made that no massive public investments took place anymore. The change in the welfare state can also be seen from the rise in the rent in Fig. 7.2. Contrary to the period before the 1980s, rents did rise much faster than the average consumer price increase as from the 1980s on.

Amsterdam, like most other big cities in the Netherlands, accelerated its housing production in these years, leading to an end of population decline (see Tables 7.1 and 7.2). Although most new construction plans contained social housing for political reasons, an increasing share of housing was constructed for the owner-occupier housing market. As one can also observe from Fig. 7.2 it also marks the end of the price fall in house selling prices in the Netherlands. It is also in these years that one can observe an inflow of wealthier households into downtown Amsterdam, and a process of downtown gentrification (Dieleman and Musterd 1992). Yet, the high share of (social) rental housing in Amsterdam in general, prevents households from easily moving up the housing ladder towards more expensive owner-occupier housing (cf. van der Vlist 2000) within the city of Amsterdam.

Vinex cities

The late-1980s marked a shift in physical planning policy towards a more market-oriented approach. Till then, most attention was paid to reduce the housing shortage, what led to increasing qualitative mismatches between housing supply and housing demand. The Vinex policy aimed at high-quality neighbourhoods by combining the compact city policy with a policy of restrictive suburbanisation near the most important metropolitan areas in the Netherlands. This planning policy led in many situations to land-speculation, or required the development of land (near Amsterdam land is reclaimed for the new suburb IJburg) resulting in excessive prices for land and higher house prices. Also, a combination of financial factors made that the construction of public transport facilities was postponed sometimes for years after the completion of the new suburbs, making the suburbs after all automobile-dependent (cf. den Hollander et al. 1996; Dijst et al. 1998).

7.3.2 Amsterdam Metropolitan Housing Stock and Population Developments

The Amsterdam metropolitan housing market centres around Amsterdam city and includes surrounding municipalities within the functional area. The metropolitan region is mainly in the province of Noord-Holland (Regional code NUTS-32 of Eurostat) and is also part of the Randstad Area; which consists of four metropolitan regions around Amsterdam, Den Haag, Rotterdam and Utrecht. From Table 7.3 one can observe that the Amsterdam metropolitan area includes part of Noord-Holland (NUTS-325 and NUTS-326) but also includes the rapidly expanding municipality of Almere which is part of another province. Throughout this chapter we refer to the Amsterdam metropolitan area (AMA) including the municipalities Amsterdam, Waterland, Amstel-Meerlanden, Zaanstreek and Almere as indicated in Table 7.3, also shown in Figs. 7.3–5.

Table 7.3. Population in Noord-Holland and Amsterdam metropolitan region 1999 (1000s)

REGION	POPULATION
Noord-Holland	2510.8
Kop van Noord-Holland	351.1
Alkmaar	229.1
Ymond	171.6
Haarlem Region	216.8
Gooi en Vechtstreek	232.8
Zaanstreek	150.1
Amsterdam Region	1151.8
Amsterdam metropolitan area	1438.0
Amsterdam	727.1
Waterland	155.4
Amstel-Meerlanden	269.3

Source: CBS.

To better understand the structural differences between Noord-Holland and AMA in general, and Amsterdam in particular, we show some informative descriptive statistics in Table 7.4. In number of housing units, Amsterdam is about one-third of Noord-Holland's total housing stock.

One of the most striking differences between Amsterdam and Noord-Holland, however, lies in the tenure structure. The rental share (of both private and social) in Amsterdam is over 80 per cent, and is much higher than the 57 per cent in Noord-Holland (and about 52 per cent for the Netherlands). Comparatively, the rental share of both social and private housing in Amsterdam metropolitan area is 66 per cent (in 2000). In consequence, the owner-occupier market in Amsterdam is relatively small.

Other remarkable differences relate to the housing stock. Amsterdam has a lot more cheaper and smaller housing units than Noord-Holland, explaining the lower average rent in Amsterdam. Over 50 per cent of the housing stock consists of units with at most three rooms.

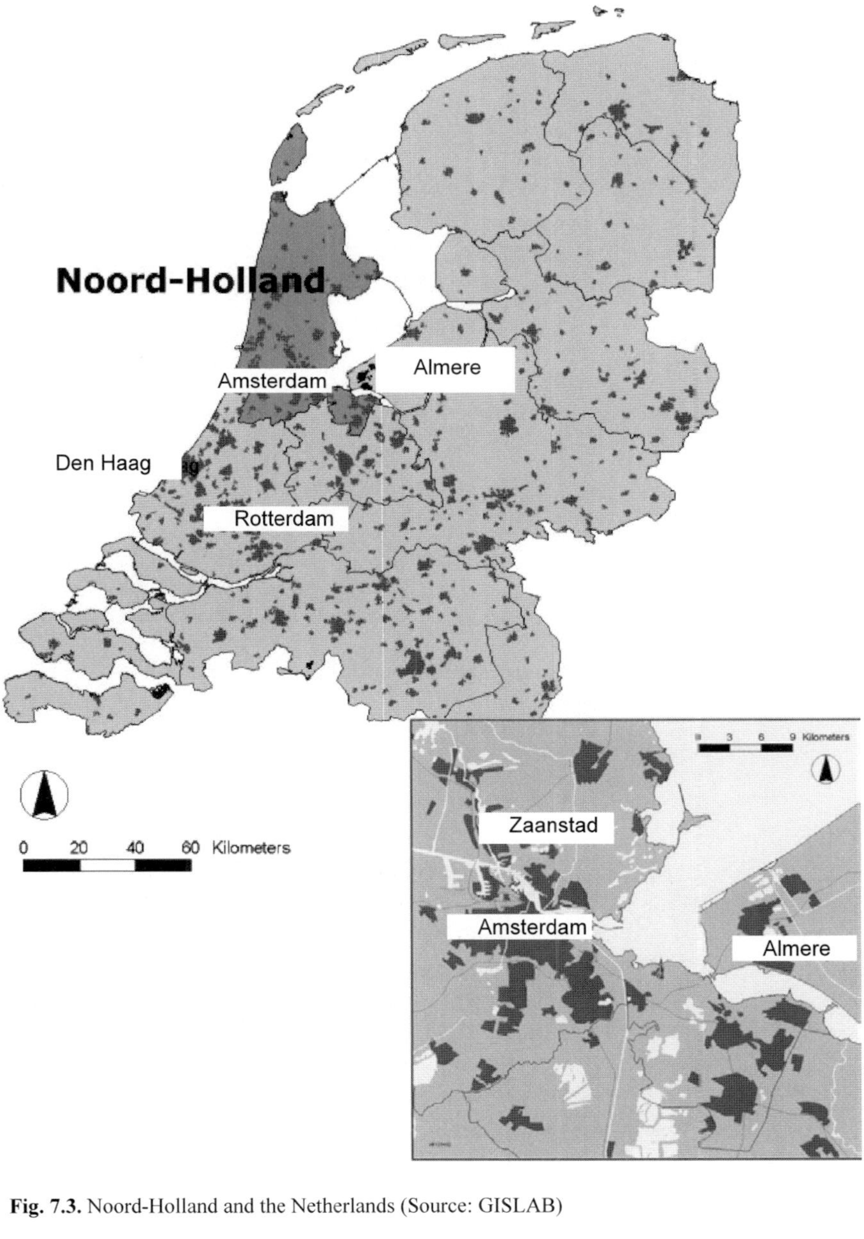

Fig. 7.3. Noord-Holland and the Netherlands (Source: GISLAB)

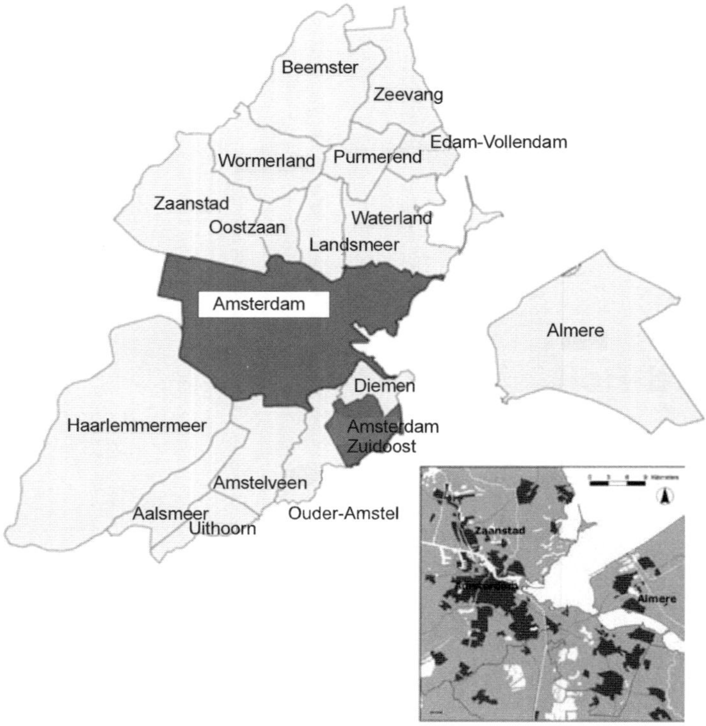

Fig. 7.4. Amsterdam metropolitan area (Source: GISLAB and O+S)

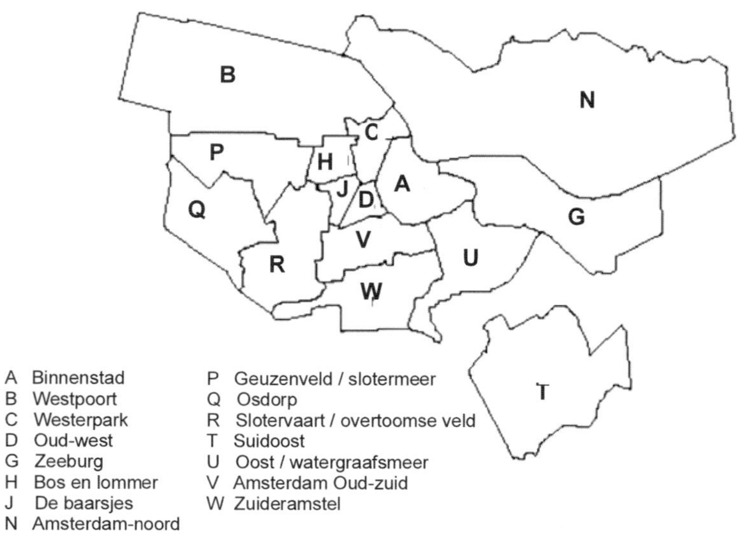

Fig. 7.5. Neighbourhoods in Amsterdam (Source: O+S)

Table 7.4. Housing market characteristics of Noord-Holland and Amsterdam 2000

	Noord-Holland	Amsterdam
Housing stock in 1000s		
Number of units	1 117	372
Tenure structure, % of housing stock		
Social rental housing	41	56
Private rental housing	16	27
Owner-occupier housing	43	17
Dwelling size, % of housing stock		
Units with at most 3 rooms	37	58
Units with 3–5 rooms	56	38
Units with more than 5 rooms	7	4
Construction period, % of housing stock		
– 1945	32	49
1945–1959	11	10
1960–1970	16	11
1971–1980	15	7
1981–1990	16	13
1991 –	10	10
Rental price structure, % of housing stock		
Cheap	30.9	53.7
Middle	19.6	20.1
Expensive	6.5	9.2
Average rent in Euros/month	314.5	289.9
Owner-occupier price structure		
Cheap	5.9	2.9
Middle	11.6	3.7
Expensive	25.5	10.4

Source: Minvrom.

Housing stock

As we showed above, the housing market of AMA consists of a number of municipalities around Amsterdam. In number of housing units, the city of Amsterdam has about half AMA's total housing stock. Table 7.5 gives descriptive statistics of the housing stock in total number of units and tenure structure.

One of the most important peculiarities of the housing stock is the large rental market. From Table 7.5 one can see that the larger rental market in AMA (relative to the national share of about 50 per cent) is basically the result of Amsterdam's tenure structure. Some large post-war neighbourhoods in Amsterdam, like Amsterdam-Noord, Geuzenveld/Slotermeer and Zuidoost have shares of about 80 per cent social housing. Contrary, older neighbourhoods downtown have much higher private rented shares of about 50 per cent of total housing. Overall, the owner-occupier market segment is relatively small in Amsterdam, ranging from eight to 25 per cent. In neighbourhoods with more recent (re)constructed areas, like Osdorp and Slotervaart/Overtoomse veld higher shares of home-ownership can be observed. Comparison with the surrounding municipalities however indicates large differences with home-ownership ranging from 41 to 77 per cent.

Table 7.5. Housing and tenure structure in Amsterdam metropolitan housing market 2000

Municipality[a]/neighbourhood	Total stock [1000s]	Owner-occupier [%]	Social rental	Private rental	Total
Beemster	3.2	67	25	8	100
Edam-Volendam	10.7	74	18	7	100
Landsmeer	4.1	64	30	7	100
Purmerend	29.3	53	44	4	100
Waterland	6.8	68	25	7	100
Wormerland	6.1	59	34	7	100
Zeevang	2.5	77	19	4	100
Oostzaan	3.6	65	26	10	100
Zaanstad	56.8	46	47	7	100
A Binnenstad	44.8	21	37	42	100
B Westpoort[b]	0.1	12	0	88	100
C Westerpark	19.2	9	65	26	100
D Oud-west	18.6	13	36	51	100
G Zeeburg	17.0	18	65	17	100
H Bos en lommer	14.6	8	60	32	100
J De baarsjes	18.7	10	40	50	100
N Amsterdam-noord	39.5	14	81	4	100
P Geuzenveld/slotermeer	17.6	15	80	5	100
Q Osdorp	19.0	25	66	9	100
R Slotervaart/overtoomse veld	19.0	24	52	24	100
T Zuidoost	38.0	11	79	11	100
U Oost/watergraafsmeer	29.4	12	60	28	100
V Amsterdam oud-zuid	47.0	14	32	53	100
W Zuideramstel	26.8	19	34	47	100
Amsterdam	369.2	17	56	27	100
Aalsmeer	8.5	65	29	6	100
Amstelveen	36.0	51	30	18	100
Diemen	9.9	41	28	31	100
Haarlemmermeer	43.5	60	26	14	100
Ouder-amstel	5.5	53	33	14	100
Uithoorn	10.8	53	38	9	100
Almere	55.6	56	37	8	100
Total[a]	662.3	34	46	20	100

[a]Excluding Almere.
[b]Westpoort is industry and office centre area.
Source: O+S.

Population facts

When discussing the population of AMA it can best be subdivided into those households living inside and those who live outside Amsterdam. Table 7.6 gives population facts by municipality and neighbourhood. Comparison across municipalities indicates that average disposable income in surrounding municipalities in AMA is higher than in Amsterdam. Comparing the AMA figures with the national average disposable household income (€21,200 per year for 1998) we note that the Amsterdam city level is about six per cent below the national level, whereas the AMA aggregate is about seven per cent above the national level.

Table 7.6. Total number of households and average disposable income of households 1998

Municipality	Population [1000s]	Number of households [1000s]	Average disposable household income [€1000]
Beemster	8.4	3.2	27.1
Edam-volendam	27.1	10.0	27.6
Landsmeer	10.3	4.1	27.9
Purmerend	68.4	28.4	24.3
Waterland	17.4	6.8	28.1
Wormerland	14.9	6.0	26.2
Zeevang	6.2	2.4	28.3
Total Waterland	152.7	60.9	26.0
Oostzaan	8.7	3.5	27.5
Zaanstad	135.1	56.7	24.2
Total Zaanstreek	143.8	60.2	24.4
A Binnenstad	75.5	43.9	20.7
B Westpoort	0.3	0.1	21.3
C Westerpark	33.8	19.2	16.7
D Oud-west	31.7	18.8	18.0
G Zeeburg	33.2	16.8	18.9
H Bos en Lommer	29.4	13.8	17.7
J De Baarsjes	35.0	18.4	17.9
N Amsterdam-Noord	89.1	41.1	20.5
P Geuzenveld/Slotermeer	39.3	17.8	19.3
Q Osdorp	41.1	18.6	21.1
R Slotervaart/Overtoomse veld	45.8	19.4	23.3
T Zuidoost	85.3	39.4	19.4
U Oost/Watergraafsmeer	58.0	30.1	19.1
V Amsterdam oud-zuid	82.3	46.3	21.2
W Zuideramstel	46.3	25.7	23.4
Amsterdam	727.1	369.9	20.0
Aalsmeer	22.5	9.0	27.8
Amstelveen	77.7	35.3	26.9
Diemen	23.8	10.4	25.6
Haarlemmermeer	109.4	42.7	27.8
Ouder-amstel	12.5	5.3	28.2
Uithoorn	25.9	10.7	28.1
Total Amstel-meerlanden	271.8	113.4	27.4
Almere	136.2	52.8	24.5
Total AMA	1431.6	657.2	22.6

Source: O+S.

Comparison of average disposable household income across neighbourhoods indicates large differences as well, ranging from €16,700 to €23,400 a year in 1998. Neighbourhoods like Westerpark, Bos en Lommer, De Baarsjes have less than 80 per cent of AMA average disposable household income. As we observed earlier when describing the history of Amsterdam in Sect. 7.2 and the urban structure in Sect. 7.3, the population of Amsterdam includes large numbers of unemployed, one-person households, and ethnic groups. Yet, lower average disposable incomes cannot be directly related to the share of total ethnic population alone. One factor that may explain differences in disposable household income for example is the large share of one-person households in Amsterdam relative to the number of dual earning households. In discussing the age structure of AMA we return to this issue.

Table 7.7. Ethnic population in Amsterdam by region 2000

Neighbourhood	Surinamese [numbers]	Antillean	Turk	Moroccan	Total ethnic population [%]
A Binnenstad	2 987	746	676	1 331	18.4
B Westpoort	1	1	6	–	12.5
C Westerpark	2 979	430	1 046	3 103	36.2
D Oud-west	1 711	341	856	1 599	25.9
G Zeeburg	4 523	494	3 050	4 968	48.9
H Bos en lommer	2 244	292	4 934	6 595	57.6
J De baarsjes	2 475	337	3 376	4 091	42.3
N Amsterdam-noord	7 451	1 044	3 843	5 597	31.9
P Geuzenveld/slotermeer	3 179	390	5 060	7 137	50.1
Q Osdorp	3 426	430	3 148	5 509	39.2
R Slotervaart/overtoomse veld	3 760	400	2 837	5 643	39.8
T Zuidoost	26 421	5 498	863	1 342	62.9
U Oost/watergraafsmeer	5 238	562	2 968	5 374	35.9
V Amsterdam oud-zuid	3 811	735	1 918	3 751	23.5
W Zuideramstel	1 735	333	493	1 053	17.6
Total Amsterdam	71 941	12 033	35 074	57 093	36.7

Source: O+S.

In Table 7.7 shares of the four most important ethnic groups in the Netherlands and total ethnic population are given by Amsterdam neighbourhood. Again, shares of total ethnic population vary widely between neighbourhoods, ranging from 17.6 per cent to 62.9 per cent of total population. From these figures one can see that in Zuidoost a large number of Surinamese and Antilleans live, whereas in the western part of Amsterdam (like Osdorp, Geuzenveld/Slotermeer, De Baarsjes, Bos en Lommer) large numbers of Turks and Moroccans reside. It has been observed that these residential patterns may be related to the large share of social rented housing (see Table 7.5) in these post-war neighbourhoods (cf. Kesteloot and Cortie 1998). Deurloo and Musterd (2001) remark in this respect that the structure of the housing market itself does not by and in itself explain the residential patterns of ethnic groups as other contextual factors play an important role. Yet, it goes too far to argue that the high share of social housing does not play a role at all in explaining residential patterns.

Another important (demographic) factor in AMA is the age distribution across municipalities. Table 7.8 gives population by age groups for AMA by municipality. Interestingly, the age distribution indicates differences in population structure; Almere with a large share of families with small children, Amsterdam with a large group between 20–39, and surrounding municipalities with a large group of aged 50+. The income distribution of AMA as we discussed just above may well be related to the age distribution whereby a large group of aged 50+ have higher (non-) labour income, explaining differences in disposable income between municipalities.

Table 7.8. Population by age groups 2001 (per cent)

Age-group	Waterland	Zaanstreek	Amsterdam	Amstel-meerlanden	Almere	Total AMA
0–4	6.5	6.4	6.1	6.5	8.3	6.5
5–9	6.8	6.2	5.1	6.4	8.3	6.0
10–14	6.3	5.7	4.8	5.8	7.7	5.5
15–19	5.7	5.1	4.6	5.1	6.3	5.1
20–24	5.4	5.6	6.8	5.5	5.5	6.1
25–29	6.3	7.1	10.3	6.2	7.3	8.5
30–34	8.0	8.8	11.1	8.3	9.7	9.9
35–39	8.8	8.7	9.8	9.0	10.8	9.5
40–44	8.2	7.5	8.1	8.2	9.8	8.2
45–49	7.5	6.9	6.7	7.4	7.6	7.0
50–54	7.7	7.7	6.5	7.7	5.8	6.9
55–59	5.9	5.8	4.4	5.5	3.2	4.8
60–64	4.9	4.8	3.7	4.6	2.5	4.0
65–69	3.9	4.0	3.1	4.0	2.3	3.4
70–74	3.2	3.3	2.9	3.6	2.2	3.0
75–79	2.4	2.9	2.6	2.9	1.6	2.6
80e.o.	2.4	3.5	3.4	3.1	1.2	3.0
Total	100.0	100.0	100.0	100.0	100.0	100.0

Source: O+S.

Comparison of the age distribution of Amsterdam with AMA in Fig. 7.6 reveals that Amsterdam has a relatively large number of inhabitants between age 20–40, but a relatively small number of small children.

Housing structure and the jobs-housing balance

In our presentation of the history of Amsterdam we have shown that the housing structure in general has a large impact on residential choice and mobility patterns of households. The development of large residential growth centres around Amsterdam without many job locations led to large commuting flows to job centres like Amsterdam. Contrary, land-use policies to balance number of jobs to number of housing units does not necessarily lead to smaller commuting flows (cf. Peng 1997). In that sense a jobs-housing balance is a necessary but not a sufficient condition for shorter commuting trips. Planned communities like Almere however, provide planners possibilities to create more self-contained communities and integrated public transport facilities (cf. Cervero 1995).

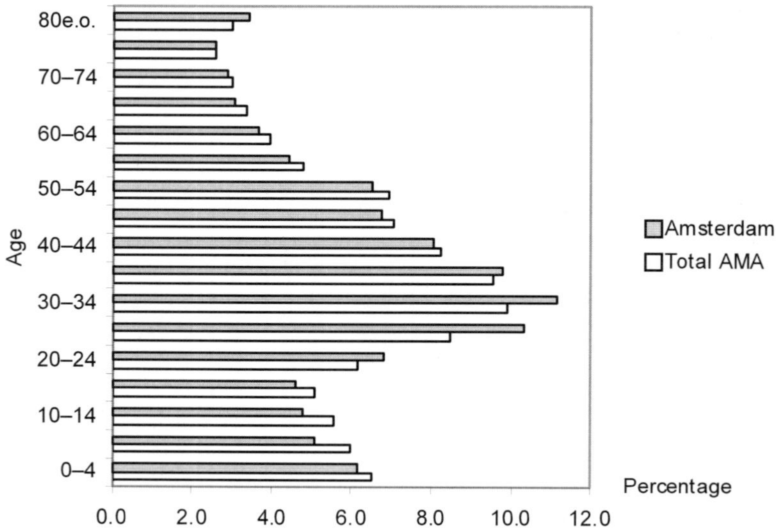

Fig. 7.6. Age distribution of Amsterdam and AMA 2001 (Source: O+S)

Table 7.9. Job location, residential location and the journey-to-work 1999 (in 1000s)

	Residential location				
Job location	Waterland	Zaanstreek	Amsterdam	Amstel-meerlanden	Almere
Waterland	28.5	1.5	1.4	1.0	0.1
Zaanstreek	2.2	39.2	4.4	0.5	0.4
Amsterdam	28.7	17.7	243.6	37.8	17.1
Amstel-Meerlanden	2.6	2.5	27.3	65.3	3.2
Almere	0.1	0.8	1.8	0.2	28.5
Outside AMA	10.9	12.2	57.2	35.0	18.5
Labour force	73.0	73.9	335.7	139.9	67.8
Out-commute	44.5	34.7	92.1	81.3	39.3
Per cent of labour force	61.0	47.0	27.0	58.0	58.0

Source: O+S.

Table 7.9 gives information on the jobs-housing balance in AMA, providing the percentage of out-commuting for each municipality. From last column one can see that about 20 per cent of the labour force works outside AMA (134.7 of the 690.4), indicating that 80 per cent live and work within the metropolitan area. For most municipalities Amsterdam is AMA's most important job centre.

7.4 Housing Demand, Housing Careers and Housing Allocation

7.4.1 Rent Regulation and Rent Allowance

Besides initiating new construction of both subsidised rented accommodation and owner-occupied dwellings, the central government intervened with rent controls and rent assistance programmes (cf. van der Schaar and Hereijgers 1991). During the 1990s, major changes took also place in the rental sector (Priemus 1996). Most public, locally-controlled rental agencies were transformed into private, non-profit housing corporations. Rents may now be set freely by the landlord within a certain range, depending on the dwellings' amenities.

In the 1970s, a rent assistance programme was introduced based on individual rent subsidies and generic subsidies. Because wealthier households also benefit from the generic subsidies, more recent rent assistance prescriptions proposed a gradual abolishment of these generic subsidies. The rent assistance programme of today originates in the rent programme (Beschikking Inviduele Huursubsidie) of 1975. In this programme, individual rent subsidies were given to households on the basis of their income and their monthly rent of the unit (cf. Minvrom 1982). The individual subsidies have given the household some freedom to choose what rented unit to accept (cf. Boelhouwer et al. 1989). This system of rent assistance weighed heavily on the national budget, leading to some changes in the programme in the 1980s. The change in welfare state led to lower rent subsidies, lower subsidies for one-person households, and a significant smaller rented housing stock for which one could opt for rent subsidies (cf. Boelhouwer et al. 1989). The late 1980s has seen a second major revision of the rent assistance programme, abolishing rent subsidies for young people below age 23 and other measures to lower the total outlay of the programme.

The number of households with rent assistance in AMA is given in Table 7.10 which also provides information over the average rent subsidy, and the average rent by municipality. Differences in the number of subsidies relate to the average rent as well as to the average disposable income of household. Amsterdam with a large share of inexpensive small rented units shows a lower average rent subsidy than in surrounding municipalities. Despite the changes in the rent assistance package in the 1980s the programme is still quite extensive with 22 per cent of all households in Amsterdam receiving rent assistance.

Table 7.10. Number of households with rent assistance by rent class 1998/99 (Source: O+S)

Region	Rent per month, € <200 [Number of households]	200–250	250–300	300–350	350–400	400–450	>450	Households with subsidy [total number]	[%]	Average rent subsidy [Euro]	Average rent [Euro]
Beemster	3	38	24	80	87	9	1	242	7.6	131	322
Edam-volendam	29	102	213	227	125	88	2	786	6.8	132	313
Landsmeer	22	46	113	61	35	2	–	279	6.8	107	285
Purmerend	263	263	800	2273	1177	435	154	5365	18.9	136	329
Waterland	14	73	122	155	60	30	4	458	6.7	119	306
Wormerland	38	99	214	132	101	4	3	591	9.9	107	289
Zeevang	3	21	41	44	47	5	–	161	6.7	128	311
Total waterland	372	642	1527	2972	1632	573	164	7882	12.9	131	321
Oostzaan	16	49	28	52	55	14	3	217	6.2	123	307
Zaanstad	387	1693	2894	2104	1332	267	111	8788	15.5	115	294
Totaal zaanstreek	403	1742	2922	2156	1387	281	114	9005	15.0	115	294
Amsterdam	8988	20088	21208	19962	9434	1891	493	82064	22.2	112	279
Aalsmeer	49	43	192	151	141	75	18	669	7.4	128	316
Amstelveen	99	352	786	1048	706	291	142	3424	9.7	131	324
Diemen	15	163	205	272	263	165	159	1242	11.9	144	343
Haarlemmermeer	444	430	622	1254	938	618	119	4425	10.4	127	321
Ouder-amstel	12	12	27	50	145	35	32	313	5.9	150	356
Uithoorn	18	105	181	511	123	35	13	986	9.2	125	317
Total amstel-meerlanden	637	1105	2013	3286	2316	1219	483	11059	9.8	130	325
Almere	93	386	944	4437	3284	1123	191	10458	19.8	149	344
Total A MA	10493	23963	28614	32813	18053	5087	1445	120468	18.3	118	293

7.4.2 Housing Allocation

In the post-war reconstruction period, both housing associations and municipal housing agencies distributed social rental housing units. These rental housing units were allocated such that the cheapest units were, if possible, offered to the lowest-income households (cf. van der Schaar 1987).

In the early 1990s the central government decided to reduce housing expenses, eliminating the operating subsidies and passing the financial risks on to the local authorities and housing associations (Priemus 1996). During these years waiting lists for rental units have been gradually replaced by a market-oriented system under which households can apply for vacant rental units, whose allocation among eligible households depends on their search/waiting period (cf. van der Vlist et al. 2002a).

The current system of allocation rules still play an important role in Dutch housing policy; regulating the entry into and the movements within local housing markets (cf. van der Vlist et al. 2002b). The main reason for these rules, the local authorities argue, is to attempt to prevent mismatches (in terms of income or household size) and to reserve part of the housing stock for locals wishing to enter the housing market or for those working in the local community. Also, this system of allocation rules is to provide affordable housing to those who need it most, and to stimulate residential mobility of households no longer eligible for those units. In reality, however, the social rented sector has provided housing also for a large share of households with above-model incomes (Dieleman and van Kempen 1994; van Kempen and Priemus 2002). Regardless of the submarket – public rental, private rental, the existing owner-occupied stock or new construction – a complex system of allocation rules exists (see van der Vlist 2001).

The most important allocation rules of AMA can be summarised as:

- *Rental sector*: To obtain a rental unit in the social sector, households must often comply with stringent, unit-dependent eligibility rules, in terms of a maximum income and a minimum number of household members. In addition, households must either live or work in the local community. Once a household has obtained a housing unit, it cannot be forced to move if eligibility rules no longer holds. Beyond a certain rent, anybody is free to move into a rental unit of the commercial market. Table 7.11 summarises the allocation rules in AMA. For rental units below 452.42 Euro per month a households must either live two years or more, work or study in AMA. In addition, the long-term unemployed, the disabled, the retired, the accepted refugees, the remigrants, and the divorced may also enter a rental unit in the social sector (SWD 2001).
- *Owner-occupier sector (existing housing stock)*: To buy a unit in the owner-occupier sector, households are relatively free in their choice. However, below a certain price threshold, which may vary among local communities, households must live or work in the local community as specified above. As from early 2002 there is no price threshold for existing construction in AMA (till 2002 the price threshold was 87.170 Euro). Transaction costs are highest in this

submarket. In addition to search costs and solicitor's costs, all transacttions are subject to a six per cent (central government) tax paid by the buyer.

- *Owner-occupier sector (new construction)*: Like in the social rental sector, households must often comply with very stringent eligibility rules in order to obtain a newly constructed dwelling. In some cases, however, no eligibility rules exist. In most cases, households must live or work in the local community, and sometimes an income maximum is set as well. Recall that most new residential construction sites are designated by the central government. As the number of newly constructed units is limited, allocation rules exist which allocate these units randomly to eligible households. Individual lots are hardly ever available for sale, and, if available, local government rules regarding dwelling type and construction materials have to be obeyed.

Table 7.11. Allocation rules of rental units in AMA

Rent, €/month	Rooms	Age	Annual Income
< 340	1–4	no restrictions	0–28,838
	5 or more	below 65	0–22,712
		65 and older	0–19,626
340–452			28,838–40,387
452			No limit

Source: SWD (2002)

7.4.3 Residential Mobility

These allocation rules most likely affect housing consumption as well as local patterns of residential mobility. Especially in the big cities like in Amsterdam eligibility rules are rather stringent and may affect mobility rates. Of course, in housing markets with an abundant supply of dwellings these rules may be less strict, enabling households from other local markets to enter the market more easily. In fact, households wishing to move between different local housing markets have greater difficulty obtaining a dwelling. In general, a household, wishing to move to a housing market in which it does not work, is only eligible for a unit of the existing owner-occupier sector (above the local price threshold) or the free-market rental housing stock. Usually, for households in a social rental unit who are no longer eligible for the social rental sector, residential mobility is associated with a steep rise in their housing outlay. In consequence, households think twice before they move out of their unit, and may hence stay much longer in a unit which is actually no longer intended for them (cf. Rietveld 1984). This seems to be supported by the statistics in Table 7.12 giving the total inflow into social rented units of AMA by origin. As one can see, a maximum of six per cent flow from other regions into a social rented unit in AMA, with most households moving within the municipality. The share of social rental housing is an important feature of the local housing market structure.

Table 7.12. Inflow in social rented sector by origin 2000

	Origin				
	Within municipality	Amsterdam	Other AMA	Total AMA	Other regions
Municipality[a]	[in %]				
Beemster	54	21	26	100	0
Edam-volendam	75	6	14	96	4
Landsmeer	79	11	6	96	5
Purmerend	75	18	4	97	2
Waterland	84	11	1	96	4
Wormerland	55	10	33	98	2
Zeevang	44	25	28	97	3
Zaanstad	87	6	2	97	3
Amsterdam	89	–	4	93	6
Aalsmeer	69	12	19	99	1
Amstelveen	75	17	6	98	2
Diemen	43	52	4	99	1
Haarlemmermeer	69	17	7	94	5
Ouder-amstel	49	27	23	99	1
Uithoorn	55	17	25	97	2

[a]No information for Almere and Oostzaan.
Source: O+S.

7.5 Amsterdam Metropolitan Area: Past Developments and Future Prospects

In this chapter we described the development of Amsterdam metropolitan housing market by considering the main contextual factors in history. We have seen that wars, financial crises and social revolts have had major effects on the course of Amsterdam metropolitan housing market. Likewise, physical planning policy, housing policy like systems of allocation, rent assistance shaped the housing market as it is today. As is observed earlier, the housing market structure has implications for residential choice and mobility patterns. Particularly in controlled housing markets with housing shortage like in AMA, does observed behaviour not only reveal household preferences for housing, but also reveals public sector interventions and other housing market factors (see van der Vlist et al. 2002). The outflow of middle-income households in the late 1960s has shown the importance of housing for the economic and social viability of the metropolitan housing market as well. Other lessons that have been learned from the past refer to early revitalisation plans – maintaining the improved neighbourhoods for the lower-income households – that turn out not to be quite successful, indicating that revitalisation needs reconstruction as well a socio-economic improvements.

Like the past has shaped the urban environment, likewise will future prospects be intimately related to changes in contextual factors. Physical planning is one of the most important factors that have formed the housing market in the Netherlands. As we have discussed above, physical planning has sometimes stimulated but also hindered the operation of the housing market. Two important conclusions will be mentioned here. First, physical planning cannot ignore residential choice and mobility patterns in relation to work and commuting choices (see van der Vlist 2001). As has been observed earlier in the literature, until recently Dutch planning policy has been exclusively oriented towards housing planning. More recent planning initiatives that focused on job centres as well failed to guide new planning initiatives, being too much based a planning approach and not so much on economic principles. Second, in physical planning government can not ignore consumer preferences, prescribing local government to allow market forces to operate.

Another important factor is housing policy. One of the most heard criticisms is that it is still planning-oriented, not giving households freedom of choice. In a recent contribution, Priemus (2001) rightly questions the freedom of households and housing associations under the revised Housing Policy Memorandum. Under the new Housing Memorandum more freedom of choice is given, but policy also prescribes housing associations to sell 500,000 dwellings in the upcoming ten years at the national level. It goes without saying that this will have large implications for Amsterdam metropolitan housing market in general and Amsterdam particularly. Lessons that we have learned from the past suggest that one should take care of selling large parts in only some of the neighbourhoods. What we have seen is that one of the great advantages of the social rented sector is the control in case of reconstruction and revitalisation initiatives, currently necessary for some parts of the social housing stock. Also, selling part of social housing may lead to stigmatisation (van Kempen and Priemus 2002). It remains a challenge to achieve a proper distribution of households in the Amsterdam metropolitan area in such a way that excessive clustering of low income households is avoided and higher income households can contribute more to the prosperity of the central city.

References

Boelhouwer P (2002) Trends in Dutch Housing Policy and the Shifting Position of the Social Rented Sector. Urban Studies 39: 219–35

Boelhouwer P, Groen A, Reith S, Wiegersma M (1989) De Individuele Huursubsidie en de Locale Woningtoewijzing [Rent Subsidies and Housing Allocation]. DUP, Delft

Cervero R (1995) Planned Communities, Self-containment and Commuting. Urban Studies 32: 1135–61

Deurloo MC, Musterd S (2001) Residential Profiles of Surinamese and Moroccans in Amsterdam. Urban Studies 38: 467–85

den Hollander B, Kruythoff H, Teulre R (1996) Woningbouw op VINEX-locaties: Effect op het Woon-werkverkeer in de Randstad [Mobility in VINEX-suburbs]. DUP, Delft

Dieleman F (1999) De Compacte Stad Voorbij? [Beyond the Compact City?]. In: Dieleman F, Musterd S (1999) Voorbij de Compacte Stad [Beyond the Compact City]. Nethur, Utrecht

Dieleman F, Musterd S (eds) (1992) The Randstad: A Research and Policy Laboratory. Kluwer Academic Publishers, Dordrecht
Dieleman F, Musterd S (1999) Voorbij de Compacte Stad [Beyond the Compact City]. Nethur, Utrecht
Dieleman F, van Kempen R (2002) The Mismatch of Housing Costs and Income in Dutch Housing. Journal of Housing and the Built Environment 13: 83–95
Dijst M, de Jong T, Maat K, van Eck J (1998) Wonen en Mobiliteit op Vinex-locaties [Living and Mobility in Vinex-areas]. Den Haag/Utrecht: Ministerie van Volkshuisvesting, Ruimtelijke Ordening en Milieubeheer/Nethur
Faludi A, van der Valk A (1994) Rule and Order: Dutch Planning Doctrine in the Twentieth Century. Kluwer Academic Publishers, Dordrecht
Feddes A (1995) Woningmarkt, Regulering aen Inflatie: het Naoorlogse Volkshuisvestingsbeleid in tien Noordwest-Europese Landen Vergeleken. PhD thesis. Universiteit Utrecht, Utrecht
Fokkema T, Gierveld J, Nijkamp P (1996) Big Cities, Big Problems. Urban Studies 33: 353–77
Jobse RB, Musterd S (1992) Changes in the Residential Function of the Big Cities. In: Dieleman F, Musterd S (eds), The Randstad: A Research and Policy Laboratory. Kluwer Academic Publishers, Dordrecht
Kesteloot C, Cortie C (1998) Housing Turks and Moroccans in Brussels and Amsterdam: The Differences Between Private and Public Markets. Urban Studies 35: 1835–53
Minvrom (1982) Individuele Huursubsidiering [Individual Rent Subsidies]. Ministerie van Volksgezondheid, Ruimtelijke Ordening en Milieubeheer, Den Haag
Minvrom (2001) Ruimte Maken, Ruimte Delen. Vijfde nota Ruimtelijke Ordening [Housing Policy: Fifth Physical Planning Document]. Ministerie van Volksgezondheid, Ruimtelijke Ordening en Milieubeheer, Den Haag
Musterd S, van de Ven J (1991) Gentrification and Residential Revitalization in Amsterdam. In: van Weesep J, Musterd S (eds) Urban Housing for the Better-off: Gentrification in Europe. University of Utrecht, Utrecht
O+S (2002) Amsterdam in Cijfers [Statistics of Amsterdam]. Amsterdam Bureau voor Onderzoek en Statistiek, Amsterdam
Peng Z (1997) The Jobs-housing Balance and Urban Commuting. Urban Studies 34: 1215–35
Priemus H, Dieleman F (2002) Social Housing Policy in the European Union: Past, Present and Perspectives. Urban Studies 39: 191–200
Priemus H (2001) A New Housing Policy for the Netherlands 2000–2010. Journal of Housing and the Built Environment 16: 319–32
Priemus H (1996) Recent Changes in the Social Rented Sector in the Netherlands. Urban Studies 33: 1891–1908
Rietveld P (1984) Vacancies and Mobility in the Housing Market: An Exploratory Analysis. Environment and Planning A 16: 673–87
SDW (2002) Uitvoeringsinstructies Woonruimteverdeling [Allocation Rules]. Stedelijke Woningdienst Amsterdam. Amsterdam
SCP (2001) De Stad in de Omtrek: Problemen en Perspectieven van de vier Grootstedelijke Gebieden in de Randstad [The City and its Surrounding]. Sociaal Cultureel Planbureau, Den Haag
van Kempen R, Priemus H (2002) Revolution in Social Housing in the Netherlands. Urban Studies 39: 237–53
van der Schaar J (1986) Huisvestingssituatie in Nederland 1900–1982 [Housing in the Netherlands 1900–1982]. DUP, Delft

van der Schaar J (1987) Groei en Bloei van het Nederlandse Volkshuisvestingsbeleid [Developments in Dutch Housing Policy]. DUP, Delft

van der Vlist AJ, Rietveld P, Nijkamp P (2002a) Residential Search and Mobility in a Housing Market Equilibrium Model. Journal of Real Estate Finance and Economics 24: 277–99

van der Vlist AJ, Gorter C, Nijkamp P, Rietveld P (2002b) Residential Mobility and Local Housing Market Differences. Environment and Planning A 34: 1146 – 68

van der Vlist AJ (2000) New Households' Residential Careers. Mimeo, Department of Economics, Vrije Universiteit Amsterdam, Amsterdam

van der Vlist AJ (2001) Residential Mobility and Commuting. PhD. Thesis, Department of Economics, Vrije Universiteit Amsterdam, Amsterdam

8 The Oslo Metropolitan Housing Market

Viggo Nordvik

Norwegian Building Research Institute, Oslo

8.1 Introductory Remarks

Housing is both a consumption good and an asset that has many characteristics. This complicates analyses of housing markets. We shall here give an overview of the situation in the Oslo metropolitan housing market. Within the given framework it is of course not possible to give any complete analysis that covers all the special features of housing markets in general and the Oslo metropolitan housing market specifically. Rather we shall present some relevant empirical facts and structures from the Oslo metropolitan housing market. In this context a relevant fact or structure is something that is important for the housing conditions of the population, or some empirical fact or structure where the Oslo market differs from other metropolitan areas in Europe.

The presentations are based upon data from many different sources. Unfortunately the most interesting data sources are not available at the time this is written. In the autumn 2001 both a survey of living conditions and a census were undertaken. The data sets from these are not yet available for research purposes. On the other hand, a recently published report on housing policy and markets (NOU 2002:2) prepared for the government offers an extensive mass of relevant empirical information.

We shall not dwell too much on the list of special features of the housing market. Readers interested in this topic are referred to general housing market texts such as Smith et al. 1988; Pitkin et al. 1991 or Miles 1994. However, for a start one feature should be pointed out: the durability of housing capital. An important implication of this is that the housing conditions and housing market opportunities of the population to a very large extent depends on the existing housing stock. The existing housing stock is a result of decision made in the past. A consequence of this is that the housing conditions at any present point in time to a very large extent depend on the housing policy of the past.

The empirical relevance of the durability dimension becomes evident when the age structure of the Norwegian housing stock is considered. Around five per cent of the housing units in use in 1995 were built before the year 1900. Every fifth housing unit in the country was more than fifty years old. The housing stock in Oslo is even older. Eight per cent of the Oslo-stock was built before 1900 and slightly more than 30 per cent of the housing units are more than fifty years old. This can probably be found in most large cities throughout Europe.

As a background for the description of the housing market in Oslo at the turn of the century, two dimensions of the Norwegian housing policy after the World War II are therefore worth a brief discussion. Following the World War II, one of the prime tasks was to rebuild and build the country. This was done during a time with severe constraints on the supply of credit and also many other goods. As an instrument in the 'building-policy', The State Housing Bank was established. Secondly, as a means in the housing policy Norway chose to establish a quite strongly regulated co-op sector rather than a public rental sector. This stands in contrast to most of our neighbouring countries that chose to build up a very much larger public rental housing sector than was done in Norway.

The State Housing Bank was established in order to allocate credit to new construction. The interest on these loans was politically determined, and it involved a substantial element of subsidisation. Loans of this type were given for construction of housing units within a medium quality segment. Scarce public funds were not to be used for construction of in the highest quality brackets, but one did want to stimulate a 'good housing quality'. This system of subsidised loans for new construction was, with some modifications, continued up to 1996. Some simple figures illustrate the significance of this system. In 1995 the Norwegian housing stock consisted of 1.9 million housing units, since 1946 the State Housing Bank had financed more than one million housing units.

In Norway as opposed to many other North-European countries there was not established any large public rental sector through the post-war years. Instead a co-operative sector was stimulated. Municipalities provided inexpensive land for new construction, and the government provided credit through the State Housing Bank. New co-ops were allocated to the members of housing societies and in accordance with municipal waiting lists. The second-hand prices where strongly regulated and allocated to the members of housing societies according to the length of their membership. During the 1980s the regulations came under political pressure, and most of them were gradually phased out. In consequence, the co-op sector in most respects today functions as a part of the ordinary owner-occupied market.

Even if both the regulations of the co-op sector and large subsidies through the State Housing Bank now are history, these policy measures to a large extent affected the size and composition of the housing stock of today. This has influenced strongly on the price structure observed in the Norwegian housing market today.

Two other factors should be noted. First, the area of Norway is large compared to the size of the population. Even if there is a discussion of whether new construction in the metropolitan Oslo area is constrained by lack of land, this is true also for part of the country. It is sometimes claimed that inside the borders of Oslo the population of Paris could be housed. Second, Norway is a quite rich society, and this affects the housing market and the housing conditions of the population.

8.2 Some Popular Views on the Oslo Metropolitan Housing Market

In this description a picture of a metropolitan housing market with a quite high price level will be drawn up. Furthermore, the price level has been growing rapidly during the last 7–8 years. Despite of this; the text will build up to a picture of fairly well working housing market where the housing conditions of the population are in a fairly good state. However, the claim that the housing conditions of the population are in a fairly good state is not a claim that there are not any problems left to solve. Especially one can say that there still are some problems connected to distributive matters.

The views on the Oslo metropolitan housing market expressed here are by no means a consensus view. Other commentators give a much darker description of the present situation at the housing markets and of the prospects for the future. As a background some of these views are presented briefly here. It is, however, probably fair to say that the description of the situation as being in a quite bad state of affairs is shared by more people than my description of a metropolitan housing sector in a fairly good state.

In Aftenposten, a major newspaper in Norway, a researcher stated in May 2000 that no one else in Europe face larger housing market problems than the youths in the Oslo metropolitan area do. Furthermore, the situation was described as far more difficult than it were twenty years ago. The main reasons for these conclusions were the high house prices and the absence of a generally accessible subsidised rental sectors.

The causes of the sad situation described above are also identified. 'First the social housing policy was abandoned, then the housing policy was abandoned, finally new construction was abandoned'. Perhaps needless to say; I do not share the analysis of this researcher.

Another commentator also claims that Norway has one of the worst social housing policies in Europe. This time social housing policy is equalised to the number of public rental dwellings. In addition this commentator states that we in Norway have not had any new construction for social purposes. This is a strong claim that really does not find any empirical support.

In the time period from 2002 up to 2015, Oslo-authorities have planned for a total new construction of 40,000 housing units. A housing market analyst has already revealed this as being far from enough to avoid serious housing shortages. In order to avoid this kind of shortages, one has to build an additional 30,000 dwellings during this time period. An addition of 70,000 housing units in Oslo, where the housing stock at the start of 1999 was estimated to consist of 271,000 housing units, is a quite high number. To put these numbers in perspective some basic facts should be noted. According to the official population prognoses the population in Oslo is expected to grow with 5.8 per cent up to 2015, a need for 70,000 new housing units equals a little more than 25 per cent of the existing housing stock in Oslo.[1]

The views on the Oslo metropolitan housing market reported above are not chosen because it in a way is easy to argue against them. They are chosen because statements and 'analysis' of this sort quite frequently are brought forward in the public debate on the housing market in the Oslo metropolitan area.

8.3 Population

During large parts of the post-war years demographics played a central role in housing studies in Norway. Housing markets were in different ways regulated. The main ambition in the housing policy was to reduce (or even to get rid of) the housing shortage. As a tool in this policy demographically based assessments and projections of the housing need in the population was frequently produced. After many of the regulations were abandoned the need for and interest of assessments and projections of the housing need in the population vanished. In a, maybe too, large extent this turned the focus of housing studies away from demographics.

Demographic factors such as size and composition of the population and aggregate mobility and its direction are really important for anybody who wants to develop an understanding of what is happening in any local housing market. Demographic factors lay the premises for what is happening in a housing market and also for our judgment of the situation in a local housing market.

At the turn of the century close to one million people lived in the Oslo metropolitan area. In Oslo there were 507,500 inhabitants while 467,000 people lived in the neighbouring municipalities in Akershus. From 1975 up to today the population in this area has grown at an annual rate of 0.74 per cent. The total population growth in greater Oslo over this period was hence 19.4 per cent. The corresponding figure for the whole of Norway was over the same period was approximately 12 per cent. Consequently there has been a trend where an increasing share of the Norwegian population has been concentrated to the Oslo metropolitan area.

Table 8.1. Share of the Norwegian population in the Oslo area (per cent)

	Oslo	Akershus	Greater Oslo
1975	11.64	8.77	20.41
1980	11.15	8.99	20.14
1985	10.79	9.32	20.11
1990	10.83	9.79	20.62
1995	11.12	9.99	21.11
2000	11.33	10.43	21.76

Source: Statistics Norway.

[1] Note that all these figures refer only to the municipality of Oslo, not the whole metropolitan area Oslo.

The national trend of concentration of the population towards the Oslo metropolitan area has really not been very strong. Furthermore, it has not evolved monotonically over the last quarter of a decade. From 1975 up to 2000 the share living in greater Oslo increased by 1.3 percentage points. More than half of this growth over the last 25 years came during the last five years of the nineties. The share of the population living in Akershus has increased steadily over the period.

The share of the Oslo population living in Oslo fell from 1975 up to sometimes between 1985 and 1990. After that the population share has grown by as much as half a percentage point. The time period over which this growth has taken place was the time period when new construction was at its lowest ever level! Of course this phenomenon must have something to do with increased household size. One probable cause of this is that the age-structure of the population in parts of Oslo has shifted. In effect many old households have been replaced by younger ones. Average number of persons in households in the age span between 30 and 50 is typically higher than in households formed by persons more than 70 years old. It has also been hypothesised that larger household size among some groups of non-Western immigrants are among the reasons for the observed development.

Hence, the aggregate population growth in greater Oslo hides an uneven development both over time and in Oslo and Akershus. Fig. 8.1 shows the annual growth rates in Oslo and Akershus over the time from 1975 up to 2000. As the figure reveals, the growth rate over the last 25 years have consistently been higher in the neighbouring municipalities than in central Oslo. A few years at the beginning of the 1990s were an exception to this.

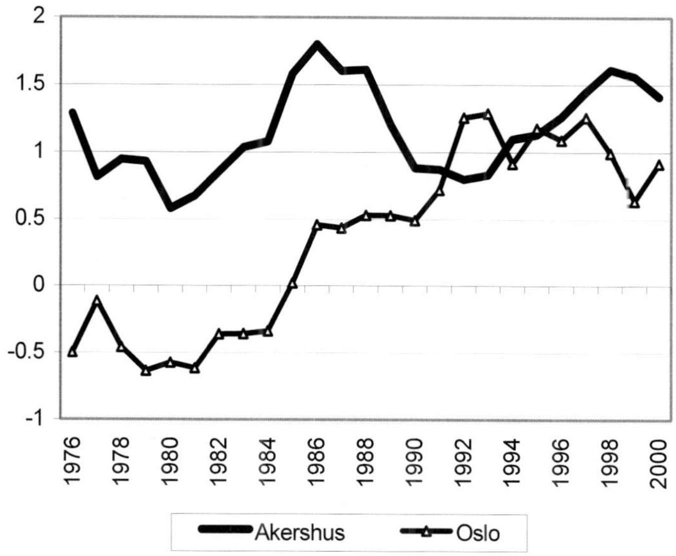

Fig. 8.1. Growth rates of the population of Oslo and Akershus (Source: Statistics Norway)

Statistics Norway makes at regular interval population forecasts. These are made both at a national and at lower regional levels. Demographic events such as births and deaths are more easily predicted than moving streams. When we here discuss the expected developments of future population in the Oslo metropolitan area, we shall use the baseline projection, and we also report expected development along two alternative scenarios. The alternative scenarios are entitled 'Low(er) degree of centralisation' and 'High(er) degree of centralisation', respectively. This enables us to show how different assumptions on mobility affect the results (Table 8.2).

Table 8.2. Population growth under different scenarios, Oslo metropolitan area

	2000–2005	2000–2010	2000–2020
Norway – baseline	2.5	4.8	9.3
Oslo – baseline	2.0	3.9	9.1
Akershus – baseline	6.5	9.6	15.7
Oslo metropolitan – baseline	4.2	6.6	12.3
Oslo – lower	0.6	1.3	4.7
Akershus – lower	4.5	7.7	12.6
Oslo metropolitan – lower	2.4	4.4	8.5
Oslo – higher	3.6	6.6	13.6
Akershus – higher	6.5	11.5	19.0
Oslo metropolitan – higher	5.0	8.9	16.2

Source: Statistics Norway.

From 2000 to 2010 the Norwegian population is expected to grow with 4.8 per cent. With a growth rate in the Oslo metropolitan area nearly 2 percentage points higher. The table also reveals the importance of intensity and direction of mobility streams. Under the low degree of centralisation scenario the population of Oslo Metropolitan area will grow with 4.4 per cent, equivalent to an annual growth rate of 0.4 per cent. Under the high centralisation scenario the total growth rate of the greater Oslo population is expected to be 8.9 per cent, equivalent to an annual rate of growth of 0.8 per cent. The expected growth rates are twice as high under the increased centralisation scenario as in the lower centralisation scenario. The differences are largest for the most central part of the metropolitan area, i.e. Oslo. Naturally the differences between these two scenarios are even higher when we look as long forward in time as to 2030. No matter which time span or scenario is considered the population of Akershus is expected to grow faster than in Oslo, the central part of the Oslo metropolitan area.

Historical and expected future developments of the population are, as already claimed, important for the understanding of a local housing market. It is also possible to extract quite a lot of information from the distribution of the population over different age groups. Fig. 8.2 shows how the distribution of the population in the Oslo metropolitan area by age groups is expected to look like over the next ten years.

Thinking about the next ten years, it is clear that some changes in the age structure of the population in the Oslo metropolitan area will take place. There is expected to be an increase in the share of people aged between 40 and 69 years. The share of the population that belongs to this age group will increase by more than 5 percentage points, over the ten years from 2000 to 2010. As a matter of fact, this growth is so strong that the share for all other age groups is expected to decrease. This pattern can be seen both in Oslo and Akershus. It is, however, most pronounced in Oslo.

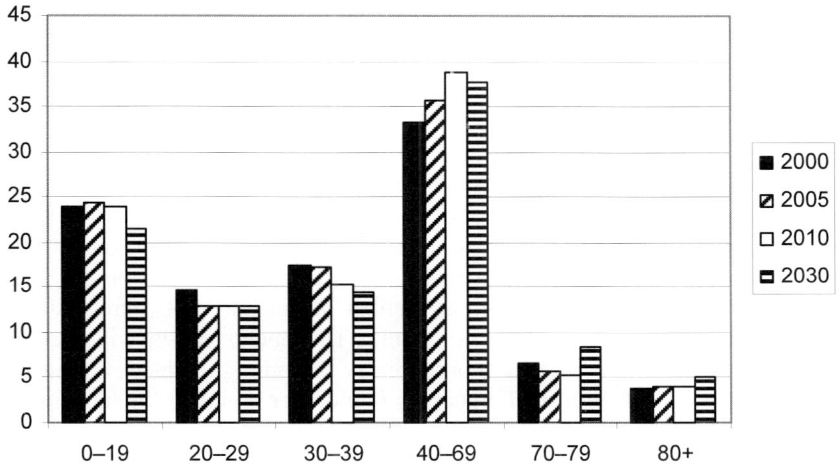

Fig. 8.2. Population in the Oslo metropolitan area, projections by age and year (Source: Statistics Norway)

When discussing these population forecasts at the individual level, in a housing market context one should bear in mind that the relation between the number of persons and the number of households vary strongly between different age groups. Some rough calculations based on the Norwegian Survey of Housing Conditions from 1995 reveal the following share of individuals in each age group who live together with a partner.

Table 8.3. Share of the population living as a part of a couple (per cent)

Age	Share
0–19	–
20–29	63.0
30–39	77.5
40–69	78.9
70–79	57.4
80+	34.6

Source: Survey of Housing Conditions 1995, Statistics Norway.

The expected future age distribution of the Oslo metropolitan area revealed that the growth comes in the age group between 40 and 69 years old. From the table above one can see that it is exactly in these age groups that the propensity to live together with a partner is at its highest level. Consequently, it is good reason to expect a lower growth in the number of households than the overall population growth. Another way to express this is to say that the demographic growth in housing demand is expected to be lower than a quick look at population projections seem to indicate.

8.4 The Housing Stock – Size and Composition

As already discussed in the introduction, together with the population the existing housing stock lays the basic premises for both the housing conditions and the housing market. In this chapter we will use information from the Census 1990 to describe the housing stock. In our context it is interesting to describe the housing stock along many dimensions, such as number of housing units, tenure distribution, house types and size of the housing units. To some extent we will also utilise information on new construction in order to say something on the development of the housing stock. This information can be found later on under the heading 'new construction'.

However, one should bear in mind that new construction cannot be interpreted as net growth of the housing stock. There also occur changes in the stock due to events such as demolition, merging of dwellings and transformations of parts of the building stock to and from housing purposes. The dynamics of the housing supply from the existing building stock are partly explained by natural life cycles of buildings. In part it can also be explained by how the profitability of different transformations is affected by the development of housing demand.

The focus of this chapter is the housing market of the Oslo metropolitan area. In the descriptions of the housing stock we find it natural to distinguish between the central part consisting of Oslo, the capital city, and the surrounding municipalities in Akershus. Our choice is guided by the fact that the housing stock in these two parts of the Oslo metropolitan area really differs. In many ways the Akershus housing stock resembles the housing stock of the rest of Norway more than it resembles the housing stock of Oslo. Still, these two parts of the Oslo metropolitan area together make up a natural local housing market.

The total number of housing units in Akershus was 166,544 in 1990. This gives an average of 2.5 persons per dwelling. The number of rooms per person amounted to 1.7. In Table 8.4 number of rooms and house types in Akershus is reported. In the number of rooms kitchen is not included.

Some comments should be made on the fact that more than ten per cent of the housing units in single-family houses have only one or two rooms. These figures do not imply that many funny-looking single-room, or double-room, single-family houses can be found around Oslo. Rather, it reveals a special feature of the Norwegian rental housing market. A large share of the single-family houses in Norway is constructed so that they offer the opportunity to let part of the house. The one and two room units in single-family houses are most certainly such secondary units. For some of the three room units in single-family houses, this can also be the case. As a matter of fact 25 per cent of the 'rental units' in Norway are such secondary units in single-family houses, and in around 10 per cent of the single-family houses a tenant is present. The share of the single-family houses where a secondary unit potentially can be let is far higher. Nordvik (2000) has, at a national level, analysed the utilisation of this part of the housing stock.

Note that a majority of the secondary units clearly have a satisfying quality and are independent housing units. They have their own entrance, kitchen and sanitary facilities (WC and bath). However, an alternative use of them is to include them as a part of the owner's own housing unit.

Table 8.4. House types and number of rooms Akershus

	Single-family houses	Other small houses	Blocks of flats	Share of housing stock[a]
One room	2 753	1 881	2 396	4.5
Two rooms	7 637	6 185	6 418	12.4
Three rooms	10 856	10 390	9 026	18.4
Four rooms	21 192	15 000	5 655	25.3
Five rooms	18 292	10 352	752	17.7
Six rooms or more				
Sum	90 139	50 087	24 566	166 544
Share of housing stock[a]	54.1	30.4	14.8	–

[a]When the share of housing stock is calculated also units in the category 'other house types' is included. This category is small (1,700 units) and is not reported in the table.
Source: Census 1990.

In short one can say that rather large single-family houses dominate the Akershus housing stock. Fig. 8.3 shows that it is also right to claim that owner-occupation is the dominant tenure form. Owners can be defined as those who either owns their housing unit alone as owner-occupiers or together with others through housing co-ops. In Akershus as much as 81.7 per cent of the households own the housing unit in which they live. As renter households on average are smaller than owner-households, 86.7 per cent of the Akershus population lives in a housing unit owned by their household.

Hence, only 18.3 per cent of households in Akershus lived in 1990 in a rental dwelling. Especially compared to the national average of 21.8 per cent and a rental share in Oslo at 24 per cent, the rental share in Akershus seems quite low.

In 1990, 94.6 per cent of the housing units in Akershus had both a WC and a bath. In 2.2 per cent of the units both of these facilities were missing. These are probably mostly 'older units' on their way out of the housing stock. The new census 2001 will give us new information on this topic.

In Oslo, the total number of housing units in 1990 amounted to 244,434. The average number of persons per dwelling was 1.9. This yields 1.67 rooms per person. Based on the 1990-census it is estimated that 1.9 per cent of the dwellings in Oslo lacked both a WC and a bathroom of their own. An additional 1.8 per cent had a bathroom but lacked a WC. These low quality dwellings are mostly found in inner city houses set up 50 years or more ago. Inner city rehabilitation programmes are strongly reducing the frequency of such problems.

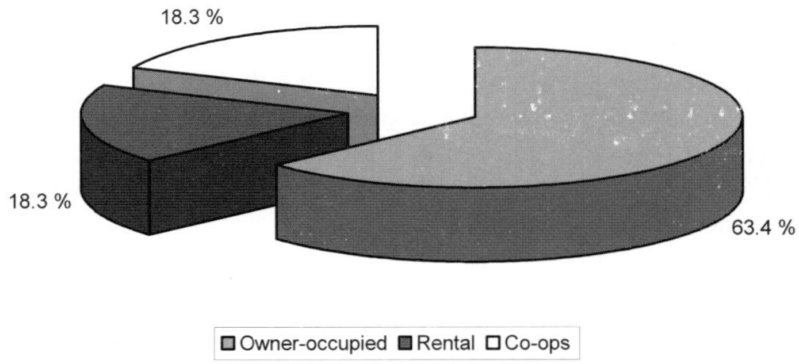

Fig. 8.3. Tenure distributions in Akershus 1990 (Source: Census 1990)

The house type composition of the housing stock in Oslo differs markedly from the corresponding distribution in the surroundings of the Oslo metropolitan area (Akershus). Two out of three housing units are in blocks of flats. Compared to other capitals of Europe a share of single-family houses of 11.4 per cent is probably quite high. The rest, about 15 per cent, is other types of small houses.

Also along the tenure dimension the Oslo housing stock differs from the housing stock of Akershus. Fig. 8.4 gives the total tenure distribution in Oslo.

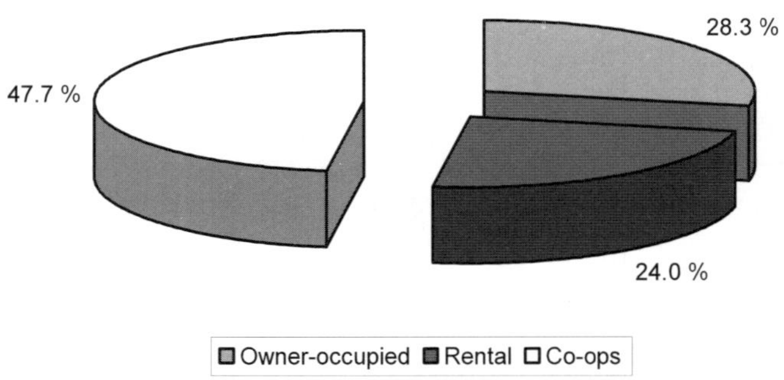

Fig. 8.4. Tenure distributions in Oslo 1990 (Source: Census 1990)

The most frequent tenure in Oslo is the co-ops. Nearly every second housing unit in the Norwegian capital is a co-op. It is natural to speculate whether this has something to do with a combination of two factors. First, the widespread preference for owning in the Norwegian housing market, which at least partly is generated by a generous tax treatment of housing capital used by the owner and her household. Second, until the 1980s Norway did not have a legal framework for owner-occupied units in multi-family houses. Consequently, condominiums are a rather new phenomenon in both the Norwegian and the Oslo metropolitan housing market. In the light of these two factors it is no surprise that co-ops are strongly present in the areas of Norway where the population density is at its highest. The rental share was in 1990 24.0 per cent.

Fig. 8.5 shows the number of rooms in the Oslo housing stock. Not very surprisingly it differs from the similar distribution of Akershus.

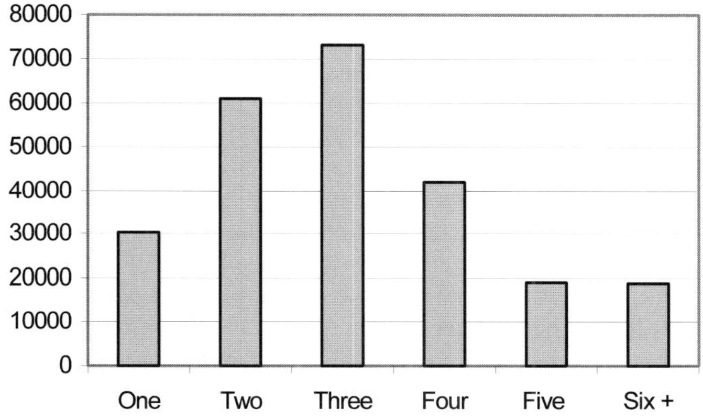

Fig. 8.5. Number of rooms Oslo 1990 (Source: Census 1990)

Dwellings with 2–4 rooms dominate the Oslo housing stock. More than 70 per cent of the housing units fall into this bracket. Applying the same definition of a large housing unit as we did for Akershus, we find that 15.5 per cent of the Oslo dwellings are classified as being large.

As were said at the start of the discussion of the housing stock in the Oslo metropolitan area, Akershus and Oslo should be regarded as two different segments of one local housing market. These two segments seen together can be seen as forming a menu of housing opportunities. Those who have preferences for high housing consumption and maybe also prefer a single-family house choose to settle down in Akershus. Preferences like this vary over the life cycle of the household. This again explains the fact that average household size is higher in Akershus than in Oslo and the fact that there are more children in Akershus than in Oslo.

Also the fact that the aggregate rental share of Akershus and Oslo is approximately equal to the national average while Oslo lies clearly above and Akershus below the national average supports the view that they make up different parts of the housing menu offered within one local housing market. Note also that the lowest rental shares in Akershus are found in the municipalities closest to Oslo. Maybe one can claim that the rental market of the neighbouring municipalities to a large extent is geographically located in Oslo. For a household the choice between

Oslo and Akershus can be viewed as a trade-off between the size of the housing unit and centrality.

8.5 New Construction

From the time of the 1990 census until year 2000, new construction in the Oslo metropolitan area amounted to 35,733 units. This equals 8.7 per cent of the housing stock in 1990. The population in the area grew during the same period by around 11 per cent. The new construction activity over this ten-year period was not, however, evenly distributed over the Oslo metropolitan area.

In Oslo new constructions amounted to only 6 per cent of the housing stock of 1990. Measured by the share of the 1990 housing stock new construction was highest at the locations most distant from the city centre. Both in the south eastern parts of the metropolitan area and in the north, new construction made up 15 per cent of the 1990 housing stock. This might of course have something to do with the opening of a new main airport, Gardermoen, at the northern part of the Oslo metropolitan area. Even though the airport was opened up in 1997 it probably affected new construction in this part of the Oslo metropolitan area during the whole period from 1991–2000. The opening of an airport is hardly an unexpected shock to a local housing market. Especially not in this case as the opening was preceded by a fifty year long decision and planning process.

According to established theories of the evolution of a monocentric city (see for example Cappoza and Helsley 1990) it should hardly be surprising that the housing stock of a metropolitan area grows at a faster speed at the 'fringe of the area'. According to a stylised picture of the growth of such a city, the land at the fringe of the city is utilised when there is no more vacant land closer to the city centre. Even though urban land use models of this kind yield understanding into the process of growth of an urban area it does not give an empirically correct picture of the situation in Oslo. It is still vacant land regulated for housing purposes in the city of Oslo. Hence it is possible to increase the supply of new housing units to a quite large extent inside the borders of the capital.

A widely used theoretical framework for understanding the determinants of housing demand, house prices and new constructions is given by Poterba (1984). In short the important mechanisms of the Poterba model can be described in the following way: The willingness to pay for housing services are determined by preferences and income. The willingness to pay for housing services determines together with the interest rate and expected appreciation of housing capital the asset prices of housing capital.

Poterba then goes on to postulate a relation for the long run marginal cost of increasing the housing stock. A (long run) equilibrium will under this framework be a situation where the asset price of housing capital equals the long run marginal cost of increasing the stock. Within this model new construction is expected to equal zero if the asset price is below the long run marginal costs and to be larger the larger a positive gap between the asset price and the marginal long run cost is.

Based upon arguments like this, the Tobin's q-value becomes a central concept in an attempt to understand new construction. The q-value is the ratio of the asset price to the marginal cost of housing stock. Another result to be extracted from the reasoning around the Poterba model is that we expect a positive correlation between second hand house prices and the level of new construction. Because of this we illustrate the development of the nominal index of house prices and new construction in Oslo over the 1990s in Fig. 8.6 below.

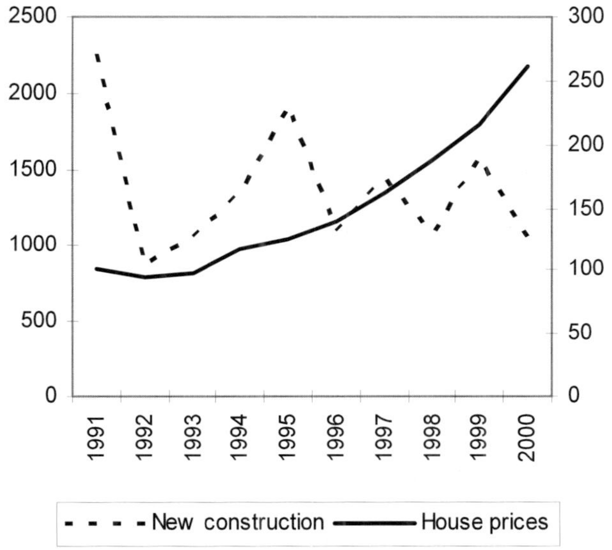

Fig. 8.6. New construction and second hand prices in the Oslo housing market (Source: Statistics Norway)

At the start of the period new constructions in Oslo fell sharply from the boom level in the late 1980s. In the first years of the 1990s new constructions was at a low level. As the prices started growing in 1993–94 new constructions also rose. Despite of an increasing growth rate of house prices after that, new constructions again fell sharply. From 1996 up to 2000 new constructions seems to have been fluctuating around a low level. Preliminary figures for the number of housing starts in 2001 indicate an extremely strong growth from 2000 to 2001. The number of housing starts is nearly twice as high as it were in 2000. The growth of housing starts in Akershus in the same year was far lower (10 per cent up).

Visual inspection of Fig. 8.7 indicates a positive correlation between new constructions and house prices in Akershus. The correlation is however, not very strong. Also here we observe a drop in new constructions in the middle of a period of rapidly increasing house prices. In Akershus it came one year later than in Oslo.

Statistics Norway produces a measure that can be interpreted as a kind of Tobin's q-measure. They report the ratio between the average price (per square metre) for second hand single-family houses and newly constructed single-family houses. These measures are only reported at a county-level and for some of the large cities and are now available only for 1999. At this point in time the (average) q-ratio was 1.05 in Oslo and 0.92 in Akershus.

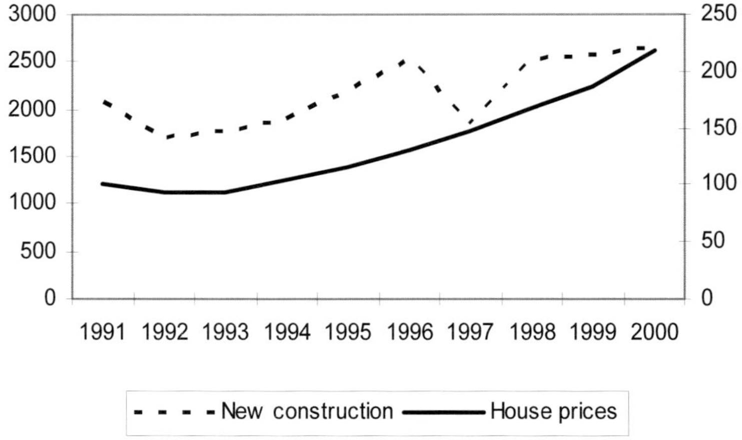

Fig. 8.7. New construction and second hand prices in the Akershus housing market (Source: Statistics Norway)

Different measures of the development of construction costs show that these costs have increased significantly over the latter half of the 1990s. This increase has not by any means been as high as the growth in the second hand house prices. Consequently, the q-measures reported here have not at any point during the 1990s been as high as they were in 1999, and the q-values have probably grown also in the time after 1999.

There are several severe problems, both theoretical and empirical, associated with the interpretation of aggregate q-measures defined in the way we do here. The most important are probably connected to the treatment of land prices. In the measure we use historical purchase prices of land. The price of a new unit, on the other hand, reflects the current land price. Moreover, second hand prices and land prices are simultaneously determined. In Poterba-terms this implies that there does not exist a long run marginal cost function of housing stock that is determined independently of the intensity of housing demand. It remains an unsettled question what consequences this should have for the interpretation of q-measures.

The second problem is connected to the use of an aggregated average q-measure. At the bottom line of a theory of new constructions based on Tobin's q lies an assumption of newly constructed and second hand dwellings being alternative assets. Taking proper account of this probably would lead us to try to develop marginal, rather than average, q-measures. Maybe one should also direct the interest towards distributions of project-specific q-measures rather than reporting and analysing Tobin's q as one single value. It is by no means obvious that the information present in such a distribution can be captured by any aggregate measure.

This can have important implication for an analysis of new constructions in a metropolitan area. High second hand prices in the most attractive central parts of a city do not necessarily make new constructions at the fringe of the city profitable. In short one can say that our q-measures are not a measure of the profitability in new constructions – but it most probably correlates positively with the profitability.

However, based on the information presented here a hypothesis that the number of housing starts in Oslo has, been quite low because the profitability has been quite low can not be rejected. That is, the low correlation between new constructions and house price growth in Oslo and Akershus over the 1993–2000 period may be due to asset prices, which were lower than the long run marginal cost of housing stock. Or in other words: the q-values have been too low to generate much new construction. This hypothesis is supported by the recent increase in the number of housing starts in Oslo. Furthermore, maybe the fact that Akershus did not experience the same type of increase in the number of housing starts can also be interpreted as a kind of support for this hypothesis.

During the time span analysed here new construction in Norway outside the Oslo metropolitan area was 154,260 units. This amounted to as much as 11.5 per cent of the housing stock outside the metropolitan area. In most counties outside the metropolitan area the average q-measure is around 0.8 or even lower. This casts some doubts on the usefulness of aggregate q-measures as a predictor for new construction. At least it casts doubt upon the use of our operational q-measure.

The working of the land markets and land use regulations also probably adds noise to the pictures of the determinants of new construction given above. Why did for example new construction fall sharply in 1996 in Oslo and in 1997 in Akershus, despite of a strong growth in house prices in both of these years and also the preceding years? One hypothesis is that as prices fell sharply from 1988 to 1992–93 many well-prepared projects were postponed. During the first years with rising prices some of these projects were completed. These projects had during the preparation period already collected sunk costs and their completion was more profitable than just waiting. Prices were however not high enough to start preparing new projects. Therefore new construction dipped when these were completed. In the following years prices continued rising and new projects were prepared. The accelerated housing starts in 2001 can be a result of this. Note that we here only bring forward a hypothesis; we do not claim to have given any certain conclusion.

The time-lag generated by the preparation process can be substantial. It might involve making new land use regulation plan or revision of prior regulations. The making of regulation plans can be especially time consuming when new construction is to take place in existing neighbourhoods. Complaints from neighbours are more the rule than it is an exception. Even if these complaints are not accepted in the end, the regulation authorities must give them a proper bureaucratic treatment. An Oslo politician once stated that even though there are only a quarter of a million households in Oslo they add up to many millions of neighbours.

Land for new construction is nowadays mostly owned by different private agents.[2] They can either sell the land to a developer or they can keep the option to sell at a later data. A quite low interest rate makes the price of waiting lower. Building companies often complain that landowners have unrealistic expectation of the value of the land. Maybe the truth is that they have high expectations and that they find it profitable to wait and see whether these expectations can be fulfilled some time in the future.

To conclude this somewhat discomforting discussion one can say that the process of new construction involves a not very well understood lag-structure.

Despite of all the problems discussed, hopefully some mechanisms relevant for the understanding of new construction in the Oslo metropolitan area have been illustrated above. Still it should be stressed, that there are several unsettled questions concerning the complexities of the interdependencies between urban land markets, planning practices, the second hand market for housing and new construction. It is beyond the scope of this survey to go any further into these questions.

8.6 The Market for Owner-occupied Housing

In Norway nearly all legal differences between the co-ops and the 'pure owner-occupied' segment of the housing market has vanished over the last twenty years. Regulations of the co-ops have been gradually phased out and the legal framework surrounding them now approximates that for owner-occupation. Neither of these two tenures is price regulated. Consequently, consumers in the Norwegian housing market treat co-ops and owner-occupied units that are otherwise equal as being perfect substitutes. Because of this, both these two segments are treated together under the heading 'The market for owner-occupied housing'. As seen earlier in this chapter the co-ops are a major part of the owner segment of the Oslo housing market.

House prices in Norway, as in most other West-European countries, went through a boom and bust cycle in the late 1980s and early 1990s. This turned around 1993–94 into a new boom period that still prevails. This pattern was, and still is, even more marked in the Oslo metropolitan area than it was in the other parts Norway. Fig. 8.8 shows real house prices in Norway from 1980 up to today.[3] The index is based on transactions of owner-occupied housing units.

---

[2] In the Oslo metropolitan housing market the lots of the existing housing units are mostly owned by the owners of the housing units, either collectively through the co-ops or directly by the owner-occupiers. Land lease arrangements do exist but are not very common.

[3] Unfortunately official house prices indexes were not published (or produced in Norway) before 1991. Because of this we are not able to give longer time series for the Oslo metropolitan area. The price index reported in the Fig. 8.8 was produced by Rolf Barlindhaug at the Norwegian Building Research Institute, using information from different sources. From 1991 and onwards the index coincides with the official index.

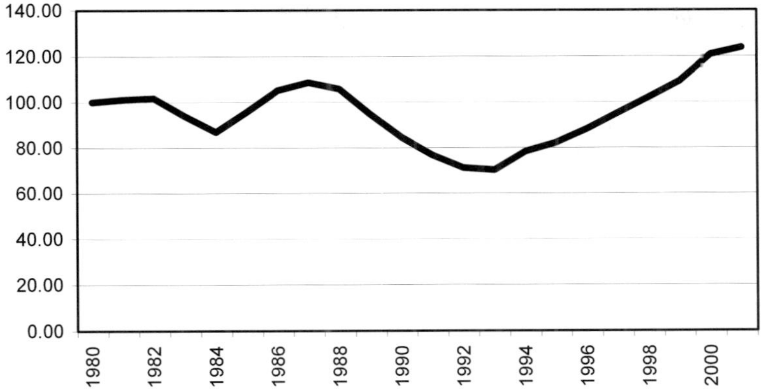

Fig. 8.8. Real house prices Norway 1980–2001 (Source: Medby 2002)

Real, after-tax, interest rates are singled out as the probably most important determinant of house prices both in theoretical and empirical studies of housing markets. Even though real interest rates in Norway have been a little bit higher than in most other parts of Europe, they have really been quite low. Furthermore, compared to the interest rate of the early 1990s, the after-tax real interest rate today lies clearly below the levels at the start of the 1990s. It is no wonder that house prices are far higher today than they were in the early 1990s.

On inspection of Fig. 8.9 there really seems to be a kind of long run relation between house prices and the real interest rate after tax. We see, however, that house prices do not react strongly to short term variations of the interest rates. The probable cause of this is that housing market behaviour reacts towards a kind of permanent long run interest rate and that not all short-run variations in the interest rate are expected to feed into the permanent interest rate. Note for example the period from late 1997 to late 1998. During this period the real after-tax interest rate more than doubled, while house prices only dipped a little bit down before they continued rising. The reason for this is that nobody really believed in December 1998 that the interest rate had risen permanently.[4] Income growth and the internal dynamics of house prices probably also smoothed the path of house prices over the period with high interest rates.

House prices are far higher in the Oslo metropolitan area than they are in the rest of the country. NOU (2002) compare 'constant quality' price levels in Norwegian counties at the turn of the century with the price level in Oslo. The price level in Akershus was found to be 68 per cent of the Oslo-level. The vast majority[5] of the other counties had price levels ranging from a little bit below 40 per cent to 50 per cent of the Oslo-level.

[4] Note that fixed interest loans are not very frequent in Norway.

[5] The lowest prices were found in the most Northern counties where the price level was about 30 per cent of the Oslo-level.

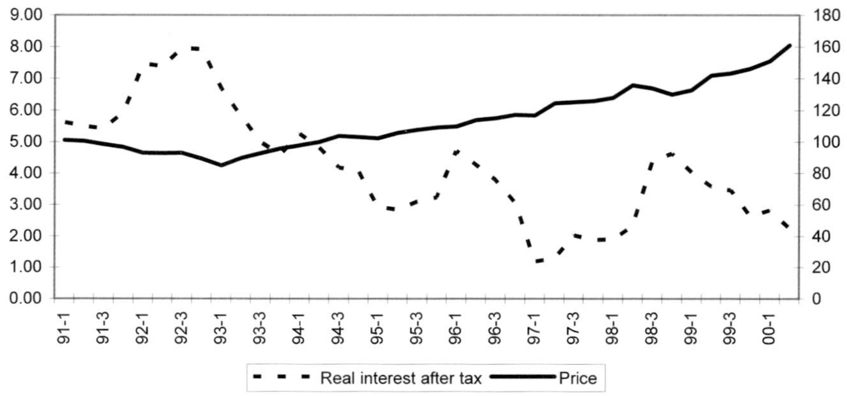

Fig. 8.9. Real house prices and real interest rates after tax (Source: Statistics Norway)

The price gap has been widened over the period analysed here. In Fig. 8.10 the nominal price development from 1991 up to 2001 is illustrated. The Norwegian housing market is spilt up in three: Oslo, Akershus and the rest of Norway. Prices are normalised to equal 100 at the start of 1991 in each of the 'regions'. Consequently the figure can only be used to compare price development, not price levels. It is clearly seen that prices has increased far strongest in Oslo, while also Akershus has had a stronger growth than the rest of the country.

As clearly documented above house prices in the Oslo metropolitan area are high and they have been growing at an extremely high rate for many years. So what are the consequences for the consumers? The answers to these questions vary over different groups, and they depend strongly on the time horizon.

The public report on housing markets and policy defines a high housing-expense-to-income-after-tax ratio to be a ratio in excess of 25 per cent. Using this benchmark they find that 50 per cent of the households in the Oslo metropolitan area have a high housing-expenses-to-income ratio. It would have been more informative if we had been able to report more information on the distribution of the expense ratios.

Based only on the level of house prices we can, however, claim that most households, who have bought their first housing unit in the Oslo metropolitan area over the last couple of years probably, have a stressed economic position. By a stressed economic position we simply mean that they have high housing expenses. On the other hand, it might be that such first time buyers are laying down a fundament for a future healthy economic position. At least this is true for those who bought a housing unit some five years ago. Because of the rapid increase of house prices, many households have experienced negative user costs because of quite high non-realised capital gains during the last few years. During this period, an owner-occupied housing unit (or a co-op) in the Oslo metropolitan area has really been a 'wealth-machine'.

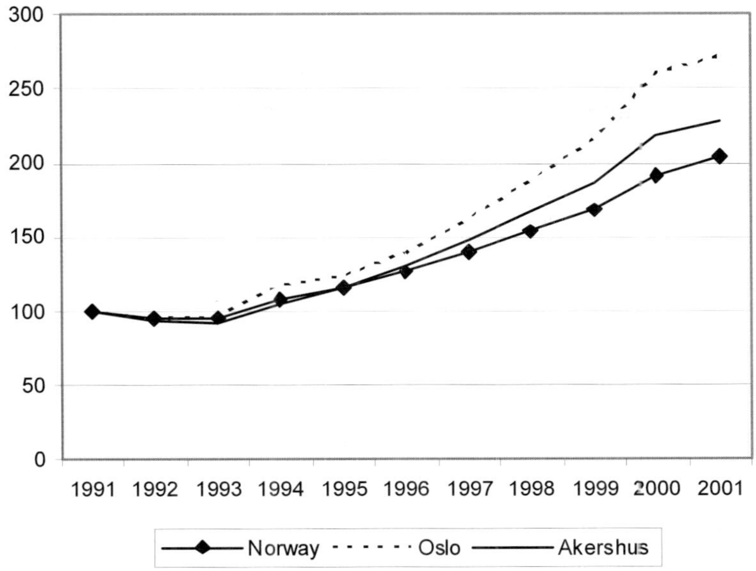

Fig. 8.10. Development of nominal house prices in the Oslo metropolitan area and the rest of Norway 1991–2001 (Source: Medby 2002)

Another noteworthy feature of the Oslo metropolitan housing market is the change of relative prices, see Medby (2002). In 1991 the price of a small housing unit in Oslo was 45.5 per cent of the price of a large unit. Ten years later the price ratio had increased and the price of the small unit was 55.7 per cent of the price of the large housing unit. Hence the price of entering the owner segments of the Oslo metropolitan housing market seems to have risen. The price of taking the next step in a housing career within the housing market has, at least relatively, fallen.

The widening of the gap between house prices in the Oslo and the rest of Norway may have consequences for both the rate of immigration to the area and for the economic position and welfare of entrants to the housing market. Think of a family from, say, North-Norway which considers moving to the metropolitan region. They can sell, say, a single-family house in North-Norway and collect a price of approximately 850,000 NOK. At the market for family units in Oslo they will compete with Oslo-households taking the next step of their housing career. The Oslo households might for example sell their two-room unit for a price of 1,500,000 NOK. This of course affects the competition between insiders and outsiders in the Oslo metropolitan housing market.

8.7 The Oslo Metropolitan Rental Housing Market

Before turning to the Oslo metropolitan rental housing market, some comments on the composition of the Norwegian rental housing market should be given. Even though more than 20 per cent of the Norwegian households are tenants, we have virtually no stock of more permanent rental housing! A very small part of the housing stock is constructed as rental housing and remains in the rental sector throughout its life span. Rather, the rental sector in Norway consists of presently rented units that tomorrow can enter the stock of owner-occupied housing.

Probably less than 25 per cent of all the rented dwellings in Norway can be classified as permanent rental housing units. The rest consists of presently rented units that can easily and immediately be transformed into owner-occupied housing. The tenure flexibility of the rented housing stock of course has serious consequences for the working of the Norwegian rental housing market.

Based on information from the Survey of Housing Conditions of Norway 1995, we can show the composition of the rented housing stock in Norway and the Oslo metropolitan area. The rental sector of Oslo and Akershus differs. Despite of this and because of the sample sizes we have chosen to aggregate the Oslo metropolitan housing market in Table 8.5.

Traditional professional landlords play a far more important role in the Oslo metropolitan rental housing market than in the rest of Norway. Despite of this, they do not play a quantitatively important role in the Oslo metropolitan housing market.

Table 8.5. Composition of the rental housing market (per cent of rented units in 1995)

	Oslo metropolitan	Norway
Secondary units in single-family houses	24.0	26.1
Other extra units owned by private households	36.5	42.3
Public social rental units	12.8	13.4
Professional landlords	18.4	9.8
Publicly owned for own employees	5.3	5.3
Privately owned for own employees	3.0	2.6
Sum	100.0	100.0
Number in thousands	94.0	418.0

Source: Survey of Housing Conditions 1995.

About one of four rented units is a secondary unit in a single-family house. Most of the secondary units in the Oslo metropolitan area can be found in Akershus, but they are also found in Oslo. These units can be included as part of the main unit whenever the owner needs it and can afford it. This is not only a hypothetical possibility. A very large part of the owners of single-family houses where such an additional unit is present lets it in periods and uses it for her own purposes in other periods. The decision to let or not is affected by stage in the life cycle of the owner household and by economic considerations. In addition: many owners who do not let say that they would consider letting ‘if somebody we know needs a rental unit’.

The most frequent type of rented dwellings is found in the category 'other extra units owned by private households'. In this category one finds many different types of landlords. Here we have households with a temporal absence from their own housing unit and we have dwellings that the owner plans to use for her own purposes some time in the future. In some cases one can say that an extra dwelling is kept not because the owner knows that she will use the unit herself in the future, but because she wants to keep the option to use it. In addition, we have households who for pure investment purposes buy, or keep, a unit for letting. What makes this different from the traditional landlord is that they typically own one unit in a house of condominiums. In Oslo there have been complaints that some houses of condominiums in reality have been transformed to a rental house. The fact that each of the units in the house has its own landlord makes administration and operating of the unit difficult. Unfortunately, we do not have information on the exact composition of this part of the rental market.

In many ways both the Norwegian rental market in general, and more specifically the Oslo metropolitan rental market are personal rental markets where ability and willingness to pay are not the only assets needed to find a rental unit. Also personal networks can be important. There are some indications that this structure causes difficulties for housing demanders of non-Western origin.

Statistical information on rent levels in Norway is very weak. Based upon data from different surveys rent levels for rented units with two rooms in different parts of Norway were calculated for the state committee writing their public report on housing markets and policy. Table 8.6 reports the results of this.

Table 8.6. Monthly rents of two-room flats

	1995	1997	2001
Oslo	3 219	4 048	6 443
Villages	2 930	2 549	2 975
Sparsely populated areas	2 422	2 731	3 126

As the table reveals, rent levels have increased very strongly over the period from 1995 to 2001. The rent level in Oslo is more than two times higher than the rent level in the rest of the country.

8.8 Some Policy Issues

In this chapter the focus has been on the workings of the Oslo metropolitan housing market and the housing conditions of the population. Many aspects of housing policy in the metropolitan area have consequently been suppressed. Some of them are briefly commented on in this last part.

From the late seventies and onwards a quite large inner city rehabilitation programme has been carried out. Grants have been given to rehabilitation of low quality housing and to development private and public outdoor areas. In many ways the programme has succeeded. The frequency of really low quality housing has been sharply reduced, also the development of house prices shows that the relative attractively of these areas has been improved. (The question of whether this has been done in a cost efficient way however remains to be settled). But there is still more to be done and the programme is not ended. As a part of the rehabilitation process many former rental properties has been transformed to condominiums or co-ops.

The backside of the urban renewal programme is of course that the most inexpensive parts of the housing stock have been upgraded and made more expensive. This has had consequences for segregation and concentration of low-income households. There has probably been a movement where many low-income groups have moved away from the city centre towards the northern and south-eastern suburban areas of Oslo. As the frequency of low income is larger among households of non-western, origin this statement probably also applies for these groups.

Rental housing units set up before 1940 were rent regulated up to year 2000. After this the regulation of rents has been gradually lifted. However, the rent-regulated units have not for many years played any quantitatively major role in the Oslo metropolitan rental market. Furthermore, as a result of the inner city renewal programme, a large share of the previously regulated rental properties is now transformed into co-ops and condominiums.

Oslo municipality is currently working on plans for redevelopments of some former industrial areas for housing purposes. This applies to the area of a former national hospital and the harbour area. A political desire to make the regulation processes work more smoothly has also been expressed. The ambition of this is to reduce the time lags in new construction.

References

Capozza D, Helsley RW (1990) The Stochastic City. Journal of Urban Economics 28: 187–203

Medby P (2002) Prisutviklingen for Selveide Boliger – En Empirisk Analyse av Perioden 1991–2000 [Price Development of Owner-occupied Housing Units – An Empirical Analysis of the Period 1991–2001]. Prosjektrapport 323, Norges byggforskningsinstitutt

Miles D (1994) Housing, Financial Markets and the Wider Economy. John Wiley & Sons Inc., New York

Nordvik V (1995) Prices and Price Expectations in the Market for Owner Occupied Housing. Housing Studies 10(3): 365–80

Nordvik V (2000) Utilisation of the Stock of Owner Occupied Single Family Houses – An Econometric Analysis. Urban Studies 37(7): 1171–83

Nordvik V (2001) Analysis of Rental Housing Markets: Five Essays. Prosjektrapport 295, Norges byggforskningsinstitutt

NOU 2002:2 Boligmarkedene og Boligpolitikken. Oslo

Poterba JM (1984) Tax Subsidies to Owner-occupied Housing. An Asset Market Approach Quarterly Journal of Economics 99: 729–52

Rothenberg J, Galster G, Butler RV, Pitkin JR (1991) The Maze of Urban Housing. University of Chicago Press, Chicago

Smith L, Rosen K, Fallis G (1988) Recent Developments in Economic Models of Housing Markets. Journal of Economic Literature XXVI: 29–64

9 The Milan Housing Market

Roberto Camagni[1] and Dino Martellato[2]

[1] Milan Technical University, Milan
[2] University of Venice Ca Foscari, Venice

9.1 Introduction

Segmentation is definitely the main characteristic of housing markets and the case of Milan is no exception. We must necessarily start looking at the territorial structure of the Milan metropolitan area, which essentially coincides with the province, by focusing the relation between the changes intervening in real estate prices and population dynamics. In doing this we not only get confirmation that there are significant differences between the different zones of the metropolitan area, but also that the recoveries of the city centre in terms of population translates into relatively larger prices increases. Although the same is occurring in other large Italian cities, Milan retains a kind of leadership over the rest of the country as it still shows some lead and a stronger cyclical behaviour.

There are other obvious distinctions and segments worth examining, besides the internal horizontal differentiation. The separation between the property market – relatively large in Milan – and the rental market (relatively small) is an obvious example. The separation between new and old housing space and the distinction between private and public housing are equally important examples. From this perspective, Milan is not very different from many other large Italian cities as the share of restructured space is comparatively large and the availability of public housing definitely small. Where the comparison between Milan and other Italian cases proves interesting is in the level and the time profile of housing prices, costs, yields and rents. In Milan the cycle leads the average one and price oscillations are comparatively larger than elsewhere.

The disparities across different Italian cities mirror differences which are both internal to the metropolitan area and external to it. What interests most is the cyclical behaviour of housing prices and rents. As price changes impinge on the propensity to invest and the willingness to hold housing property, it seems worthwhile to look closely at the current price recovery and, in particular, at the role of price expectations in the real estate market. The case of Milan could again foreshadow something which is going to occur elsewhere. There is evidence of diffused systematic errors in price expectations showing that investors form them more by extrapolating current prices than by looking at relation between the fundamental relation which ought to exist between price and rent. Milan looks different from other large cities. The large housing ownership in Milan also seems to reflect a stronger advantage for owner-occupiers over renters. In this particular phase, the uneven recovery of housing prices reveals that investors see the housing equity as a safe haven, i.e. a low risk-asset able to out perform both high-risk equities and low-yield government bonds. It seems safe to argue that the recovery is better fuelled where the pressure coming from the demand side is higher, as is probably the case in Milan.[1]

9.2 Basic Features of the Housing Market

Durable, immobile and expensive goods supply housing services. The services are differentiated as houses are supposed to be bundles of joint intrinsic qualities and neighbourhood features. Housing prices certainly reflect different mixes of those characteristics and, at the same time, a common or market trend. Because of their changes, housing values are more similar to those of assets than those of final goods and services, rents included. On average, the changes in market values seem to be greater in the larger metropolitan areas, such as Milan. Changes are not the same in the different zones of any metropolitan area. While some of the qualities and features of houses are impossible to alter, others are simply expensive to change, particularly in historical cities. This is why observed changes in prices can be explained more by the presence of rationing phenomena and expectations dynamics than by fluctuations in those characteristics, particularly in cities where net investment adds little to the existing stock.

Other aspects of the housing market are worth noting. There are obvious construction lags and an equally obvious rigidity in supply, which may add to price instability. The rigidity of supply is compounded by the fact that what we call the housing market is a rather abstract concept. Indeed, many tiny and loosely related sub-markets exist in any single metropolitan area. In the case of Milan, the fashion district, for instance, has average prices and dynamics which cannot be easily compared to those of other residential zones. Although it is possible to think about a common trend of a metropolitan area, there are obvious differences in different segments of the same area. In Milan, for instance, although the last market slump brought about a price contraction larger than that at national level, the fashion district did not share the same price fall.

Besides the obvious geographical segmentation, any urban housing market is formed by a property market where developers and investors supply a quantity of

[1] This chapter is the result of a common research project of the two authors. Sects. 3 and 4 have been written by R Camagni while the others have been contributed by D Martellato.

housing space. In the case of many Italian cities, new additions are rather limited both from the qualitative and the quantitative points of view. A further useful distinction is that between new and restructured housing. The geographical segmentation is also important. The housing market of the municipality of Milan is formed by a number of zones: around the city centre there is a ring divided into seven radial sectors, all of which are served by the underground railway network. The metropolitan area embraces a large number of medium and small-size municipalities around Milan and almost coincides with the province.[2] Like many other large Italian cities, Milan underwent a suburbanisation phase lasting thirty years, during which the population slowly moved from the central districts to the periphery as well as towards the smaller towns of the metropolitan zone and the province as well.[3]

One distinctive feature of old industrial cities is the presence of abandoned old industrial and commercial sites. In Milan, some of these sites have been renovated and have now become service or residential areas. More than 20 business areas have been realised in the last few years and others are being created. They spread from the seven radial zones of Milan to its outer periphery and further out towards the municipalities surrounding the city.

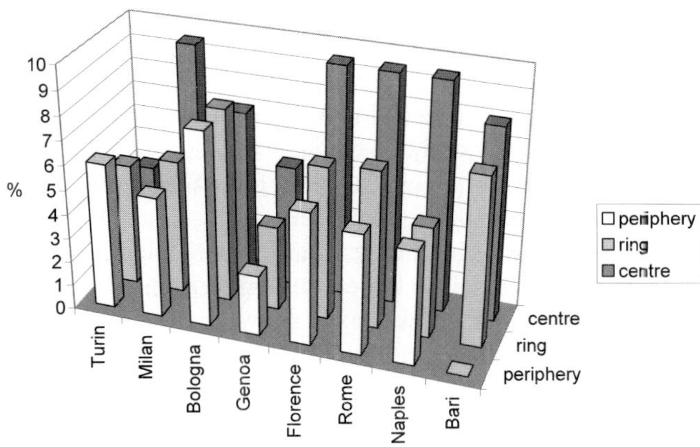

Fig. 9.1. Average rate of change of housing prices in large Italian cities 2000–01

The residential choices of the population, the new business areas and infrastructure investments have introduced new complexities into the hierarchical structure of the metropolitan housing market. The profiles of rents and values, as usual, give an indication of the spatial hierarchy and the intrinsic residential quality of different zones. Fig. 9.1 shows the changes in average market values in a number of Italian cities. It shows how different are the dynamics of market values as only

[2] In the next section the municipalities around Milan will be divided in two rings.
[3] This aspect will be dealt with in the next paragraph.

Milan, Florence Rome, Naples and, to a certain extent, also Genoa, show a clear advantage of the city centre over the periphery. This indicates how across-the-board differences could be cancelled out by simple city averages.

9.3 Population Dynamics and Location

In terms of urban life-cycle, the metropolitan area of Milan has experienced a process of suburbanisation since the 1970s. With the exception of a few single years, in which the growth of the external rings was not able to overcome the demographic loss of the core, in general it is possible to affirm that Milan never really experienced a process of disurbanisation (cf. Camagni 1985): the total metro area, approximately defined by the Milan province, never declined in terms of total population for long periods.

In the two decades following the end of the World War II, suburbanisation happened with respect to the municipalities located in the northern part of the metro area, but the central city was still increasing its population (what is called 'relative' suburbanisation); but during the 1970s it started losing population to the benefit of the hinterland and other provinces in the Lombardy area.

In recent years (1993–2001: see Table 9.1), the population of the metro area increased by 1 per cent. This overall rate resulted from a decrease of 2.44 per cent in the city centre and an increase of 3 per cent in the hinterland. It is interesting to note that the northern part of the first ring, which encompassed the first suburbanisation of the 1950s and 1960s and represents nowadays a continuous conurbation with respect to the centre[4], followed the same reduction trend (–1.27 per cent in the 1993–2001 period), while the southern part of the first ring and the entire second ring grew substantially. This process can be seen clearly in Fig. 9.2, which show growth rates by municipality: the entire northern ring drops, similarly to the central city, while some radial growth axes show up along some main corridors, such as the north-eastern one (served by a metro line), the south-eastern one (towards Cremona) and the south-western one (towards Pavia).

The demographic decrease of the central city was determined both by a negative natural balance, of above 5,000 persons a year until 1998 – due to an ageing population – and by a negative migration balance (about 10,000 persons a year in the early 1990s). But in most recent years this almost structural condition changed: since 1999 the yearly death-birth balance fell below the –5,000 persons mark, thanks to the higher fertility rate of foreign immigrants and apparently also to signs of an increasing fertility rate among the indigenous population; since 1997 the immigration balance has turned to a positive sign (with the exception of 1999). In 2000, for the first time in thirty years, the population in the centre actually increased: a rise of only 500 inhabitants. As is shown in Table 9.1, total decrease in population amounted to only –0.18 per cent during the period 1996–2001, in line with the general recovery of the local economy.

[4] See the map in Fig. 9.1, showing urban densities in the Milan metropolitan area in 2001.

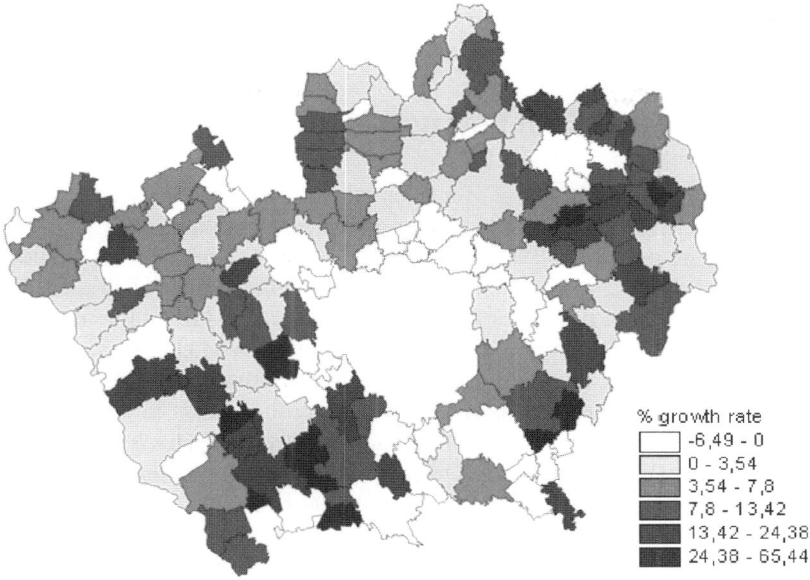

Fig. 9.2. Growth rates by municipalities 1993–2001 (per cent)

Table 9.1. Population growth rates

	Population growth rate [%]		
	1993–2001	1993–1996	1996–2001
Milan municipality	–2.44	–2.27	–0.18
First ring north	–1.27	–0.47	–0.81
First ring south	2.59	1.27	1.31
First ring	0.31	0.25	0.07
Second ring north	3.74	1.18	2.54
Second ring south	4.77	1.71	3.01
Second ring	3.93	1.27	2.62
Hinterland (total)	3.01	1.01	1.98
Total metropolitan area	1.06	–0.16	1.22

In all probability, a new cycle of urbanisation has started, very different from the preceding one. As before, the attractiveness of the centre lies in its economic and employment performance, with the financial, communication and 'new economy' sectors leading in relative terms and mainly seeking a 'central' location. But unlike previous years, the advantages of suburbanisation are no longer so clear. Congestion of the outer rings is substantial, increasing and probably higher than that of the central city; real estate price differentials between centre and periphery of the metro area have shrunk substantially, as consequence of the crisis of the sector in the early 1990s in the city centre and of the rise in suburban prices; an explicit policy of relaunching residential construction in the municipality of Milan started in the late 1990s and is now beginning to give some early results.

9.4 Residential Real Estate Prices: Structure and Trends

Let us now turn to the analysis of residential real estate prices, which may be seen as both cause and effect of the location preferences of populations.

Purchase prices in the 1993–2001 period were collected for the central zones and the peripheral zones of each of the 186 municipalities of the metropolitan area, and an average price was calculated in each case. The source is the real estate bulletin 'Borsa Immobiliare' of the Milan Chamber of Commerce.

In the last two decades, real estate prices in the municipality of Milan followed a similar cycle with respect to all major metropolitan cities in Europe (Camagni and Gibelli 1996): in particular, they boomed after the launch of the European Single Market Project in 1985 in Delor's White Paper, as a consequence of a policy of anticipation of its effects by multinational firms and their strategy of locating headquarters in the main international 'gateways' of European countries. Office rental values in particular rose substantially, generating a boom in office construction and a parallel rise in residential values. All this came to an end in 1992–93, with the economic slump that followed eight years of continuous and strong economic growth, the crisis of over-production in office space, the exchange rate crisis in countries such as Italy and Spain.

The cumulative rise in prices in the centre (we cannot speak about a 'speculative bubble' as in the Japanese case) suddenly stopped, but its effects on the suburbanisation of population were relevant (as we saw in the preceding section).

In this chapter, we concentrate on the 1993–2001 period, encompassing the slump and the recovery of Milan's economy and of its real estate market.

In Table 9.2 the ratio between residential real estate prices (Italian lire per sqm) in the central city and in each ring is computed for both central location and peripheral locations. In this way, any problem of comparing absolute values in time is overcome, and ratios are perfectly comparable. In Table 9.3 the growth rates of prices are nevertheless computed: the interest in this case lies mainly in the direction of changes and in a comparative reading of data among the different subareas.

As far as central locations are concerned, prices in Milan in 2001 are three times higher (200 per cent) than prices in the first ring, and 3.75 times higher than in the second ring. In peripheral areas of the single municipalities, on average, the difference is much smaller: 20 per cent higher in Milan with respect to the first ring and 50 per cent higher with respect to the second. The northern part of the metro area shows higher prices than the southern.

It is interesting to note that the slump in residential prices (in central zones) that happened in the first sub-period 1993–96 was substantial for the core city (–21 per cent) and the first southern ring (–0.96 per cent, see Table 9.3). For the other rings and in particular for the entire northern part of the metro area it resulted only in limited growth rates of prices. In the case of the Milan municipality, the subsequent recovery (+25 per cent) was not sufficient to overcome the previous slump, and average price levels are still lower in absolute terms than in 1993.

Table 9.2. Residential real estate prices: ratio Milan/Rings

	City centre prices 1993	1996	2001	Periphery prices 1996	2001
First ring north	3.50	2.58	2.78	1.16	1.11
First ring south	3.48	2.78	3.18	1.26	1.28
First ring	3.49	2.68	2.99	1.22	1.20
Second ring north	4.57	3.26	3.67	1.44	1.45
Second ring south	5.16	3.57	4.00	1.54	1.55
Second ring	4.73	3.34	3.76	1.46	1.48

Table 9.3. Growth rates of residential real estate prices in Milan metropolitan area (per cent)

	City centre 1993–96	1996–01	1993–01	Periphery 1996–01
Milan municipality	–21.02	25.44	–0.93	13.44
First ring north	6.99	16.42	24.56	19.05
First ring south	–0.96	9.64	8.58	11.77
First ring	3.00	12.40	15.77	15.04
Second ring north	10.92	11.18	23.33	12.63
Second ring south	14.38	11.70	27.76	12.09
Second ring	11.82	11.31	24.46	12.44

As a consequence of these trends, the ratio of land prices (the reference is still to central zones) between Milan and the different rings fell quickly between 1993 and 1996. Although it subsequently rose again, it has remained in all cases significantly lower than in 1993.

These trends have a double economic meaning. On the one hand, they show the relative superior strength of demand for suburban locations with respect to locations in the centre, in particular in the first sub-period. On the other, they show that the locational advantage of the hinterland – at least as far as relative prices of residential estates are concerned – shrank considerably during the last decade, in particular with reference to the first northern ring – the northern Milanese conurbation – and the second northern ring. This fact would explain in past the return to the city centre (or at least its demographic re-equilibrium) in the last two or three years that we have mentioned in the previous section.

If we look at maps depicting both price levels and price growth rates for central and peripheral zones in each municipality, we can see the following elements, which confirm what was previously stated:

- Average prices for central zones in Milan reached 8.16 millions lire (€4,200) in 2001, while the highest prices in the hinterland were in the northern conurbation, encompassing the large municipality of Monza, where they ranged from 2.8 million and 4 million (€1,500 to €2,000 respectively); in most of the other municipalities prices for central zones ranged from 2 to 2.8 million (€1,000–€1,450) (Fig. 9.3).
- Average prices in peripheral zones are much more similar in the central and north eastern part of the metro area, ranging from 2.3 to 3 million, including the Milan municipality (Fig. 9.4).
- Growth rates for the entire 1993–2001 period show that Milan and Monza experienced a reduction in land prices in central zones (Fig. 9.5), resulting from a substantial fall between 1993 and 1996 and a lower subsequent recovery for Milan and an opposite trend – increase first and slump subsequently – for Monza (maps for sub periods are not included).
- If one excludes Monza, almost all northern municipalities experienced a rise in prices for central zones in both sub periods; southern municipalities on average saw a rise in central prices only in the second sub-period.
- Prices for peripheral zones are available only for the second sub-period 1996–2001, and show a similar or higher increase with respect to Milan in the majority of municipalities.

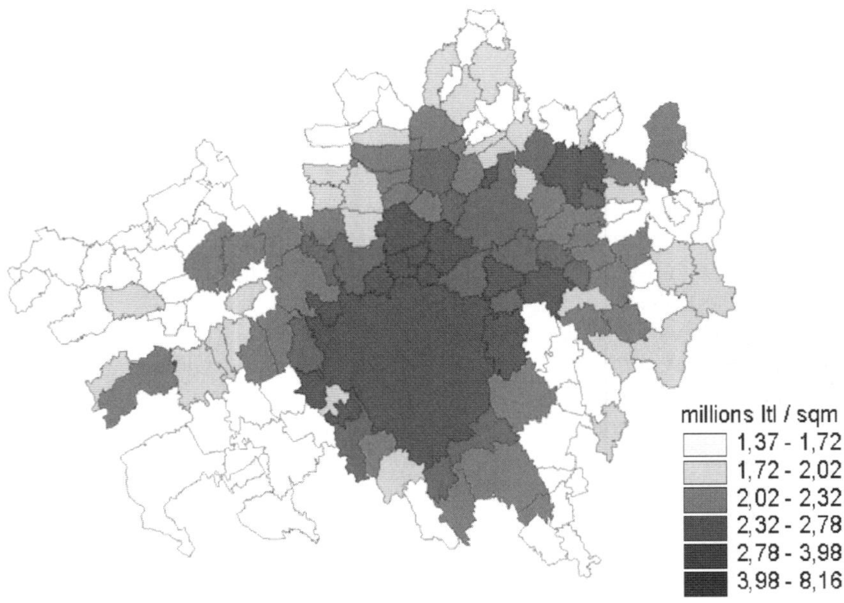

Fig. 9.3. Residential real estate prices 2001 city centre (million lire/sqm)

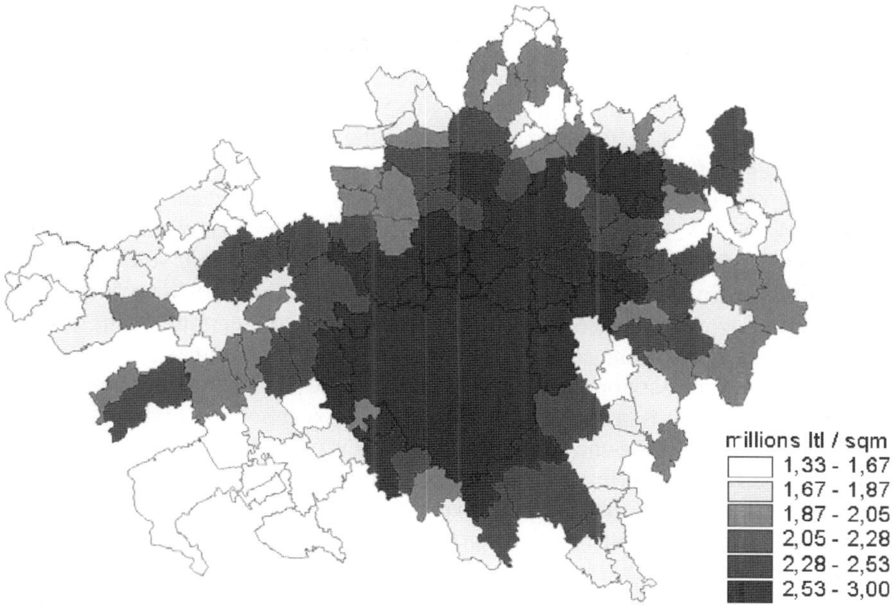

Fig. 9.4. Residential real estate prices 2001 periphery (million lire/sqm)

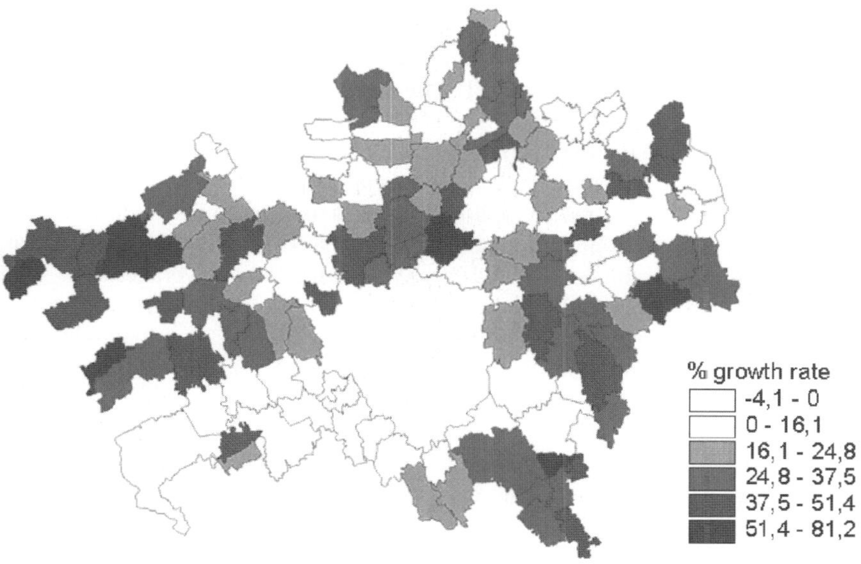

Fig. 9.5. Growth rates of real estate prices 1993–2001 city centre (per cent)

9.5 House Ownership

There are two aspects involved in tenure choice. The decision of the saver to buy a house rather than other financial assets, or vice versa, is a portfolio decision, i.e. a decision which should be taken on the basis of the mean returns of the different assets and their statistical variance. Rational investors need worry only about these two aspects and will prefer the asset that offers the highest mean return for the level of risk they prefer. It is debatable, however, whether this principle reflects how house owners behave. First of all, savers who decide to hold some housing equity in his portfolio are also consumers and if they are looking for a home and can afford to buy, the decision to be house-owners will, to a certain extent, be biased by the fact that housing services satisfy one of their primary needs.

There are also transaction costs. Will rational house-owners reduce their housing equity holdings at times when house prices are exceptionally high in relation to the rate of return and bound to decline? No, this is not usually the case. Indeed, there is evidence that during a cyclic slowdown or recession investors become more risk averse and look for a safe heaven. As the housing market often moves in a counter-cyclical way, just like the mortgage interest rate, equity setbacks bring property back into fashion. Investors tend to extrapolate price increases and invest more when prices are on the up as they cling to property. They often forget that on all assets, property included, the rate of return cannot permanently diverge from the fundamental value and when market values go up as a consequence of a price surge, it eventually will revert to the mean.[5] Owners will sell neither during a price surge, particularly if they are owner-occupiers and if transaction costs are high, nor during phases of low prices. The above is particularly true for real investors, i.e. for investors who buy houses not for personal use. To own more housing space than required for personal needs implies that owners rent out. This is the case where the owner is a real investor. The decision of the consumer to own, instead of renting, is clearly a consumption decision.

The province of Milan appears to be relatively ahead of the other large Italian metropolitan areas as regards house ownership. Fig. 9.6 shows that the ratio of owners to inhabitants is rather high and, in particular, is higher than that of any other large Italian metropolitan area, except Genoa. House ownership in the large metropolitan areas, with few exceptions, exceeds the Italian average. How should these figures and, in particular, the position of Milan be interpreted?

There is a vast literature (see, for instance Henderson and Ioannides 1983; Rosen 1985; Mills and Hamilton 1994; Flavin and Yamashita 2002) indicating that many aspects, such as tax treatment of owner-occupied housing, transaction costs, rental externality and pride in ownership, put constraints on the individual's rational behaviour and distort investment and consumption choices. This explains the high ownership in general and also why the equilibrium rate of utilisation of housing stock for owners is lower than that for renters.

---

[5] These technical aspects are briefly considered in the final section, where a simple model of the housing market is presented.

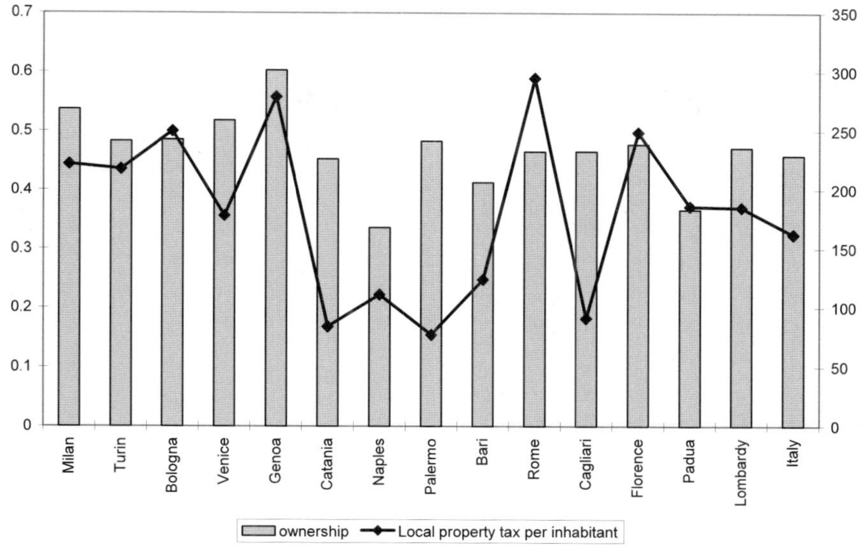

Fig. 9.6. Ownership and local property tax in large Italian cities 2001

Another implication of the tenure choice is that the equilibrium level of housing stock is higher than the optimal level from the portfolio point of view. On the basis of Italian data, Weber and Pelizzon (2002) found that diversified portfolios (housing included) are not mean-variance efficient. They found, however, that diversified portfolios (i.e. portfolios able to hedge the risks connected with the illiquid housing investment) are mean-variance efficient in many cases (from 1/2 to 1/3 of the total).

The main determinants of tenure choice are the advantages or disadvantages of owning and the sharing of the cost of utilisation between owners and renters. It is generally assumed that the owner-occupier pays lower taxes than pure owners. The owner, however, bears transaction costs that are higher than those charged to the renter. The owner consequently has a low propensity to change his location. The high owner-occupancy rate that can be observed in Italy may also account for the observed low average spatial mobility of Italian workers.

The owner who rents, furthermore, charges a high rent in order to recover not only the financial opportunity cost but also the cost of utilisation not directly covered by the tenant.

A high rate of owner-occupancy should not be directly interpreted as an indication of the overvaluation of the advantages of owning and the effects of distortions and biases. It should probably be considered as an indication that people correctly perceive the relative convenience of owner-occupancy in comparison to renting. At the same time, the low rate of rental housing should be interpreted as an indication of a correct perception of the low profitability of housing investments.

Mills and Hamilton (1994 p. 233) report that about 65 per cent of Americans were owner-occupiers in the early 1990s while the ownership rate for the inhabitants of Milan was 55 per cent in 2001 (Fig. 9.6). As usual, space introduces a complication. The single units forming the housing stock of a metropolitan area or city can obviously be owner-occupied or rented. However, the inhabitants normally own the stock of houses of a specific city only in part as some people own houses in more than one city. There are then four possibilities: some houses are owned-occupied by local inhabitants while some others are owned-occupied by people who are not inhabitants. This is the case of holiday homes or business property. By the same token, some renters are inhabitants while some others are not, as individuals may own or rent houses outside the city where they live. To say that the inhabitants of Milan are owners does not necessarily mean that 55 per cent of the houses in Milan are owner-occupied.

9.6 The Property Market

Market values are seldom constant. As with the price of any other asset, house prices are unstable and the experience amply shows that the housing market is even prone to bubbles. This is a little surprising as housing stock is an intrinsically useful asset and only a small share of the stock is traded on the market. It is well known that in a dynamically inefficient economy, i.e. an economy where there is an over-accumulation of capital[6], there can be bubbles. It is rather interesting to understand why it is this and, in particular, what role prices play.

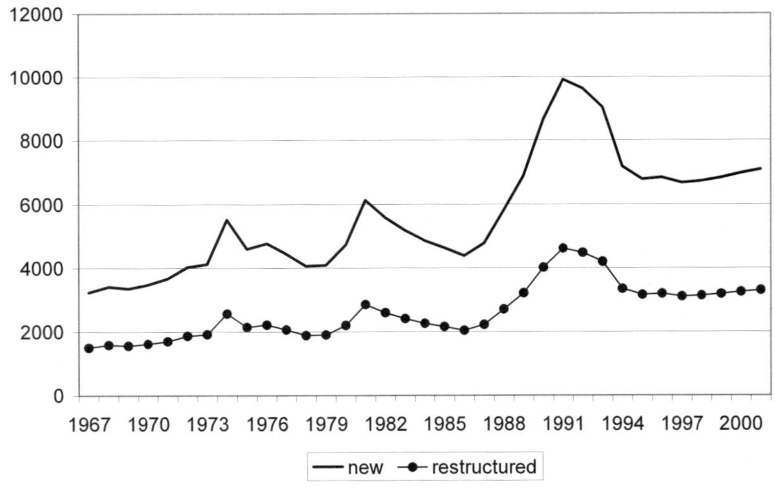

Fig. 9.7. Prices for new and restructured housing space at constant prices in Milan 1967–2001

[6] In such an economy, useful assets typically pay a dividend which does not grow at the same rate as the economy.

As Fig. 9.7 shows, Milan is no exception to the rule according to which a property market, like any other asset market, shows fluctuations in prices. The last five years have seen price fluctuations of increasing amplitude. Price fluctuations have large effects on the whole local economy from at least two different viewpoints. From one side, house ownership is large and entails a large wealth effect on consumption and a large effect on housing investment. In Italy more than 50 per cent of households (and more than 55 per cent in Milan) own a house. We have argued that this large ownership does not reflect a particularly high rate of return on housing equity as it reflects a kind of bias in favour of real estate investment, but, nevertheless, house property is considered as wealth. Aggregate consumption is held to be more sensitive to property valuation than to financial wealth and the instability of housing prices. From another viewpoint, the market value of the existing stock of houses feeds back on investment and thus on building sector activity and thus on aggregate demand. All this implies that the specific impact on the local economy of the metropolitan area of Milan underwent cyclical shocks larger than those of other metropolitan areas.

Housing prices obviously vary across space but it is easy to see that there is a common trend. Fig. 9.8 shows that price fluctuations from 1967 to 2001 in four selected metropolitan areas are clearly well-tuned even though the amplitude is not equal or even the same average level. Fig. 9.9 shows nominal market values in prime Italian property in a number of Italian metropolitan urban areas. In the data reported in Fig. 9.9, Milan emerges as the prime housing market in Italy. Unlike Fig. 9.8, Fig. 9.9 shows that there really is a common trend as the average price is up everywhere. The spatial variations at the level of the metropolitan area are strong, which mirrors a structural factor that can be related to dimension and rank. There is a common trend, but the variations at the very local level, i.e. inside a specific urban area, also reflect conditions in the neighbourhood.

Standard economic theory assumes that market equilibrium is reached whenever demand equals supply. In a typical Italian housing market, however, the market supply of new housing is a tiny fraction of the existing stock; nevertheless market demand and supply jointly determine the market value of the existing stock in any sub-market. Equilibrium implies that values are constant and the yield on the housing equity, which is simply the ratio between rent and the value of the house, is equal to the user's cost of one unit of capital.[7] There is no doubt that if the price equals the present value of future services or rents, irrespective of whether they are changing or not, the market is in equilibrium. However, this is a rare situation and the changes in prices may even be large. In the simple model of the final section it is shown that there can be equilibrium even in a market where prices are changing, if the owner's foresight is perfect. A commonly observed situation is that in which investors are particularly keen to invest in housing equity when prices are on the rise, irrespective of the market fundamentals. In doing so, investors increase prices, and also building costs, but prices will eventually revert to the mean. Historical evidence only serves to confirm the logical argument that, in the long run, no investment can deliver a return the growth of the economy.

[7] This is shown in the model presented at the end of the chapter.

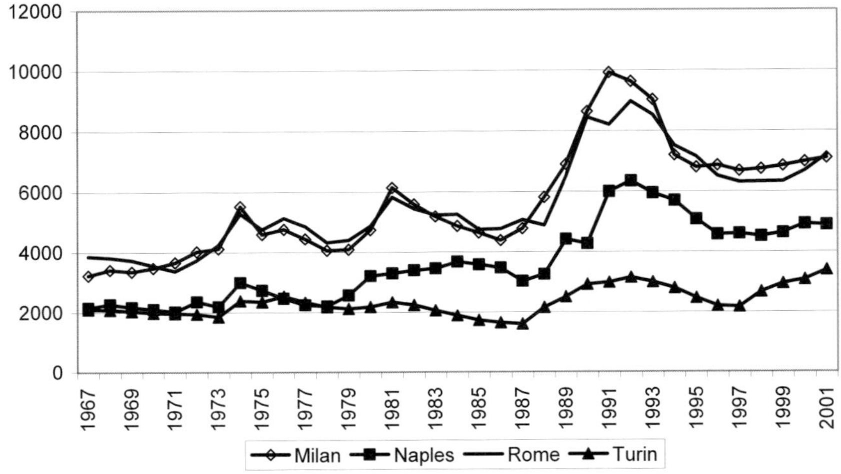

Fig. 9.8. Prices of new housing space at constant prices in four selected metropolitan areas 1967–2001

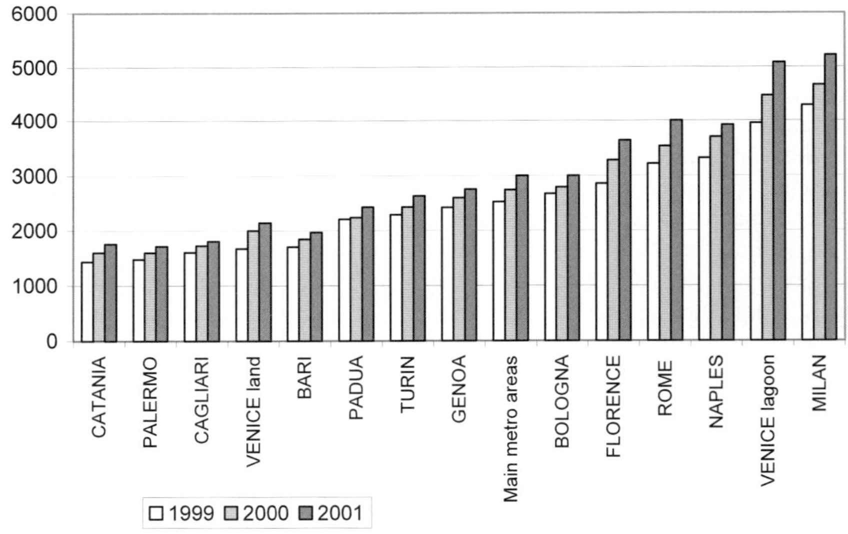

Fig. 9.9. Market values on prime housing property in large Italian cities 1999–2001

9.7 Shocks to the Housing Market

The preceding paragraph may be summarised by saying that equilibrium is an uncommon situation in the housing market not least because there is a diffuse misperception of market fundamentals. Equilibrium is definitely uncommon in the housing market as some net investment always takes place and some shocks always occur.

Shocks come from many sources and can be more or less permanent. Housing market fundamentals such as rents and the rates of return on competitive assets change in relation to the conditions prevailing in the rental market and in asset markets other than the housing market. General liquidity and credit conditions have an obvious impact on the mortgage market. Other shocks come from property and income taxation. Real estate investment may be the target of specific public policies. Public sales, for instance, represent an injection of housing space capable of altering the size of some segments of market supply. Other shocks come from changes in the urban structure, commercial centres, facilities, infrastructures and the derived demand for housing and commercial space. In brief, all the different elements entering the basic equilibrium condition between the yield and the user's cost of capital[8] can change.

The available statistical evidence suggests that, at least in the OECD countries, changes in real house prices appear to be closely correlated to business cycles. This is particularly visible in some Nordic countries, as well as in the United Kingdom, Canada, Germany and Spain over the period 1970–99 (OECD 2000 p. 171) and also France, Japan and Italy since 1980. To say that the housing market cycle is strongly influenced by the general business cycle is not equal to saying that the same is true for each sub-market of the building and real estate markets. Even the various segments of the housing market are affected differently by the common shock. Fig. 9.1, for instance, shows that different zones in different cities reacted in a very unequal way to the general conditions. It has been noted many times that housing price cycles appear to be driven by irrational expectations (Meese and Wallace 1994; Clayton 1997) as the housing market does not appear to be efficient.

The mechanism through which the effects of shocks are passed on to the market seems to be one according to which shocks induce some expected price changes and these changes, in turn, induce current demand and supply to change,[9] if individuals are not constrained by the credit market conditions. However, the high cost of investing in the real estate market implies that conditions prevailing in the credit and mortgage markets are able to influence actual market behaviour. In conclusion, it is likely that expectations are a major source of shocks if the market is not efficient in its ability to process information and prices. Ultimately, expectations, particularly those regarding the credit market conditions, govern the actual house market prices and this is why it is important to know how people form their expectations of change.

[8] See Eqs. 9.1 and 9.2 of the model presented at the end of the chapter.

[9] This is the logic of the model at the end of this section.

Supply and demand are sensitive to the state of the economy, but they interact in showing a strong internal cycle in asset prices. There is a partial symmetry: the cycle in asset markets, and particularly in the building sector, is represented by changes in the level of assets prices and in the level of investment, while the general business cycle is represented by the rate of inflation and the rate of real growth. As measured on the basis of housing prices, it can be said that there have been four complete building cycles, during the last forty years, in the main Italian urban areas (Fig. 9.8). By considering the housing sector alone, one finds the first peak in 1974. In constant 2001 Euro prices, the average price in Milan was then at about €2,000 per square metre. The second peak was in 1981 at about €6,000 and a third peak was in 1991 at about €10,000 per square metre. The market for both new and old housing bottomed again in 1997 and started to recover the following year. In April 2002 it neither peaked nor regained the level touched in 1991. This is particularly evident for the larger urban areas. Fig. 9.10 reports the price for the sub-market of new housing. As in the entire Italian market for new housing, the crisis was milder, and one could argue that the last crisis was rather concentrated in urban centres. It has always appeared to be difficult to tune supply to housing demand and the larger Italian urban areas, Milan included, are no exception to this rule.

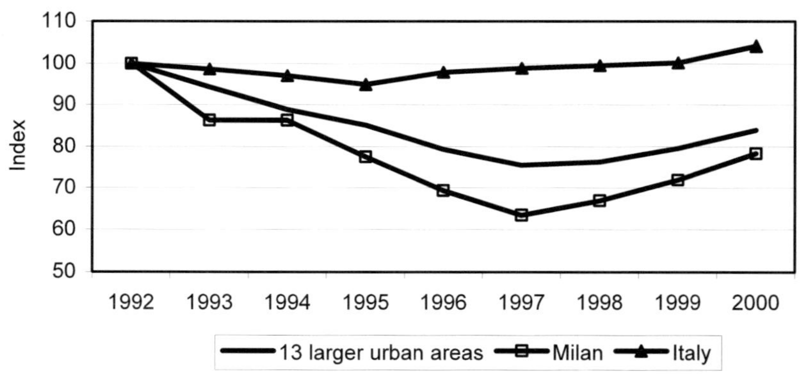

Fig. 9.10. Prices of new housing in Italy 1992–2000

9.8 Market Efficiency and Expectations

There is an obvious lack of information in real estate markets even though new technology has brought new possibilities. Investors and households now share an amount of information which is much larger than in the past. However, what really matters to participants is the market's efficiency in transferring it on to prices. From this point of view, the property markets are still not efficient as they are both illiquid and tiny. Transactions in each sub-market are likely to be few and not enough to make the market efficient in transferring available information on to prices. In this respect, they fall short of many other financial markets. The inefficiency of property markets is compounded by the inability of individuals to be forward-looking and, at the same time, correct in processing existing information on market fundamentals. This is a further element making current prices biased indicators of market fundamentals. In the simple model described in the final section of this chapter, it is shown that expectations are crucial in shaping market's behaviour. If individuals simply extrapolate current price changes, market equilibrium is unstable in the sense that any excess in current values over market fundamentals commands further price increases. Only if individuals are rational and correct in looking forward, do market values appear to be entirely based on market fundamentals.

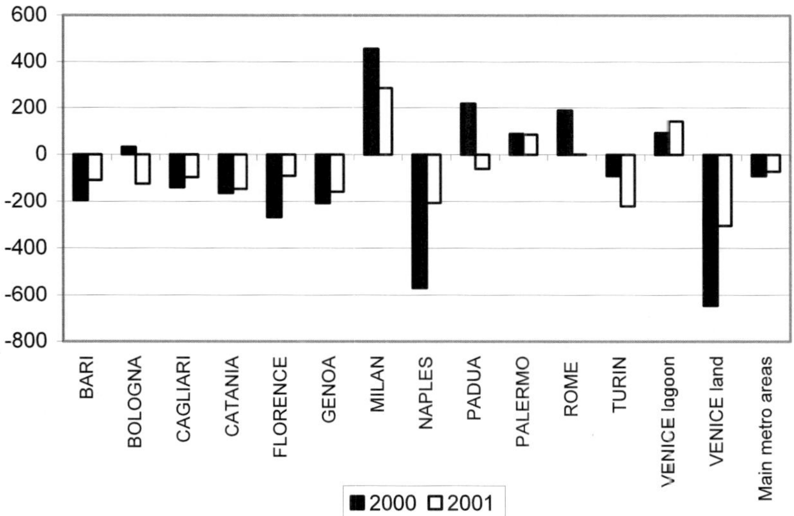

Fig. 9.11. Differences between expected and effective property values in large Italian cities 2000–2001

In Milan, and in all other large Italian metropolitan areas, prices have started to rebound in the late 1990s. Fig. 9.9 compares price changes in Milan to those of other Italian urban areas, showing how the price fluctuation is larger than elsewhere in Italy. The recent price surge is a general phenomenon (OECD 2000) and the statistical evidence which always shows large fluctuations in prices raises the problem of understanding whether the current price recovery is a further example of how expectations fail to fit market fundamentals. There is abundant statistical evidence showing that the housing market is a cyclical one. Usually property values rebound at the end of a cyclical and long recovery in the general business cycle and, more in general, when people see real estate as a safe haven and make prices rebound. If liquidity is abundant (as now), the initial price rise brings about a further increase in the expected capital gain and a rise in the current price.[10] An obviously simple way of looking of expectations is to compare effective market values to those implied by the expectations of one period earlier. In this way, one can assess the capability of housing markets to correctly anticipate any future price movements and the existence of errors. Fig. 9.11 indeed shows that there is a persistence in the sign of the errors. In many cases the error is negative, but lower in 2001 than in 2000. Milan, in particular, not only shows the largest percentage rate of price increase but also a systematic tendency to an over-valuation of housing space. Naples and Florence are in the opposite situation, as are many other metropolitan areas. If expectations were correct, the market value would reflect market fundamentals. The observed error and its systematic character can be interpreted as a confirmation of how current prices do not correctly reflect market fundamentals.

9.9 Housing Investment

Investment in financial assets representing real estate is becoming a real possibility. Stocks in building companies, investment funds holding stocks in real estate companies and, particularly, real estate investment trusts (REITs), are collecting the savings of an increasing number of households. Nonetheless, physical housing remains the favourite form of investment, at least in Italy. It is necessary to make a distinction between investments in houses to rent out and houses to be owner-occupied. In the latter case, the real motivation behind the decision to buy is not a pure portfolio decision. Investment in buying houses to be rented is different. From a statistical point of view it is worth noting that this form of investment is only a small share of overall housing investments, probably no higher than 10 per cent. Investment in commercial space is larger as it offers higher after-tax yields and lower transaction costs than those of housing space.

To make the investment profitable, the market value of new housing must be higher than the construction cost and usually the profitability is assessed by using the ratio between market values and the implicit residential investment deflator.[11] Investment in housing space to be sold or rented appears to be loosely associated to that indicator of profitability. In the last few years, construction has faced rising costs both in Italy and in Milan, but at the same time, market values have increased faster than costs (see Fig. 9.12).

The supply curve of the building sector in historical cities has not yet been carefully investigated. Is it steeper than the average one? If a given expansion of the sector's output caused a price rise of one or more than one of the many input factors of the building sector, then housing space supply would not be perfectly elastic, i.e. rising. This is the case where costs move with prices and thus in a pro-cyclical way. This is particularly true when people extrapolate current price

[10] See Eq. 9.5 in the last paragraph of this chapter.
[11] OECD 2000 p. 179.

changes, thus translating current changes into expected further changes and added demand. The new building activity triggers the price rise of inputs whose supply is not perfectly elastic thus yielding the increase housing prices. The larger part of market deals in historical cities comes from restructured space, which means that a market recovery shows up more in price increases than in volumes and implies a rising market value of old space. The statistical evidence seems to indicate that the assumption of a rising supply curve is a correct one as the correlation between market prices and building costs is quite striking in the case of Milan (Fig. 9.13).

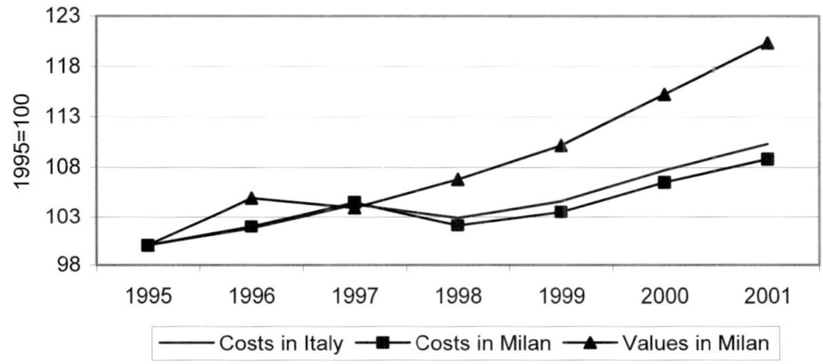

Fig. 9.12. Building costs of a residential building in Milan and in Italy 1995–2001, 1995 = 100

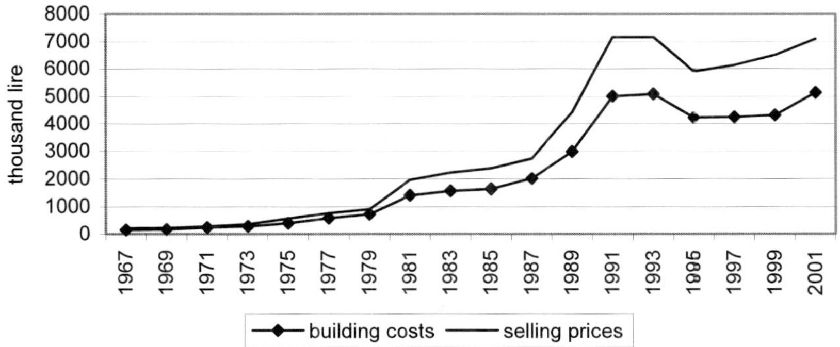

Fig. 9.13. Building costs and housing prices in Milan 1967–2001 (thousand lire)

The effects on the supply of new housing space in the municipality and the province of Milan is reported in Fig. 9.14, where it can be seen that the municipality has not suffered the slow-down of the province. There is an obvious and sizeable difference between the new and restructured components of the market supply as shown in Fig. 9.15 which is typical of Italian cities.

Fig. 9.16 compares the offered space to the bought space and shows that bought space grew faster than offered space even though prices were rising. A possible explanation could be one of a strong cyclical rise in demand attracted by expectations of a further price increase. As we will see later on, the demand surge is tempered neither by the rise in costs and market prices nor by the low after-tax yield on real-estate.

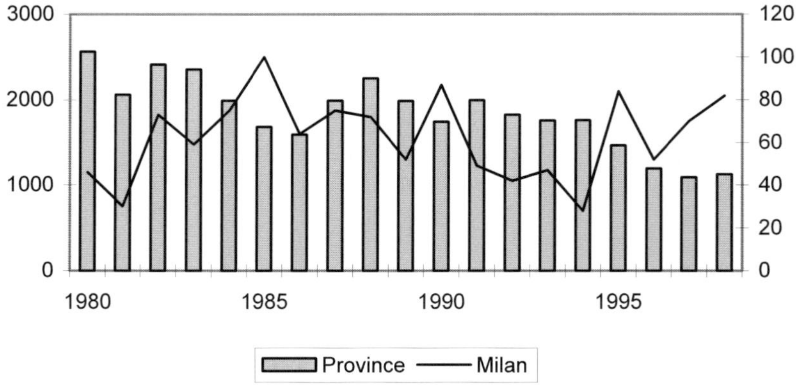

Fig. 9.14. New buildings in the province and municipality of Milan 1980–1998

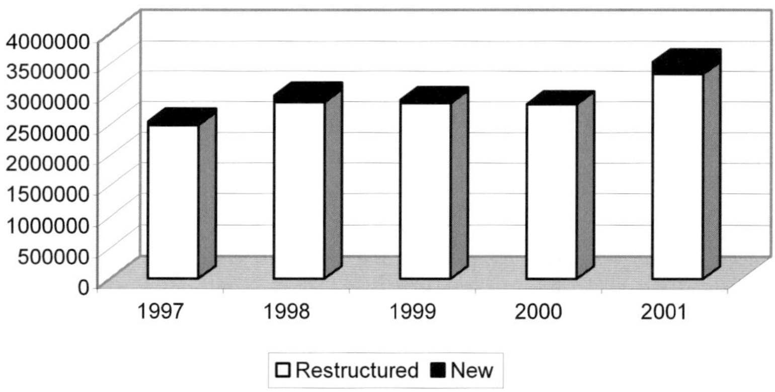

Fig. 9.15. New and restructured housing space in Milan 1997–2001

As an investment good, house values should be sensitive to the joint distribution of returns from housing and from other real and financial assets. The capability of housing equity to reduce overall portfolio risk or to be a safe haven asset may also be an element helping to explain housing investment. The statistical evidence shows (see below) that the after-tax rate of return of housing equity does not compare with that of other assets, but house ownership is large. How can this large ownership be reconciled with the low rates of returns? A tentative explanation may be along the following lines. People face obvious constraints in adjusting their portfolio composition. The first is the consumption demand for housing according to which the real estate ownership, which is optimal from the point of view of the consumption of housing services, may differ from the optimal level of housing stocks from a portfolio point of view. If, as a tenant, the owner pays a lower rent than he would pay if he were not the house owner, he has an incentive to own the house simply because he occupies it. This is particularly true if the tenant is careful. A careful tenant has a further incentive to own the house since free market rents are set to provide the owner with a rate of return sufficient to compensate for the wear and tear caused by the average renter. The mechanism works also for holiday homes and for houses purchased for one's offspring. It seems apparent that the consumption demand for housing adds a bias in favour of real estate share portfolios as, in Italy, family ties compound the basic effect.

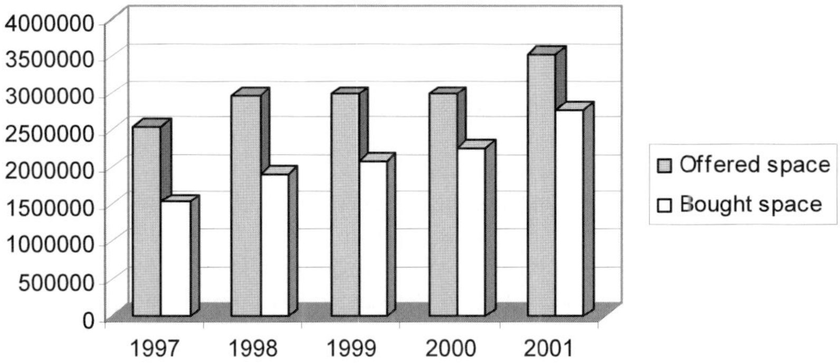

Fig. 9.16. Offered and bought space in Milan 1997–2001

A further constraint is the level of transaction costs. In the Italian housing market, these introduce a large bias in the sense that households may be unable to adjust not only the wealth share represented by housing equity, but also the location or dimension of the house they occupy as owners. The obvious result of these two constraints is that a large share of housing is owner-occupied and it is possible to say that in Italy portfolio considerations are of secondary importance.

9.10 The Rental Market

According to SUNIA[12] there are more than 4.3 million rented houses, a mere 20 per cent of the total Italian housing stock. On the basis of 1998 figures, SUNIA reckons that more than 51 per cent of those houses are in the north of Italy and about 18.9 per cent in Lombardy. The eleven larger metropolitan areas concentrate

---

[12] SUNIA is the Union of Italian Tenants.

about 2 million rented houses, i.e. about 46.6 per cent of the total. The largest share is held by Milan (see Fig. 9.17).

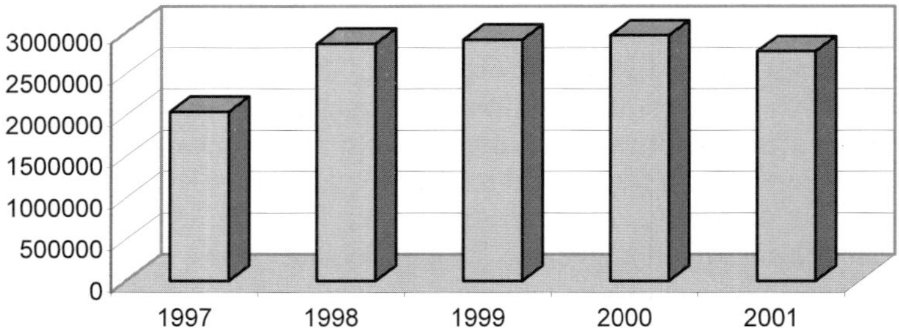

Fig. 9.17. Rented space in Milan 1997–2001

Houses for rent are most often located in the periphery or the near periphery. In 1998, slightly fewer than 80 per cent of houses were in the periphery or near it and about 19 per cent were in the city centre.

As far as the ownership composition is concerned, SUNIA reckons that, on average, about 70 per cent of rented houses are owned by single households. Less than 10 per cent are owned by companies, insurance companies included. The remaining 20 per cent are owned by the state and other public institutions.

The Italian rental market has a long tradition of regulation. In the 1960s, when inflation was still relatively moderate, the rents were simply fixed at their historical levels. After the inflation rise of the mid-1970s – to be exact, from 1978 to 1992 – rents were still regulated, but adjustable, and were not allowed to exceed the fair rent level. The fixing of rents favoured the surge of a severe rationing of households looking for a house to rent. Some deregulation took place in 1998 and landlords can now choose between various regimes. There is a free market regime for four – or eight-year contracts. There is the possibility of a mildly regulated regime implying a fixed rent and a shorter duration of the contract. Other possibilities exist for municipalities facing severe rental rationing (transitory use), for students and for other special cases (historical buildings, buildings for tourists). There is still, however, a black market. SUNIA reckons that, no later than 1998, the fair rent regime applied to about 35 per cent of Italian housing stock and the free market regime accounted for 37 per cent. About 13 per cent was offered in the black market and only 12 per cent was offered by either local or central government. At present, the most common regime is held to be the free market rent.

The factors which still hinder the full development of the rental market are strikingly different according to which side of the market they are viewed from. From the viewpoint owners, the high level of transaction costs, i.e. the costs owners have to face when they rent out and when they wants the house free of tenants, is considered a serious obstacle, but the low after-tax yield accruing to him is no less critical.

On the other hand, tenants complain about the effects of a rent deregulation that has lifted rents without increasing, for the time being, the actual amount of space available. Renters, particularly young households and households with one salary, are at present certainly overburdened by the cost of housing, particularly in the larger metropolitan areas. Taking into account the impossibility of finding a house at an affordable rent or simply a house in a place where they would be able to limit their commuting, consumers are certainly rationed. On this basis, one could argue that the population move from the heart of the metropolitan area to its periphery is explained more by plain displacement than by real qualitative choice. Another aspect of the problem is that of the cost incidence of renting: according to SUNIA, about 14 per cent of households spend more than one-third of their income on rent.

9.11 Public Housing and Transaction Costs

Public housing is unable to give help to low-income households. Lack of funding and mismanagement has led public institutions to a poor situation, with a further negative effect on the efficacy of public sector intervention in the housing market. Private investment in housing does not adequately feed the rental market, particularly for the low-income segment. Public housing is also unable to supply the market with a sufficient quantity of low-cost rented accommodation. The rental market indeed appears to be rather small and expensive, particularly for younger people and immigrants. This is clearly a problem, as by displacing younger individuals the city will inevitably face a long-run population problem, as the case of Venice shows only too well.

One possibility that has been advanced several times is the tuning of the local property tax to target the owners of empty houses. The efficacy of such a policy, however, has not been fully demonstrated as owners do not rent because the tax burden is low (the contrary, indeed, is true) but because renting implies a loss in the market value of the property. Addressing the wrong target will not help as the expected supply increase will be missing. Tuning the local property tax in order to reduce the rent may be more effective. The incentive will accrue to the owner, which could reduce his tax burden. In principle, any measure which implies a reduction in the market value of property could be ineffective in pursuing the enlargement of the market supply of rental housing.

Both lenders and renters in the property market incur various transaction costs. Search and negotiation entail monetary and non-monetary costs. Moving, per se, is costly. Taxation compounds all these costs by introducing rigidities in the market. Transaction costs, furthermore, inflate the owner-occupied real estate stock and deflate the rental space on offer. Investors are probably obliged to partially adjust their portfolios, and households are forced to consume housing services either more than desired if they are owner-occupiers or less so, if they are renters.

The following list of items is probably sufficient to give an overall idea of the fiscal regime prevailing in Italy.

- Negotiation costs. The main negotiation costs are the brokerage commission, notary fees and registration fee of the purchase contract (the normal rate is 7 per cent, but it is reduced to 3 per cent for the first time buyers). VAT replaces the registration fee if the seller is a building company or a developer (from 4 to 20 per cent).
- Income tax. Income tax is levied on the market rent for rented houses and on the book rent for empty or owner-occupied houses. The book rent depends on the area in square meters of floor space, quality, zone and the specific municipality where the house is located. For a tax rate equal to 35 per cent it is: rent × (1 – 15 per cent) × 35 per cent.
- Local property tax. Local property tax is levied on the book value and computed on the book rent defined as above. It is proportional to the length of the time period of possession and varies from 0.4 to 0.7 per cent of the book value multiplied by the factor 1.05.
- Registration fee of the rental contract: 5 per cent × 1 per cent.
- Value added tax. VAT is an alternative to the registration fee of the buying contract and it varies from 4 (for the first house) to 20 per cent.
- Waste disposal tax. The tax aims at sharing the waste disposal costs between owners and renters and varies according to local council decisions.

After-tax rents are reduced to a fraction as low as 35 per cent of the original market level. As a result, the net yield, i.e. the relation between the after-tax rent and the user cost, is significantly lowered. To see this we can compare before-tax yields in prime Italian property (Fig. 9.18) to after-tax yields on housing equity (Fig. 9.19 and Fig. 9.20) in a larger number of cities and regions.

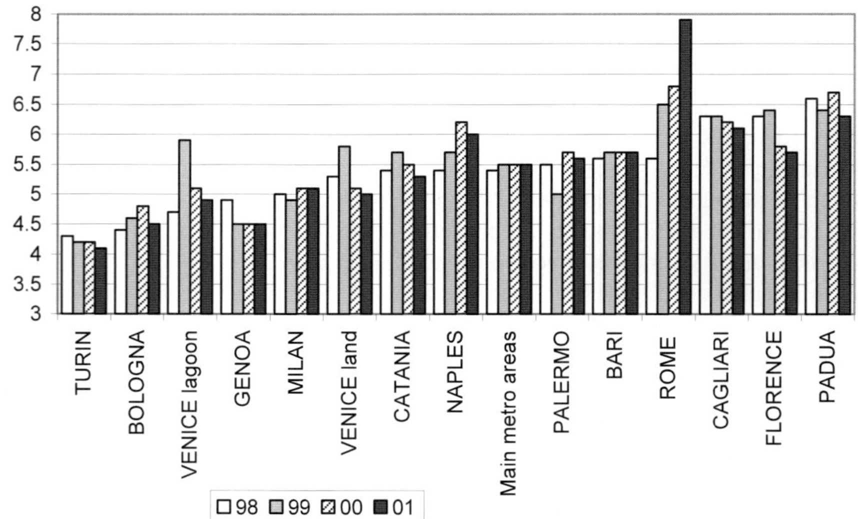

Fig. 9.18. Before-tax yields on prime housing property in large Italian cities 1998–2001

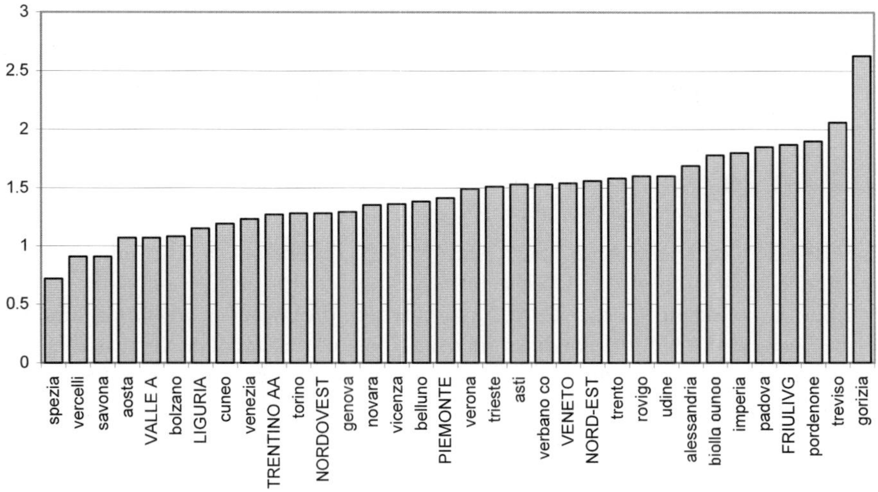

Fig. 9.19. Net yields on housing equity in medium and small size cities 2001

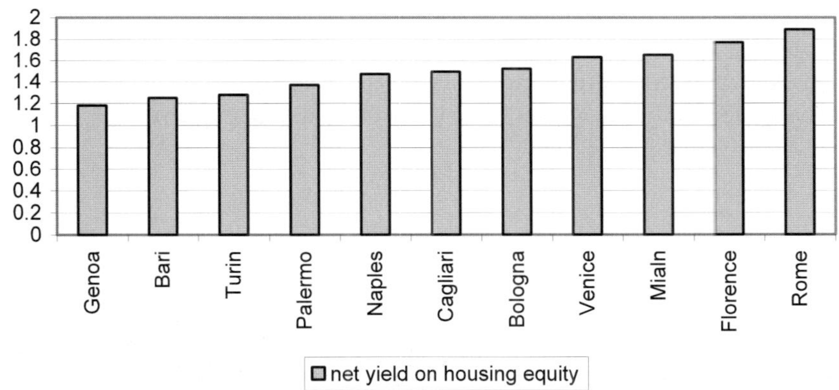

Fig. 9.20. Net yields on housing equity in large Italian cities 2001

Evidence suggests that owners face greater transaction costs than renters. As households that are more likely to move are also more likely to rent, it is probable that the higher the level of transaction costs in the property market, the greater the difference in the propensity to move between owner-occupiers and renters. High transaction costs help to explain the low geographical relocation of workers, particularly where the level of home ownership is high, as it is in Italy. High commuting, therefore, can be explained not only by the obvious time lag with which families fit their place of residence to their work place, by the obstacles they face, but also by a likely structural reduction in owner-occupiers' propensity to move.

Transaction costs, furthermore, help to explain the observed low mobility between the sub-markets. The elderly and widowed, for instance, do not move to smaller houses; many houses are neither rented nor owner-occupied. As a consequence some people are obliged to commute more than desired.

9.12 A Toy Model for the Housing Market

Standard economic theory assumes that market equilibrium is reached whenever demand equals supply. In the case of a sub-market formed by only one house, equilibrium is meant to describe a situation where the owner is willing to hold the house because the yield is equal to the user's cost of capital. The yield is the ratio between the rent R_t and the market value of the house V_t. The user's cost is the rate of return on the capital and it is assumed as given in that it is the sum of the nominal interest rate on risk-free assets, the risk premium, the depreciation cost augmented by the maintenance cost not incurred by the renter and is indicated with (i_t). In symbols the equilibrium reduces to:

$$R_t = i_t V_t \tag{9.1}$$

In equilibrium, the market value is also perfectly constant. What about net investment? To be in a perfect stationary equilibrium, net investment in a housing market should be zero. In the other cases equilibrium is only a possibility. In an asset market out of equilibrium the owner expects a change in the market value of the existing stock, yet he does not sell the asset if the expected change in value (g_t^e) satisfies the following condition:

$$R_t / V_t + g_t^e = i_t \tag{9.2}$$

The percentage rate of change in the market value is defined as follows:

$$V_{t+1}^e = V_t (1 + g_t^e) \tag{9.3}$$

Eqs. 9.2 and 9.3 combined, yield a relation between the current and the expected future price. One should choose which variable determines what, as the resulting equation simply states the equilibrium relation between them.

The resulting equation can first be solved for the expected future market value, given the current price:

$$V_{t+1}^e = V_t (1 + i_t) - R_t \tag{9.4}$$

The equation gives the expected price level capable of inducing the owner to hold the house, on the base of the expected rate of return i_t. The owner will be willing to hold the house only in the case of rising prices. When out of equilibrium, prices must go up sufficiently rapidly to make him happy with his asset holding. If the current market value is high enough, the rate of return applied to that value exceeds the current rent: $i_t V_t > R_t$, a further price increase is expected and new housing investment becomes profitable. If the current market value is the equilibrium one, $V^e_{t+1} = V_t$, then $i_t V_t > R_t$. In any other case, equilibrium is lost because any item of information able to change the current market value is passed on to the future market value even if there is no warranted effect on market fundamentals, i.e. rents and rate of return. This is the case of extrapolative expectations, which are rather common in real estate markets.

However, Eqs. 9.2 and 9.3 can be solved also for the current market value and by assuming as given the expected future market value:

$$V_t = \frac{R_t}{1+i_t} + \frac{V^e_{t+1}}{1+i_t} \tag{9.5}$$

Eq. 9.5 shows that any change in the rent or in the price expectation has a bearing on the current market valuation. By assuming that the owner is perfectly rational, i.e. by assuming that his expectations are consistent with market fundamentals, one can also assume that they are formed according to Eq. 9.5 itself. In this case one gets the equilibrium solution. Repeated forward substitution yields under the simplifying assumption of a constant rent $R_t = R$ and a constant rate of interest $i_t = i$:

$$V_t = \sum_{k=1}^{\infty} \frac{R}{(1+i\ )^k}, \text{ or } V = \frac{R}{i} \tag{9.6}$$

This is the fundamental equation stating that real market value of a house obviously equals the present value of its future net services (rents) discounted at the homeowner's real after-tax rate of return. A market satisfying this condition can be defined as an efficient market.

References

Camagni R (1985) Innovation and the Urban Life-cycle: Production, Location and Income Distribution Aspects. In: Nijkamp P (ed) Technological Change, Employment and Spatial Dynamics. Springer Verlag, Berlin, pp 382–400.

Camagni R, Gibelli MC (1996) Cities in Europe: Globalisation Sustainability and Cohesion. In: European Spatial Planning, Presidenza del Consiglio dei Ministri, Roma, Il Poligrafico dello Stato

Clayton J (1997) Are Housing Price Cycles Driven by Irrational Expectations? Journal of Real Estate Finance and Economics F(3): 341–63

Flavin M, Yamashita T (2002) Owner-occupied Housing and the Composition of the Household Portfolio over the Life Cycle. The American Economic Review 92: 345–62

Henderson JV, Ioannides YM (1983) A Model of Housing Tenure Choice. The American Economic Review 73: 98–113

Mees R, Wallace N (1994) Testing the Present Value Relation for Housing Prices: Should I Leave my House in San Francisco? Journal of Urban Economics 35: 245–66

Mills ES, Hamilton BW (1994) Urban Economics. Fifth edn. Harper Collins College Publishers, New York
OECD (2000) House Prices and Economic Activity. Economic Outlook. June, Paris
Pellizzon L, Weber G (2002) Are Italian Household Portfolios Efficient? A Mean-variance Analysis Conditional on Housing. University of Padua, presented at WFA, 2003
Rosen HS (1985) Housing Subsidies. Effects on Housing Decisions, Efficiency, and Equity. In: Auerbach AJ, Feldstein M (eds) Handbook of Public Economics vol. I, Elsevier Science P, North Holland, Amsterdam

10 Housing in Vienna

Hanns Abele and Andrea Höltl

Vienna University of Economics and Business Administration, Vienna

10.1 Introduction: History and Topography

Without some consideration of the historical development of the 20th century it is almost impossible to understand the Viennese metropolitan housing sector. (A short historical outline in English can be found on the web pages of the municipality of Vienna; see http://www.wien.gv.at/english/history). Both World Wars led to significant interruptions in the housing situation and are therefore important time points for structuring the development.

The end of World War I brought about the end of the Hapsburg Empire. The monarchy was broken up in a number of small national states. One among them, the Republic of Austria, inherited the capital of the empire, Vienna. This was not only a natural refugium for the German speaking population all over the monarchy but seemed also attractive for a great number of other parts of the population like intellectuals or artists being lured by the chances of a centre. Thus Vienna faced an influx of people which had to be coped with. On the other hand some members of the bureaucracy were induced to join the newly established states. Although the stock of houses was not damaged as during World War II the effects of the war threw the housing market into disequilibrium (cf. Türr 1933). Rent increases reduced the supply of affordable apartments and created excess demand for the cheaper segment of the market dominating the housing situation. Policy in Vienna reacted with two measures both of historical dimension: rent control and so-called 'Sozialer Wohnbau' (public housing) which was a programme to offer people housing directly by the municipal authority (For a European comparison see Zimmermann 1997). Both policy instruments are still in use today.

Since the building activities were an activity of the socialist dominated municipality they were stopped after 1933 and during the Nazi-regime which interrupted the socialist dominance in Vienna. Economic depression especially the high unemployment was countered by other construction projects.

In the final weeks of World War II the housing stock in Vienna was heavily damaged, 20 per cent of the housing stock partly or completely destroyed. Nearly 87,000 flats were in ruins and uninhabitable. Together with a wave of refugees from the Eastern countries again huge excess demand characterised the housing situation. It was not surprising that the policy instruments having been in use some forty years earlier again seemed to provide a promising cure for the looming problems. Like Berlin Vienna was divided by the allied occupation forces in four zones. This was not enhancing a fast and regionally equal reconstruction of the housing stock. One new policy instrument, however, was created. This was a system of subsidies which have dominated the decades after the war like the continuation of rent control. This approach to housing established a dominating influence of administrative and hence political forces on the housing sectors. Public means were channelled into organisations and enterprises themselves closely affiliated with political parties. Continuous excess demand forced people to try the offer of these organisations because otherwise the rationing would prohibit them from finding an apartment. The political parties, the in Vienna dominating socialist party and the conservative party were able to get a firm grip on their electorate.

For quite some time now there are cautious attempts to get rid of the inherited market distortions. The excessive use of deficit spending constrains further budget deficits and thus the room for providing public housing and high subsidies shrinks. In addition to these constraints doubts started to loom about the adequacy of housing policies in reaching the proclaimed goals whether they themselves make sense or not.[1]

With a little simplification Vienna in its present appearance can be viewed as a system of three concentric circles cut by a chord, the Danube, in two parts roughly in the relation 2:1. The smaller part consists of former suburbs north of the Danube. The first district being the centre, the districts two to nine the medium circle, and the districts 10 to 23 comprising the outer circle. The area of 415 km^2 is inhabited by a population of 1.6 million people. The enlargement took place in several steps but the manifestation of the development of the last 150 years still shapes the present Viennese metropolitan housing sector.

In the middle of the 19th century Vienna was still surrounded by a city wall as it used to be in a medieval town. By incorporating suburbs both area and population of Vienna started to grow (see Table 10.1 and Fig. 10.1).[2] The largest population of slightly more than 2 million people was counted 1910. Because of the incorporation of the suburbs population density decreased. This effect was dramatic between 1938 and 1951 whereas since 1961 both area and population densities are almost constant (Fig. 10.2).

---

[1] See Bingley and Walker (2001), Best (1996) and Currie and Yelowitz (2000) for some interesting theoretical discussions.

[2] Source of all data is 'Statistik Austria' except when otherwise stated. A list of Viennese districts and a map of the town is given in the Appendix.

Table 10.1. Growth of the city territory 1869–2001

Year	Change of territory	Number of districts	Area km²	Circumference km
till 1849	–	district 1 and glacis	3.60	–
1850	Incorporation of 34 suburbs	–	55.40	38
1863	Division in districts	9	55.40	38
1874	Separation district 10 from 4	10	55.40	38
1890	Incorporation of suburbs	19	178.12	63
1900	Separation district 20 from 2	20	178.12	63
1904	Incorporation of Floridsdorf (district 21)	21	273.08	96
1910	Incorporation of Strebersdorf and Mauer	21	278.05	101
1938	Incorporation of 98 surrounding villages of Lower Austria	26	1,215.41	226
1954	Separation of 80 former villages of Lower Austria	23	414.95	133

Source: Stadt Wien (2002).

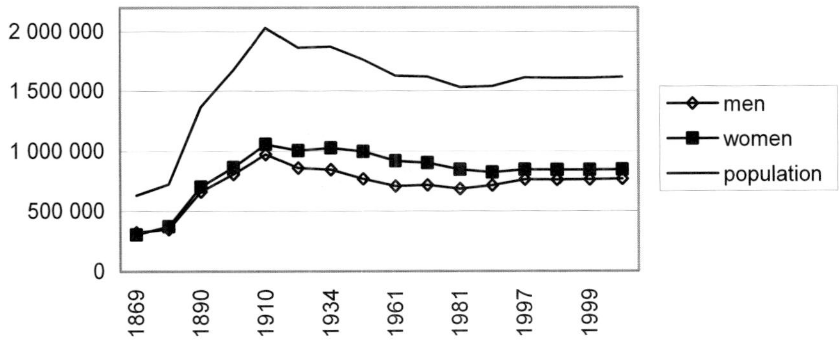

Fig. 10.1. Development of the population of Vienna 1869–2000

Intensive construction tried to keep pace with population growth. Predominantly new land was developed at the outskirts of Vienna making construction very demanding on the provision of infrastructure. This approach to create new housing was only reversed in the last two decades when revitalisation of the inner districts has become more important. As a consequence of construction population moved within Vienna.[3]

[3] The central districts 2–9 are loosing population at least since World War I, the first district already since 1869. The increase of population in the group of districts 10, et al., is correlated with the intensified construction in areas of relatively cheap land in the out-

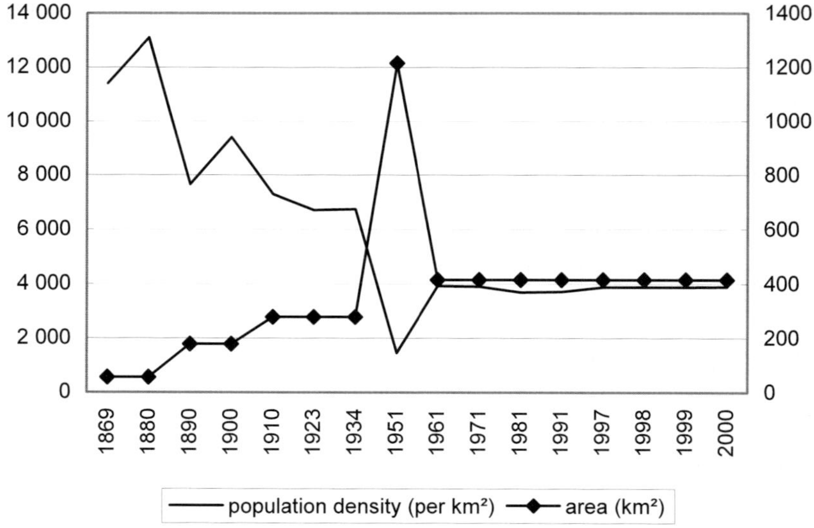

Fig. 10.2. Population densities 1869–2000

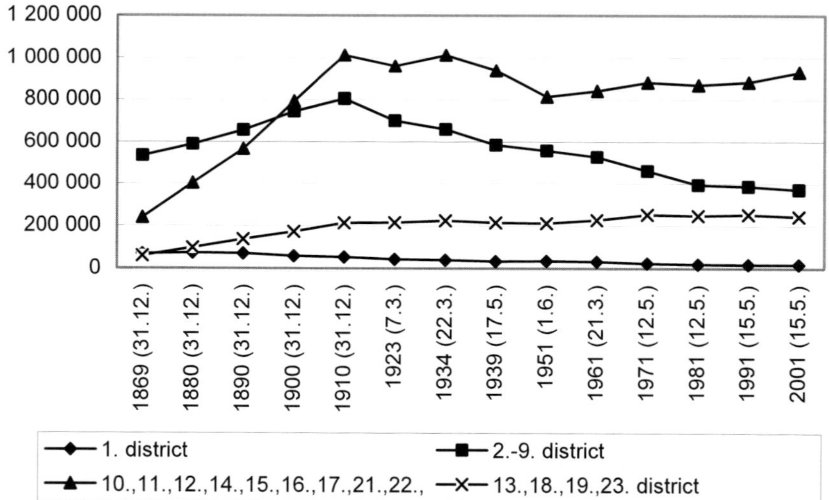

Fig. 10.3. Centre vs. periphery 1869–2001

---

skirts of Vienna. The increase in the group 13, et al., can be interpreted as a move to the 'west end'.

Summing up, the long run development in the Viennese housing sector can be viewed as a gradual adjustment process after being exposed to severe external shocks.

The chapter is organised as follows: An exposition of the main structural elements of the housing sector in Vienna is given following the introduction. Then an analysis of the population dynamics which is relevant for the housing sector during the last decade at a micro level is presented. Construction and the development of important economic determinants like prices, costs and incomes are studied next. Finally, regulation and policy measures like rent control and the subsidy system are discussed. A short evaluation concludes the chapter.

10.2 Some Structural Analysis

Basically modelling the housing market consists of analysing the dynamics of two sets, population and houses and apartments respectively and their mapping. Social and economic factors act as filters governing both the developments of population and houses as well as their matching. These determinants are embedded in a spatial framework, which in itself is not invariant in time. Thus the analysis uses the following transformation:

Expanding population density to include the other important structural factors determining the housing sector of an economy results in the relations:

$$\text{population } (POP) \, / \, \text{households } (HHO), \tag{10.1}$$

$$\text{households } (HHO) \, / \, \text{apartments } (APA), \tag{10.2}$$

$$\text{apartments } (APA) \, / \, \text{buildings } (BLD), \tag{10.3}$$

$$\text{buildings } (BLD) \, / \, \text{area } (ARA). \tag{10.4}$$

Eqs. 10.1 to 10.4 multiplied are equal to population density that is:

$$POP/ARA = (POP/HHO)\cdot(HHO/APA)\cdot(APA/BLD)\cdot(BLD/ARA). \tag{10.5}$$

Eq. 10.4 is nothing else than the degree of land used for constructing buildings. It is governed by zoning laws and construction activity. Clearly the ratio is higher in metropolitan areas than in rural ones. Eq. 10.3 describes the use of buildings for housing purposes. Rise in demand for office space creates intensified construction of buildings not for residential purposes. Eq. 10.2 represents the quantitative balance of the residential market. Every household should have one apartment to live in. Thus a value of Eq. 10.2 close to 1 indicates absence of market imbalance at least at the aggregate level. Eq. 10.1 is an important demographic characteristic whose small changes may create enormous disequilibrium in the housing sector.

In addition to a description of the essential stocks this framework can be used to study dynamics and questions of policy as well. It is clear that subsidies for buildings or apartments influence Eq. 10.3 whereas subsidies given to individuals or households will manifest themselves in Eq. 10.2. In order to explain the dynamics of the housing sector one has to analyse the influence of economic and social variables on these stocks. Among them are prices, incomes, interest rates, expectations, etc. Regulation and institutional factors matter a great deal. Even if population and area are constant over time they may generate extraordinary dynamics within the housing sector of the economy.

Fig. 10.4 illustrates the main relation of Eq. 10.5 and Table 10.2 informs about the values of the stocks in Eq. 10.5 over the last three decades.[4]

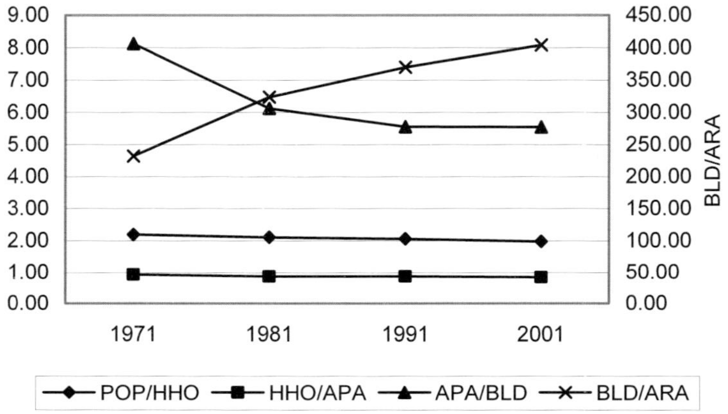

Fig. 10.4. The ratios of Eq. 10.5 1971–2001

Table 10.2. The ratios of Eq. 10.5 in 1,000 per km^2

YEAR	POP/ARA	POP/HHO	HHO/APA	APA/BLD	BLD/ARA
1971	3 903	2.20	0.94	8.12	231.83
1981	3 690	2.11	0.88	6.11	323.67
1991	3 710	2.06	0.88	5.55	370.34
2001	3 765	1.98	0.85	5.54	403.74

Looking at the distribution of population at the district level details the development of Fig. 10.5 further. It gives an illustration of the different development of the centre and the periphery. It can be viewed as a long run 'petrifaction' of the Viennese housing sector.

The development of the share of people of foreign nationality in Vienna reflects

[4] All numbers for 2001 should be regarded as preliminary since the definite results of the last census are not available yet.

the fact that Austria is a leading host country for refugees (see Fig. 10.6). But seeking asylum is not the only reason for moving to Austria. So it is not surprising that foreigners are found very unequally distributed in the districts of Vienna. The shares vary from 8 per cent (district 23) to 37 per cent (district 15). In addition the shares also differ for different nationalities like people from other EU countries or of Asian nationality. Sometimes this creates some friction among the inhabitants of areas with a high share of foreigners.

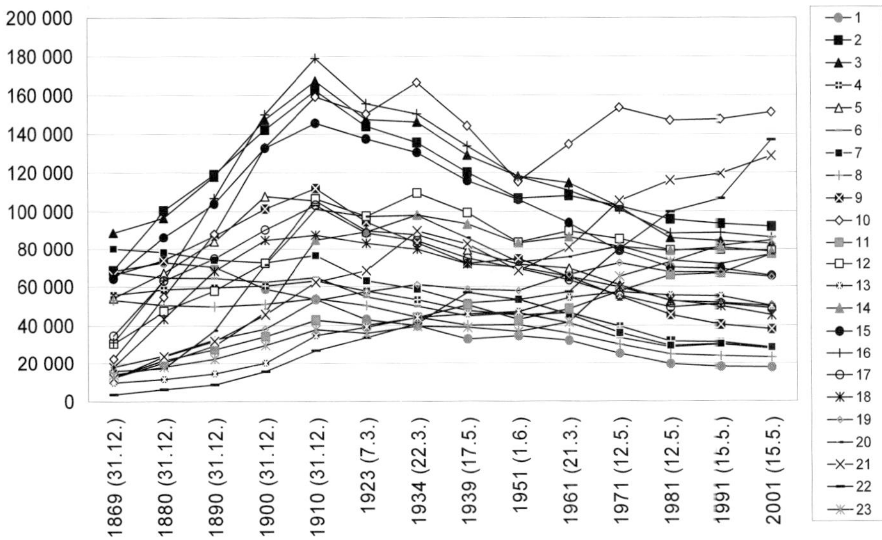

Fig. 10.5. Population by district 1869–2001 (Source: Magistat der Stadt Wien 2001)

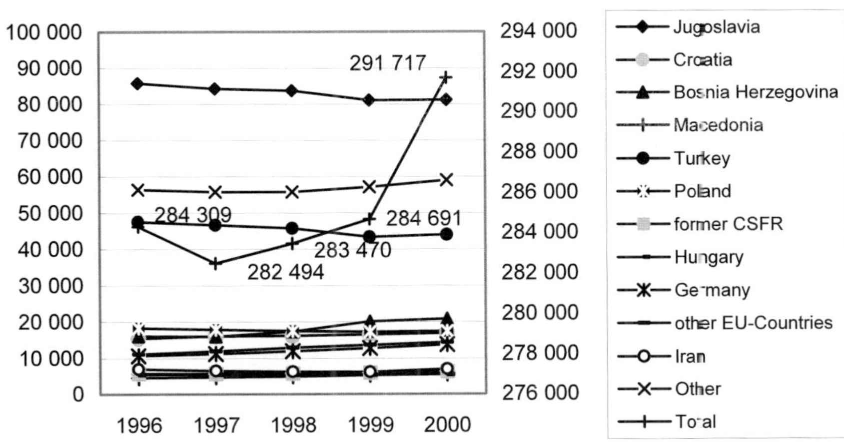

Fig. 10.6. Foreign population according to nationality 1996–2000

As can be seen from Table 10.1 and Fig. 10.2, the area of the municipality of Vienna did not change for the last half century. This does not mean that there were no changes in the area of districts. However, they were small and are disregarded in this context.

The decline of the size of households is a typical phenomenon of modern industrial societies. The extreme value would be a one person household. Till 2001 there is no sign of a reversion of the trend and an average size of 1.98 has been reached. Although this development causes additional demand for housing the aggregate situation in the housing sector has eased. Since the 1970s the ratio *HHO/APA* has been constantly below one. This implies a reduction of excess demand and has allowed market forces to have a greater influence despite rent control and other regulatory measures being still in effect.

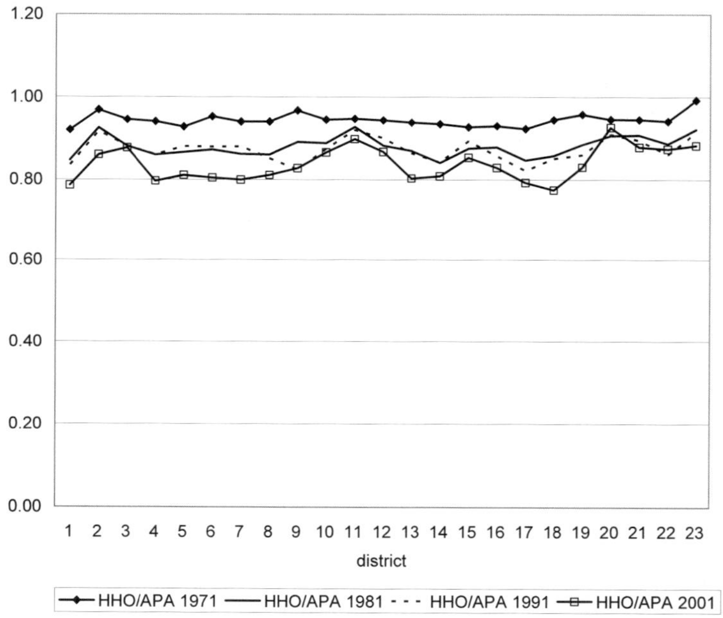

Fig. 10.7. Housing market equilibrium: households/apartments 1971–2001

Besides households, the other central figure of the housing sector is the number and quality of apartments. During the time span from 1971 to 2001 the number of buildings in Vienna increased by 75 per cent whereas the number of apartments grew by roughly 20 per cent only. The huge differences reflect the strategies to increase the housing supply primarily at the outskirts where land was available and cheap. However, the development after 1991 indicates that there has been some change in the fundamental orientation of construction activity.

It is interesting that most of Viennese apartments were built in two periods, one from 1880 to 1918, and the other from 1961 to 1980 (see Fig. 10.8). Almost 40 per cent of the apartments in the centre (district 1) were built before 1880! This need not imply inferior quality. According to the most recent available detailed data (1991) the apartments in district 1 are roomier than in other districts. A similar result is reached when the number of square metres per apartment is the ranking criterion. The largest share of apartments in all districts covers between 60 and 90 sqm. This is in part a consequence of the size limits which are imposed by subsidies for construction of apartments. One of the changes in rent regulations introduced different limit prices for apartments of different standards. Four categories were introduced. In 1991 there were – with two exceptions – at least 50 per cent of the apartments in the best category. The middle two groups had roughly 10 per cent each and in the worst category only 11 districts had shares above 10 per cent.

Table 10.3. Buildings and apartments 1971–2001, 1971 = 100

District	BLD 1981	APA 1981	BLD 1991	APA 1991	BLD 2001	APA 2001
1	112.0	91.2	109.3	88.8	109.3	93.9
2	179.7	101.0	207.7	101.4	204.9	108.1
3	122.6	97.4	126.1	95.7	130.5	97.4
4	111.6	96.2	119.9	95.0	119.8	98.6
5	107.7	97.5	110.3	93.7	114.4	99.9
6	113.1	98.5	119.7	101.4	124.8	109.2
7	105.2	93.1	112.8	94.5	117.0	102.3
8	118.0	96.9	118.9	95.5	102.7	99.6
9	119.2	95.6	122.6	93.8	124.5	94.4
10	167.5	108.3	189.6	113.5	204.7	122.9
11	143.2	118.6	174.0	132.0	196.5	163.9
12	145.0	103.4	154.1	102.1	163.4	108.4
13	125.1	110.9	134.1	119.6	140.2	127.9
14	154.4	112.3	174.6	118.9	181.4	127.5
15	112.6	96.6	111.2	89.9	141.3	90.6
16	138.5	96.2	151.1	97.2	153.1	98.7
17	130.7	99.0	147.1	103.6	152.1	104.3
18	127.8	100.4	133.3	96.1	135.6	100.4
19	151.0	108.6	166.9	118.5	173.0	124.7
20	137.8	101.6	150.8	100.5	161.5	108.8
21	158.3	120.1	195.8	135.8	220.8	155.6
22	131.7	135.3	170.7	162.2	211.4	217.3
23	146.8	123.9	175.3	148.5	190.7	173.2
Total	139.6	105.1	159.7	109.2	174.2	118.8
Absolute numbers	134,321	821,175	153,693	853,091	167,554	928,479

Construction in the last decades led to a significant improvement in the available housing stock. The districts where the new developments took place profited most; because of new construction their housing stock exhibits a relatively high quality. Most of their inherited substandard dwellings were replaced during the construction boom.

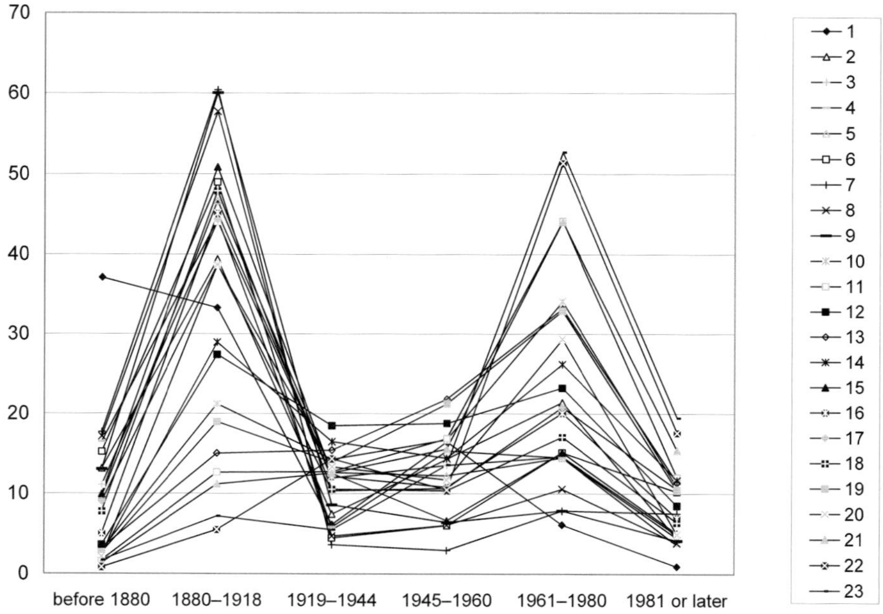

Fig. 10.8. Share of apartments by period of construction and district

For several reasons construction of new apartments has not been a continuous process. Because of the stringency of the Maastricht criteria the building activities of the municipality had to be reduced. Only with some time lag construction demand reacted to the changed circumstances like the sharp reduction in inflation and changes in the budget situation of public households.

Part of the construction boom has been the result of increased demand for office space. Thus high rising buildings were erected and some are still in the pipeline. After the abolishment of the city walls new houses for living were built instead, but contrary to the intentions within a short time business tenants moved in. There is a similar tendency driven by intensive demand for office space nowadays.

Finally turning to the last fraction of the right hand side of Eq. 10.5, it is important to note that the number of buildings in relation to the available area almost doubled from 1971 on. One reason could be that more buildings have been erected per unit of area; however, this is only marginally correct. The main reason for this development is an intensified land use. Not only have all the ruins of World War II been removed and new buildings erected, but even small lots in the inner parts of the town have been used for construction purposes. The number of buildings in almost all districts increased from 1971 to 2001, which is reflected in an increase in the value of Eq. 10.4 of more than 70 per cent from 1971 to 2001. However, the ratio *APA*/*ARA* has grown only less than 20 per cent in the same time. This increases the density of population and reduces the possibilities of recreational space in some parts of the town. A disaggregated picture of the spatial distribution of Vienna's population is provided by Table 10.4 and Table 10.5.

Table 10.4 summarises the detailed development of the left hand side of Eq. 10.5. This ratio varies less than 6 per cent over three decades. Therefore most of the large changes have been compensated for by developments of the other ratios. For the understanding of the dynamics a detailed look into population dynamics and the correlation to building activities may be helpful.

Table 10.4. Area and population of Viennese districts 1971–2001

District	Viennese population				% change		
	1971	1981	1991	2001	1981/1991	1991/2001	1971/2001
1	25 169	19 537	18 002	17 693	–7.9	–1.7	–29.7
2	102 730	95 892	93 542	92 057	–2.5	–1.6	–10.4
3	102 223	86 054	84 500	82 953	–1.8	–1.8	–18.9
4	39 619	31 800	31 410	28 448	–1.2	–9.4	–28.2
5	60 529	52 436	51 521	49 745	–1.7	–3.4	–17.8
6	33 633	28 771	30 298	27 838	5.3	–8.1	–17.2
7	36 255	29 490	30 396	28 576	3.1	–6.0	–21.2
8	30 151	24 769	23 850	23 112	–3.7	–3.1	–23.3
9	54 788	45 314	40 416	38 089	–10.8	–5.8	–30.5
10	153 695	147 101	147 636	151 208	0.4	2.4	–1.6
11	57 540	65 859	66 881	77 120	1.6	15.3	34.0
12	85 500	79 408	79 592	79 095	0.2	–0.6	–7.5
13	57 068	55 331	54 909	49 839	–0.8	–9.2	–12.7
14	81 310	78 996	80 822	78 548	2.3	–2.8	–3.4
15	78 981	70 066	69 309	65 566	–1.1	–5.4	–17.0
16	101 017	88 587	88 931	86 346	0.4	–2.9	–14.5
17	55 532	49 337	50 944	48 668	3.3	–4.5	–12.4
18	59 237	52 548	49 761	45 134	–5.3	–9.3	–23.8
19	72 387	67 522	67 377	64 839	–0.2	–3.8	–10.4
20	81 647	73 696	71 876	77 108	–2.5	7.3	–5.6
21	105 510	116 033	119 415	128 644	2.9	7.7	21.9
22	80 200	99 801	106 589	136 998	6.8	28.5	70.8
23	65 164	72 998	81 871	84 858	12.2	3.6	30.2
Total	1 619 885	1 531 346	1 539 848	1 562 482	0.6	1.4	–3.7

Table 10.5. Population density of Viennese districts 1971–2001

District[a]	ARA	POP/ARA 1971	POP/ARA 1981	POP/ARA 1991	POP/ARA 2001
13	37.70	1 514	1 468	1 456	1 322
22	102.34	784	975	1 042	1 339
14	34.00	2 391	2 323	2 377	2 310
19	24.90	2 907	2 712	2 706	2 604
23	32.01	2 036	2 280	2 558	2 651
21	44.46	2 373	2 610	2 686	2 893
11	23.24	2 476	2 834	2 878	3 318
17	11.36	4 888	4 343	4 485	4 284

Table 10.5. (Cont.)

District[a]	ARA	POP/ARA 1971	POP/ARA 1981	POP/ARA 1991	POP/ARA 2001
10	31.77	4 838	4 630	4 647	4 759
2	19.27	5 331	4 976	4 854	4 777
1	3.01	8 362	6 491	5 981	5 878
18	6.28	9 433	8 368	7 924	7 187
12	8.21	10 414	9 672	9 695	9 634
16	8.64	11 692	10 253	10 293	9 994
3	7.42	13 777	11 598	11 388	11 180
9	2.99	18 324	15 155	13 517	12 739
20	5.67	14 400	12 998	12 677	13 599
4	1.80	22 011	17 667	17 450	15 804
7	1.61	22 519	18 317	18 880	17 749
15	3.69	21 404	18 988	18 783	17 769
6	1.49	22 572	19 309	20 334	18 683
8	1.08	27 918	22 934	22 083	21 400
5	2.03	29 817	25 831	25 380	24 505
Vienna Total	414.95				

[a]Sorted according to last column.

10.3 An Analysis of the Micro-dynamics

Since housing belongs to basic needs any movement of a household implies normally a change of the apartment being inhabited. The dynamics of the housing sector should therefore be studied at the micro level.[5] As several contributions in the literature suggest a detailed study of household formation is indispensable.[6] Lacking such studies a possible approximation is to substitute for households by using population dynamics. The dynamic evolvement of population is given by Eq. 10.6, where the stock (*POP*) is modified by migration, immigration (*IMI*) and emigration (*EMI*), and the difference of births (*BIR*) and deaths (*DTH*).

$$POP(t+1) = POP(t) + IMI(t) - EMI(t) + BIR(t) - DTH(t). \tag{10.6}$$

Transforming this accounting relation by separating migration into migration within a district, within the town and across the border of the town it is possible to formulate Eq. 10.6 analogous to a Markov process. This is the idea of Eq. 10.7.

$$POP(t+1) = M(t)POP(t) + NMI(t) + BIR(t) - DTH(t), \tag{10.7}$$

where *NMI* being net migration across the borders. All other migration is taken

[5] Fischer et al. (1988); Aufhauser (1986). However, very often the necessary data do not exist as is the case in Vienna for the last census 2001 at least for the moment.

[6] For modelling the household formation see Keilman et al. (1988).

care of by M. The elements m_{ij} of M give the share of the population of district j moving to district i within the year t. The diagonal elements m_{ii} are the shares of people staying in the same district over the period under consideration either by not moving or moving within the district. An estimate of a time invariant matrix of transition probabilities M for the last decade is given in Table 10.6.

Table 10.6 reveals realisations of the market dynamics of the underlying structure of the Viennese housing sector. The advantage of such an approach lies in paving the way for a theoretically more satisfactory analysis of the housing sector. Demand and supply normally violate one of the fundamental requirements of economic theory for the market model namely independence. In most cases demand of a new apartment is conditional on the supply of the old one. Hence the use of the typical economic models would suffer from serious misspecification.[7]

An inspection of M reveals the different mobility of inhabitants of Viennese districts. Fig. 10.9 gives the ranking of the districts according to the share of the population staying inside the district within the year. It is important to note that migration within Vienna is a local affair.

The direction of migration, of both immigration and emigration, is to neighbouring districts. The largest three coefficients in the columns of M for all districts are those for the neighbouring districts. This is an astonishing result because it implies a village-like, even rural character of the housing market in Vienna!

Another result is the importance of migration to and from outside for the development of population and housing in Vienna. As is clear from the figures of M without immigration, Vienna's population would shrink. Assuming, ceteris paribus, that M is constant, but disregarding births and deaths, which in sum have a negative influence anyway, and setting immigration to zero, would slightly decrease the population in Vienna till 2011. Without immigration there would be, however, an incessant reduction in the population further on!

Looking at migration activities in more detail reveals (Table 10.7) that the districts 15, 6 and 7 are relative to their population the most attractive to outsiders and loose most to the outside. This can be a consequence of the quality and the price of housing they offer or circumstances which make them a good point to start with in Vienna but not a place for permanent residence. In absolute numbers district 10 is ranked top.

---

[7] It is not possible to further elaborate this point in this context but see Abele in Abele and Winckler (1976).

Table 10.6. Transition probabilities for the last decade

district	1	2	3	4	5	6	7	8	9	10	11	12	13	14	15	16	17	18	19	20	21	22	23
1	0.9460	0.0006	0.0008	0.0009	0.0005	0.0009	0.0009	0.0012	0.0012	0.0003	0.0002	0.0003	0.0008	0.0004	0.0003	0.0003	0.0004	0.0009	0.0010	0.0003	0.0002	0.0002	0.0002
2	0.0048	0.9453	0.0050	0.0029	0.0041	0.0037	0.0041	0.0032	0.0044	0.0025	0.0021	0.0027	0.0017	0.0022	0.0038	0.0029	0.0032	0.0025	0.0019	0.0077	0.0024	0.0025	0.0011
3	0.0053	0.0043	0.9428	0.0042	0.0043	0.0041	0.0041	0.0035	0.0041	0.0027	0.0038	0.0033	0.0020	0.0021	0.0035	0.0026	0.0027	0.0023	0.0018	0.0032	0.0016	0.0017	0.0014
4	0.0027	0.0010	0.0017	0.9458	0.0030	0.0024	0.0019	0.0015	0.0015	0.0010	0.0007	0.0009	0.0009	0.0007	0.0009	0.0009	0.0010	0.0008	0.0008	0.0007	0.0004	0.0004	0.0005
5	0.0021	0.0021	0.0026	0.0050	0.9259	0.0049	0.0040	0.0024	0.0025	0.0027	0.0014	0.0032	0.0015	0.0020	0.0033	0.0023	0.0022	0.0016	0.0012	0.0020	0.0008	0.0009	0.0011
6	0.0020	0.0011	0.0014	0.0018	0.0028	0.9298	0.0038	0.0024	0.0021	0.0010	0.0006	0.0012	0.0009	0.0011	0.0020	0.0013	0.0012	0.0010	0.0008	0.0009	0.0005	0.0004	0.0005
7	0.0020	0.0011	0.0014	0.0018	0.0020	0.0038	0.9258	0.0041	0.0023	0.0008	0.0005	0.0011	0.0010	0.0012	0.0024	0.0016	0.0016	0.0013	0.0011	0.0011	0.0005	0.0004	0.0006
8	0.0020	0.0007	0.0008	0.0011	0.0010	0.0016	0.0028	0.9387	0.0020	0.0004	0.0002	0.0007	0.0007	0.0006	0.0009	0.0009	0.0012	0.0012	0.0008	0.0006	0.0003	0.0003	0.0003
9	0.0033	0.0017	0.0016	0.0018	0.0018	0.0025	0.0028	0.0040	0.9300	0.0010	0.0007	0.0011	0.0012	0.0011	0.0019	0.0016	0.0021	0.0028	0.0024	0.0020	0.0009	0.0007	0.0006
10	0.0025	0.0042	0.0060	0.0062	0.0100	0.0056	0.0049	0.0031	0.0038	0.9560	0.0067	0.0076	0.0030	0.0038	0.0066	0.0045	0.0042	0.0029	0.0020	0.0045	0.0022	0.0024	0.0041
11	0.0009	0.0023	0.0054	0.0023	0.0032	0.0019	0.0018	0.0015	0.0019	0.0044	0.9615	0.0029	0.0012	0.0014	0.0026	0.0020	0.0019	0.0014	0.0010	0.0025	0.0015	0.0013	0.0012
12	0.0017	0.0024	0.0029	0.0023	0.0057	0.0042	0.0036	0.0026	0.0027	0.0036	0.0021	0.9408	0.0038	0.0033	0.0059	0.0034	0.0030	0.0023	0.0014	0.0027	0.0013	0.0012	0.0035
13	0.0032	0.0021	0.0025	0.0027	0.0031	0.0030	0.0028	0.0026	0.0027	0.0022	0.0017	0.0041	0.9582	0.0040	0.0032	0.0025	0.0026	0.0022	0.0021	0.0022	0.0014	0.0012	0.0031
14	0.0018	0.0021	0.0024	0.0025	0.0039	0.0042	0.0047	0.0031	0.0031	0.0022	0.0017	0.0038	0.0050	0.9515	0.0080	0.0060	0.0044	0.0032	0.0022	0.0026	0.0013	0.0011	0.0019
15	0.0016	0.0024	0.0026	0.0020	0.0042	0.0053	0.0056	0.0031	0.0032	0.0024	0.0015	0.0038	0.0020	0.0050	0.9248	0.0061	0.0051	0.0028	0.0015	0.0029	0.0010	0.0010	0.0012
16	0.0017	0.0026	0.0024	0.0020	0.0042	0.0041	0.0061	0.0051	0.0043	0.0023	0.0016	0.0034	0.0020	0.0049	0.0080	0.9379	0.0105	0.0051	0.0023	0.0033	0.0012	0.0012	0.0012
17	0.0012	0.0014	0.0014	0.0013	0.0022	0.0023	0.0028	0.0030	0.0029	0.0011	0.0010	0.0016	0.0010	0.0019	0.0033	0.0056	0.9312	0.0050	0.0020	0.0018	0.0009	0.0007	0.0006
18	0.0024	0.0013	0.0014	0.0015	0.0019	0.0020	0.0023	0.0029	0.0045	0.0009	0.0007	0.0013	0.0011	0.0013	0.0020	0.0025	0.0045	0.9416	0.0039	0.0016	0.0008	0.0006	0.0007
19	0.0040	0.0016	0.0017	0.0018	0.0017	0.0019	0.0025	0.0027	0.0049	0.0009	0.0009	0.0012	0.0016	0.0016	0.0019	0.0022	0.0033	0.0063	0.9583	0.0023	0.0013	0.0009	0.0007
20	0.0017	0.0063	0.0033	0.0017	0.0034	0.0025	0.0032	0.0024	0.0055	0.0022	0.0018	0.0024	0.0013	0.0020	0.0038	0.0034	0.0035	0.0032	0.0029	0.9371	0.0030	0.0023	0.0010
21	0.0018	0.0049	0.0033	0.0022	0.0032	0.0027	0.0029	0.0023	0.0041	0.0025	0.0028	0.0027	0.0016	0.0023	0.0035	0.0036	0.0038	0.0036	0.0036	0.0087	0.9663	0.0072	0.0014
22	0.0021	0.0065	0.0040	0.0031	0.0042	0.0032	0.0031	0.0022	0.0035	0.0036	0.0037	0.0033	0.0022	0.0026	0.0039	0.0035	0.0037	0.0033	0.0030	0.0072	0.0089	0.9699	0.0015
23	0.0014	0.0013	0.0019	0.0019	0.0032	0.0023	0.0021	0.0015	0.0015	0.0029	0.0017	0.0059	0.0049	0.0025	0.0028	0.0019	0.0018	0.0016	0.0011	0.0014	0.0011	0.0010	0.9713

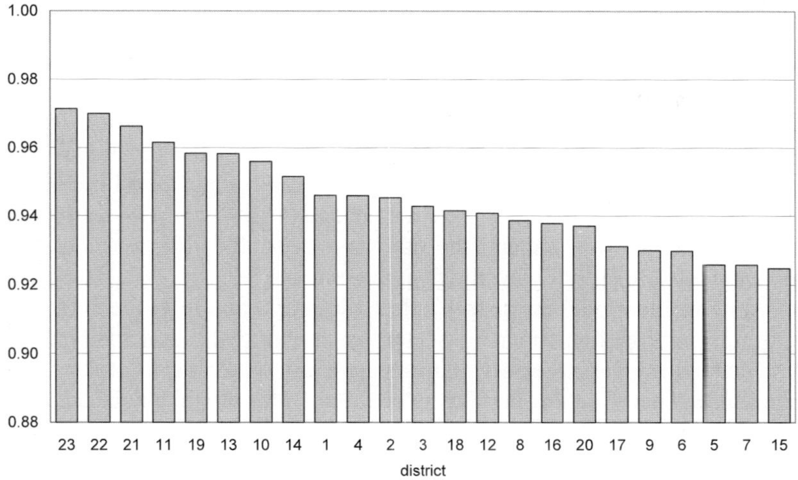

Fig. 10.9. Share of residents staying in the same district

Table 10.7. Total migration 1991–2000

District	Emigration Mean	Standard Deviation	Immigration Mean	Standard Deviation
1	1 822	181.43	1 901	239.39
2	9 615	586.61	9 849	639.57
3	9 543	661.97	9 836	1 387.15
4	2 825	287.70	2 994	315.51
5	6 520	351.17	6 513	267.83
6	3 870	253.21	3 993	400.37
7	3 871	296.53	4 008	327.00
8	2 594	158.35	2 671	314.74
9	4 847	428.81	4 954	342.74
10	16 122	884.64	16 848	1 801.18
11	6 464	788.16	7 505	1 353.23
12	8 686	493.77	8 835	534.80
13	5 041	829.00	6 555	725.80
14	8 398	460.21	9 209	1 229.57
15	10 600	850.90	10 733	1 956.02
16	10 471	622.30	10 624	723.27
17	6 229	460.28	6 200	830.49
18	4 994	431.97	5 067	351.88
19	6 170	352.12	6 528	535.62
20	9 027	577.56	9 768	1 362.78
21	11 068	1 005.34	12 108	913.66
22	9 632	1 504.16	12 333	2 191.40
23	6 191	513.78	6 985	1 199.49

Finally, the analysis of the micro dynamics allows a rough estimate of the yearly turnover in the Viennese housing market. During the years from 1991 to 2000, seven to eight per cent of the population moved within Vienna. Including migration across city borders this number increased to 11 to 12 per cent every year. Using the average size of households to get an estimate of households moving, one ends up with a figure of roughly 55,000 to 60,000 and 85,000 to 90,000, respectively. This means that some 85,000 to 90,000 dwellings or a little bit more than 10 per cent of the available stock change hands every year, two thirds of this figure are satisfying local demand the other meet demand from outside. Newly supplied were 6,000 to 12,000 dwellings in the nineties.[8]

Ideally one would model the supply side analogously and infer the determining factors of the metropolitan housing sector by studying the matching process.[9] However, at present the necessary data are still not available to make this approach possible. Therefore this part has to be dropped for the time being.

10.4 Construction Activities

During the nineties there was an enormous boom in housing construction driven by an increase in population by immigration. The opening of the eastern borders and the influx of refugees from the Balkan countries intensified demand generated by a reduction of household size and the entrance of larger cohorts into adolescence. The years before were characterised by relatively low construction even in the subsidised sector and in addition there were some projects like a world exhibition, the joining of EU, all of which worked together to create expectations of further increases of demand as well.

In order to make increased construction possible the volume of subsidies was raised dramatically. The municipality of Vienna opted for a doubling of the housing investment in the form of development at the periphery. This effort paralleled private construction leading to an increase of constructed apartments to 10,000 per year which may be seen in Fig. 10.10.

However, this boom is not sustainable. The long run level of demand for new dwellings will stabilise at some 6,000 apartments per year being sufficient to satisfy demand for replacement, substituting higher quality, enlarging dwellings by mergers and decreasing household size. Therefore a shift started to redevelop more central urban areas and to improve the existing housing supply there. The intensified construction and renewal activities led to a significant improvement of the quality of the housing stock in Vienna. By 2000, 83 per cent of the apartments

---

[8] See below the discussion of construction activities.

[9] There is a further dimension to be considered. Housing is part of the economy and society and their development. It exerts influence inter alia on the labour market and in the financial sector of an economy. A discussion of these interrelations, however, is beyond the scope of this study; for some recent analysis see Bingley and Walker (2001), Maclennan et al. (2000), Girouard and Blöndal (2001), Jensen et al. (1996), Hofmann (2001).

belonged to the top quality group with respect to equipment like central heating, bath etc. and 9.7 per cent only were substandard.

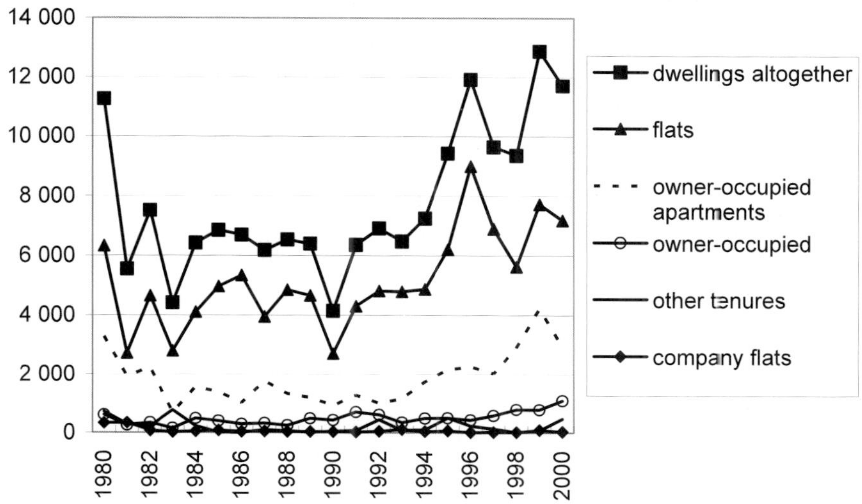

Fig. 10.10. Dwellings completed by tenure of dwelling 1980–2000

Half of the new construction in the nineties took place at the outskirts in the districts 10, 11, 21, 22 as already mentioned. More than 75 per cent of these new dwellings are up for renting. In contrast in the western part of the town more than half of the new construction is sold. This is a consequence of the larger share of commercial building contractors there. In the aggregate the share of rented apartments is unchanged at approximately 80 per cent.

Most dwellings are constructed by limited profit building societies. They increased their activities during the last two decades from 2,400 to 4,500 units on average per year. On the other hand public housing construction was reduced from 2,500 units to 1,000. The share of other constructors, mainly private ones, increased as well.

Limited profit building societies are strictly regulated.[10] They have to ask rents and prices on a cost basis and are allowed to calculate interest on their capital of only 3 per cent, but are obliged to build dwellings not larger than 150 sqm offering 'normal equipment'. Since 1985 their activities were extended to renovation of buildings. In 2001 they were allowed to sell their housing assets under certain conditions to the tenants. This marks an ideological shift accepting the role of property and was brought about by changes in the financial market conditions and

[10] Recent information on their activities may be found in Österreichischer verband gemeinnütziger Bauvereinigungen (2001).

the public budget situation. It is a long way from providing subsidised housing to the present more competitive environment for building societies. At the end of 2000 their stock of apartments was roughly 172,000 in Vienna almost 80 per cent of which were rented out.

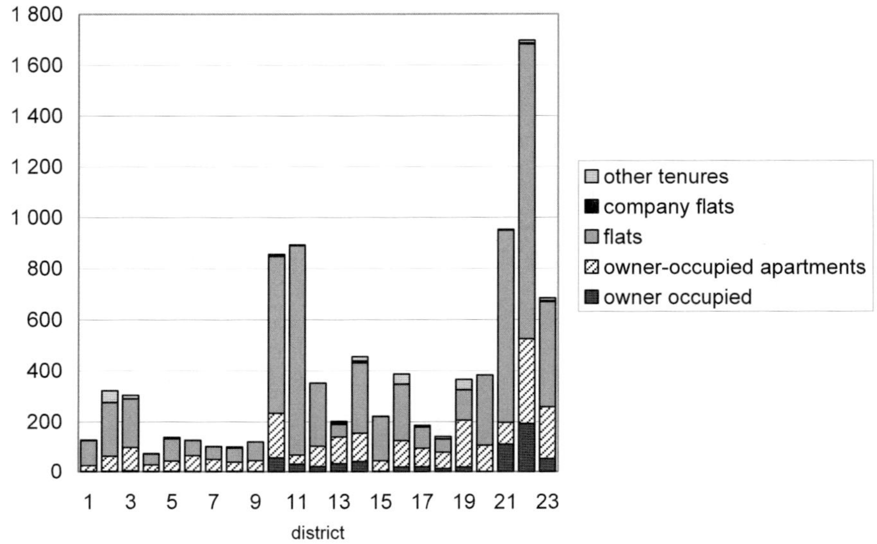

Fig. 10.11. Dwellings completed by district and by tenure of dwelling, mean 1991–2000

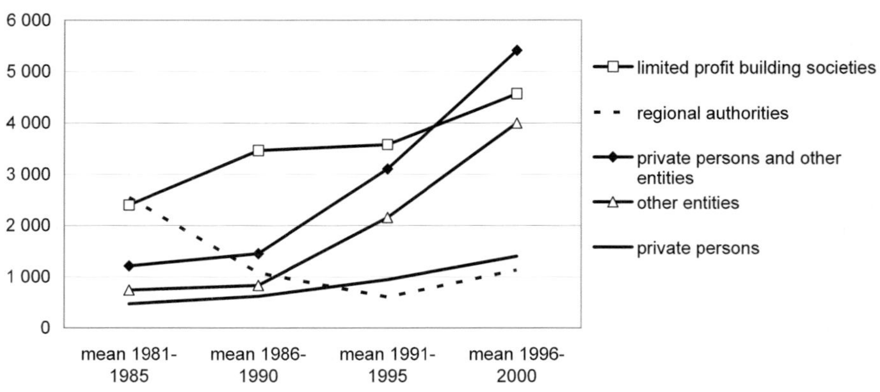

Fig. 10.12. Housing constructions by building contractors 1980–2000 (Sources: Magistrat der Stadt Wien 1990–2000; Stadt Wien 2001a)

One of the trademarks of the Viennese municipality has been public housing. After World War I up to 26 per cent of the budget of the city were devoted to the construction of public housing. These amounted to 64,000 units from 1919 to 1934 (Blaas et al. 1991). From 1950 to 1970 3,000 to 6,000 flats were built, but the average trend was decreasing. In the 1980s the number of new dwellings built by the municipality shrank to 2,000, at the beginning of the 1990s it was 600 units only. From 1996 to 1999 the number of new housing units constructed by the municipality averaged 1,250. All in all, the municipality owns approximately 220,000 dwellings which represent roughly 25 per cent of the total housing stock. Therefore the city government is an important factor in the metropolitan housing market.

A change in the legal requirements helped the municipality to outsource the financing of the housing construction because the community was allowed to use special dedicated subsidy funds for housing construction and thus it was no longer necessary to use budgetary means for financing since 1972. The disadvantage was, however, that the rents asked from the tenants of the new dwellings almost reached market level. Some critique that the community no longer pursued the goal to supply affordable housing to low income groups has been raised. In response the city government offered its housing stock to foreigners and people living in very bad conditions.

For a long time private and commercial building contractors were squeezed out of the market because of rent control. Only after they were allowed to apply for subsidies – that was after 1929 and again after 1968 – they were able to compete and supply housing in the range of the limited profit organisations. As regulation of the housing sector has been reduced more and more they became an important supplier of new apartments. In the second half of the 1990s they built on average 5,400 units which were more than the building societies.

10.5 Costs, Prices and Incomes

The construction boom in the nineties caused different price increases in the housing sector.[11] The prices for land ready for construction doubled or tripled whereas market prices of apartments stagnated or even fell as a consequence of the ample quantitative supply creating a buyers market. The housing segment of the consumer price index (CPI) increased in the last decade twice as high as the CPI (Fig. 10.13). Very recently this has changed and the increase was not only reduced but even lower than CPI's increase. Basically the increase reflects the beginning phasing out of rent control. Construction costs increased on average by 3.7 per cent which was between the increase of housing prices (4.8 per cent) and CPI (2.6 per cent). Increases of incomes in Vienna were slightly lower than the development of CPI which implies a slight increase in the share of housing expenditures. The

[11] For the effects of a large 'external shock' caused by the integration of the former Eastern Germany in the nineties in the housing sector of a big economy see Deutsche Bundesbank (2002).

1999/2000 household budget survey put the figure for housing expenditures at 23.5 per cent of Austrian household budgets.

Continuing deregulation started to close the gap between prices in the different segments of the housing sector.[12] Easing rent control increased the prices in the huge part of old apartments even at times when prices in the segment for unregulated new apartments stagnated. The difference between prices for new apartments and old ones sank from 50 per cent to 30 per cent during the last decade (Fig. 10.14).

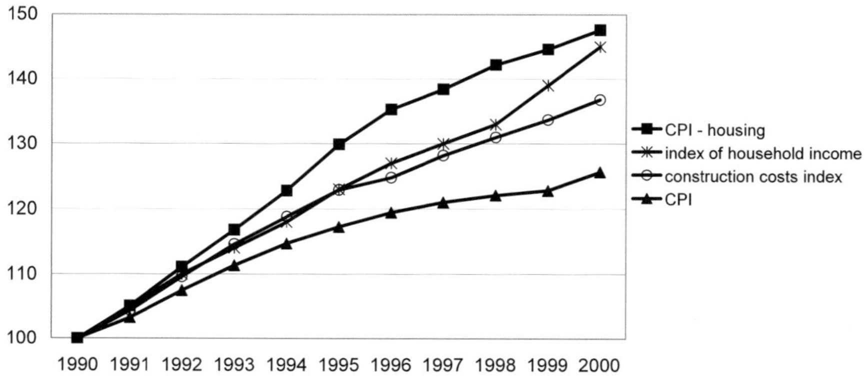

Fig. 10.13. Construction costs index, consumer price index, housing cost index, index of household income 1990–2000 (Sources: Donner 1995; Stadt Wien 2001; Statistik Austria 1998, 1999)

Illegal side payments at the time of contracting had been a serious problem for the segment of old flats. By these payments compensation for the artificial low rents had been sought. The adjustment of rent levels in the wake of partial deregulation removed their justification. There are, however, down payments for subsidised new housing which are used to finance costs of land. They can be quite reasonable and are now on average €259 per sqm. According to a recent study (Amann and Skopek 1999) of a sample of old (top category) and new apartments the average costs per sqm of subsidised apartments are €3.7 and €5.2 respectively. In relation to average incomes of the tenants this represents 21 per cent and 23 per cent. A similar picture emerges for the lowest income quartile which indicates that supply for their housing needs is available in enough quantity. With respect to the size distribution of incomes the group profiting most from the supply of subsidised housing are middle or high income groups.

[12] See Steiner and Troper (1991) for a general discussion.

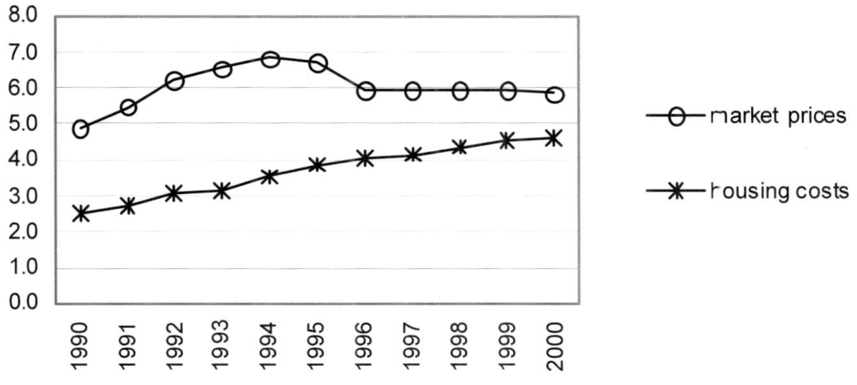

Fig. 10.14. Market prices and housing costs for flats by square metres in Euro 1990–2000 (Sources: Bundesinnung der Immobilien- und Vermögenstreuhänder (2001); Statistik Austria)

Another source of information about market conditions and prices is the yearly report of estate agents (Bundesinnung der Immobilien- und Vermögenstreuhänder 2001). In 2001 they report the price range for new property with three living-rooms in medium quality environments from €1,550.33 to €3,197.50 per sqm, in top quality environments €2,034.84 to €4,287.70 per sqm. The range for used apartments in the medium segment is €962.92 to €2,216.52. Market rents can be found between €5.16 and €10.68 per sqm.

There is some constraint on price increases because subsidies are granted only when the prices of land used do not exceed €218 per sqm, which limits construction to the availability of cheap land for development (Blaas 1997). Such land may be found in suburbs only.

Financing conditions reflect the high degree of regulation in the housing sector in Austria. Most of the construction activities are highly subsidised. A change to increased market conditions is already under way (Url 2001). Hypothetically calculated interest rates on the basis of a weighted mixture of sources of finance resulted in a nominal interest rate of close to 6 per cent 1993 and from then on in a reduction to 4 per cent. Real rates reached 2 per cent and fell to 1 per cent because of the reduction of inflation. In 2000, the municipality of Vienna spent €734 million for housing subsidies, 65 per cent of which were used for new construction, 30 per cent for redevelopment and the final 5 per cent for subsidies to individuals.

10.6 Institutions and Policy

For a long time the supply of adequate housing was the prime goal of housing policy. From these times a number of institutions has been inherited whose justification is more and more questionable. In addition the obligation of public budgets to fulfil deficit criteria limits the options for deficit spending. Thus there is some discussion for a basic reform of the policies for the housing sector.[13] Since basic legal provisions are the competence of the federal government the metropolitan options are limited.

One important area for municipal policies is the regulation by zoning. This creates the opportunities for development and influences land use and provides guidelines for urban infrastructure and separation of office and housing areas (Bundeskanzleramt der Republik Österreich 2002). Construction technique and style is regulated as well. By these means there is an opportunity to pursue environmental goals. A special organisation (Wiener Bodenbeschaffungs- und Stadterneuerungsfonds – WBSF) (Stadt Wien 2002a) tries to secure the availability of affordable land for subsidised construction. By its activity it provided land for 43,000 new subsidised apartments. Its reserves are about 2 million sqm at present.

In order to preserve or even improve competitiveness Vienna has given itself a development plan and started co-operation with the neighbouring provinces. From 1996 to 2001 population in Vienna increased by 1.6 per cent, in the surrounding area by 14 per cent! The expected access of the neighbouring countries to EU enforces planning perspectives which think in larger areas and include the influences and developments there as well.

The most important law regulating the housing sector in Vienna is the so-called 'Mietrechtsgesetz' (MRG). It is applicable for rented flats. This is the legal title for the use of more than 60 per cent of all Viennese dwellings (Stadt Wien 2001). Since the very beginning of rent control in 1917 the legal framework was revised several times. The last changes aim at phasing out of the strict control by simulating market conditions. A reduction of the heterogeneity of the housing sector is an additional goal of reform, because it can happen that very similar apartments are rented at very different prices. A detailed presentation of all consequences of rent control is beyond the scope of this chapter but it should be mentioned that it offered additional political influence in times of excess demand because of the ample options in manipulating rationing schemes.

The two other important laws concern limited profit building contractors and the conditions to buy and own flats. The latest revisions of these laws liberalise the regulation according to the general policy principles.

The main channel of influence on the housing sector is a wealth of subsidies. More than 95 per cent of all subsidies are directed to the supply side and only recently aim more in the direction of redevelopment. Long duration of credit, low interest rates and limited annuities are instruments used (Blaas et al. 1991). Since these conditions are not commercially viable this approach established political influence. All political parties tried to satisfy the interests of their clientele. Both owners of houses as well as tenants were able to profit by acquiring subsidies. As an example of the conditions to be met Table 10.8 presents the limits of incomes for several cases in order to become recipient of a subsidy for new construction.

[13] An important source of information is the contributions in Czerny (2001).

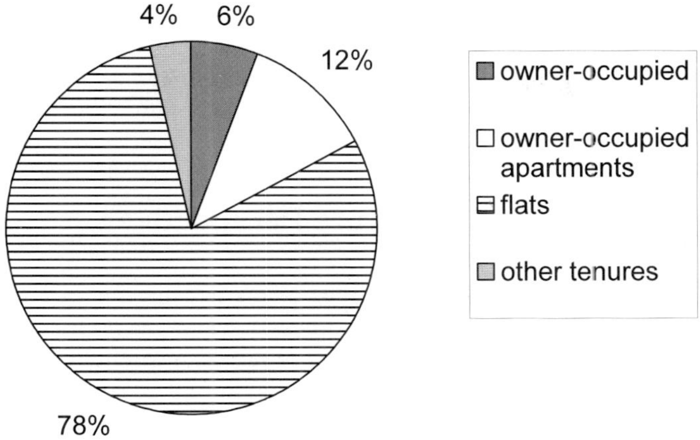

Fig. 10.15. Dwellings (main residence) by tenure of dwelling 2000

In the nineties the policy was adapted. Because of the big role of immigration for the population development in Vienna it became necessary to care more for the needs of this group of persons leading to innovative pilot projects (Stadt Wien 2002). In addition environmental concerns became more and more important. Simultaneously a shift back from expansion at the border to the centre and the older parts of the metropolitan area started (Stadt Wien 2001). It is an attempt to stop the deterioration of larger parts of the city and to make them attractive to a younger generation.

Table 10.8. Limits of annual income for households applying for subsidised new apartments in Euro 2002

	Public housing	Flats	Owner-occupied
1 person	25,500	30,600 to 35,700	35,700 to 40,800
2 persons	38,000	45,600 to 53,200	53,200 to 60,800
3 persons	43,000	51,600 to 60,200	60,200 to 68,800
4 persons	48,000	57,600 to 67,200	67,200 to 76,800
Every additional person	2,800	3,360 to 3,920	3,920 to 4,480

In the 1990s the policy was adapted. Because of the big role of immigration for the population development in Vienna it became necessary to care more for the needs of this group of persons leading to innovative pilot projects (Stadt Wien 2002). In addition environmental concerns became more and more important. Simultaneously a shift back from expansion at the border to the centre and the older parts of the metropolitan area started (Stadt Wien 2001). It is an attempt to stop the deterioration of larger parts of the city and to make them attractive to a younger generation.

Finally it should be mentioned that there are special programmes aimed at individuals lacking the means for affordable housing. They get support if they have an income but the costs of housing are higher than a share of the income regarded as 'reasonable' which is defined depending on household size and other characteristics.

10.7 Conclusion and Future Perspectives

It is fair to diagnose that the institutions of the housing sector are changing profoundly. The assumption of a general excess demand can no longer be maintained and the shift in the perception of the role of the state can be felt in the metropolitan housing market as well. Consequently, the process of deregulation of the housing market is well under way and seems to be not reversible barring external shocks (see Donner 1995; Czerny 2001).

The big challenge for the future will be to cope with the changes in population and the redevelopment of the older part of the urban area. Eastern enlargement of the EU may offer an opportunity and a threat as well for Vienna because it can generate new dynamics but may put strain on the urban structures. Redevelopment may be used as a chance to earn a double dividend contributing to meet the Kyoto reduction criteria. Housing has a share of more than 30 per cent of the final energy consumption in Vienna and offers great potential for CO_2 reduction as well. However, the different interests of owners and tenants pose big problems which need to be solved in an incentive compatible way if the necessary investments should be generated. This may indicate that there is still some latent imbalance in the housing sector in Vienna although aggregate excess demand no longer exists.

References

Abele H, Winckler G (1976) Wohnungsmarkt 1. Ansätze zu einer Mikroanalyse der Wohnungswirtschaft. Institut für Stadtforschung, Wien

Amann W, Bauernfeind S (2001) Wohnkosten und MRG-preisregelung. Forschungsgesellschaft für Wohnen, Bauen und Planen, Wien

Amann W, Skopek A (1999) Kosten von Mietwohnungen. Kammer für Arbeiter u. Angestellte für Wien, Wien

Aufhauser E, Fischer MM Schönhofer H (1986) A Disaggregated Probabilistic Approach to a Regulated Housing Market with Emphasis on the Demand side: The Vienna Case. Papers of Regional Science Association 60: 133–53

Best R (1996) Successes, Failures, and Prospects for Public Housing Policy in the United Kingdom. Housing Policy Debate **7**(3): 535–62

Blaas W, Rüsch G, Brezina B, Doubek C (1991) Mehr Markt oder mehr Staat im Wohnungswesen? Böhlau, Wien

Blaas W (1992) Determinanten des Bodenpreises in Wien. Kammer für Arbeiter u. Angestellte für Wien, Wien

Blaas W, Kramar H, Davy B (1997) Beiträge zur Wiener Bodenpolitik Kammer für Arbeiter u. Angestellte für Wien, Wien
Bingley P, Walker I (2001) Housing Subsidies and Work Incentives in Great Britain. Economic Journal 111 May, C86–C103
Bundesinnung der Immobilien- und Vermögenstreuhänder (2001) Immobilien-preisspiegel 2001. Pressekonferenz am 21 Mai 2001, http://www.wkimmo.at
Bundeskanzleramt der Republik Österreich (2002) Bauordnung für Wien. http://www.ris.bka.gv.at/lr-wien/
Currie J, Yelowitz A (2000) Are Public Housing Projects Good for Kids? Journal of Public Economics 75: 99–124
Czerny M (ed) (2001) Wohnungswirtschaft vor neuen Herausforderungen. Österreichisches Institut für Wirtschaftsforschung, Wien
Deutsche Bundesbank (2002) Der Wohnungsmarkt in den neunziger Jahren. Monatsbericht Januar, 29–39
Donner Ch (1995) Das Ende der Wohnbauförderung. Selbstverlag, Wien
Donner Ch (2000) Wohnungspolitiken in der Europäischen Union. Selbstverlag, Wien
Fischer MM, Aufhauser E (1988) Housing Choice in a Regulated Market: A Nested Multinominal Logit Analysis. Geographical Analysis 20(1): 47–69
Girouard N, Blöndal S (2001) House Prices and Economic Activity. OECD Economics Department Working Papers (279) January, http://www.oecd.org/eco/
Hofmann B (2001) The Determinants of Private Sector Credit in Industrialised Countries: Do Property Prices Matter? BIS Working Papers 108
Jensen SEH, Nielsen SB, Pedersen LH, Sorensen PB (1996) Tax Policy, Housing and the Labour Market: An Intertemporal Simulation Approach. Economic Modelling 13: 355–82
Keilman N, Kuijsten A, Vossen A (1988) Modelling Household Formation and Dissolution. Oxford: Clarendon Press
Kleinman M (1996) Housing, Welfare and the State in Europe. Edward Elgar, Cheltenham
Magistrat der Stadt Wien (2001) Statistisches Jahrbuch der Stadt Wien. Different volumes. Wien
Magistrat der Stadt Wien (2002) Voranschlag 2002. http://www.magwien.gv.at/
Matznetter W (1991) Wohnbauträger zwischen Staat und Markt. Campus-Verlag, Frankfurt
Maclennan D, Muellbauer J, Stephens M (2000) Asymmetries in Housing and Financial Market Institutions and EMU. http://www.housingoutlook.co.uk/
Österreichischer Verband gemeinnütziger Bauvereinigungen, Revisionsverband (2001) Die gemeinnützige Wohnungswirtschaft Österreichs in Zahlen, Wien
Schopper M, Eigler R (1996) Baulückenkataster für das dichtbebaute Wiener Stadtgebiet. Wien
Stadt Wien (2001) Stadtentwicklungsbericht 2000. Beiträge zur Fortschreibung des Wiener Stadtentwicklungsplans, Wien
Stadt Wien (2001a) Statistische Mitteilungen der Stadt Wien. 2, 3
Stadt Wien (2002) Homepage of the City of Vienna. http://www.wien.gv.at
Stadt Wien (2002a) Wiener Bodenbereitstellungs- und Stadterneuerungsfonds. http://www.wbsf.wien.at/
Statistik Austria ISIS Datenbank, http://www.statistik.at
Statistik Austria (1998) Statistische Nachrichten (2)
Statistik Austria (1999) Statistische Nachrichten (4)
Steiner W, Troper R (1991) Entwicklung der Wiener Altmiethäuser – Probleme und Szenarien. Institut für Stadtforschung, Wien
Türr H (1933) Die Wohnungsprobleme Österreichs vor und nach dem Krieg. Heymann, Berlin, Wien

Url T (2001) Der Einfluss öffentlicher Fördermittel auf die Finanzierungskosten von Wohnbauinvestitionen. In Czerny M (ed) (2001) Wohnungswirtschaft vor neuen Herausforderungen. Österreichisches Institut für Wirtschaftsforschung, Wien

Zimmermann C (ed) (1997) European Housing Policy in Comparative Perspective 1900–1939. Fraunhofer-IRB-Verlag, Stuttgart

Appendix

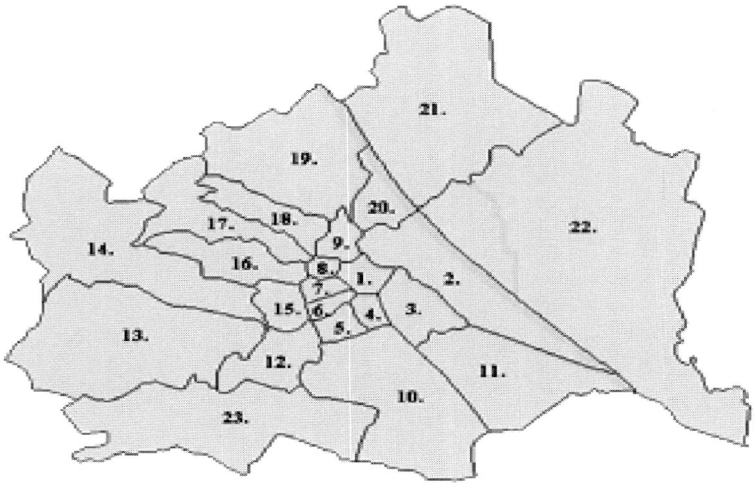

Fig. 10.16. Map of Vienna (Source: http://www.wien.gv.at/english/map/)

district 1: Inner City
district 2: Leopoldstadt
district 3: Landstraße
district 4: Wieden
district 5: Margareten
district 6: Mariahilf
district 7: Neubau
district 8: Josefstadt
district 9: Alsergrund
district 10: Favoriten
district 11: Simmering
district 12: Meidling
district 13: Hietzing
district 14: Penzing
district 15: Rudolfsheim-Fünfhaus
district 16: Ottakring
district 17: Hernals
district 18: Währing
district 19: Döbling
district 20: Brigittenau
district 21: Floridsdorf
district 22: Donaustadt
district 23: Liesing

11 Housing Market and Housing Policy in Hamburg. Evidence and Prospects

Annekatrin Niebuhr

IAB Nord, Kiel

11.1 Introduction

The housing market and housing policy strongly influence the social and economic conditions of regions. Housing in turn is affected by the economic development of regions, i.e. by income growth, labour market conditions and population growth. The present situation in Germany indicates these relations conspicuously. Housing markets are marked by pronounced regional disparities at present. In East Germany, still suffering from economic decline and high unemployment, the housing market is currently characterised by high vacancy rates, indicating low housing demand respectively excess housing supply because of unfavourable social and economic conditions. At the same time, excess demand and high real estate prices persist in large agglomerations in West Germany, especially in the southern part. These tight housing markets are evidence of a favourable economic development. With respect to economic development also the wealth boosting effect of rising housing prices respectively the positive impact on consumer demand might be relevant. For corresponding argumentation, see Economist (2002). However, simultaneously high land and housing prices, associated with excess housing demand, might become a growth impediment in the long run. This applies in particular to metropolitan regions that are frequently marked by extremely high rents and real estate prices. Even the present conditions, characterised on average by rather balanced housing markets, are accompanied by bottlenecks in major metropolitan regions in West Germany. Since human capital is an essential factor of economic success, especially in agglomerations specialised in sophisticated production services, sufficient supply of adequate housing is of utmost importance. Thus, a functioning and relatively balanced housing market is an important prerequisite for a favourable social and economic development.

The present chapter deals with the housing market and housing policy in Hamburg – one of the major metropolitan areas in Germany. With roughly 1.7 million inhabitants living on an area of 755 km^2, Hamburg is the second largest city and second smallest federal state in Germany as well as the economic centre of northern part. Due to the relatively wide urban area, the population density is lower than in most German cities. Hamburg's economy has experienced a prolonged period of structural adjustments, mainly pertaining to the shipbuilding industry and other productions related to the port. Nevertheless, the port is still an important element of the regional economy. The harbour is the main hub of German overseas trade and a significant part of Hamburg's economy, especially wholesale and related financial services are directly or indirectly connected to the port. Moreover, Hamburg is specialised in services and one of the major locations of both traditional and new media industry, in particular as regards publishing, advertising, film industry and internet firms. With respect to the relatively small industrial base, the civil aviation industry increasingly gains in importance. As a location of these branches, Hamburg attracts highly qualified labour. Especially for this population group housing market conditions are important determinants of location decisions.

Hamburg is a wealthy and economically successful region, both measured on the national and the European scale. Hamburg's GDP per capita was more than 80 per cent above the average level of the European Union in 1999. However, like other large metropolitan regions, Hamburg has to cope with serious social problems: poverty and unemployment polarise in specific city districts and many immigrants have to be integrated. The housing market and housing policy are highly relevant in this context as well.

Regarding the region under consideration, the empirical analyses focus in principle on the core city (NUTS-1 region) because of data restrictions. In case the investigations consider the hinterland of Hamburg as well, this is mentioned explicitly in the corresponding sections of the chapter. The hinterland comprises several NUTS-3 regions in the neighbouring federal states bordering directly on the core city. Most analyses have to be restricted to the core city since many indicators relevant for housing market issues are only available on the NUTS-1 level in Germany.

The rest of the chapter is organised as follows. The analysis of Hamburg's housing market starts with an inspection of the long-term development of housing demand and housing supply in Sect. 11.2. Sect. 11.3 focuses on the current market conditions regarding rent level, real estate prices and vacancies. Housing policy in Germany and the specific design of policy measures in Hamburg are outlined and evaluated in Sect. 11.4. The section deals with the tenancy law, tax allowances, demand subsidies and supply subsidies. Social problems associated with the housing market in Hamburg are investigated in Sect. 11.5. In Sect. 11.6 another important issue of housing in the Hamburg region is discussed: the relationship between suburbanisation, land use and urban development policy. Sect. 11.7 concludes.[1]

[1] I would like to thank Ulf Teubel, Silvia Stiller and an anonymous referee for valuable comments and suggestions on an earlier version of this chapter.

11.2 Housing Demand and Housing Supply in Hamburg

11.2.1 Housing Demand

With respect to housing demand, a number of determinants have to be considered. Population, the number of households, household structure as well as disposable income substantially influence the demand side of the housing market. Population growth can convey a first impression of the demand development. The city of Hamburg has experienced a prolonged period of declining population figures, like other large West German cities in the 1970s. Between 1970 and the mid of the 1980s the number of inhabitants decreased by about 12 per cent (see Fig. 11.1). In contrast, the subsequent period until 1993 was marked by high population growth of more than 7 per cent. This pronounced increase was caused by several immigration flows. An east–west migration within Germany started in 1989. Moreover, with the fall of the iron curtain a strong influx of immigrants from the Middle and East European countries set in. Between the end of the 1980s and mid-90s also many asylum seekers and refugees from former Yugoslavia came to Germany and Hamburg. However, since the mid of the 1990s, the number of inhabitants only slightly increased from about 1,708 million in 1995 to 1,726 million in 2001.

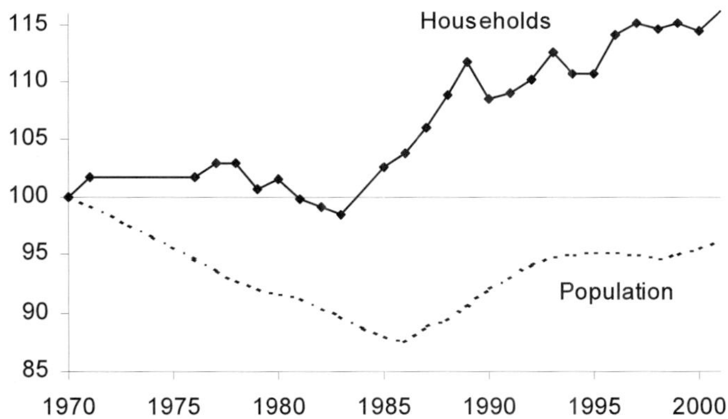

Fig. 11.1. Development of population and households in Hamburg 1970–2001, 1970 = 100 (Source: Statistisches Landesamt Hamburg (2002), own calculations)

Whereas net migration gains for Hamburg, originating in other federal states and foreign countries, have been characterised by pronounced fluctuations during the last three decades, the migration losses to the hinterland constitute a steady phenomenon. Almost 25,000 people have moved on average from Hamburg to the hinterland every year since 1970.[2] In contrast, only 16,000 people moved from the urban fringe to the city of Hamburg. Thus, the region is marked by a strong and

[2] The hinterland of Hamburg comprises six immediately neighbouring districts in the federal states Lower Saxony and Schleswig–Holstein. The hinterland and the core city are linked by intensive commuting flows.

continuous suburbanisation with an annual migration loss to the hinterland of more than 8,000 inhabitants. A significant proportion of the high population growth in the urban fringe is due to this suburbanisation process. The rate of population growth in the hinterland (16 per cent) was clearly higher than growth in the core city (7 per cent) between 1987 and 2000. The increase in housing demand that is caused by more than 300,000 additional inhabitants in the region since 1987 is, therefore, to a high degree effective in the hinterland (see also Gemeinsame Landesplanung Hamburg/Niedersachsen/Schleswig–Holstein 1999 p. 9 f.).

However, population is only a crude indicator for housing demand. More important than population growth is the change in the number of households. With respect to housing demand, both the absolute number of households and structural changes concerning the average size of households matter. Although the population in Hamburg slightly declined between 1970 and 2001, the number of households increased by more than 16 per cent due to major structural changes (see also Fig. 11.1). The number of one-person households increased by more than 57 per cent and two-person households showed an above average growth as well (almost 19 per cent). In contrast, the number of households with three or more persons declined by 29 per cent. The share of single-person households in all households rose from 36 per cent to 48 per cent[3] and the average number of persons per household decreased from 2.3 to 1.9. Currently, almost 80 per cent of all households in Hamburg comprise one or two persons. Thus, especially the demand for rather small dwellings has probably increased during the last decades.

Up to now, it is not demographic ageing, i.e. a rising percentage of old people living in single- or two-person households that causes the changes in average household size. Instead, the share of households consisting of a single person older than 65 years in all single-person households decreased between 1970 and 2001 from 43 per cent to 28 per cent. On the contrary, the age group up to 35 years contributed significantly to the increasing weight of single-person households in Hamburg. Their share in all households raised from 21 per cent (1970) to 30 per cent (2001). Another important aspect regarding the declining household size is probably the number of single parents that increased from about 30,000 in 1976 to 47,000 in 2001.

Furthermore, disposable income is highly relevant for housing demand. Disposable income per capita in Hamburg amounted to more than €17,700 in 2000 (see Table 11.1). This level is significantly above the German average (€15,800). Total disposable income increased by 18 per cent between 1991 and 2000. This expansion of total income as well as the increase in disposable income per capita (15 per cent), have probably raised total housing demand and demand per capita in Hamburg. A demand dampening effect presumably emanates from the relatively high unemployment in Hamburg since purchasing power of unemployed persons is lower and the unemployment risk is higher. The unemployment rate amounted

[3] The high percentage of one-person households is quite typical of large agglomerations in Germany. In the cities Hanover, Frankfurt and Munich the share has even surpassed 50 per cent. Ratios of this magnitude are well above the average level in Germany (36.6 per cent). Moreover, there are significant differences between city districts in Hamburg. The percentage of one-person households ranges from 17 per cent to almost 70 per cent. The share is higher than 50 per cent in all districts close to the city centre.

to 7.0 per cent in 2000. At present, unemployment in Hamburg is high compared with the federal states in the southern part of Germany and also with respect to other large metropolitan regions in Europe. However, labour market conditions have slightly improved during the last decade. In 1990, the unemployment rate in Hamburg was 7.5 per cent.

Table 11.1. Determinants of housing demand and housing supply in Hamburg

Variable	1990	2001	Growth 1990–2001 [%]
Population (in 1000)	1652	1726	4.5
Households (in 1000)	864	924	7.0
Housing space per inhabitant (m^2)	33.6	35.6	6.0
Disposable income (million Euro)	25629[a]	30311[b]	18
Disposable income per capita (Euro)	15433[a]	17723[b]	15
Unemployment rate (per cent)	7.5	7.0[b]	–
Dwellings (in 1000)	790	864	9.4
Average size of dwellings (m^2)	70.4	71.1	1.0
Share of dwellings in single- and two-family houses (per cent)	20.7	20.5	–

[a]Disposable income in 1991.
[b]Figures refer to 2000.
Sources: Statistisches Landesamt Hamburg 2001b, 2002; Statistisches Landesamt Hamburg, Homepage: http://www.hamburg.de/fhh/behoerden/behoerde_fuer_inneres/statistisches_landesamt/zeit/inhalt.htm; Statistisches Landesamt Baden-Württemberg (2002), Eurostat Regio database, own calculations.

Simultaneously, income per capita and housing demand per inhabitant have substantially increased in Hamburg. Housing space per person rose by more than 10 square metres (m^2) since 1970 and amounts to 35.6 m^2 currently. However, this level is rather low compared to the national mean (more than 39 m^2 per person) or other German cities.[4] Rising size and quality of dwellings have contributed to the considerable growth of rents that has resulted in a significant increase of the financial burden of housing expenditures. Whereas in the early 1970s approximately 17 per cent of disposable household income was spent on housing in West Germany, this percentage has increased to almost 25 per cent in 1998. The burden of rent expenditures in Hamburg does not significantly differ from the West German average. Low-income households and retired persons have to cope with an above average rent burden.[5]

The ownership rate, i.e. the share of dwellings occupied by proprietors, is relatively low in Germany (41 per cent, 1998), and Hamburg is a lagging region even compared to this low nationwide level. The corresponding percentage amounts to merely 20 per cent. Although the ownership rate increased in Hamburg since the

4 The housing space per inhabitant in other large cities ranges from 35.8 m^2 in Frankfurt to 40.4 in Hanover; see Statistisches Landesamt Hamburg (2002), p. 62.

5 See Haspa (1998), p. 31 f. This study is based on a survey and points to an above average burden for single parents as well. However, official statistics suggest that their rent burden corresponds with the average level in Hamburg.

end of the 1970s (level in 1978: 14.5 per cent), the region could not catch up in absolute terms to the national average. Several factors contribute to the low ownership rate in Germany and Hamburg: a focus on the construction of rental housing, high land prices and partly excessive visions regarding quality and amenities of owner-occupied housing. Owner-occupied apartments are a relatively low-priced alternative to single-family houses, especially in large cities. This is reflected by the relatively great importance of owner-occupied apartments in Hamburg. About 12 per cent of all dwellings accounted for this type of housing at the end of the 1990s (national average: 10 per cent; see Statistisches Bundesamt 2000 p. 71 f.).

To sum up, the long run development of housing demand in Hamburg is characterised by a continuous increase. Even in periods of constant or slightly declining population figures, demand for housing tended to rise since changes in household structure, income and preference for additional housing space more than compensated negative effects caused by a modest development of population.

11.2.2 Housing Supply

The number of dwellings in Hamburg increased quite continuously since 1970 from roughly 700,000 to more than 860,000 in 2001 (+24 per cent). Between 1990 and 2001, the quantitative housing supply rose by approximately 9 per cent (see Table 11.1). However, the steady development of the total housing stock hides pronounced fluctuations of construction activity. As Fig. 11.2 shows, the number of completed dwellings per year declined considerably since the beginning of the 1970s. The minimum level was reached in 1987 with less than 3,000 dwellings. The low level of construction activity around the mid of the 1980s was based on the general perception that insufficient housing supply was no longer a severe problem. The following years are marked by a sharp rise of completed dwellings in response to the strong population growth starting in 1986. The construction figures reflect that reunification and the fall of the iron curtain respectively the corresponding increase in housing demand was completely unanticipated by developers. In the period before the pronounced population growth set in, construction activity was particularly low. Moreover, the price index for the construction of new dwellings almost stagnated around the mid of the 1980s. Since housing supply can adjust to demand changes only with a certain time lag and construction activity was marked by massive increases starting at the end of the 1980s, housing prices and construction prices rose significantly in the first half of the 1990s. With stabilised population figures in mid-1990s, construction activity dropped again to a level of approximately 5,000 finished dwellings in 2001.

The structure of new housing in Hamburg differs significantly from the average pattern in Germany. Whereas 65 per cent of all new housing in Germany is situated in small buildings, i.e. in one- or two-family houses, in Hamburg these dwellings only amounted to less than one third of new housing in 2001.[6] In other words,

[6] With respect to the motives of suburbanisation a comparison with the hinterland is important. The supply of large dwellings and of one- or two-family houses, the preferred housing of highly mobile, young families, is substantially lower in Hamburg than in the

about 70 per cent of all new apartments in Hamburg are located in larger buildings with at least three flats. Regarding the construction of small buildings, there are also pronounced distinctions between Hamburg and the German average. The distribution of new small buildings on terraced houses, single- and two-family houses is rather uniform in Hamburg. The mean weight of single-family houses is by far larger in Germany (64 per cent of all small buildings in Germany, 34 per cent in Hamburg). In contrast, the construction of terraced houses tends to be more important in Hamburg (34 per cent of all small buildings in Hamburg, only 15 per cent in Germany).

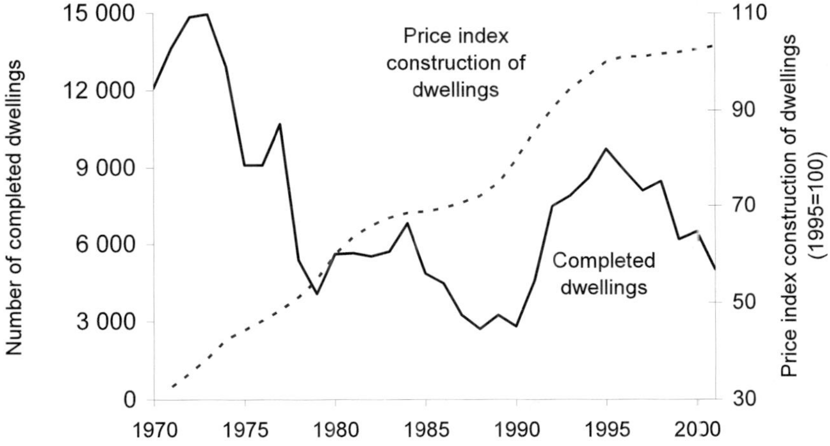

Fig. 11.2. Construction activity and price index for construction of dwellings in Hamburg between 1970 and 2001 (Source: Statistisches Landesamt Hamburg (2002); own calculations)

Corresponding differences mark the housing stock as well. The share of one- and two-family houses in total housing is about 20 per cent in Hamburg. This is far below the percentage achieved in the urban fringe of Hamburg (almost 60 per cent) and also below the German average (about 45 per cent) in 1999. However, a low share of single- and two-family houses is characteristic for large German cities and Hamburg achieves a higher percentage than most agglomerations in Germany.[7] The compressed house building in Hamburg aims primarily at low- and medium income households. Families with a relatively high income prefer offers in the hinterland since prices are relatively low, dwelling size tends to be higher and there is a considerable supply of owner-occupied housing. In order to provide attractive housing for young families and to adjust supply to the increasing demand for this type of dwelling, Hamburg is currently zoning more building land

neighbouring districts of the hinterland. See also Technische Universität Hamburg–Harburg (1999) p. 40.

[7] The share of single- and two-family houses in large German cities ranges between 11 per cent in Dresden and more than 35 per cent in Bremen.

for owner-occupied housing and especially for terraced houses (see Gemeinsame Landesplanung Hamburg/Niedersachsen/Schleswig–Holstein 1999 p. 31).

Due to the large scale reconstruction during the 1950s and 1960s, the housing stock in Germany and Hamburg is relatively new and well equipped. In 1998, less than 30 per cent of all dwellings in Hamburg were built before 1949 and more than 88 per cent had central heating (see Table 11.2). Already at the beginning of the 1990s, more than 98 per cent of the housing stock had a bathroom in West Germany. Moreover, the size of dwellings has considerably increased during the last decades. In 1970, the average size of dwellings in Hamburg was 62.5 m^2. At present, the average size is 71 m^2 (2001). New dwellings even have a mean size of almost 96 m^2. Compared with the national mean (average size of the housing stock: 84.8 m^2), dwellings in Hamburg are rather small. But a below average size is characteristic for housing in large German cities.[8]

Table 11.2. Structure of housing supply in Hamburg and Germany 1998 (in per cent)

	Share of category in total dwellings	
	Hamburg	Germany
Dwellings built		
before 1900	5.4	9.3
between 1901 and 1918	8.5	6.9
between 1919 and 1948	14.1	13.4
between 1949 and 1978	57.9	48.3
between 1979 and 1986	5.8	10.7
between 1987 and 1990	1.7	3.2
1990 and later	6.6	8.2
Owner occupied dwellings	20.3	40.9
Rented dwellings	79.7	59.1
Public housing[a]	17.9	–
Dwellings with central heating	88.8	86.9

[a]Figure refers to 2000.
Source: Statistisches Bundesamt 1999.

Construction costs are high in Germany compared to other European countries. However, construction costs in Hamburg are extremely high. On average, construction costs per m^2 housing space amounted to €1,240 in Germany in 2000.[9] In contrast, €1,625 had to be paid for one m^2 in Hamburg. This is more than in all other federal states. The construction of single-family houses is particularly cost-intensive with €1,646 per m^2. Concerning small buildings, the lowest alternative in Hamburg is the terraced house with €1,510 per m^2. Large buildings with more than three flats present a relatively cost-saving type of construction as well (€1,606 per m^2). Between 1991 and 2001 price indices for the construction of new dwellings significantly increased, by 21 per cent in Hamburg and by 16 per cent on average in Germany. Thus, costs differences between Hamburg and the mean level in Germany even tended to rise in the 1990s. Moreover, whereas construction prices for new housing continued to increase in the second half of the 1990s

[8] The average size in large German cities ranges between 63.9 m^2 in Dresden and 76.1 m^2 in Bremen, see Statistisches Landesamt Hamburg (2001).

[9] Construction costs are the estimated costs at the date of building permission.

in Hamburg, on average, the price indices slightly declined in Germany during that period.

Several factors contribute to the high level of construction costs in Germany. Firstly, public regulations define quality standards that are frequently quoted as one major reason for high construction costs. Secondly, German consumers have a preference for expensive individual housing. This applies in particular to single-family houses. And finally, housing policy has possibly also cost-enhancing effects since the subsidisation of housing construction might reduce the incentive for cost-saving production of dwellings.[10] Moreover, specific factors in Hamburg aggravate the cost conditions. Since large areas are marsh land or need flood protection, planning and development costs are relatively high as well.

To sum up, housing supply in Hamburg has steadily increased during the last decades. Moreover, this applies to both quantity and quality of dwellings. Due to the substantial growth of housing supply, excess demand, that was a central feature of housing markets for a long time in Hamburg, was successfully reduced. However, if the currently extremely low construction activity will persist, this might result again in a significant excess demand in foreseeable future.

11.3 Real Estate Prices, Rents and Housing Market Equilibrium

The development of German housing markets during the last decade is characterised by two rather contrasting periods. Until mid-1990s pronounced increases in housing demand, rising rents and real estate prices were main features of housing markets. Since mid-1990s the tight market conditions have slackened to some degree. A stabilisation of demand, increasing supply and a modest development of rents marked the second half of the 1990s. In 2002, rents are on average 4 per cent to 6 per cent below the level in 1993/94. In some segments of Hamburg's housing market, real estate prices and rents declined during the last years as well.

Central features of present housing market conditions in Germany are the pronounced regional disparities. First, significant differences exist between East and West Germany. Whereas in the western part housing markets are on average more or less balanced, the federal states in the eastern part are marked by a substantial excess supply of housing. The high vacancy rates in East Germany constitute probably the most acute problem regarding current housing market conditions in Germany.[11] Second, there are also noticeable regional distinctions in West Germany. Fairly different housing market conditions prevail in agglomerations and less densely populated areas. In general, rents and real estate prices in large agglomerations are significantly above the average level. And finally, there are also systematic differences between the northern and southern part of West Germany.

---

[10] See Donner (2000) p. 178; Grosskopf and König (2001a) p. 174. Cost reduction has received more attention in the 1990s. There have been efforts to search for possible costs reduction regarding regulations, housing design and land policy.

[11] In order to achieve more balanced housing markets in East Germany a subsidy for the demolition of large residential buildings was introduced recently (see DIW 2001).

Agglomerations in southern Germany are still marked by relatively tight housing markets.

By far the highest rent level can be observed in Munich: the average rent per m^2 was €10 in 2002 for a standard dwelling of about 70 m^2 and almost €12 for a new dwelling of the same type.[12] On average, the rent in large German metropolitan regions varies currently between €5.8 and €6.3, depending on the age of the housing, and €7.7 for new dwellings. In Hamburg, a level well above the average is achieved, with about €6.7 (€8.8 for new dwellings). Rents of the same dimension prevail only in a few other agglomerations, i.e. in Düsseldorf, Frankfurt, Cologne and Stuttgart (see Ring Deutscher Makler 2002b).

A similar regional pattern marks the prices of owner-occupied houses and flats. More than €237,000 had to be paid in West Germany on average for a standard single-family house with roughly 125 m^2 in 2002. The prices in the northern part of Germany (€182,000) were significantly below the level in south (€302,000). Highest prices are currently realised for real estate located in large agglomerations in southern Germany. Again, Munich holds the top position with €500,000. A rather high level can be observed also in Frankfurt (€410,000) and Stuttgart (€350,000). The average price in Hamburg is rather modest (€280,000) compared to the level in other metropolitan regions in West Germany. Approximately €2,100 has to be paid per m^2 for a single-family house in Hamburg, €1,900 per m^2 for an owner-occupied apartment. The comparatively low price level for real estate is partly caused by the relatively large area covered by the city of Hamburg. Moreover, the hinterland provides a number of alternative locations, thus, leading to an extensive supply and relatively low prices in Hamburg as well. This is also reflected by the price level for building land in Hamburg that is below the average for large metropolitan regions in West Germany. In Hamburg, the mean price of one m^2 building land is €220 at present. On average, €180 have to be paid in Germany. The highest price levels prevail in Munich and Stuttgart with more than €500 (see Ring Deutscher Makler 2001a, b; LBS 2002).

Significant price differences also persist within the Hamburg metropolitan region. The intraregional price structure is marked by a more or less clear centre-periphery gradient. Average prices for owner-occupied apartments and houses tend to decline with increasing distance from the city centre. Moreover, there are significant differences between the northern and the southern part of Hamburg. Prices per m^2 are on average lower in southern city districts. In first-class locations prices per m^2 range between €2,500 and more than €4,100 for single- or two-family houses. Owner-occupied apartments in these areas achieve €2,300 to €3,200 per m^2. However, at the most popular locations, along the rivers Elbe and Alster, high quality apartments realised prices of up to €10,000 per m^2 in 2001. In the outer districts, close to the outskirts, real estate prices tend to be substantially below these maximum levels. Prices between €1,500 and €2,400 per m^2 have to be paid for houses and apartments. In the southern part of Hamburg corresponding prices vary from less than €1,250 to €2,000. The prices in immediately neighbouring districts of the hinterland do not significantly differ from these levels. Consistent with the structure in the core city, prices decline in the hinterland with in-

[12] All presented rents do not include costs for heating, other running costs and public charges for waste disposal or sewerage

creasing distance to the city centre. In locations at the outer border of the urban fringe, prices range between €1,000 and €1,600 (see Vereins- und Westbank Hamburg 2001 and LBS 2002).

The housing market in Hamburg is characterised by large differences regarding the rent per m^2 as well. The intraregional rent structure closely resembles the disparities with respect to real estate prices. Rents range between €7 per m^2 for a new standard flat in lowly districts and up to €16 in the most preferred locations in 2001. Table 11.3 shows the current level and growth of rents for various categories of dwellings in Hamburg between 1989 and 2001. The rent level depends on equipment, residential area, age and size of dwellings. The lowest average rent per m^2 was €3.4 in 2001 for medium-sized dwellings with low equipment (no bathroom and central heating) that were built before 1919 and are located in a standard residential area. In contrast, more than €11 per m^2 had to be paid on average for fairly new and small dwellings (25 to 41 m^2, built after 1987) located in a good residential area.

Table 11.3. Rent structure and rent increase 1989–2001 in Hamburg

Dwellings[a]	Average rent per m^2 2001 [€]	Growth 1989–2001 [%]	Growth 1989–1995 [%]	Growth 1995–2001 [%]
Construction year before 1919				
Low equipment, standard location, 66–91 m^2	3.39	38.1	27.7	8.2
Standard location 66–91 m^2	6.08	57.3	36.2	15.4
Good location > 131 m^2	6.13	50.6	32.3	13.9
Construction year 1948–1960				
Standard location 66–91 m^2	4.86	25.0	22.5	2.0
Good location > 91 m^2	7.05	58.7	45.9	8.8
Construction year 1968–1977				
Standard location 66–91 m^2	4.86	8.8	20.8	–9.9
Good location > 91 m^2	7.86	51.8	47.5	2.9
Age < 14 years[b]				
Standard location 66–91 m^2	7.67	27.5	26.0	1.1
Good location 25–41 m^2	11.07	8.9	8.4	2.6
Good location > 91 m^2	9.15	31.7	21.0	8.8

[a]All presented categories of dwellings have standard equipment, i.e. bathroom and central heating, if not stated otherwise.
[b]Growth rates for dwellings of age less than 14 years are calculated for dwellings with this feature in 1989.
Source: Own calculations based on data of the Hamburger Mietenspiegel, various volumes.

There is no simple relationship between specific housing characteristics and the rent level as one might expect against the background of these cases, representing the lower and upper bound. The rent level is not declining steadily with rising age of housing. Dwellings built before 1948 are marked frequently by higher rents than comparable housing built in the 1950s and 1960s. For more recent vintages, however, the rents are relatively high. The maximum rents are realised for dwellings up to 14 years age. Size of dwellings and residential area are also important features affecting the rent level in Hamburg. Moving from a standard to an above average residential area can increase ceteris paribus the rent by up to €2.4 per m^2. Furthermore, the rents per m^2 of small dwellings (25 to 41 m^2) tend to be higher than the rent level of larger dwellings. This possibly reflects a strong and rising demand for small flats due to an increasing number of one- and two-person households in Hamburg. However, large apartments with more than 91 m^2 are relatively expensive as well. Thus, with respect to the rent per m^2 medium sized flats are the cheapest category.

More or less pronounced rent increases mark the development of the housing market since 1989. Again, significant differences persist between various types of dwellings. The average rent of a medium size flat, built between 1968 and 1977, located in a standard residential area, shows a modest increase of about 9 per cent between 1989 and 2001. In contrast, tenants of large dwellings, built in the 1950s and located in an above average residential area, had to cope with a growth rate of almost 59 per cent. There is a tendency for above average rent increases in good residential areas, especially with respect to housing built in the 1960s and 1970s as well as to large dwellings. A pronounced rent growth also marks old dwellings with more than 91 m^2. The period between 1989 and 2001 can be divided into two rather contrasting sub periods. Until the mid of the 1990s, rents increased rapidly due to strong growth of population and housing demand. The rent level rose especially in highly agglomerated areas in West Germany because migration flows concentrated in these regions. The subsequent stabilisation of population figures and housing demand is reflected by fairly modest rent increases in Hamburg. Rent growth slowed down significantly between 1995 and 2001. For some housing categories average rents even declined for the first time since more than 20 years. Changes in housing supply have contributed to this development as well. A large number of new dwellings became available during the 1990s because of massive construction activity that followed the strong influx of people (see also Sect. 11.2.2).

The appraisal that housing markets in Germany and in Hamburg are more or less balanced at present is confirmed by a relatively high vacancy rate. In general, it is assumed that a share of about 3 per cent vacant dwellings in total housing stock is compatible with housing market equilibrium in Germany since this percentage is necessary for renovation and relocation. In 1987, the vacancy rate was 1.8 per cent in West Germany, pointing to excess demand due to the strong population growth and low construction activity around mid-1980s. The rate increased to 2.9 per cent in 1993. This suggests that the pronounced increase in construction activity starting at the end of 1980s already significantly reduced excess demand. The vacancy rate continued to rise to 6 per cent in 1998, in East Germany even to more than 13 per cent.[13] The housing market in Hamburg remained tighter in the 1990s. In 1993, only 1.8 per cent of all dwellings were vacant. However, the market conditions converged towards a more balanced situation in subsequent years as well. At the end of the 1990s the vacancy rate in Hamburg was clearly above the assumed equilibrium level of 3 per cent (4.2 per cent in 1998).

These facts point to a housing market that is rather balanced at the moment. But it should be noted that some market segments are still rather tight. Moreover, gen-

[13] More current data on vacancies are not available because the corresponding surveys are carried out irregularly.

eral conditions for housing investment have deteriorated during the last years. Market prices of real estate as well as rents tended to stagnate or even slightly declined. In contrast, construction costs for new dwellings continued to rise in Hamburg. Besides, investors argue that recent reforms in housing policy reduced investment incentives since the changes have a negative impact on expected returns on housing investment (see Sect. 11.4). This is in line with the most recent figures on construction activity. Between 2000 and 2001 the number of new dwellings in Hamburg decreased further by 22 per cent to about 5,000 (Statistisches Landesamt Hamburg 2002).

Summarising, one can state that the housing market in Hamburg is fairly balanced at present. However, investment incentives have probably declined during the 1990s because of increased housing supply, a modest development of demand and a slow growth of rents and real estate prices, partly even declining prices and rent levels. Furthermore, negative effects might also arise from recent policy changes. Against this background, the issue is raised again whether the low construction activity prevailing presently will result in excess housing demand and insufficient supply especially regarding low-income households in the foreseeable future.

11.4 Housing Policy

The design of housing policy in Germany has been heavily influenced for more than five decades by the conditions prevailing immediately after the World War II. Large-scale destruction of housing stock and massive population influx resulted in a severe housing shortage. Housing policy, therefore, concentrated primarily on providing adequate housing for large parts of the population. Only recently reforms of housing policy changed this general focus. The reforms aim at a housing policy that concentrates more on low-income households and problem groups (Deutscher Bundestag 2000 p. 14).

Housing policy is a common task of the federal government, the federal states and local authorities. However, the federal government is not directly involved in housing policy implementation. In principle, the federal government determines the general conditions of housing policy by corresponding legislation and contributes to housing policy funds. Housing policy is mainly based on four different instruments. Firstly, the tenancy law aims at protecting tenants against eviction and regulates rent adjustments. Supply subsidies and tax policy are applied to promote the construction of rental and owner-occupied housing. Finally, housing benefit, i.e. demand subsidies, support low-income households in financing of adequate housing (Donner 2000 p. 177).

11.4.1 Tenancy Law

The tenancy law has two main elements: the protection of tenants against eviction and regulations regarding rent adjustments. Apart from a few exceptions tenancy agreements are unlimited. Termination of the tenancy has to be justified by the landlord. In case of legal grounds for termination, the periods of notice range between three and nine months. The rent level of new tenancy agreements is relatively unregulated. In contrast, later rent adjustments are strictly regulated for the duration of the agreement. Tenancy agreements can not be terminated in order to raise rents. Rent adjustments have to consider the local comparable rent. The comparable rent is the amount usually demanded for a comparable dwelling in the region. The corresponding rent listings (Mietenspiegel) base on a regular survey. In Hamburg, this service is provided for more than 20 years by the responsible housing authority. With certain limitations, rents of existing tenancies can be raised up to the comparable rent level. However, the increase must not exceed a specific amount within three years. Only the rent determination for new tenancies is fairly unrestricted. However, also new contracts with a rent level exceeding the comparable rent by more than 50 per cent are illegal (Donner 2000 p. 155).

In 2001, several changes regarding the tenancy law have been introduced by the federal government. Firstly, landlords now have to state explicitly the comparable rent level if they demand a higher rent. Secondly, the maximum increase of rents allowed within three years was reduced from 30 per cent to 20 per cent. Finally, periods of notice have been shortened one-sided in favour of the tenants. At present it is discussed whether this extension of tenant protection might have negative effects on housing investment. Moreover, flexibility of rent adjustments is increasingly restricted to new tenancy agreements and new dwellings. This results in a relatively high rent level of new tenancy agreements and probably reduces the mobility of tenants. Thus, tenants might stay in flats although they would prefer e.g. a smaller dwelling (Expertenkommission Wohnungspolitik 1995 p. 118).

11.4.2 Housing Benefit

An important instrument of German housing policy is the housing benefit. These income transfers aim at the provision of adequate housing for low-income households. Eligible for housing benefit payments are households with an income below a specific income ceiling. The income ceiling depends on household size. In 2000, the housing benefit system was adjusted to changes in rent levels and income. Housing benefit increased on average by more than €40 per month, and more households became eligible for housing benefit. Income ceilings range between €882 and €4,142 monthly gross income. The intention of housing benefit is to ensure that housing expenditure does not exceed a maximum percentage of 35 per cent of household income (Donner 2000 p. 162; Fuchs 2001; Bundesministerium für Verkehr, Bau- und Wohnungswesen 2000). Thus, housing benefit serves to cover the part of housing expenditure that low-income households can not bear up. Tenants always have to pay a certain part of rent. The calculation of the subsidy rests upon on the monthly rent, household income and household size (Bundesministerium für Verkehr, Bau- und Wohnungswesen 2000). Funds for this demand subsidy are provided by the federal government and the federal states. The local authorities are responsible for the implementation.

In 2000, 4.5 per cent of all inhabitants in Hamburg received housing benefit. Total housing benefit amounted to about €137,000,000. Thus, on average an eligible person received approximately €146 housing benefit per month. In Hamburg, the demand subsidy is slightly more important than on average in Germany where 3.5 per cent of the population was recipients in 2000, receiving a mean housing benefit of €104 per month. In the course of recent reforms of housing policy, housing benefit gained in importance compared with other measures of housing policy.

11.4.3 Tax Policy

Tax policy relevant for the housing market in Germany comprises various instruments. A detailed description of all corresponding measures is beyond the scope of the present chapter. Important with respect to the housing market is, among other things, a municipal real estate tax that is due on all properties. However, the tax rate is relatively low. This implies that the incentive to sell unused building land is fairly small in Germany. Moreover, transaction costs have to be considered that become due with the transfer of dwellings. The buyer has to pay a property acquisition tax that amounts to 3.5 per cent of the real estate price. Altogether, taxes and fees associated with the transfer sum up to approximately 7 per cent of the price (see Donner 2000 p. 163 f.; Expertenkommission Wohnungspolitik 1995 p. 318).

Different tax benefits granted in conjunction with the construction of rental housing and the formation of owner-occupied housing are also associated with significant effects on the housing market. These tax regulations have been subject of considerable changes in 2002. Until 2002, the construction of rental dwellings was promoted by an accelerated depreciation. This accelerated depreciation has been replaced by a linear depreciation for rental housing in 2002. Furthermore, gains from selling real estate have become subject to taxation with the exception of owner-occupied housing. Until 2002, a tax liability pertained to sales within a speculative period of 10 years. The promotion of owner-occupied housing, i.e. the construction of new owner-occupied dwellings and the acquisition of dwellings from the existing stock, is supported by allowances that were formerly composed of a basic component and an allowance for children. The basic component has been cancelled recently. Thus eligibility for the promotion is restricted to parents now. The promotion has also been restrained by a reduction of the corresponding income limits. Only households with a two years income below €70,000 (single parent households) or €140,000 (larger households) are eligible. With these changes the promotion of house building was significantly decreased. The shift in basic conditions will probably reduce investment incentives and dampen the long-term development of housing supply (see Bartholmai 2002).

11.4.4 Housing Construction Policy

Housing construction policy focuses on supply subsidies and promotes the construction of rental housing and owner-occupied housing for low-income households. The modernisation and maintenance of the existing housing stock is supported as well. The intensity of subsidisation varied considerably during the last decade. The promotion was substantially increased in response to the massive population influx starting at the end of the 1980s and steadily declined again between 1993 and 2000 (Stern 2001 p. 67). The subsidisation of rental housing construction establishes a commitment to rent out to low-income households and reduces rents in corresponding dwellings. Moreover, local authorities can receive the right to decide on the occupancy of subsidised dwellings in exchange for supply subsidies. These occupancy rights can be used to provide housing for problem households that are not able to find a dwelling because of specific characteristics. Until 2002, rents in subsidised housing were determined according to the concept of cost rent, i.e. they covered costs of equity and foreign capital as well as operating expenses. Subsidised dwellings are freed of rent limitations and become part of the private rental market as soon as subsidisation expires (Donner 2000 p. 154).

Social housing for low-income households is primarily subsidised rental housing. Only persons eligible for social housing get a housing eligibility certificate that allows them to move into a subsidised flat. Eligibility is restricted by an income ceiling. The general income ceilings are fixed by the federal government. Since the beginning of 2002, the income ceiling amounts to an annual income of €12,000 for a one-person household, €18,000 for two persons and €4,100 for every additional household member. The federal states can deviate from these general stipulations in order to take into account specific regional housing market conditions (Bundesministerium für Verkehr, Bau- und Wohnungswesen 2001). However, often household income increases over time and exceeds the corresponding income ceilings. Thus, some subsidised flats become inaccessible to entitled households since tenants, although no longer eligible for social housing, are protected against unwarranted eviction by tenancy law. Therefore, compensation payments, i.e. misallocation charges, were introduced. The revenues from misallocation fees are used for social housing provision (Donner 2000 pp. 154, 161). In addition to social housing for low-income households, local authorities provide housing for some population groups that are unable to obtain adequate accommodation because of specific personal characteristics, e.g. alcoholics or socially disruptive persons. The local authorities can use occupation rights associated with subsidised dwellings in these cases. Funds required for these measures have to be provided by the local authorities.

The subsidisation system distinguished between several promotion schemes until 2002. The federal legislation provided a more or less detailed framework of subsidisation depending on the promotion scheme. The schemes differed with respect to target group, intensity of subsidisation and size of dwellings. Since 2002, there is no explicit differentiation between promotion schemes. However, their presentation offers comprehensive information on the current subsidisation because the current promotion combines elements of the former schemes. In principle, the federal government determines the general conditions of subsidisation and the federal states are responsible for actual design of promotion and implementation. The federal funds are allocated to the federal states which have to provide at least an equal amount from their own funds. The subsidisation comprises interest-free or low-interest public loans, guarantees as well as grants towards construction costs and operating costs. Subsidised loans generally carry no interest initially. Maturity is usually less than 45 years, in Hamburg the terms of the loans are relatively short.[14]

The first promotion scheme (FPS) was highly regulated by federal legislation and focused on the construction of rental housing for low-income households and the provision of housing for problem households. The second promotion scheme (SPS) aimed primarily at owner-occupied housing for middle-income households. The permitted size of dwellings and subsidies were lower, rents were higher and social commitment periods shorter compared to the FPS. However, the strict cost rent regulations applied to flats subsidised through the SPS as well. The SPS has steadily become less important and was of minor interest with respect to the construction of rental dwellings in the last years. Hamburg provided a subsidisation of rental flats within the SPS until 1997 (Behring et al. 1998 p. XIII; Hamburgische Wohnungsbaukreditanstalt 2001). The third promotion scheme (TPS) was introduced in 1989 and considerably gained in importance during the 1990s. The TPS was more flexible than the other programmes and aimed at both rental housing and owner-occupied dwellings. The intensity of subsidisation was lower than in the FPS and the SPS. The scheme involved flexible agreements with private promoters of new rental housing. Investors and local authorities agreed on the amount of subsidies, rent level, eligibility and duration of social housing commitment. The cost rent regulations did not apply to the TPS (see Donner 2000 p. 152; Behring et al. 1998 p. XIII/XIV).

Until 2002, the subsidisation of rental housing in Hamburg was primarily realised through the first and third promotion scheme. The promotion involved both grants towards operating expenditures and low-interest public loans covering in principle 80 per cent of total construction costs. In contrast to other federal states, in Hamburg the TPS was restricted to rental dwellings in multi-storey buildings. The programme exclusively aimed at low-income households. The level of subsidies depends on the tenant's income. Eligibility for housing is restricted to households with an income exceeding the general income ceiling defined by the federal government at most by 20 per cent. Rent increases in subsidised dwellings are determined by the reduction of subsidies, i.e. two years after completion grants decline yearly by €0.15 per m^2 and rents rise correspondingly. Moreover, in the TPS the tenant's income is checked every second year, and exceeding the relevant income ceiling results in a rent increase as well. In the FPS, tenants with an income above the corresponding income ceiling had to pay a misallocation fee. However, this fee was gradually reduced and finally cancelled in 2002. The rate of misallocation in Hamburg was almost 15 per cent in 2000, and the associated sum of charges amounted to more than €18,000,000.[15]

Owner-occupied housing is promoted by loans for construction and operating costs in Hamburg. The construction of houses and purchase of real estate can be

---

[14] Among others, the terms of the loans depend on the kind of construction activity promoted. For maintenance measures maximum terms of loans range between six and nine years in Hamburg. In contrast, promotion programmes by the Kreditanstalt für Wiederaufbau (KfW) include terms of loans up to 30 years. See Donner (2000) p. 159 and Hamburgische Wohnungsbaukreditanstalt (2002).

[15] See Hamburgische Wohnungsbaukreditanstalt (2001) p. 9 ff. The abolition of the misallocation fee was decided because of unfavourable effects the charge might have regarding social segregation (see also Sect. 11.5).

subsidised if the income of the respective household does not exceed the general income ceiling by more than 20 per cent (FPS) or at most 60 per cent (SPS). Furthermore, the construction of houses is only promoted in Hamburg if they correspond with a special low-energy standard. The loans for construction are interest-free during the first 10 years. The amount of the loans depends on the number of household-members and dwelling size.[16] The loan was up to €740 (FPS) respectively €460 per m^2 (SPS) in 2001. Families with children can get additional loans. At least 15 per cent of total costs have to be covered by own capital. The subsidisation of owner-occupied houses and flats in Hamburg comprised more than 900 dwellings in 2001.[17]

The promotion of modernisation and maintenance aims at improving housing conditions, energy saving and providing low-priced housing for large parts of the population in Hamburg. Subsidisation is associated with limited rent regulation, as in the case of subsidised construction of new dwellings. Some measures focus on specific city districts that suffer from a deteriorating housing stock and social problems (Hamburgische Wohnungsbaukreditanstalt 2001 p. 24 f.). In 1999, the federal government started the programme Soziale Stadt (social city). This programme focuses on large cities as e.g. Hamburg that suffers from a concentration of unemployment and poverty in some districts. In Hamburg the programme is used to support the modernisation of dwellings in city districts that are affected by economic decline and social problems.

Altogether, more than 2,300 dwellings in Hamburg were subsidised in 2001. The subsidisation focused on rental dwellings in multi-family buildings (55 per cent of all subsidised dwellings). The second important group of subsidised housing was single-family houses with a share of approximately 38 per cent. The initial rent level in new subsidised dwellings ranged between €5.06 and €7.11 per m^2. The funds for the construction of new dwellings amounted to roughly €204,000,000 for loans and more than €163,000,000 for grants. Moreover, substantial funds were also provided for modernisation, maintenance and environmental measures (Hamburgische Wohnungsbaukreditanstalt 2002).

11.4.5 Recent Reforms and Evaluation of Housing Policy

Recent changes in housing policy focused on three areas: reforms of housing construction policy, increasing funds for housing benefit and a reform of the tenancy

[16] The size eligible for promotion depends on the number of household members: 60 m^2 for one person and 10 m^2 for every additional person; see Hamburgische Wohnungsbaukreditanstalt (2001) p. 20.

[17] In principle, owner-occupied housing is promoted in several ways in Germany. Besides public grants towards financing, indirect subsidisation through building society financing (Bausparkassen) and tax allowances are provided. Building society financing is one of the main financing forms in Germany. The federal government supports this form of financing by income tax allowances or premiums on deposits in housing savings plans. In addition, owner-occupied housing is promoted by the housing property programme of the KfW. The KfW provides low-interest loans of up to 30 per cent of total costs (maximum €100,000) with a maximum term of 30 years. See Donner (2000) p. 153 f. and Hamburgische Wohnungsbaukreditanstalt (2001, 2002).

law. The reforms of housing policy are associated with a gradual shift in emphasis from supply subsidies to demand subsidies, i.e. housing benefit gained in importance relative to the subsidisation of housing construction. Deregulation of housing markets concentrates presently on housing construction policy. In contrast, there are no significant liberalisation efforts regarding the tenancy law. The reform of housing construction policy, in force since 2002, aims at a more efficient and flexible use of subsidies in view of rather differentiated housing market conditions. The general focus changed from housing for large parts of the population to specific target groups: low-income households and problem groups. In addition, regarding supply subsidies more attention is paid to the existing housing stock. Furthermore, the heavily criticised concept of cost rents in social housing was abolished and the federal states get more scope for an individual design of housing policy. With the new housing construction law the federal government determines general conditions, like e.g. income ceilings, whereas the federal states define the specific organisation of the promotion, e.g. deviations from the general income ceilings in accordance with regional or local housing market conditions. The determination of conditions regarding occupation of subsidised dwellings and rent level is also task of the federal states.

The recent reforms have certainly removed some deficiencies of German housing policy, like the former cost rent regulation that split the housing market in two segments. The costs rent overrode investment decisions based on profitability under market conditions. By abolishing the cost rent the general rent regulations of the tenancy law apply to social housing now as well (Vesper 2001 p. 140). However, with respect to efficiency and market distortions there are still fairly problematic instruments of housing policy. The criticism regarding the current policy focuses on the supply subsidies and the tenancy law. According to results of several studies, the subsidisation of social housing results in a crowding out of privately financed housing supply. Moreover, promoting the construction of social housing has no justification as a means of providing accommodation for problem households since this can be solved by purchasing occupation rights for the existing housing stock. The supply subsidies have proven to be an inefficient instrument of housing policy. The amount of subsidies is by far higher than the resulting rent reductions for low-income households. Rents for social dwellings partly even exceed the local comparable rent level. The attempt of covering the housing demand of low-income households by new dwellings is fairly questionable.[18] Furthermore, due to misallocation only a part of rent reduction is actually to the benefit of target groups. The social accuracy of supply subsidies is low compared with the housing benefit. The misallocation fee is a questionable solution of this problem since the fee might reinforce social segregation. Thus, there is clearly a discrepancy between reducing the misallocation of supply subsidies and attempts to avoid social segregation.

Another problem of social housing derives from the fact that the number of eligible households is around five times higher than the number of subsidised dwellings. Thus, there is intense competition among households for social housing. In

[18] According to estimates, the fiscal burden of social housing construction in Germany was approximately €10 billion in 1993, whereas the benefit for tenants amounted to just €2 billion. See Stern (2001) p. 68; Donner (2000) p.178.

contrast to housing benefit, supply subsidies do not allow to treat all eligible households equitably (Eekhoff 2001 p. 147). In addition, since the period of social commitment is limited, a persistent subsidisation of housing construction is required in order to provide sufficient social housing.[19] Moreover, the level of social rents is more affected by the construction year than by housing quality. Consequently, young families moving into new social dwellings have to pay relatively high rents. The effects of housing policy regarding the mobility of tenants have to be considered as well. The rent level of existing tenancy agreement is relatively low compared to new contracts since rent adjustments within the scope of current contracts are highly regulated. The resulting immobility applies especially to social housing. Tenants often stay in rather large dwellings although a smaller apartment would be more reasonable. Finally, the joint funding of housing policy by the federal government and the federal states is problematic. The increased responsibility of the federal states should also apply to the financing of housing policy. The currently practiced mixed financing is criticised because it tends to result in wasting public funds (Stern 2001 p. 70 f.; Keil 1996 p. 15 ff.; Eekhoff 2001 p. 146).

11.5 Social Segregation in the Hamburg Region

Social structures prevailing in the districts of metropolitan regions are closely related to housing policy. The degree of residential segregation indicates the social mixture of a metropolitan region's neighbourhoods. A region is marked by a high degree of segregation in case social groups are divided in rather homogeneous neighbourhoods. Thus, social disparities are reflected by an uneven spatial distribution of different social groups. A popular measure of segregation of two social groups is the index of dissimilarity. The index shows the percentage of either social group that would have to relocate in order to achieve complete integration, i.e. a proportional representation of all social groups in each neighbourhood.[20]

The degree of social segregation in Hamburg, measured by the dissimilarity index, is moderate. The analysis is based on data on foreign population and welfare recipients in 98 city districts in Hamburg. According to the results 16 per cent of the foreign and German population would have to relocate to achieve complete integration. With respect to the population being on welfare, a proportional representation in each city district would require that more than 19 per cent of the population has to move. Although the extent of social segregation is moderate in Hamburg, compared e.g. to the degree of racial segregation in some US cities, there are considerable social disparities within the city (see Table 11.4).

---

[19] In Hamburg, the social commitment of more than 40,000 subsidised dwellings will expire between 2000 and 2007 (see Bürgerschaft der Freien und Hansestadt Hamburg 2000).

[20] See O'Sullivan (1996) p. 390; Mills and Hamilton (1994) p. 256. The dissimilarity index is given by: $D = 100 \cdot \sum_i N_i \left| (b_i - b) \right| / 2Nb(1 - b)$, where N is the population of the metropolitan region and b is the share of a specific social group in total population. The metropolitan region is divided into a number of areas. N_i and b_i are the population and the fraction of population in area i.

Table 11.4. Social disparities and housing. Hamburg, the hinterland and Germany

Variable	Hamburg	District minimum	District maximum	Hinterland	Germany
Share of foreign population in 2001 [%]	15.7	1.0	78.3	5.4[a]	8.8[a]
Share of welfare recipients in total population in 2001 [%]	6.9	0.6	16.1	3.2	3.3
Unemployment rate in 2001[b] [%]	9.1	1.8	18.3	7.3	10.0
Share of social housing in 2000 [%]	17.9	0	71.9	–	–
Average income of tax-payers 1995 in Euro	33,500	21,300	81,100	35,500	30,500
Average size of dwellings in sqm in 2000	71.0	52.2	118.7	92.3	84.6
Dwelling area per inhabitant in sqm in 2000	35.4	19.3	54.6	40.5	39.0
Crime per 1000 inhabitants in 2000[c]	167	27	5,038	68	77

[a]Data refer to 2000.
[b]The unemployment rate of the city districts in Hamburg refers to 2001 and is calculated by using the population between 15 and 65 years, since there is no data on working population available for the city districts. The underlying definitions of unemployment in Table 11.1 and 11.3 therefore differ.
[c]Crime data for the hinterland and Germany refer to 1999.
Source: Statistisches Landesamt Hamburg (2001b, 2002), own calculations.

The share of foreign population in Hamburg's districts ranges from around 1 per cent to more than 78 per cent. Disparities are less pronounced regarding the poor population. The share of welfare recipients in the city districts varies between less than 1 per cent and about 16 per cent. Substantial differences persist also with respect to unemployment, income level and crime rate.

These disparities are reflected by significant differences between the housing conditions. Whereas in some city districts no social housing at all is provided, in other districts more than 70 per cent of all housing is social housing. Substantial differences likewise exist in terms of housing space per inhabitant and average size of dwellings. Furthermore, the findings suggest that social problems tend to accumulate in some districts. There is a significant positive correlation between the share of poor people, unemployment and the percentage of foreign population. In addition, housing conditions are closely linked to the social structure of city districts. The quality of housing, measured by size of dwellings, area per person or share of social housing, is positively correlated with average income in the city district. Housing conditions tend to deteriorate with increasing social problems (see Figs. 11.3 and 11.4).

Similar relations are also detected regarding differences between the hinterland of Hamburg and core city. To sum up, average income is higher and social problems tend to be lower in the hinterland compared with the core city. Moreover, housing conditions are rather favourable on the outskirts of Hamburg. The disparities between core city and urban fringe, e.g. with respect to the percentage of welfare recipients, are also fairly stable. Suburbanisation tends to reinforce social segregation within the city and between the core city and the hinterland since households with a relatively high income primarily move from the city to the hinterland (Technische Universität Hamburg-Harburg 1999 p. 34). Thus, social segregation is at least partly caused by segregation with respect to income. However, segregation might also reflect preferences for living in a rather homogeneous neighbourhood to some extent.

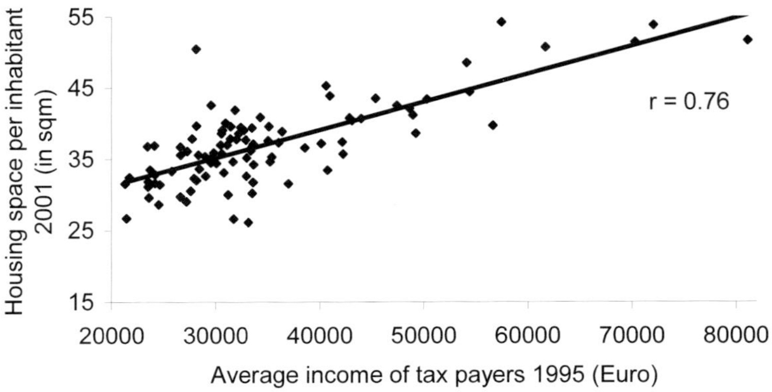

Fig. 11.3. The relation between income and housing conditions in Hamburg's districts (Source: Statistisches Landesamt Hamburg (2001b, 2002), own calculations)

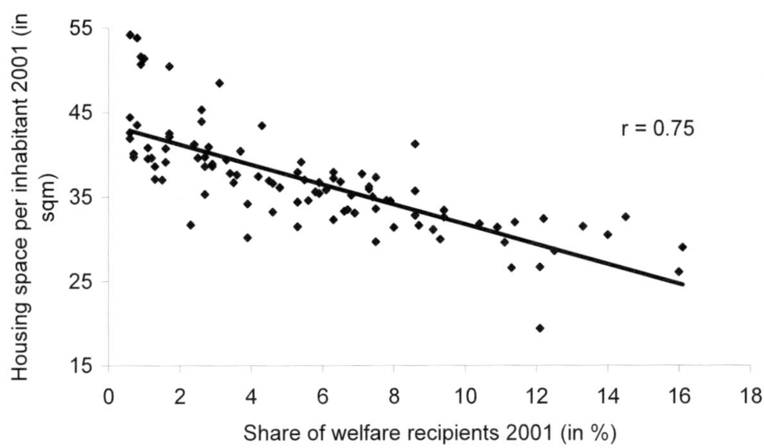

Fig. 11.4. The relation between poverty and housing conditions in Hamburg's districts (Source: Statistisches Landesamt Hamburg (2001b, 2002); own calculations)

Especially in periods of balanced housing markets, a misallocation fee tends to intensify social segregation. Since the number of vacant dwellings is relatively high, more medium and high income households, not eligible for social housing, leave districts characterised by a high percentage of social housing. In contrast, only poor people can move into the vacant subsidised flats because new tenants must have an eligibility certificate. In order to reduce social segregation, Hamburg abolished the misallocation fee in 2002. The misallocation fee probably contributed to a polarisation of poor households in city districts marked by a relatively high share of social housing (Donner 2000 p. 166). The provincial governments of Hamburg and the neighbouring federal states stress that the planning of new residential areas should, therefore, aim at a wide variety of dwelling sizes and types in order to achieve a heterogeneous population and avoid polarisation processes.

11.6 Suburbanisation, Land Use and Urban Development Policy

An important aspect of housing in the Hamburg region is the continuous suburbanisation of population. Especially young families leave the city in order to settle in the hinterland. About 50 per cent of the migrants moving from the core city to the hinterland belong to two age groups: adults between 30 and 50 years and children/young persons up to 18 years (Gemeinsame Landesplanung Hamburg/Niedersachsen/Schleswig–Holstein 1999 p. 10). There is also a migration flow in the opposite direction which is dominated by young people up to 24 years starting education in Hamburg. Several factors are presumably relevant regarding the steady process of suburbanisation. An important motive for suburbanisation is probably the differential in real estate prices between Hamburg and the urban fringe (see Sect. 11.2). Furthermore, the supply of large dwellings that meet the requirements of families with children, is limited in the core city. There is an enormous deficit of large apartments particularly in districts close to the city centre. Large dwellings are primarily located on the outskirts, in districts with a high percentage of one- and two-family houses. Thus, the structure of housing supply in Hamburg encourages suburbanisation of households searching for more housing space (Technische Universität Hamburg-Harburg 1999 p. 107).

Another motive of suburbanisation is the desire for housing property that will probably gain in importance as a way of private retirement provisions in Germany. However, the financial burden associated with the purchase or the construction of real estate requires a minimum household income. Consequently, only high-income households can afford the relatively expensive property in Hamburg. Analyses point to significant differences regarding the annual financial burden, depending on the location in Hamburg or the hinterland.[21] The estimated burden ranges between €22,000 in areas close to the city centre and €12,000 in the outer hinterland. Assuming a maximum share of housing costs in income of 35 per cent,

[21] See Leutner (1999). The analyses base on the regional price structure in 1998 and assume the purchase of a dwelling with 140 m^2, 40 per cent financing by own capital and 6 per cent loan interest.

the required annual net income varies between €61,000 near the city centre and €33,000 in the hinterland. Therefore, only about 7 per cent of all households in Hamburg could afford real estate in the inner city at the end of 1990s. In contrast, approximately 28 per cent of the households could afford housing property in the periphery. The desire for housing property and substantial price differences might, therefore, result in massive suburbanisation. Additional factors discussed in this context are social tensions in some city district and less environmental problems in the hinterland (Technische Universität Hamburg-Harburg 1999 p. 100 ff.).

The consequences of suburbanisation for both the core city and the hinterland are considered to be one of the major problems in the region for decades now. On the one hand, suburbanisation has unfavourable effects on tax revenues, social segregation and public expenditures (e.g. regarding public transport) in Hamburg. According to estimates, the city looses annual revenues of approximately €2,800 to €3,300 per migrating inhabitant. This sum bases on reduced income tax and turnover tax, but also on less funds from the system of financial transfers between the federal states since the amount of transfers depends on the number of inhabitants.[22] On the other hand, local authorities in the hinterland are frequently concerned about additional expenditures caused by the immigrants that might exceed the additional revenues. The willingness of local authorities to supply building land is low in some municipalities in the urban fringe of Hamburg. They fear high costs since the zoning of building land involves considerable investments in local infrastructure. Therefore, new housing may impose a fiscal burden on the municipalities in the hinterland. It seems doubtful whether this constellation of different interests is consistent with an appropriate provision of building land and housing space in the entire region. Furthermore, the present land use and urban development policy is unsuitable for coping with the associated problems.

The organisation of land use and urban development policy in Germany is a complex hierarchy comprising various tasks of national, regional and local authorities. The federal government is responsible for national plans and general conditions, as e.g. plans for long-distance transport infrastructure. With their individual zoning plans and development targets the federal states provide the framework for local authorities, e.g. a system of central places. However, the local authorities determine the actual land use and provide the local infrastructure, i.e. public transport, local road network or sewage system. Plans of the federal government, the federal states and local authorities have to be coordinated. Regarding the coordination between different local authorities, Hamburg and the hinterland represent a special case. A consistent policy for the entire region calls for close cooperation across the borders of federal states and between a number of local authorities. The relevant region regarding housing market and physical planning process is larger than the federal state Hamburg. The relevant area also comprises the hinterland, i.e. several districts in the neighbouring federal states Lower Saxony and Schleswig–Holstein.

[22] With respect to the entire region, these losses are compensated to some degree by additional tax revenues and transfers for the municipalities in the hinterland. But altogether, the core city and the hinterland loose financial resources because inhabitants of the urban fringe have less weight in the system of regional transfers than the population in the core city. See Technische Universität Hamburg-Harburg (1999) p. 30 ff.

The present organisation of physical planning is likely to result in scarce land and relatively high housing prices in the region. Investors, therefore, turn to less expensive but also less accessible sites at the periphery, between the axes of public transport (Gemeinsame Landesplanung Hamburg/Niedersachsen/Schleswig–Holstein 1999 p. 10). However, this development is problematic regarding environmental compatibility since it involves increased traffic and a dispersed landscape due to urban sprawl. Moreover, especially the population in the core city might be affected by scarce housing supply that results in higher rents since a relatively high percentage lives in rented flats. In contrast, the urban fringe is dominated by owner-occupied housing. The corresponding households do not suffer from higher rents. They may even benefit from rising prices for real estate. To sum up, demand for building land is primarily located in the core city that has no sufficient land resources, whereas there may be no incentive to supply more building land in the urban fringe, although there are land resources. Interests in the region are at least partly conflicting (Donner 2000 p. 157 or Expertenkommission Wohnungspolitik 1995 p. 85 ff.). Hamburg should be interested in a sufficient supply of building land and dwellings in the hinterland in order to avoid high rents and estate prices in the core city. At the same time, high housing supply and low prices in the hinterland involve suburbanisation, declining tax revenues and social segregation in the city.

The current organisation of regional and local planning does not meet the requirements of metropolitan regions that do not correspond with the historic borders of districts and authorities of local decision makers. The large agglomerations in Germany have grown across city borders. City and urban fringe have become a socio-economic entity. In such regions, the planning process on a correspondingly higher (regional) level should get more influence (Expertenkommission Wohnungspolitik 1995 p. 349). For most of the German metropolitan regions, this implies an increasing influence of the federal states. However, regarding the specific structure of the Hamburg region, i.e. an area extending across the borders of three federal states, a single regional authority does not exist. Physical planning that takes into account the needs of the entire region can only base on intense cooperation of the federal states Schleswig–Holstein, Hamburg and Lower Saxony.

The provincial governments have realised the need for cooperation and agreed on a common regional development concept for the Hamburg metropolitan region in 2000. The concept considers several policy areas and includes a model of spatial development for the area. This model comprises a system of central places and emphasises settlement in existing centres along the main transport axes of the region. The zoning of land for different uses should involve coordination between all responsible authorities. The zoning of building land should focus on gaps in the housing estates of the core city and conversion of former industrial and military sites. New residential areas should have a good access to the traffic system and a functional mixture of housing, work, shopping and leisure facilities (Gemeinsame Landesplanung Hamburg/Niedersachsen/Schleswig–Holstein 1999 p. 17). The regional development concept defines targets and general conditions of cooperation, but it does not involve a direct legal commitment for the various public planning authorities. It remains an open issue whether such non-committal measures are adequate with respect to land use, urban development and the housing market in the Hamburg region. Projects involving actually a practiced cooperation are still scarce. The federal governments of Hamburg and Schleswig–Holstein have started a close cooperation regarding subsidised social housing. The common project comprises the construction of up to 500 dwellings for social housing in the northern hinterland. See Gemeinsame Landesplanung Hamburg/Niedersachsen/Schleswig–Holstein (1999).

11.7 Conclusions

The development of housing demand and housing supply in Hamburg is characterised by a continuous growth during the last decades. Due to the substantial increase of quantitative and qualitative housing supply, excess demand, that was a central feature of the housing market at least until mid-1980s, was successfully reduced in Hamburg. At present, the housing market is fairly balanced, although there are still some tighter market segments. However, incentives for housing investment have probably declined during the 1990s because of increased housing supply and a modest development of demand, rents and real estate prices. Furthermore, negative effects might also arise from recent policy changes. Against this background, the issue is raised again whether the low construction activity prevailing presently will result in excess housing demand in the foreseeable future. Assuming that general demand conditions do not significantly change, persistently low housing investments will soon involve an insufficient supply especially regarding the target groups of housing policy, i.e. low-income and problem households.

Future housing policy has to cope with a number of challenges that arise from demographic changes. Housing demand will change because of an ageing population, the decreasing significance of traditional family relationships and immigration. This applies in particular to the large metropolitan regions in Germany. Recent reforms of housing policy have removed some deficiencies of German housing policy such as the cost rent regulation. However, there are still problematic elements with respect to efficiency and market distortions. The changes of housing policy extend the scope for policy design at the federal states level. The provincial government in Hamburg has to seize this chance in order to remove current deficiencies as far as possible within the limits of federal legislation.

Housing policy in Hamburg should focus on measures with a relatively high social accuracy. Moreover, the present market condition, i.e. a fairly balanced housing market, also offers an opportunity for reducing supply subsidies and increasing the importance of measures with less problematic side effects, such as housing benefit. Demand subsidies should gain in importance relative to supply subsidies since their social accuracy is higher and negative consequences of supply subsidisation like misallocation and social segregation are avoided. Furthermore, the dimension of problems related to the housing market frequently exceeds the border of the federal state Hamburg. Thus, the coordination of housing policy and urban development policy of the concerned federal states is of utmost importance. Finally, a primary objective of housing policy should be to guarantee favourable basic conditions for housing investment in order to secure a sufficient unsubsidised housing supply.

References

Bartholmai B (2002) Bauwirtschaft: Statt Stabilisierung erneut kräftiger Einbruch zu erwarten. DIW-Wochenbericht 45/2002, pp 780–90

Behring K, Kirchner J, Ulbrich R (1998) Förderpraxis des Sozialen Wohnungsbau. Duncker & Humblot, Berlin, München

Bodewig K (2001) Die Neue Ausrichtung des Sozialen Wohnungsbaus. Wirtschaftsdienst 81: 135–38

Bundesministerium für Verkehr, Bau- und Wohnungswesen (2000) Wohngeld 2001. Ratschläge und Hinweise, Berlin

Bundesministerium für Verkehr, Bau- und Wohnungswesen (2001) Gesetz zur Reform des Wohnungsbaurechts vom 13. September 2001. http://wwwbmvbw.de/

Bürgerschaft der Freien und Hansestadt Hamburg (2000) Mietpreisbindungen in Hamburg. Bürgerschaftsdrucksache 16/4439, Hamburg

Deutscher Bundestag (2000) Wohngeld- und Mietenbericht 1999. BT-Drucksache 14/3070, Berlin

DIW (2001) Zur Wohnsituation in West- und Ostdeutschland – Anstieg der Mieten zum Stillstand gekommen. DIW-Wochenbericht 41/2002, pp 625–33

Donner C (2000) Housing Policies in the European Union. Theory and Practice. Ernst Becvar Verlag, Vienna

Economist (2002) Going Through the Roof. Special Report. House Prices. The Economist March 30th

Eekhoff J (2001) Anmerkung zum geplanten Wohnraumförderungsgesetz. Wirtschaftsdienst 81: 146–48

Expertenkommission Wohnungspolitik (1995) Wohnungspolitik auf dem Prüfstand. Report by order of the federal government, Mohr, Tübingen

Freie und Hansestadt Hamburg, Behörde für Bau und Verkehr, Amt für Wohnungswesen, Mietenspiegel. Several volumes, Hamburg

Fuchs A (2001) Unzureichende Mindestförderung des Bundes. Wirtschaftsdienst 81: 141–43

Gemeinsame Landesplanung Hamburg/Niedersachsen/Schleswig–Holstein (1999) Metropolregion Hamburg. Regionales Entwicklungskonzept REK 2000. Hamburg

Grosskopf W, König P (2001a) Die Wohnungspolitik in der Bundesrepublik Deutschland. In: Gondring H, Lammel E (eds) Handbuch Immobilienwirtschaft. Gabler-Verlag, Wiesbaden, pp 165–84

Grosskopf W, König P (2001b) Der Wohnungsmarkt – Grundstrukturen und Funktionsweise. In: Gondring H, Lammel E (eds) Handbuch Immobilienwirtschaft. Gabler-Verlag, Wiesbaden, pp 75–94

Hamburgische Wohnungsbaukreditanstalt (2001) Jahresbericht 2000. Hamburg

Hamburgische Wohnungsbaukreditanstalt (2002) Jahresbericht 2001. Hamburg

Haspa (1998) Wohnungsnachfrage in Hamburg. Ist-Zustand und Trends der nächsten Jahre. Hamburg

Haspa (2000) Wohnungsnachfrage in Hamburg und Umgebung. Status quo und Trends der nächsten Jahre. Hamburg

Keil K (1996) Sozialer Mietwohnungsbau in der Krise. IFSt-Schrift No 346, Institut für Finanzen und Steuern, Bonn

LBS Bausparkasse Hamburg (2002) LBS-immobilienpreisuntersuchung August 2002. http://www.lbs-hamburg.de/PL9D/pl9d.htm?detail_snr=52

Leutner B (1999) Immobilienmarkt und Umlandwanderung. In: Technische Universität Hamburg–Harburg (ed) Auswirkungen der Umlandwanderungen auf den Hamburger Wohnungsmarkt. Hamburg, pp 88–99

Mills ES, Hamilton BW (1994) Urban Economics. Harper Collins College Publishers, New York
O'Sullivan A (1996) Urban Economics. Irwin, McGraw-Hill, Boston
Ring Deutscher Makler (2001a) Immobilienmarkt: Belebung läßt immer noch auf sich warten. Pressemitteilung vom 05.07.2001, Hamburg
Ring Deutscher Makler (2001b) Bauplätze: Stabile Aufwärtsentwicklung der Baulandpreise. Pressemitteilung vom 26.10.2001, Hamburg
Ring Deutscher Makler (2001c) Wohnungsmieten steigen wieder. Pressemitteilung vom 28.09.2001, Hamburg
Ring Deutscher Makler (2001d) RDM kritisiert Mietvertragsrecht als einseitig und investitionshemmend. Pressemitteilung vom 30.03.2001, Hamburg
Ring Deutscher Makler (2002a) Immobilienmarkt: Aufschwung frühestens im kommenden Jahr. Pressemitteilung vom 10.07.2002, Hamburg
Ring Deutscher Makler (2002b) RDM-Marktanalyse: Wohnungsmieten steigen schwächer als im Vorjahr. Pressemitteilung vom 08.11.2002, Hamburg
Ring Deutscher Makler (2002c) Markt für Einfamilienhäuser: Schwache Konjunktur dämpft Nachfrage. Pressemitteilung vom 15.02.2002, Hamburg
Statistisches Bundesamt (2002) Preisindizes für Wohngebäude. http://www.destatis.de/indicators/d/bpr110ad.htm
Statistisches Bundesamt (1999) Bautätigkeit und Wohnungen, Mikrozensus – Zusatzerhebung 1998. Fachserie 5 Heft 1, Bestand und Struktur der Wohneinheiten, Wiesbaden
Statistisches Bundesamt (1999) Bautätigkeit und Wohnungen. Fachserie 5 Reihe 1, Bautätigkeit, several volumes, Wiesbaden
Statistisches Bundesamt, Bautätigkeit und Wohnungen, Fachserie 5 Reihe 3, Bestand an Wohnungen, several volumes, Wiesbaden
Statistisches Bundesamt (2000) 50 Jahre Wohnen in Deutschland. Ergebnisse aus Gebäude- und Wohnungszählungen, -Stichproben, Mikrozensus – Ergänzungserhebungen und Bautätigkeitsstatistiken, Wiesbaden
Statistisches Landesamt Baden–Württemberg (2002) Verfügbares Einkommen 1991 bis 1999. http://www.statistik-bw.de/VolkswPreise/ArbeitskreisVGR/einkommen.asp
Statistisches Landesamt Hamburg (2000) Einkommens- und Verbrauchsstichprobe 1998 in Hamburg. Hamburg
Statistisches Landesamt Hamburg (2001a) Hamburger Statistisches Jahrbuch 2001/2002. Hamburg
Statistisches Landesamt Hamburg (2001b) Die Stadtteil-Profile 2001. Hamburger Statistische Porträts, Hamburg
Statistisches Landesamt Hamburg (2001c) Preisindizes für Bauwerke in Hamburg. Statistische Berichte M I4–vj 3/01, Hamburg
Statistisches Landesamt Hamburg (2002) Hamburger Statistisches Jahrbuch 2002/2003. Hamburg
Statistisches Landesamt Hamburg (2002) Zahl der neuen Wohnungen rückläufig. Press release 01.03.2002, Hamburg
Stern V (2001) Wohnungsbauförderung auf dem Prüfstand. Publications of the Karl-Bräuer-Institut des Bundes der Steuerzahler, Volume 93, Wiesbaden
Technische Universität Hamburg–Harburg (1999) Auswirkungen der Umlandwanderungen auf den Hamburger Wohnungsmarkt. Dokumentation des Workshops vom 6/7 July 1998 und Abschlußbericht, Hamburg
Vereins- und Westbank Hamburg (2001) Immobilienmarktübersicht. Oktober 2001, Hamburg
Vesper M (2001) Das zukünftige Profil der Wohnungsbauförderung. Wirtschaftsdienst 81: 138–40

12 Housing Market and Housing Policy in Copenhagen

Hans Skifter Andersen

Danish Building Research Institute, Hørsholm

12.1 The Greater Copenhagen Region

12.1.1 Copenhagen and the Øresund region

Copenhagen is the capital of Denmark and the political and financial centre of the country, with a population of half a million inhabitants. Together with the neighbouring municipality of Frederiksberg, Copenhagen city forms the centre of the greater Copenhagen region. This region is made up of the counties of Copenhagen, Frederiksborg and Roskilde, and constitutes an infrastructural and geographical entity with around one third of the country's population, more than 1.7 million people. The region can be divided into centre, suburbs and outer region. There are 50 municipalities in the region.

In 2000 Denmark was connected to Sweden with a bridge over the Øresund. This bridge is also connecting the two cities of Copenhagen and Malmø, and the travel time from Copenhagen centre to Malmø centre is now about half an hour. The two cities are now working to integrate the two sides of the Øresund into one urban region with more than 2.2 million inhabitants.

Table 12.1. Population in the Copenhagen metropolitan area and the Øresund region 1997

	Greater Copenhagen	Malmø region	Øresund region
Centre	568 900	251 400	820 300
Suburbs	821 512	81 364	902 876
Outer region	362 720	177 336	540 056
Total	1 753 200	510 100	2 263 232

Source: Skifter Andersen and Borgegård 1999.

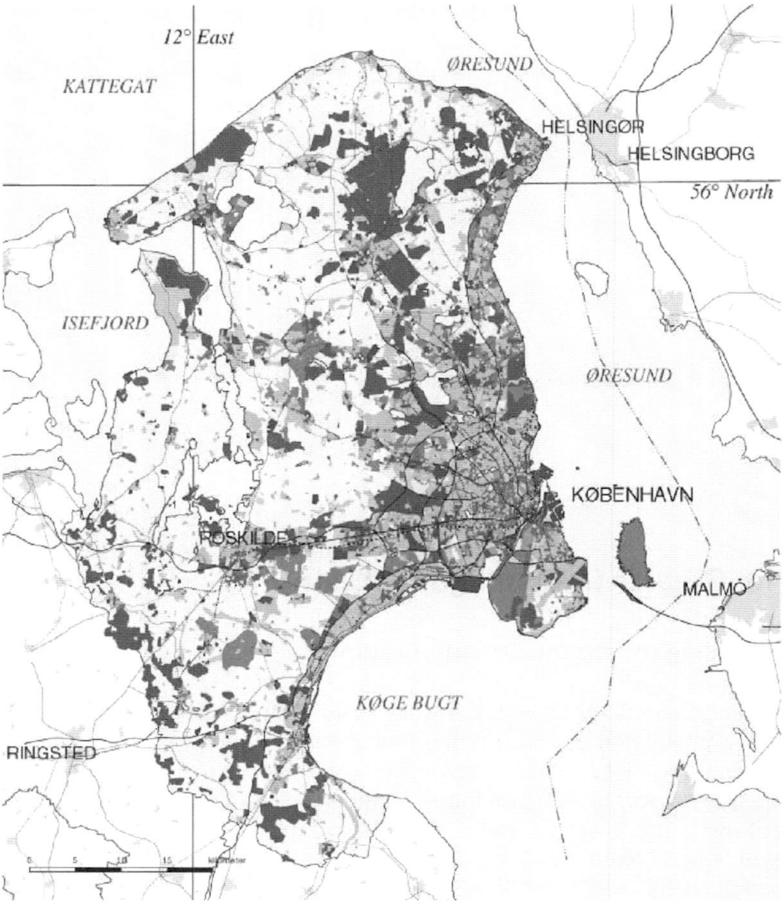

Fig. 12.1. The greater Copenhagen area (Source: Greater Copenhagen Authority)

During the period from 1975 to 1990 there was a declining population in the Copenhagen region. In the 1990s this was turned into a new growth.

In the last part of the 1990s there have also been high economic growth rates in the region, partly due to the new Øresund Bridge. There is a little less than one million jobs in the region and the number of jobs has been growing in the last five years with 1.5 per cent per year as is illustrated in Fig. 12.3.

In the middle of the 1990s the growth of jobs primarily happened in the suburbs and outer parts of the region, but in recent years the growth has been just as high in the centre. This development has resulted in a decline in unemployment in the region and especially in the centre. The unemployment rate has decrease to 4.7 in the region. It has also fallen much in the centre, which earlier had a higher unemployment than the country as a whole, but now has a lower rate. It is, however, still somewhat higher than in the rest of the region.

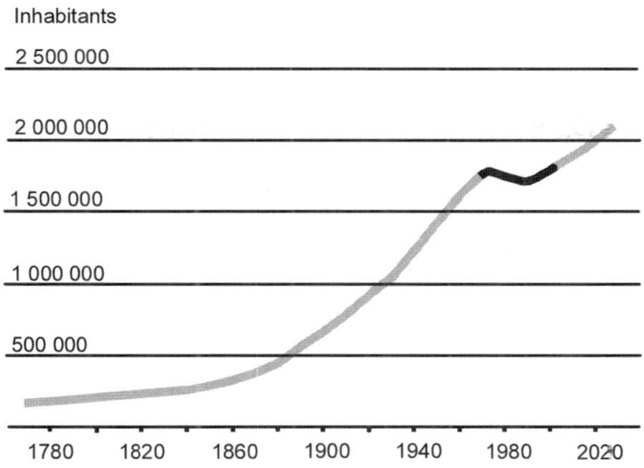

Fig. 12.2. Population development in greater Copenhagen 1769–2028 (Source: Greater Copenhagen Authority)

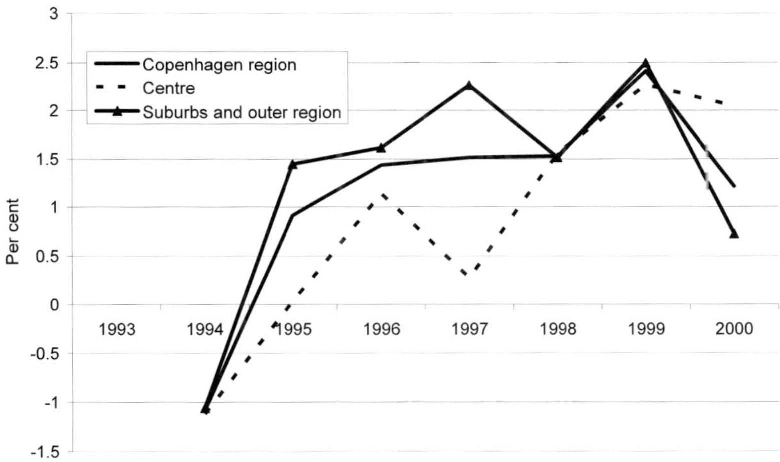

Fig. 12.3. Annual growth of jobs in Copenhagen region 1994–2000 (Source: Greater Copenhagen Authority)

Table 12.2. Unemployment rate in Copenhagen region in the first quarter of 2001 (per cent) and average taxable income 1999 in Euro for all residents more than 15 years old

	Unemployment rate [%]	Average income [1000 Euro]
Denmark	6.0	19.8
Copenhagen region	4.7	23.7
Centre	5.8	21.7
Suburbs and outer region	4.1	24.7

Source: Greater Copenhagen Authority.

Also the incomes in the region has increased in recent years and has now (1999) reached a level of about €24,000 per year for all residents more that 15 years old. The incomes in the centre are lower, but still higher than the average for Denmark.

12.1.2 Physical Planning in the Region

A regional plan for the greater Copenhagen area has been worked out and revised since 1961. The basic principle in the plan is that the built-up areas of the region are situated along five 'fingers' that radiates from the central part of the region along the major transport corridors. This area contains 85 per cent of the population.

One of the major problems for the region has been the absence of a central authority to co-ordinate the development of the region. For a period in the 1980s a directly elected council for the whole region existed, that had the overall planning authority. This was cancelled in 1989 do to conflicts with the counties and municipalities. In 1998 a new council called Greater Copenhagen Authority was formed made up by representatives from the counties and the City of Copenhagen but it only has a weak authority. It is still the counties that have the power to control the plans and how they are used by local authorities in the municipalities.

Denmark has a relatively strict zoning law that makes it difficult for local authorities to permit new buildings in land zones without the permission of counties, and the Ministry of the Environment can intervene. In greater Copenhagen many municipalities in the inner rings of the suburbs have used up their urban zone and can not use the available rural zone. Some municipalities in the outer rings have a large reserve of urban zone, but choose for different reasons not to develop the municipality to avoid too fast a growth in the population and needs of public services. There is thus a scarcity of available land for building purposes in the region that tend to increase prices of land and housing. This is reinforced by the fact that many local authorities tend to speculate in land for financial purposes.

12.2 The Danish Housing Market, Housing Policy and Urban Policies

12.2.1 The Housing Market in Denmark

The dominant tenure in Denmark is owner-occupied housing of which the vast majority is single-family houses. About 5 per cent of the dwellings are located in blocks of flats.

Denmark has a relatively large social housing sector, which is organised as non-profit housing associations. These are subjugated to a strong public regulation and local authorities are empowered to supervise their activities and administration.

Table 12.3. The Danish housing stock split up into tenures 1998

	Number of 1000 dwellings	Per cent
Owner-occupied dwellings	1270	55
of this flats	107	5
Rented dwellings	941	41
Private renting	474	21
Non-profit ass., social housing	392	17
Publicly owned	75	3
Private co-operatives	95	4
In total	2306	100

Source: Ministry of Housing.

Only a few dwellings are owned directly by local authorities. It is mostly old housing build before 1930 where non-profit housing took over the supply of social housing. Especially in Copenhagen city there has been a larger stock of publicly owned housing, but in recent years these dwellings have been sold to private investors or to the tenants as co-operative housing.

The total share of private lettings in Denmark constitutes about 21 per cent of the housing. Some of these dwellings are either one-family houses (4 per cent) or owner occupied flats (3 per cent) that are let out. Private rented dwellings in blocks of flats, which only constitutes 14 per cent of dwellings in the housing stock in Denmark.

Finally there is a small private co-operative sector. This tenure is a cross between owing and renting. The dwellings are owned by the co-operative association and each resident owns a share of the association. There are three origins of these dwellings. Some of them were built as co-operatives in blocks of flats before 1940. Others have been built since 1983 within a public subsidy programme. Finally some have been transformed from private renting.

12.2.2 Regulation of Private Renting

Since 1939 there have been different kinds of regulation of the Danish private rented housing sector. There has over the years been much public discussion on these regulations and many changes have been made during the last 20 years.

The most important element in the regulation of private renting is rent control. Other kinds of regulation concern tenants' rights and influence. Especially important is tenants' security against being evicted from their apartment. Other rules exist concerning tenants' rights to information and influence on maintenance, improvements and administration in general.

The use of vacant dwellings has also been regulated. In Denmark tenants have a right to change apartments with other tenants from inside and outside their estate, which means that the landlords in many cases are not able to decide on who is going to move in.

Lastly there is a legislation that limits landlords' ability to make changes in their estate. For example, it is not allowed to convert rented dwellings into owner-occupied flats.

Landlords also must have permission from local authorities to abolish an apartment or to put two apartments together. If a landlord wishes to sell the estate he must first offer it to the tenants at the same price as another buyer would pay. The tenants then have the opportunity to form a co-operative.

Since 1976, rents in private renting have been regulated after a principle called 'rent determined by expenditures'. Certain rules are laid down by legislation on how to calculate the rent in every estate. The rent is determined by adding up budgeted expenditures – like cleaning, taxes, insurances etc. – plus a certain amount per dwelling for administration. Furthermore, fixed transferences for maintenance and for renewal of installations are included and there is a fixed so-called capital yield to the landlord, which has been the same amount since 1976.

The rent can be raised at any time, but the landlord has to inform the tenants in advance and to provide them with written proof that the new rent is justified by higher expenses. Furthermore, it is possible to raise the rent in connection with improvements. The allowed increase is in principle – within certain limits – calculated on the basis of the repayments and interests on the loans taken to finance the improvement and the interests on capital contributed by the landlord himself. In case of disagreement over the budget and rent increase the tenants can complain to a board of appeal – a rent tribunal – that can settle the dispute.

12.2.3 Price Control on Co-operative Housing

In co-operative housing the property or estate is owned by the housing co-operative and each resident owns a share of the co-operative. When a dwelling is sold the newcomer has to pay a price for this share. The prices of shares are regulated and are determined as the difference between the mortgage debts in the property and the taxable value fixed by the authorities. This value is determined by principles used for private renting with rent control and is fairly low. That is why prices of shares often are well below market values.

12.2.4 Rent Setting in Social Housing

The rent for public, social housing is fixed and controlled according to the 'rent balance' principle, whereby the overall rent for every single housing estate must at all times be sufficient to cover the unit's operating expenses and savings for future maintenance. The rents are thus dependent on the historical costs and funding of every estate, which produce big differences in capital costs and rents between newer and older estate. These differences are to some extent equalised by transfers to a central fund for all social housing.

12.2.5 Individual Housing Benefits

Two types of individual housing benefits are available in Denmark: rent allowance and rent subsidy. Rent allowances are granted to pensioners and rent subsidies are awarded to non-pensioners. Both rent allowances and rent subsidies are primarily aimed at households in rented dwellings.

In 1998, an average of 333,000 households received rent allowances, while an average of 166,000 households received rent subsidies. The total 499,000 households, equivalent to approximately 21 per cent of all households in Denmark, received an average of DKK 17,000 in individual housing benefits in 1998. For households that received housing benefits in 1998, the average benefits covered 50 per cent of the rent (60 per cent for pensioners and 30 for non-pensioners).

Table 12.4. Rent allowance 1999 for typical pensioners in Denmark (1000 Euro per year)

	Pensioner single	Pensioners couple
Household income	12.8	18.5
Rent	4.0	4.7
Rent allowance	2.7	2.2

Source: Ministry of Housing.

Table 12.5. Rent subsidy 1999 for typical non-pensioners in Denmark (1000 Euro per year)

DKK per year	Unemployed single without children	Unemployed single with 2 children
Household income	19.3	19.3
Rent	4.7	5.4
Rent subsidy	0.7	2.6

Source: Ministry of Housing.

12.2.6 Consequences of Regulations on Price and Rent Settings

As a consequence of the regulation a distorted rent structure has been created in the rental market. The average rent for all rented properties in 1995 was DKK 437/sqm/year. This average rent covers a relatively large spread which is partly due to differences in the age of the building, ownership structure, and geographical location as well as differences in the quality, size, etc. of the dwellings. As can be seen from Fig. 12.4 there are considerable differences between rents in older private rented dwellings and newer ones – differences that only partly can be attributed to differences in quality and location. In fact much of the older housing stock has an attractive location central in cities.

For public housing, rents averaged DKK 445/sqm/year in September 1995. For private rented dwellings the rents were DKK 426/sqm/year. The difference between the average rents for the two categories of housing was thus only DKK 19/sqm/year, equivalent to 4.5 per cent.

Like most other countries in Europe the Danish private rented sector has been in decline for many years. Before World War II it was the dominant sector but after the war new social housing begun to take over on new housing. The real blow to private rented housing came in the last part of the sixties when increased inflation and favourable tax deductions made owner-occupied housing much more attractive at the same time as interest rates were raised substantially. New private rented housing did not get increased subsidies as social housing. In this situation it was difficult to built new private renting with affordable rents.

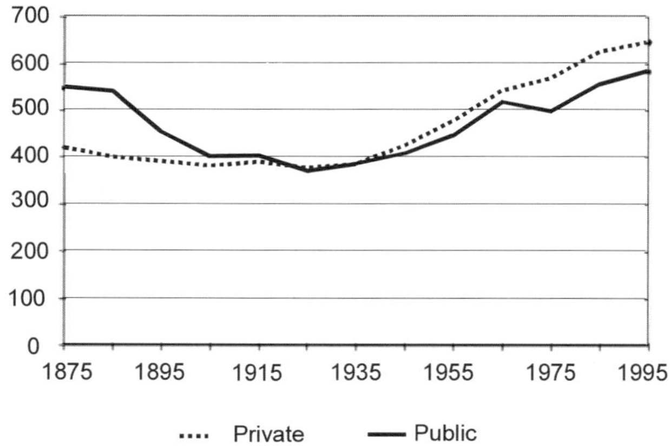

Fig. 12.4. Average rent 1995 for public, social housing and private rented dwellings categorised by period of construction, DKK/sqm/year (Source: Ministry of Housing and Urban Affairs 1999)

Moreover, private renting in the older stock decreased with about one-third from the middle of the sixties to the end of the eighties. Besides demolition of old and worn-down buildings the main reason was a transformation of dwellings to owner-occupied flats, which were made possible from 1966. This transformation of tenure was, however, partly stopped in the seventies and totally prohibited after 1980. Instead a great number of private lettings in the following years were transformed to co-operatives after an act was passed in parliament. This act ordered landlords, with the intention of selling their property, first to give an offer to sitting tenants who want to form a co-operative.

12.2.7 Housing Construction and Modernisation of Dwellings

Since the last part of the 1960s only very few new private rental dwellings have been constructed (about 20,000 since 1970). The reason is not rent regulation because there are no restrictions on rents in private renting built after 1991 and only a very weak one on dwellings built after 1963. The explanation is rather the economic unfavourable conditions for investments in private renting compared to other tenures. Social housing gets high subsidies in new housing. Moreover, tax subsidies for owner-occupied housing have been very large in Denmark – the level has been the highest in Europe (see Haffner 1991). The competitiveness of new rented housing, however, has improved in recent years as tax subsidies were very much reduced.

The typical investor in new dwellings in recent years has been pension funds and insurance companies. It is investors who can finance the projects with their own capital and are not in need of funding from other sources. Usually the state collects a so-called 'real interest tax' from these investors. In principle 40 per cent of the real incomes, after the actual inflation has been deducted, is taxed. But for investments in new housing this tax is abolished.

The present state (in 2002) is that housing construction is at a relatively low level. Non-profit housing has been reduced to the lowest level since the 1950s because the municipalities do not want to finance their part except for houses for elderly and the disabled. Private housing construction has increased a little but probably not enough to satisfy long-term demand.

The housing renewal policy has in recent years been changed from comprehensive and costly district plans to more moderate modernisation of single properties with partly private investments and with contributions via negotiated rent increase. As shown in a European comparative study (Skifter Andersen and Leather 1999) the Danish urban renewal policy for a long period, compared to other countries, was dominated by programmes with a high degree of public control, quite extensive and expensive renovations and very high subsidies. As a consequence it has only been possible to renovate relatively few properties with public support. Moreover rent control to some extend has hampered private investments in maintenance and renovation of private renting (see Skifter Andersen 1998). For these reasons Denmark, especially in the 1980s has lagged behind other countries concerning modernisation of unfit dwellings and facilities. In 2001 nearly 8 per cent of the Danish stock still lacks modern facilities (WC, bath or modern heating).

Many of the non-profit residence areas erected during the 1960s and 1970s are upgraded to make them more competitive on the local markets to be attractive for more diverse groups of households. This is mostly financed by refinancing of the total stock of social housing that have been organised in an non-profit fund to allow transference for renewal, new construction and reduction of rent for areas that is difficult to let out.

12.2.8 Urban Policies

The urban committee

In 1993 the Danish government established the so-called Urban Committee with the purpose of addressing increasing social problems and concentration of immigrants and refugees in a number of social housing estates primarily located in the suburbs. The programme was launched in 1994 and nearly 500 housing estates were given some kind of support. Objectives differed between individual housing estates but efforts were concentrated on rent reduction, building renovation and improvement, employment of area based social workers and setting up social activities.

The committee proposed a whole range of initiatives for improving the situation of the estates. They were focused on:

- Physical renovation.
- Rent reduction and economic rehabilitation.
- Social empowerment: employment of special social workers and support for social activities, especially among immigrants and socially excluded residents.
- Special education initiatives for immigrants and refugees, including efforts to solve problems following a concentration of foreign speaking children in certain schools.
- Measures against crime.
- New rules and institutional framework regulating immigration and housing for immigrants.
- New rules regulating rules for municipal referral to social housing.
- Increasing state funds for local authorities with problem estates.

The initiatives were not based on a coherent strategy and understanding of the problems. When looking at the proposed initiatives and the expressed grounds for them it can, however, be argued that there were at least four different strategies embedded in the initiatives:

- Local network strategy: Strengthening local networks to combat social exclusion.
- Improved competition strategy: Improving competitiveness for the estates on the housing market.
- Reduce segregation strategy: Changing the assignment of dwellings to combat segregation.
- Reduce consequences strategy: Reducing undesirable consequences for the municipalities.

The local network strategy had the aim to establish permanent co-operation between the housing estates, local authorities and other local actors on solving the problems of the estates. It was intended to strengthen the activity of and social relations between residents in the areas to improve living conditions for deprived tenants and immigrants, living on the estates. Moreover, it should reduce social problems by locally-based efforts and by mobilising local resources. The main efforts in this strategy were the support for social workers on the estates and for social activities, and also the demands on local co-operation between local authorities, housing associations, tenant's local organisations (estate boards etc.) and other local parties.

The improved competition strategy had the aim to improve the ability of the estates to compete in the housing market to attract groups other than the poor and jobless and also to reduce the high moving frequency on the estates. The most important initiatives were physical renovation and rent decreases. But also the support for social activity was seen as an instrument to increase the quality of life on the estates and to improve their reputation.

The reduce segregation strategy primarily consisted of changes in rules and administrative practices to limit a concentration of marginalised people and immigrants on these estates. It should later on show up that these initiatives were difficult to implement because they could be seen as discrimination against the groups that one wanted to keep away from the estates.

Finally the efforts to reduce the consequences were concentrated on support for schools with many foreign speaking pupils, on education and training of immigrants and on increased funds for municipalities with problems.

The Urban Committee thus realised that there were economic problems at some of the social housing estates that need to be addressed in order to make them more attractive also for people with employment and normal income. It was furthermore realised that at the core of much of the urban districts' problems is a strong social dimension.

Altogether six ministries were involved in the programme for which funding (approximately €95,000,000) was provided by the state (28 per cent), local authorities (43 per cent) and the National Fund of Housing Associations (29 per cent). Moreover €847,000,000 was saved by remorgaging of loans.

Implementation of the programme was originally planned for the period 1994 to 1998. However, support for most of the social efforts has been extended to year 2003 because, although the negative social, physical and economic development on the estates has been stopped and the efforts have prevented problems from escalating, the social problems have not been solved.

The 'Kvarterløft' programme

The Urban Committee launched a new 'urban area improvement programme' (Kvarterløft) in 1996, and the following year, seven larger urban areas around the country were selected for improvement. Of these three are in Copenhagen city and one in the suburbs. Furthermore, in 2000 there has been a new round of the urban area improvement programme where five additional areas have been selected for improvement – three of these in the Copenhagen metropolitan area.

- Kvarterløft addresses the neighbourhood, not the single citizen or the single property owner.
- It is comprehensive in the sense that it is to be based on a co-ordinated and integrated effort.
- It is based on the participation and strength of local actors.
- Its point of departure is an analysis of the neighbourhood's potentials and problems.

The fundamental idea in the Kvarterløft programme is to combine aid to both people and places and moreover explicitly aims at doing it in a way that involves the community. In this sense urban renewal policy has moved much closer to the citizen compared to earlier urban renewal in inner city neighbourhoods. Moreover, it is not only concerned with physical improvements but also with social and economic changes. Kvarterløft can be characterised as a 'bottom-up' strategy which favours the active participation by residents and development of partnerships. Kvarterløft seeks to capture a broad range of problems in individual areas with the aim of integrating means and aims across sectors and projects.

The first phase in all seven projects was a planning phase. Local residents, local firms and public schools, kindergartens, libraries and other local institutions were invited to participate in public meetings and bring forward suggestions, ideas, and wishes to the future development of their neighbourhood. The first phase ended during spring 1998 with the completion of plans and approval of them in the different city councils. Finally in summer 1998 the minister and the mayors of the five cities signed agreements of co-operation (contracts) which since then have been re-negotiated once a year. The contracts specify activities, funding as well as criteria for success of the planned activities, e.g. in terms of number of jobs created or physical regeneration activities implemented. The plans of the seven Kvarterløft projects share some similarities especially regarding their focus on outdoor regeneration projects that aim at stimulating the sense of belonging of residents as many of the seven neighbourhoods are characterised by being split in two or more sub-neighbourhoods.

The Kvarterløft programme has the following dimensions:

- A social dimension targeted at integration of immigrants and strengthening social contacts by means of activities, in schools and improvement of the 'social infrastructure' with emphasis on drug- and alcohol addicts as well as residents with mental illnesses.
- An employment dimension targeted at creating local jobs through co-operation between local businesses and job referral services.
- An architectural dimension by building improvement and by creation of recreational and other public spaces.
- A traffic dimension aimed at reducing traffic noise.
- An ecological dimension which is considered in relation to renewal of both housing and buildings.
- A cultural dimension targeted at creating cultural activities and institutions as well as sports and recreational facilities.

12.3 The Housing Market in Greater Copenhagen

In total the housing market in the region consists of about 840,000 dwellings of which 325,000 are located in the centre.

Table 12.6. Dwellings in the Copenhagen region and in the centre distributed on tenures 1997

	No. of 1000 dwellings		Distribution [%]	
Tenure	Whole region	Centre	Whole region	Centre
Owner-occupied one-family houses	258	20	31	6
Owner-occupied flats	112	59	13	18
Co-operatives	101	82	12	25
Social housing	203	59	24	18
Private renting	166	105	20	32
Total	840	325	100	100

Source: Skifter Andersen and Borgegård 1999, Appendix 4.

12.3.1 Tenures

Only one third of dwellings are situated in owner-occupied one-family homes and 13 per cent in owner-occupied flats. Social housing makes up a quarter of the stock and private renting one fifth. The composition of tenures in the centre is somewhat different with a dominance of private renting and co-operatives transformed from private renting.

12.3.2 Housing Quality

An important problem for the whole region and especially for the centre is that a considerable share of the housing stock has a low standard. According to the housing and building register about 12 per cent of dwellings in the region had unsatisfactory facilities in 1997 and in the centre it was nearly 24 per cent. Even if there are grounds to believe that these figures are exaggerated, because some improvements have not been registered, these are fairly high figures. As can be seen from the table it is especially private renting where standards are low. This also seems to be the case in co-operative housing, of which many has been transformed from private renting in recent years, but it is probable that the figures are exaggerated. Social housing has the most modern housing stock.

Table 12.7. Housing standard in the greater Copenhagen region 1997

	Unsatisfactory facilities[a] [%]	Built before 1940 [%]	Share in detached buildings [%]	Share of small dwellings[b] [%]	Average size[c]
Owner-occupied one-family houses	6	27	96	1	131
Owner-occupied flats	7	45	5	28	80
Co-operatives	31	80	8	30	75
Social housing	3	8	19	19	77
Private renting	25	64	13	31	81
Whole region	12	38	38	18	95
Centre	24	71	7	30	79

[a]Without toilet, bath or modern heating.
[b]Less than 60 sqm gross floor space.
[c]sqm gross floor space.
Source: Skifter Andersen and Borgegård 1999, Appendix 4.

Another major problem for the centre is the high amount of small dwellings. In Copenhagen city nearly half the dwellings only have one or two rooms. The average size of the dwellings shown in the table could seem quite large compared to other countries. It is important, however, to notice that in Denmark a gross measure of floor space is used, which is 15–20 per cent higher than the net measures used in other countries.

12.3.3 Rents and Prices

Table 12.8 presents some figures on rents and prices in different parts of the region. The average rents in the region are not very high, which is due to regulation. Due to the special Danish floor space measure the figures in the table should be increased by 15 per cent to be comparable with other countries (about €75 per net sqm/year). Sales prices for owner-occupied dwellings were around €1,300 per square metre in 1998 (1,500 per net sqm).

Table 12.8. Rents and house prices in Euro

	Suburbs				Outer region	Whole region
	Centre	North	South	East		
Standardised rents 1995 per sqm /year[a]	65	66	64	60	65	65
Sales prices 1998 one-family houses[b]	1262	1497	1285	1382	1141	1305
Sales prices 1998 owner-occupied flats[b]	1238	1371	1064	1194	1159	1228

[a]Rents for dwellings in Euro with average standard per gross square metre.
[b]Price of sold dwellings; Euro per gross square metre.
Sources: Ministry of Housing; The Danish Mortgage Credit Council.

The northern part of the suburbs is the most attractive part with the highest sales prices. The southern part of the suburbs is dominated by social housing and does not have the same access to lakes and forests as in the north. The outer parts of the region also have lower prices due to larger distance from the centre.

The development of house prices

In the period from 1986 to 1993 there was a decline in house prices in Denmark and in Copenhagen. As can be seen from Fig. 12.5 the market changed after 1993 with a dramatic increase in prices in recent years.

For the whole region the average price increase per year in the period has been about 11 per cent. Inflation has been at a low level in the same period – about 2.3 per cent per year.

12.3.4 Subsidies and Housing Costs in Different Tenures

As in many other countries Denmark has a subsidy system that results in differences in housing costs in different tenures as it is illustrated in Table 12.9.

New private renting is not under rent control, but in general there are no subsidies either. There are some subsidies for new co-operatives but they are somewhat lower than for social housing. As a result of subsidies and tax rules housing costs in social housing and owner-occupied housing are much lower than in co-operatives and especially in new private renting. This has had a pronounced importance for the housing market and new building in the region.

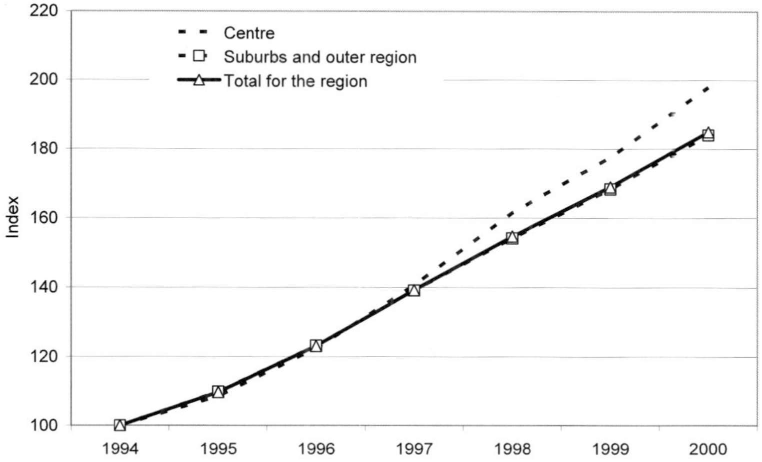

Fig. 12.5. Development in house prices in the Copenhagen region 1994–2000 (Source: Denmarks Statistics)

Table 12.9. Yearly housing costs in different tenures in Denmark 1998 as a percentage of initial purchase price or costs

Years after purchase	Owner-occupied	New private renting	New co-operatives	Social housing
1	7.4	11.6	9.0	6.7
10	7.9	12.1	9.8	7.2

Source: Lunde and Hvidt 1999.

12.3.5 Housing Construction

Housing construction in the Copenhagen region dropped in the beginning of the 1990s to a lower level in spite of a growing population in the region. As can be seen from Fig. 12.6, about 4,000 dwellings have been built per year corresponding to 2 per cent of the stock.

As can be seen from Table 12.10 nearly 80 per cent of the dwellings are built by private firms and individuals. 50 per cent is private housing in detached or semi-detached buildings as either owner-occupied housing or co-operatives. 23 per cent is private in blocks of flats as either owner-occupied flats or private renting. Some private renting has been built by pension funds with special tax arrangements, but not much.

Table 12.10. Distribution of new built dwellings 1998 on building owner and type of building (in per cent)

	Detached	Semi-detached	Blocks of flats	Student hostels etc.	Total
Private	38.5	12.2	22.9	4.9	78.5
Social	0.1	1.9	8.5	2.5	12.8
Public	0.4	0.6	7.5	0.1	8.7
Total	38.9	14.7	38.9	7.5	100.0
Centre	0.5	0.9	19.7	2.5	23.6
Rest of the region	38.4	13.8	19.2	5.0	76.4

Source: Skifter Andersen and Borgegård 1999, appendix 4.

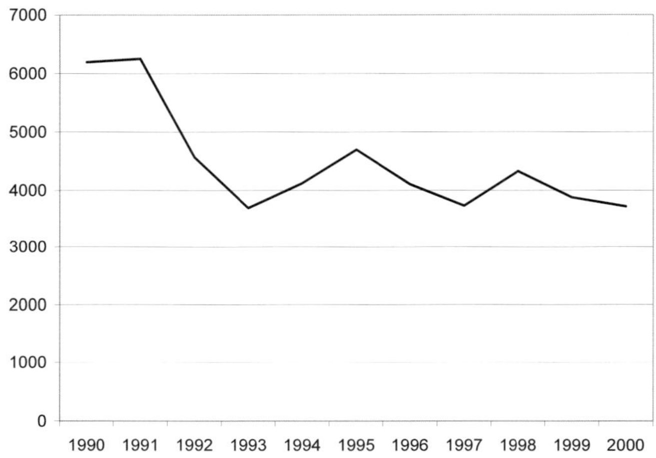

Fig. 12.6. Construction of new dwellings per year in the Copenhagen region 1990–2000 (Source: Statistical Office of Denmark)

12.3.6 Construction Costs and Housing Costs in New Housing

Statistics about housing costs are good for the social housing sector, but does not exist for the private sector.

Table 12.11. Construction costs in social housing in Euro per square metre (gross measure) in the Copenhagen region 1999

	Semi-detached	Blocks of flats
Site costs	67	97
Building costs	1692	1447
Total costs	1759	1544
Average size gross sqm	74	79

Source: Federation of Social Housing Associations.

In social housing the construction costs in 1999 were about €1,800 per gross square metre in low buildings and €1,600 in blocks of flats. Transformed to net square metre this corresponds to respectively €2,000 and €1,800 per square metre.

The estimates in Table 12.12 shows that on average a house could be build in the region in 1999 for about €1,600 per gross square metre (€1,900 per net square metre).

It was shown in Table 12.8 that the average sale in the region was about €1,300 per gross square metre. The estimates thus points to that new build houses should be quite competitive with supply from the existing stock. But for some reasons house building has remained at a quite low level at the same time as house prices have continued to rice in 2000 and 2001. The reasons for this will be discussed below.

Table 12.12. Estimated site and construction costs in Euro for private house building in the Copenhagen region 1999

	Site price /sqm	Site price for 700 sqm, €1000	Price for dwelling 150 sqm*€1000	Price /sqm
Centre	106	74	276	1837
Copenhagen county	80	56	257	1715
Frederiksborg county	18	12	214	1426
Roskilde county	31	22	223	1488

Source: Skifter Andersen and Borgegård 1999, appendix 4.

12.4 Segregation in Copenhagen

The Danish tax rules, housing subsidies and regulations of the housing market has resulted in a strong distortion of the demand for housing among different groups of the population. Households with higher incomes and tax payments have greater economic incentives and possibilities for buying a home than low-income groups. On the other hand the housing benefit system induces people with low incomes to settle in rented dwellings, in particular in the social sector. This benefit system in combination with the rent structure tends to concentrate marginalised groups, e.g. people on welfare, with early retirement, with low income, in the newer part of the social sector while the middle class and employed people avoid this kind of tenure. Moreover, it has been more difficult for immigrants than Danes to get access to private rented housing.

As a consequence there is a pronounced segregation between different tenures in the region, as can be seen from Table 12.13.

Owner-occupied housing in one-family buildings is the most segregated tenure with a massive over-representation of high-income groups and few residents with lower incomes, mostly pensioners. On the other hand social housing also is very segregated with a concentration of lower incomes. In co-operatives and private renting the middle income groups have settled. In dwellings with low standard, however, it is the lower income groups who are over-represented. Many of these are students.

Thus, the location of housing of different tenures has a significant influence on spatial segregation in the region.

Table 12.13. Segregation among tenures in the Copenhagen region: overrepresentation and index of segregation

	Over-representation in tenures [%]					
Income DKK	Owner-occupied one-family houses	Owner-occupied flats	Co-operatives	Social housing	Private renting, good standard	Private renting, bad standard
Less than 100,000	–11.7	–11.7	–3.2	23.4	1.6	14.3
100–150,000	–35.4	3.8	27.4	28.5	19.1	57.0
150–220,000	–6.8	8.0	22.4	–2.3	4.4	–7.7
Over 220,000	43.1	11.3	–25.6	–51.9	–16.2	–48.9
Index of segregation	39.0	4.0	8.0	25.0	5.0	5.0

Note: The index of segregation measures how large a share of the residents in each tenure that should be replaced before it is possible to obtain the same income distribution as the average population in the region.
Source: Skifter Andersen and Borgegård 1999, appendix 5.

12.4.1 The Influence of Local Authorities on Housing Supply in the Municipalities

In Denmark local governments have had a considerable influence on the composition of the local housing market in their municipality. They can through physical planning measures control type of tenure and size of sites for all new housing. Local governments are able to promote social housing as they have to give permission and to provide a part of the finance. By denying this they can prevent social housing from being built in their municipality.

These powers have been used by local governments in the greater Copenhagen area to create local housing markets that are extremely different. Especially in the period before 1980, when private house building boomed, some local governments chose not to accept any new social housing. In the same years house building in other municipalities was heavily dominated by social housing. There was a strong connection between the leading political party at the local level and the kind of housing prevailing, although after 1980 this pattern has been somewhat relaxed. It is thus possible for local governments to attract people with higher income and at the same time force low-incomes groups to leave the municipality by promoting owner-occupation. Consequently, the distribution of tenure is more a result of political regulation than of market processes.

In the appendix it is shown how the municipalities in the region can be divided into four ring zones, dependent on the distance from the centre, and six sectors transversely to this. The composition of the housing stock in these zones and sectors is showed in Figs. 12.7 and 12.8.

The chronological development of the city has resulted in pronounced differences between the different rings. The centre is dominated by private renting (and co-operatives). Owner-occupied housing is most common in the outermost ring. There are quite a few in the centre and the majority of these are owner-occupied flats. Social housing is most common in Ring 3 where most of the larger problem estates built in the 1960s and 1970s are located. Social housing in Ring 2 and in the centre is older.

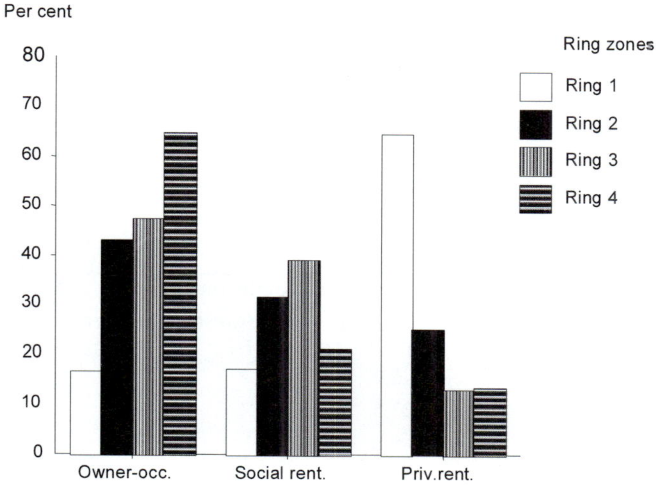

Fig. 12.7. The composition of the housing stock in different ring zones in the Copenhagen region 1996 (Source: Skifter Andersen, Andersen and Ærø 2000)

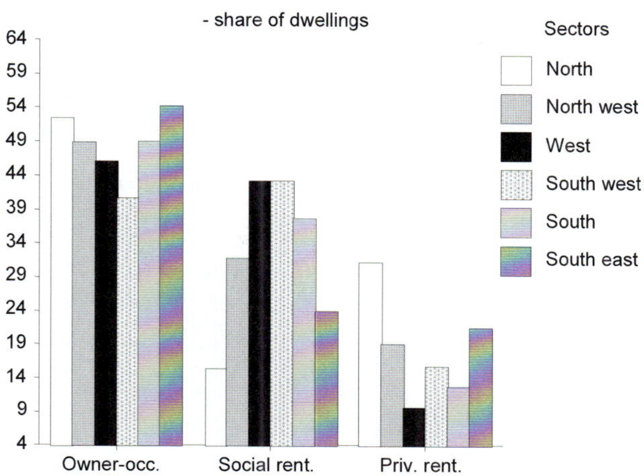

Fig. 12.8. The composition of the housing stock in different sectors in the Copenhagen region 1996 (Source: Skifter Andersen, Andersen and Ærø 2000)

More interesting are the differences between the different sectors. From the middle of the 19th century the more wealthy part of the population began to settle in the more attractive surroundings of the region north of the city. This was the beginning of a development where the rich moved to the north and occupied the land for owner-occupied housing. Social housing was instead located mostly in the western and to some extent in the southern part.

In Table 12.14 the segregation of income groups between different parts of the region is illustrated. It can be seen from the table that the most segregated parts of the region are the centre and the northern part of the suburbs. The centre has many residents with low incomes, while the northern part has an overrepresentation of people with high incomes. The south–western suburbs do not have as many residents on low incomes as the centre, but the difference is that in the centre it concerns students and old-age pensioners, while there are many more unemployed, receivers of welfare benefits and early pensioners in the suburbs.

Table 12.14. Segregation of income groups in the Copenhagen region 1998

	Over-representation in parts of the region [%]				
Income	Centre	Northern suburbs	South-western suburbs	Eastern suburbs	Outer region
Less than 100,000	7.4	–6.9	0.7	–11.3	–3.5
100–150,000	22.6	–23.5	–4.0	–3.5	–6.0
150–220,000	0.2	–9.6	2.1	6.5	6.8
Over 220,000	–24.4	30.8	–0.4	15.7	4.1
Index of segregation	17.7	15.5	1.6	1.1	4.1

Source: Skifter Andersen and Borgegård 1999, appendix 5.

The segregation of ethnic groups are, however, more extensive than that of the income groups. Table 12.15 shows that immigrants from poorer countries are very much concentrated in the centre and in the south western suburbs. They are more seldom found in the northern and eastern suburbs or in the outer region. In contrast to this, immigrants from more wealthy countries often have settled in the northern part. They are also found in the centre, but more seldom in the south

Table 12.15. Segregation of ethnic groups in the Copenhagen region 1998

	Over-representation in parts of the region [%]				
Nationality	Centre	Northern suburbs	South-western suburbs	Eastern suburbs	Outer region
Denmark	–4.5	2.5	–0.7	6.1	4.4
High developed countries[a]	33.1	18.9	–32.4	–18.6	–35.9
Eastern Europe	57.7	–46.8	–2.4	–73.0	–29.0
Third world countries	35.9	–39.5	32.1	–66.5	–41.1
Index of segregation	42.8	23.6	15.0	4.9	22.1

[a]Western Europe, USA, Canada, Australia, Japan and New Zealand.
Source: Skifter Andersen and Borgegård 1999, appendix 5.

12.5 Housing Market Problems and Policies in the Copenhagen Region

12.5.1 Regulation of the Housing Market Has Led to Shortages and Lower Quality

The housing market in the Copenhagen region is to a great extent influenced by the problems created by the above described general regulation of rental dwellings in Denmark. Especially in the Copenhagen area a distorted rent structure has been created which has led to severe unbalances between supply and demand for rental dwellings. Also co-operative housing is subject to price regulation with the same consequences. The result is that there has been a permanent shortage of rental housing, especially in the municipality of Copenhagen, where only 25 per cent of the dwellings are owner-occupied.

Another consequence of regulation, especially the rules in use before 1990, has been reduced maintenance and improvement of private rental housing in the region. Landlords have had fewer incentives to make investments in the housing stock because of the regulation and especially earlier it also meant reduced cash flow. The state and the municipalities have tried to encounter these problems by giving subsidies to renovation and renewal of housing, but in the central parts of the region it still remains many very small dwellings with lower quality.

12.5.2 Increasing House Prices and Shortage of Dwellings

After a long period where housing market problems have not been mentioned in the press, there has in recent years been much focus on housing markets problems and shortage of dwellings in the Copenhagen metropolitan area. The long period from 1992 with high economic growth and increasing incomes in the region has led to an increased demand for dwellings – especially for rented dwellings but also for owner-occupied dwellings.

Regarding the supply of rented dwellings this is mainly restricted to social housing, as new private rented dwellings are too expensive for normal incomes. But the construction of new social housing has declined. The problem is that local authorities block new social housing in their municipalities because they are afraid of attracting people with social problems and needs of public assistance (see PLS-Rambøll 2001). Moreover they have to finance part of the expenses for construction, which is difficult for many municipalities with fiscal problems. In 2001 the government has reduced the financial burdens for local authorities in connection with social housing to reduce this barrier.

What has been more surprising is that the construction of owner-occupied dwellings in the region has not been increased in recent years despite high demand and increasing house prices. One of the most probable explanations of this paradox is that local authorities control the supply of building sites. Some municipalities have no or little available land for new construction, while others have plenty.

Many local governments with much free land in the urban zone only want to sell it in small portions because it will disturb the municipal plans for development of schools and institutions if the population increases too fast. Moreover, many local governments have speculated in buying land and tend to keep back sites to increase land prices, which furthermore increase house prices.

12.5.3 Local Housing Policy Has Led to an Unequal Spatial Distribution of Social Housing

The Danish system for allocation of new social housing and funding of local authorities has, like in many other cities, led to a very unequal distribution of social housing among municipalities in the region. This is a result of increased economic expenditures for a local authority to built new social housing, and it is impossible to build without their permission. Local authorities has to pay a part of the investment and they do not control who is moving in, so they fear that there will be newcomers from other municipalities with social problems that will result in increased social expenses. Especially local governments controlled by right-wing parties have preferred to build owner-occupied housing to attract people with higher incomes and to increase their own electorate (Skifter Andersen and Als 1987). The result has been that a few municipalities in the western and southern part of the region have got a high concentration of social housing.

12.5.4 Problems of Deprived Housing Areas

As a consequence of the segregation between tenures and between different parts of the region, as shown above, there has been a concentration of immigrants and of social problems in certain neighbourhoods in the region. Some of these neighbourhoods are found in Copenhagen city. As the older parts of the city have been renewed during the last 30 years these problems have been moved to the rings of the city build in the period 1920–40. Most of the deprived housing areas are, however, found in the southern and westerns suburbs. These housing estates has come into a negative spiral of decline where social problems and physical deterioration increases in pace with that people with work and better incomes moves away and are replaced by households without work and by immigrants (see Skifter Andersen 1999b).

Many deprived housing areas in Copenhagen city and in the rest of the region have received support under the urban policy programmes described above – the Urban Committee Programme and the 'Kvarterløft' Programme. The first programme has been evaluated by the Danish Building and Urban Research Institute (Skifter Andersen 1999a; Skifter Andersen 2002), and this evaluation have shown positive effects of the programme. It has succeeded in stopping the negative development in the composition of residents and social problems have been reduced.

12.5.5 The Housing Market and the Fiscal Problems of the City of Copenhagen

The revision of the structure of municipalities in Denmark in 1971 was uncompleted in the metropolitan area. The city of Copenhagen was left as a smaller part of the area with the oldest and worst housing stock and with an elderly population. Many young people moved to the city, but they moved away as soon as they were established with family and higher income, partly because the housing market in the city was not able to adapt to the housing demand from young families. This was mainly due the extensive regulation of private renting and co-operatives. Like in many other cities in the same situation this led to fiscal problems in the city because of a declining tax base (in Denmark there is a special income tax for local authorities).

In the last part of the 1990s the city formulated a new housing policy to reverse this development (see Københavns Kommune 1999). The main objective of the policy was to establish a better housing supply that would attract more affluent newcomers from the rest of the region, and to prevent that young families moved away from the city. The main means were:

- To built new dwellings with high quality and attractive location, for example at the harbour.
- To promote joining of small apartments to larger dwellings.
- To improve the quality of outdated dwellings by public support or by encouragement of private investors.
- To improve the attractiveness of the city in general by embellishment of green spaces, streets and squares.
- To make special regeneration and renewal efforts in parts of the city were special problems of social and physical decay had appeared.

This policy has to some extent been a success. In recent years there has been an increase in immigration to the city and the fiscal situation has been bettered. The increasing demand for dwellings has resulted in a dramatic increase in the prices of owner-occupied flats and a further shortage of rented dwellings. A considerable amount of new expensive rental dwellings have been built along the harbour side, but these dwellings are not affordable for households with normal incomes.

12.5.6 Expected Consequences for the Housing Market of the Øresund Bridge

As described above the Øresund Bridge has created a physical connection between Copenhagen and Malmø in Sweden. It is the vision that a common region around Øresund should be created and also a common housing market. A research project (Skifter Andersen and Borgegård 1999) has shown considerable differences between the housing markets on each side of the Øresund. In Sweden there is a much better connection between quality and price for housing in the rental and cooperative sectors, the prices are lower and the quality higher. As a consequence one should expect increased demand and higher prices in Sweden and reduced demand, lower prices and efforts to increase quality on the Danish side. There has, however, proved to be different barriers to integration of the Øresund region – especially tax rules and cultural differences – that has reduced the demand of Swedish housing from Danish families. There has actually been a movement of people from Copenhagen to Malmø, which in 2004 has increased to about 3,000 persons per year.

References

Haffner MEA (1991) Fiscal Treatment of Owner-occupiers in the EEC. OTB, Delft

Københavns Komune (City of Copenhagen) (1999) Boliger for Alle. Boligpolitisk Strategiplan 2001–04 [Housing for All. Strategic Plan for Housing Policy]

Lunde J, Hvidt A (1999) Privatøkonomiske Konsekvenser af Bosætning Forskellige Steder i Hovedstadsregionen og Boligpolitikkens Betydning for Dette [Private Financial Consequences by Taking Up Residence in Different Parts of the Metropolitan Region and the Importance of Housing Policy for This]. Appendix no. 9 to Skifter Andersen and Borgegård 1999

Ministry of Housing and Urban Affairs (1999) Housing, Building and Urban Affairs in Denmark

PLS–Rambøll (2001), Kommunernes Boligpolitik [Local Housing Policy]

Skifter Andersen H (1992) Regulation of the Private Rental Housing Market – Some Danish Experiences. Scandinavian Housing and Planning Research 9: 41–5

Skifter Andersen H (1998) Motives for Investments in Housing Rehabilitation Among Private Land-lords Under Rent Control. Housing Studies 13(2)

Skifter Andersen H (1999a) Byudvalgets Indsats 1993–98. Sammenfattende Evaluering. SBI-rapport 320 [Final Evaluation of the Results of the Efforts Made by the Goverments Urban Committee], Danish Building Research Institute

Skifter Andersen H (1999b) Virkninger af Byudvalgets Indsats i Almene Boligafdelinger 1994–97 [The Effects of Urban Regeneration Projects in 500 Social Housing Estates]. SBI Rapport 321, Danish Building Research Institute

Skifter Andersen H (2001) Can Deprived Housing Areas be Revitalised? Efforts Against Segregation and Neighbourhood Decay in Denmark and Europe. Urban Studies 39(4): 767–90.

Skifter Andersen H, Munk A (1994) The Welfare State Housing Policy versus the Social Market Economy – A Comparison of Denmark and Germany. Scandinavian Housing and Planning Research 11(3)

Skifter Andersen H, Borgegård L-E (1999) Boligmarkedet i Øresundsregionen [The Housing Market in the Oresund Region]. SBI rapport 315, Danish Building Research Institute

Skifter Andersen H, Leather P (eds) (1999) Urban Renewal Policies in Europe. Policy Press, Bristol

Skifter Andersen H, Andersen HT, Ærø T (2000) Social Polarisation in a Segmented Housing Market: Social Segregation in Greater Copenhagen. Danish Journal of Geography 100

Appendix

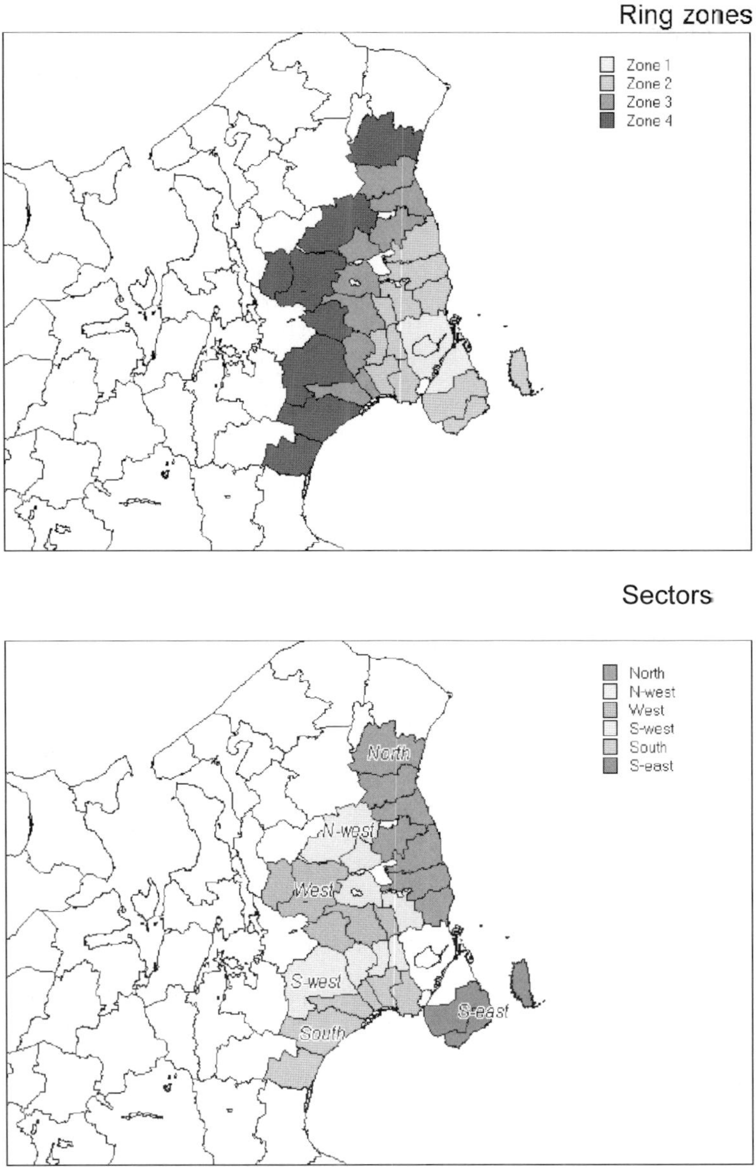

Fig. 12.9. Spatial division of Copenhagen centre and suburbs in sectors and ring zones

13 The Stockholm Housing Market

Stellan Lundström and Mats Wilhelmsson

Royal Institute of Technology, Stockholm

13.1 Introduction

Stockholm is the administrative and cultural capital of Sweden, but Stockholm is also a central hub in a region (Mälardalen region) with rapid economic growth. Some 40 per cent of the Swedish GDP is produced here. Economic growth is positive for Sweden as a nation but it also has generated problems and debate. Much of the debate focuses on the escalating regional differences inside Sweden. Some of the discussion boils down to questions about housing.

Sweden is currently divided into at least three different economic, as well as housing regions:

1. The Stockholm and Mälardalen region with fast economic growth, high house prices, low construction and an escalating housing shortage.
2. The Göteborg and Malmö–Lund regions together with major region cities that in general have balanced housing markets.
3. The rest of Sweden with 225 out of 289 municipalities that have a decreasing population, weak economic base and consequently, low transaction prices in the housing market, high vacancies in the rental market and no housing construction.

An increasingly divided housing market obstructs all efforts to introduce nation-wide housing policies. It also makes the public housing debate more fragmented and local. When it comes to Stockholm, the following issues are frequently discussed:

- How should infrastructure and housing be provided for the extra 500,000 people that are expected to live in the region by 2030? This is a strategic question concerning the balance between public and private transportation, density of the city and its suburbs as well as environmental issues. Much of the debate is about federal versus local responsibility for financing of new infrastructure.

- Historical low numbers of new construction is a fact at the same time as there is a housing shortage with increasing house prices and no vacancies at all in the rental sector within a distance of 100 km from Stockholm CBD. This situation occurs when a supply oriented federal housing policy is phased out and replaced with market-oriented policy. The question then is, if the institutional framework already is adapted to this recently new situation with local and market oriented solutions of housing issues?
- In the inner city of Stockholm there is a very quick transformation of rented apartments to tenant-ownership (co-operatives). Given the current speed of transformation there will be in ten years almost no rented apartments at all in the inner city. The transformation, and the prevalence of a black market for rental contracts, is mainly dependent on an increasing difference between contractual rent levels and market rents.
- Several of the Stockholm suburbs are heavily segregated from ethnic, social and economic point of view. Neighbourhoods with high unemployment and crime rates are a wider problem in society, but the problems are also housing issues, as they seems to be almost exclusively limited to housing companies owned by the municipality.
- Land prices for housing in the city of Stockholm have since the beginning of 1990s risen from some 1,000 SEK per square metre of building area to about 10,000 SEK. This marked price increase is partly due to a shortage of land and partly due to the fact that land prices are no longer subsidised by the city. Another circumstance is that an increasing part of new construction is undertaken on old, but centrally located, industrial land that in several aspects can be contaminated. Land prices set on the market clearly hamper new construction of rented apartments as they are regarded by investors as having a regulated income side.

It is obvious that an increasing and long lasting housing shortage in the Stockholm area can have a huge effect on the economic growth in Sweden and the position of the Mälardalen region as one of the most attractive regions for new enterprises in northern Europe. A well functioning housing market is regarded as key for further economic growth and prosperity.

The Stockholm housing market will, first, be described by analysing the inter-regional differences in Sweden as well as intra-regional differences. Second, the most important changes on the housing market and housing policy will be discussed.

13.2 Inter-regional Differences

Sweden's administrative structure is made up of 21 counties and 289 municipalities. Approximately 30 per cent of the entire population lives in the three metropolitan areas (Stockholm, Göteborg and Malmö) and almost 20 per cent of all households live in the greater Stockholm area. There is also a clear trend that the

Swedish population growth is concentrated to the Stockholm and Göteborg regions. By 2010, the forecast is that the population in Stockholm county will be 2 007,000 inhabitants. That is equivalent to a yearly increase of 18,400 or one per cent (RTK 2001). However, the main reason for this is not immigration but a rising birth rate. As a consequence, the supporting burden will be getting higher when the older age group is getting larger. Lindh and Malmberg (2000) discuss how demographic aspects affect housing demand. Besides the population increase effect, which will increase housing demand in all housing segment, the changing population structure will especially increase the demand in the higher housing segments in Stockholm. In other parts of Sweden, the population increase is very modest, that is, housing demand will not rise as dramatically as in Stockholm.

13.2.1 Housing Expenditures

In Table 13.1, the number of households and housing expenditures in Stockholm and in the rest of Sweden are presented. In total, around 600,000 households exist in the metropolitan area of Stockholm. One out of five household lives in single-family houses compared to one out of three in Sweden as a whole. Hence, living in apartments is more common in Stockholm compared to other parts of Sweden. The net housing expenditures are higher in Stockholm for all tenure forms, 17 per cent higher on the average compared to Sweden as a whole and almost 35 and 20 per cent higher housing costs for single-family and tenants-ownership households, respectively. However, housing expenditures, as a part of disposable income, is the same in Stockholm compared to the rest of Sweden due to higher average incomes. If the housing expenditures are related to the average disposable incomes, one can observe that the expenditure quotes for Sweden are higher compared to other European countries (van der Heijden and Haffner 2000).

The housing allowance system in Sweden is open to both tenants and owner-occupiers and overall the allowances in SEK per household are on the average lower in Stockholm compared to the average in Sweden.

13.2.2 The Stock of Apartments

In Table 13.2, the number of apartments in tenants-ownership (co-operatives) and in municipal (limited-profit) companies is presented.

In Sweden as a whole, the number of tenant-ownership apartments has decreased by 2,000 apartments between 1999 and 2000. At the same time the number of apartments has increased in greater Stockholm by 4,000. More than one out of four tenant-owned apartments can be found in the Stockholm region even though less than one out of five household live in Stockholm. Hence, tenant-ownership is more common in municipalities with a large number of inhabitants.

Table 13.1. Housing expenditures and allowances 1999

	No. of households	Gross housing expenditures [SEK]	Net housing expenditures [SEK]	Housing expenditures of disposable income [%]	Housing allowance [SEK]
Sweden					
Single-family houses	1 275 000	58 400	57 800	20	440
Tenant-ownership	617 000	49 600	46 300	23	2 190
Rental apartments	1 672 000	47 900	42 500	26	5 440
Total	3 563 000	52 000	48 600	23	3 090
Greater Stockholm					
Single-family houses	126 000	76 800	77 300	21	82
Tenant-ownership	152 000	59 400	55 200	22	1 410
Rental apartments	329 000	53 600	49 400	26	4 140
Total	608 000	59 800	56 700	23	2 610

Source: Statistic Sweden.

Table 13.2. Number of tenant-ownership and rental apartments

Region	Tenant-ownership 1999	Tenant-ownership 2000	Rental 1999	Rental 2000
Sweden	714 000	712 000	1 579 000	1 556 000
Greater Stockholm	183 000	187 000	390 000	381 000
Greater Göteborg	61 600	61 500	168 000	168 000
Municipalities with population > 75000	473 000	475 000	985 000	970 000
Municipalities with population > 75000 (excl. greater Stockholm and Göteborg)	228 000	227 000	427 000	422 000
Municipalities with population < 75000 (excl. greater Stockholm and Göteborg)	241 000	236 000	595 000	586 000

Source: Statistic Sweden.

One reason why the number of tenant-ownership apartments has declined in municipalities with less than 75,000 inhabitants is that some tenant-ownership companies faced economic problems and bankruptcy after the real estate crisis in the beginning of the 1990s.

The number of rental apartments decreased slightly between 1999 and 2000 in Sweden as a whole and in the greater Stockholm area. However, the reason for this development is not the same. In Stockholm, a large number of public and private rental apartments have changed ownership status to tenant-ownership housing over last couple of years. On the other hand, in small municipalities a rather substantial number of rental apartments have been demolished.

13.2.3 Construction and Construction Costs

The construction of apartments has fallen dramatically during the 1990s, both in Sweden and Stockholm as well as in the other metropolitan areas. In Fig. 13.1, an index of apartments constructed since 1991 is shown.

In Sweden as whole, the number of newly constructed housing units has decreased from more than 65,000 units in the beginning of 1990s to as low as 13,000 units in 2000. That is equivalent to a reduction of 80 per cent. The reduction is more or less the same for multi-family and single-family housing units. However, what can be seen is that the decline in new construction has been less in the three major urban areas.

The number of constructed apartments was especially reduced during the first part of 1990s and then started to increase again, but not to the same level as in the beginning of the 1990s. It is also interesting to observe that in 1991 almost 65 per cent of the newly constructed apartments in Stockholm consisted of rental apartment, while in 2000 only 26 per cent of the constructed apartments were rental. The same pattern cannot be observed in the rest of Sweden.

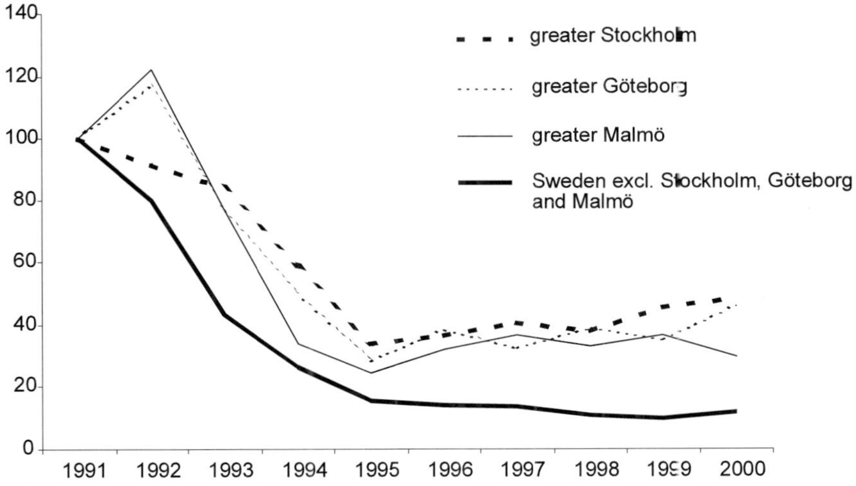

Fig. 13.1. Construction of apartment units, 1991 = 100 (Source: Statistic Sweden)

Why was the construction of new apartments at such a low level and why are public rental apartments not being produced in Stockholm? Of course, there exist many different reasons why this happened.

First, the macroeconomic situation in Sweden has changed. In the beginning of 1990s, Sweden went in to an economic recession that affected the whole economy. At the same time, we had a de-regulation of the financial market that strongly affected the real estate market.

Second, due to the economic recession, subsidies to the property market ceased out, which had a direct effect on the volume of new construction. This is not something unique for Sweden. Generic subsidies have been cut back in a number of European countries (van der Heijden and Haffner 2000).

Third, because the public rental companies are limited-profit companies, the reduction of the subsidies had an indirect effect on the construction, namely, the public companies has a low liquidity that make it difficult for them to put in a high equity in new construction projects. To be able to raise capital to construction of apartments they have to sell parts of the existing stock of apartments to private or tenant-ownership companies.

Rent structure also has a large effect on the construction. The rents on the Swedish market are not market-oriented, i.e., the weights for location are very low. This means that, and maybe particularly for Stockholm, that rents are substantially lower than the market rents, which makes it difficult to find project in Stockholm that are economically justified.

Table 13.3. Construction costs per square metre in multi-family houses (SEK)

Region	Builder	1998	1999	2000
Sweden	Private	11 395	11 398	11 473
	Tenant-ownership	13 488	15 488	16 132
	Public	14 700	12 384	15 991
Greater Stockholm, Göteborg and Malmö	Private	13 717	12 214	13 988
	Tenant-ownership	13 805	16 184	17 994
	Public	13 197	12 703	19 448

Source: Statistic Sweden.

Even though the number of newly constructed apartments is on a low level, the construction cost per square metre of living area has increased. The change in construction costs has been higher in the metropolitan areas compared to Sweden as whole. The construction cost per square metre of living area is on average around 10–20 per cent higher in the metropolitan areas compared to Sweden as a whole. One explanation is of course the cost of land, which is higher in more dense areas. Another explanation is that a higher demand in Stockholm creates inflation from the cost side.

Berger (2000) analyses the single-family market and the Tobin's q between 1981 and 2000 and what can be observed is that the aggregated Tobin's q has not been greater than 1, that is, the average single-family price has not been larger than the average production cost. However, if we analyses the Tobin's q per municipality we can see that in 2000, 12 per cent of the municipality had a Tobin's q higher than 1, but the median value is as low as 0.5. The highest Tobin's q value is 2.37 that could be found within the county of Stockholm.

13.2.4 Rents in the Public Rental-Housing Sector

The rents in the rental-housing sector are set through negotiation between the local tenant organisations and the local organisations of municipal housing companies. The negotiations take place every year and the negotiated rents serve as a yard-stick for private rents (Donner 2000). In Table 13.4, the yearly rents in Stockholm and in the other parts of Sweden are presented.

The yearly rents were in Stockholm on the average around 52,000 SEK compared to 48,000 SEK in Sweden as a whole in 2000. The rents were around 18 per cent higher in Stockholm compared to municipalities with a population less than 75,000 and 8 per cent higher compared the average yearly rent in Sweden as a whole. On reason behind the rent differentiation is that, since 1995, a more market-oriented approach where location is given a greater weight in determining the rents is utilised. Especially, in newly constructed apartments is it possible to set rents that are more market-oriented. Another reason is that age structure of the stock of buildings differs in different parts of Sweden. The higher the average age of the houses, the lower the average cost that affect the rents and vice versa. That means that Stockholm where most of the newly constructed apartments are located has a higher average cost and higher rents as a consequence of that. That is, the rent differentiation is high but probably not as high as they would be on a free market (Fransson, Rosenquist and Turner 2001).

Table 13.4. Average yearly rents

Region	Yearly rent [SEK]	
	1999	2000
Sweden	47 262	47 774
Greater Stockholm	51 214	51 949
Greater Göteborg	51 354	51 592
Municipalities with population > 75000	49 556	50 097
Municipalities with population > 75000 (excl. greater Stockholm and Göteborg)	47 330	47 827
Municipalities with population < 75000 (excl. greater Stockholm and Göteborg)	43 463	43 924

Source: Statistic Sweden.

Not only have the rents fluctuated across regional housing markets. Turner (2000) investigates the determinants of residential income property prices. What he observes is a price differentiation from 1,000 to 8,000 SEK (Stockholm) per square metre over the period 1995 and 1998. Of course, a greater part of this can be explained by the rent differentiation. Interestingly, much of the price differentiation can be described by factors that are not directly connected to the rents. Determinants that influence the price are remaining subsidies, age structure, the micro location in the sub-market, the sub-market itself and determinants that indicate prosperity of the region.

13.2.5 Single-Family House Prices and Macroeconomic Determinants

During the late 1990s demand for housing increased rapidly, especially in the Stockholm region. One result of this is that the prices of single-family houses have increased constantly since 1993. As can be seen in Figure 13.2, property prices have risen faster in the metropolitan areas compared to Sweden as a whole. Furthermore, the single-family house prices vary substantially in Sweden.

The single-family housing prices (in real terms) have decreased by more than 8 per cent over the period 1989 to 1998. In 1993, when the prices where at it lowest level, the price range across regions were also small. However, when the prices started to rise, the price differentiates started to widen. During the same period, the real gross regional product has increased by 12.9 percent. However, employment decreased by 9.9 percent, which indicates that productivity has increased. The vacancy rates in the municipal rental sector climbed from as low as 0.3 per cent to 5.3 per cent at the same time as the stock of apartments increased by 3.4 per cent. The change in real estate prices can, for the most part be explained by macroeconomic determinants.

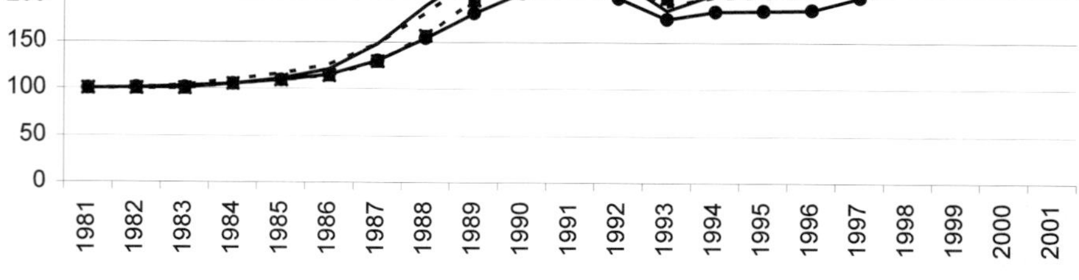

Fig. 13.2. Property price index (Source: Statistic Sweden)

Hort (2000) analyses single-family house prices across 20 regional housing markets over the period 1970–94. What she found out is that a greater part of the price fluctuation can be explained by fundamental factors such as changes in demand and supply. However, she also found that in the short term there have been speculative bubbles, perhaps especially in the Stockholm housing market. But the adjustment speed to long-term equilibrium is rather short, compared to other European housing markets and the American market.

Table 13.5. Single-family house prices and macroeconomic variables 1998

County (Largest city)	Nominal prices Mean 1000 SEK	Vacancy Within the public rental stock	Public rental apartments Total stock	Population	Employment	GRP 100,000 SEK
Stockholm	1,444	2,067	219,271	1,769,379	944,245	500,901
Uppsala	693	1,110	20,070	290,955	119,804	53,875
Eskilstuna	681	2,475	20,773	236,851	97,399	41,959
Linköping	602	2,396	41,714	404,847	175,090	79,223
Jönköping	521	1,886	22,979	328,088	156,554	69,221
Växjö	498	760	17,298	178,566	85,166	38,133
Kalmar	476	1,359	18,912	227,724	102,293	45,463
Karlskrona	549	913	13,455	151,565	68,837	30,631
Malmö	697	2,408	78,392	1,118,583	481,984	217,370
Halmstad	723	649	19,701	271,944	108,619	51,304
Göteborg	627	7,520	14,249	1,472,438	680,998	305,239
Karlstad	462	2,570	25,849	279,280	116,979	52,043
Örebro	467	1,982	34,794	267,822	121,025	52,657
Västerås	535	2,075	23,008	258,122	111,552	52,376
Falun	477	2,533	27,547	284,099	121,769	55,271
Gävle	460	3,946	42,683	283,455	123,753	58,325
Sundsvall	420	1,806	18,162	253,130	121,666	54,328
Östersund	399	1,189	11,201	132,468	58,951	25,904
Umeå	414	2,130	18,971	258,514	115,389	49,035
Luleå	409	2,742	27,818	261,421	113,801	53,899

Source: Statistic Sweden.

In Table 13.5, average nominal single-family house prices are presented together with their standard deviations within the county.

In 1998, the average price in Stockholm was four times as high compared to prices in the northern parts of Sweden. The average price for a single-family house was around 1,400 million SEK in the county of Stockholm. The prices in Stockholm are more than twice as high as in any other county, even if the spread within the county of Stockholm is rather high. Nominal housing prices are highly correlated with population size, vacancy rate within the public rental apartment sector and gross regional product (GRP).

In March 2002, the price of a single-family house was on average 18,000 SEK per square metres in greater Stockholm and around 12,000 in greater Göteborg and Malmö. In Sweden, the metropolitan areas excluded, one has to be able to pay 6,500 SEK per square metres. The prices on tenant-owned apartments show the same pattern. The average price in March 2002 is in greater Stockholm around

20,000 SEK per square metres compared to 10,000 in Sweden as a whole and only 5,000 in the rest of Sweden (Stockholm, Göteborg and Malmö excluded). The prices are highest in the inner city of Stockholm where on average an apartment cost 30,000 SEK per square metres. Hence, there is a quite substantial price differentiation among the Swedish municipalities and the differences in price is much larger compared to the rent differentiation in the rental housing sector.

13.3 Intra-regional Differences

Even if the region of Stockholm is quite unique in comparison to other areas in Sweden when it comes to the housing market, there are some substantial differences within the region and within the municipality of Stockholm.

13.3.1 The County of Stockholm

The county of Stockholm consists of 25 municipalities in 1998. The population in these municipalities varies from some 730,000 inhabitants to only 8,000. In Table 13.6, single-family house prices and macroeconomic determinants are showed.

The variation in single-family house prices varies substantially in the county of Stockholm from as high as 3 million SEK to only 0.8 million SEK. The variation is very much explained by the differences in income and of course the distance to the centre of Stockholm. However, there is also a difference between the southern suburbs and the north. Single-family prices are normally higher in the northern parts of Stockholm compared to the southern parts. To some extent, that is a result of socio-economic segregation and income tax differences.

Housing vacancies are highly concentrated to certain sub-markets. As can been seen in the tables, the vacancy rates vary substantially both in Sweden and within the county of Stockholm. Problematic sub-markets are characteristically neighbourhoods built in the sixties, the so-called million-programme. That often means that the area has a less attractive location or appearance, or neighbourhoods built later, which often means high rents. The residential companies have handled the vacancy rates by either price adjustments or quantity adjustments, i.e., demolishing apartments. The latter is more common in municipalities outside the three metropolitan urban areas (Klingborg 2000).

Table 13.6. Single-family house prices within the county of Stockholm and macroeconomic variables 1998

Municipality	Price [1000 SEK]	Total stock	Vacancy [%]	Employ-ment	Population	GRP [Mill. SEK]
Upplands-Väsby	1 090	7 638	1.3	14 425	36 583	7 229
Vallentuna	1 083	156	0.6	5 937	24 076	2 383
Österåker	1 073	2 061	3.8	8 457	33 232	3 726
Värmdö	1 252	1 363	0.0	7 464	28 889	3 443
Järfälla	1 235	6 725	0.8	20 599	59 484	10 546
Ekerö	1 250	890	0.0	5 948	21 315	2 301
Huddinge	1 208	12 040	17.6	34 631	80 723	14 043
Botkyrka	1 032	11 657	3.8	19 614	70 867	8 174
Salem	1 121	1 686	0.0	2 255	13 113	912
Haninge	1 044	9 601	3.8	21 463	67 236	10 599
Tyresö	1 269	3 589	1.1	8 637	37 816	3 771
Upplands-Bro	1 261	1 727	1.1	6 458	20 433	2 713
Täby	1 783	2 177	0.0	21 941	60 047	10 397
Danderyd	2 979	1 215	0.0	16 149	29 492	8 420
Sollentuna	1 555	6 790	0.0	21 696	56 682	10 692
Stockholm	1 587	107 625	0.1	526 948	731 729	295 389
Södertälje	1 027	12 221	1.6	38 923	79 412	23 171
Nacka	1 999	869	0.1	26 659	72 632	13 848
Sundbyberg	1 983	9 429	0.1	16 004	32 680	9 347
Solna	2 136	6 791	0.1	54 881	55 493	26 742
Lidingö	2 409	1 467	0.0	11 476	40 106	5 517
Vaxholm	1 771	1 145	0.1	2 769	8 627	1 369
Norrtälje	802	2 288	9.1	17 899	51 412	8 105
Sigtuna	1 241	5 131	1.1	25 340	34 058	13 605
Nynäshamn	927	2 990	41.5	7 672	23 242	4 459

Source: Statistic Sweden.

13.3.2 The Municipality of Stockholm

The municipality of Stockholm consists of 17 different administrative areas. Table 13.7 describes the socio-economic profile of these areas.

Analysing the socio-economic characteristics within the municipality of Stockholm shows that there is a huge variation. For example, income differentials are rather substantial. In the inner parts of Stockholm, the average income is twice as high compared to some of the suburbs. One can also observe that workforce with higher education shows the same pattern as well as the number of foreign nationals (including former immigrants that have become Swedish citizens). On the average, 36 per cent of the workforce has higher education (university degree) with a variation from 15 per cent to 56 per cent. The percentage of foreign nationals is on the average 23 per cent, with a variation from 12 per cent to 70 per cent. Hence, the socio-economic segregation is notable within the municipality of Stockholm.

Table 13.7. The municipality of Stockholm

	Population 2000-12-31	Foreign nationals 2000-12-31 [%]	Unemployment 2000-12-31 [%]	Income 1999 [1000 SEK]	Higher education 2000-01-01 [%]
Kista	29 473	47.1	3.83	171	27
Rinkeby	15 605	70.6	4.04	113	15
Spånga-Tensta	33 949	40.8	2.54	185	26
Hässelby-Vällingby	57 849	18.2	1.80	206	32
Bromma	58 506	12.1	1.45	246	49
Kungsholmen	52 245	12.8	1.95	230	51
Norrmalm	61 038	14.5	1.74	240	54
Östermalm	61 519	14.4	1.49	257	56
Maria-Gamla Stan	63 898	13.5	2.42	210	47
Katarina-Sofia	38 646	12.3	2.34	212	46
Enskede-Årsta	45 685	16.4	1.63	194	37
Skarpnäck	39 839	18.6	1.90	181	36
Farsta	45 447	18.9	2.32	181	27
Vantör	34 899	26.3	2.83	172	24
Älvsjö	20 744	14.2	1.37	213	34
Liljeholmen	29 918	17.9	2.27	190	38
Hägersten	29 964	15.4	1.83	196	35
Skärholmen	31 124	38.5	2.84	166	22

Source: RTK Stockholm County.

The number of apartments within the city centre of Stockholm has increased by only 10,000 units over the last ten years. That is a very small change compared to changes in population and households. However, there are some interesting facts to be noticed. First, 5,000 apartments in municipal multi-family houses have disappeared. Second, apartments in private housing companies have been reduced by more than 20,000. Third, apartments in tenant-ownership companies have almost doubled. In 1990, only one third of the apartments were in tenant-ownership compared to the situation today where almost every second apartment is a tenant-owned apartment.

Today it is very common in the inner city of Stockholm that public and private housing companies sell properties to tenant-ownership companies (see Table 13.9). Between 1990 and 1999, some 23,800 apartments changed ownership. Most of the properties were located in the city centre. The main motivation behind these changes in ownership is that the actual rents in the city of Stockholm are lower than the market rent. That mean that a conversion from a regulated market to an open market give a value increase that can be divided between the seller and the buyer. A second, but less important, motivation is that the tenant-ownership companies may be more efficient in property management (Donner 2000).

Table 13.8. Stock and construction in the municipality of Stockholm

Area	Stock 1990	Construction 1990–98	Reconstruction 1990–98	Stock 1998-12-31
City centre	166 266	6 434	705	173 405
Multi-family	165 701	6 431	699	172 831
Municipal housing	27 858	2 115	–50	29 923
Private housing	90 332	1 467	503	92 302
Tenant-ownership	47 511	2 849	246	50 606
Suburb (south)	137 591	4 902	541	143 034
Multi-family	118 122	4 535	479	123 136
Municipal housing	56 613	1 036	–60	57 589
Private housing	37 898	822	379	39 099
Tenant-ownership	23 611	2 677	160	26 448
Suburb (west)	82 781	3 514	–72	86 223
Multi-family	60 753	3 060	–105	63 708
Municipal housing	33 443	510	–343	33 610
Private housing	14 000	1 334	65	15 399
Tenant-ownership	13 310	1 216	173	14 699
Municipality	386 638	14 850	1 174	402 662
Multi-family	344 576	14 026	1 073	359 675
Municipal housing	117 914	3 544	–453	121 005
Private housing	142 230	3 857	947	147 034
Tenant-ownership	84 432	6 625	579	91 636

Source: USK Municipality of Stockholm.

Table 13.9. Change of ownership 1990–99

Area	Change of ownership to tenant-ownership	Rest	Total
City centre			
Municipal housing	–800	800	0
Private housing	–18 600	–800	–19 400
Tenant-ownership	19 400	–	19 400
Suburbs			
Municipal housing	–500	–7 100	–7 600
Private housing	–3 900	7 100	3 200
Tenant-ownership	4 400	–	4 400
Stockholm			
Municipal housing	–1 300	–6 300	–7 600
Private housing	–22 500	6 300	–16 200
Tenant-ownership	23 800	–	23 800

Source: USK Municipality of Stockholm.

All actors and organisations (from private landlords to tenant organisation) are very much concerned that the rental apartments are disappearing in the inner city of Stockholm. It will most certainly be a new socio-economic structure of the households living in the inner city. Today, households in the inner city have higher incomes and it could be observed that the mobility on the housing market is higher (Hellström and Gustavsson 2002). The former may lead in the future to a more segregated housing market. The latter is most certainly a consequence of the rent structure in the rental housing market where current rents reduce the mobility because there is large overvalues that could not be realised. One major municipal rental housing company observed a mobility rate of only 7 per cent in Stockholm compared to around 20 per cent in the rest of Sweden.

13.4 Discussion

The main picture of the Swedish housing policy for the last 25 years is a gradual shift from a strong and supply oriented federal regime to more or less local and market oriented polices. This main picture is built on a big set of changes in systems and institutions. The most important changes, that explain the current housing situation in the city of Stockholm, can be summarised as follows:

13.4.1 The Risk Shift

The main reason for the low level of housing construction can be attributed to an extensive risk shift. The financial risk for new construction has generally speaking been shifted from the society to the individual housing consumer and the developers. During the last 40 years almost 100 per cent of all new housing construction has been undertaken within a programme with general and comprehensive subsidies, mainly in the form of an interest cap. During the same time the municipalities have acted as creditors for their own housing companies as well as for the co-operative sector. With interest guarantees and mortgage loans backed by external creditors it has been possible to accomplish extensive new construction with a minimum of equity capital of 1 to 5 per cent.

The new agenda is that each housing project should be evaluated on its own economic merits to be profitable. Governmental subsidies have been reduced and are no longer general. A lump sum subsidy is now given to rental housing projects that meet certain cost criteria and the municipalities are no longer keen to guarantee mortgage loans.

The main effect of the risk shift is that the need for risk capital has increased dramatically. The need for equity capital is in the range of 25–50 per cent of the total investment cost. The key issue is then access to risk capital. So far is it obvious that the regular venture capital market pays no attention to the housing sector. Risk capital then has to be provided by the individual households who invest in detached houses or co-operative apartments. Rental projects have during a couple of years been regarded as very risky, mostly due to the rent formation system, and thus not attracted investors.

In the city of Stockholm is it evident that the lump sum subsidies are too small to encourage new construction of rental apartments. High land prices and inflated construction costs, due to high demand from the tenant-ownership sector, provides no conditions for profitable development of rental projects.

13.4.2 The Rent Formation System

The Swedish rent formation system was formulated during the 1960s as a 'use-value system'. Basically the system is a market oriented with caps for increased rents in areas with excess demand. By law and practice the rents in the private sector are dependent on the rents in the municipal housing companies. These rents are fundamentally cost related and a product of collective negotiations between the tenant organisation and the local municipal housing company (Bejrum, Cars and Kalbro 1995).

The product of 30 years with negotiated rents, with strong links to cost, is a flat rent structure compared to the price differences observed in the markets for co-operative apartments and detached houses. This flat rent structure has gradually been relaxed during the last 10 years, especially in cities with a balanced housing market. However, in the inner city of Stockholm is it obvious that a market oriented rent is far above the outgoing rent. On the other hand the market rent is below outgoing rents in 225 municipalities that have a weak economic base. This situation escalates as the regional economic differences increase. This is also a structural problem for the rental sector in its competition with the co-op and ownership sectors. In fact the rental sector loosing terrain in all sub-markets due to the rigid rent formation system.

The landlord and the tenant are free to agree about the rent in new apartments. However, the tenant has the right to appeal the rent level in a couple of months. The new rent level is then judged in a comparison with rents in similar apartments. The effect can thus be a radical cut down on the agreed rent level. It follows that from the investors' perspective the outcome of the appeal process is very uncertain with the consequence that investment in new rental housing does not attract capital.

13.4.3 Tax Effects

The Swedish tax system is much the same as systems found in the rest of Europe. However, from a housing market perspective, some conditions can have an effect on the consumers' choice between housing and other goods and services. Most evident is that the total tax pressure is ten per cent higher compared with the EU-average. One obvious effect of the tax is that the Swedish housing cost, as a percentage of disposal income, is among the highest in Europe. The tax pressure was not so evident when the government gave extensive interest subsidies.

The Swedish property tax has since the beginning of the 1980s been at the federal level. In most other countries the property tax is on the local level and partly considered as a charge for the local infrastructure. The argument for a local property tax is that the municipality should have incentives to create an infrastructure that contributes to high property values and high tax income. A local property tax that creates incentives for the municipalities to attract new housing, is perhaps most important in a situation with a market oriented system with no general subsides.

The property tax for detached houses is on the level of one per cent of an assessed value that in general is 75 per cent of the market value. That level is regarded as an imputed income that should correspond to the value of tax deductions for interest payments. So far the property tax is part of the taxes on capital. In order to encourage new construction there are no payments of property tax the first five years and half tax is paid during years six to ten.

By way of an equalisation system the municipalities in growth areas (Stockholm and others) are paying part of their income to municipalities with a weak economic base. This equalisation system is among the municipalities with growth regarded to have negative incentives for increased population and new housing.

13.4.4 Municipal Housing Companies

Sweden is characterised by the huge stock of rental apartments owned by municipal housing companies. Some 900,000 apartments or one out of five of the total housing stock is owned by the municipal housing companies. Yet another characteristic is that these companies are not providing social housing in a general European sense.

The municipal housing companies have since the beginning of 1990s no special rules related to taxes or financing that differentiate them from private owners. With no special rules for financing and with an owner that is reluctant to act as creditor the municipal housing companies have the last years acted like private companies. The municipal housing companies are reluctant to undertake new construction and they care for the income statement and balance sheet in the same way as private owned companies do.

There are three major municipal housing companies in Stockholm with some 110,000 apartments. These companies are acting differently depending on which political party has majority of the seats in the City Hall. The present right wing majority has pursued a policy with the conversion of rental apartments to tenant-ownership. The current left wing majority in the Swedish parliament has disliked this policy and implemented laws to obstruct the conversion. In a way the municipal companies and the rent formation system in Stockholm are in the middle of a political debate that does not exist in the rest of the country.

13.4.5 Building Contractors as Housing Developers

Since the beginning of the 1990s, due to low numbers of new housing, the municipal housing companies and the co-operative sector gradually have lost their competence to undertake an effective procurement process. One of the effects is that the traditional building contractors have created their own development departments that create new housing in market segments with high payment capabilities. In this new market structure the emphasis is on detached houses and tenant-owned apartments in high prestige areas. The focus on the wealthier part of the market has, as a by-product, given high land prices that hamper the production of rented apartments for the middle-class segment.

13.5 Conclusion

Sweden appears to be increasingly regionally differentiated with the Mälardalen and west-coast regions as extreme growth areas. Especially in the city of Stockholm it is obvious that the conditions in the housing market can have a hampering effect on the economic growth. Almost all the important actors, organisations and government bodies agree about the problem definition, as above, but the formation of political blocks delays necessary solutions to more or less acute problems. Most evident is that:

- A radical increase of the volume of new housing can only be achieved if risk capital is attracted to the sector.
- The municipalities in the Stockholm region need economic incentives to promote an increased supply of land for new construction.
- The current rent formation policy in the inner city of Stockholm result in the conversion of almost all rented apartments to tenant-owned.
- A prerequisite for new construction of rented apartments in a market-oriented system is that quality differences in the stock are expressed at different rental levels.

It is also evident that a well-functioning labour market is dependent on a well-functioning housing market. Clearly the Stockholm housing market does not function well at the moment. The problem is well understood, but there is still disagreement about the solutions.

References

Bejrum H, Cars G, Kalbro T (1995) In European Cities, Planning Systems and Property Markets In: Berry J, McGreal S (eds) Stockholm

Berger T (2000) Tobin's q på Småhusmarknader. In: Lindh T (ed) Prisbildning och Värdering av Fastigheter. Research Report 2000:4, Uppsala University

Donner C (2000) Housing Policies in the European Union – Theory and Practice. Ernst Becvar Verlag, Vienna

Fransson U, Rosenquist G, Turner B (2001) Hushållens Värdering av Egenskaper i Bostäder och Bostadsområden. Research Report, Uppsala University

Hellström A, Gustavsson Y (2002) Ombildning av Hyresrätter till Bostadsrätter – Konsekvenser för Omflyttning och Befolkningssammansättning. Report 142, Royal Institute of Technology, Stockholm

Hort K (2000) Prisbildning på Egnahem i Sverige. In: Lindh T (ed) Prisbildning och Värdering av Fastigheter. Research Report 2000:4, Uppsala University

Klingborg K (2000) Vakanser på Bostadshyresmarknaden – I Praktik och Teori. Research Report 5:55, Royal Institute of Technology, Stockholm

Lindh T, Malmberg B (2000) Demografin och Bostadsefterfrågan. In: Lindh T (ed) Prisbildning och Värdering av Fastigheter. Research Report 2000:4, Uppsala University

RTK (2001) Befolkningsprognos 2001–2010. Report 6:2001, The Office of Regional Planning and Urban Transportation, Stockholm

Turner B (2000) Hyreshusens Överlåtelsepriser – En Studie av Prisbildningen. In: Lindh T (ed) Prisbildning och Värdering av Fastigheter. Research Report 2000:4, Uppsala University

van der Heijden H, Haffner M (2000) Housing Expenditure and Housing Policy in the West European Rental Sector. Journal of Housing and the Built Environmental 15: 71–92

Figures

Tables

Contributors

Abele, Hanns
Department of Analytical Economics, Vienna University of Economics and Business Administration, Augasse 2-6, 1090 Vienna
Austria

Andersson, Åke E.
Department of Economics, Jönköping International Business School
P.O. Box 1026, 551 11 Jönköping
Sweden

Baudewyns, Didier
Department of Applied Economics, Free University of Brussels
AV. F.D. Roosevelt, 50 – CP194/7, 1050 Brussels
Belgium

Camagni, Roberto
Department of Management, Economics and Industrial Engineering
Milan Technical University
Piazza Leonardo da Vinci 32, 20133 Milan
Italy

Friedrich, Peter
Department of Public Economics, Bundeswehr University Munich
Werner-Heisenbergweg 39, 85579 Neubiberg
Germany

Höltl, Andrea
Department of Analytical Economics, Vienna University of Economics and Business Administration
Augasse 2-6, 1090 Vienna
Austria

Lönnqvist, Henrik
Urban Research Unit, The City of Helsinki
PB 5530, 00099 Helsinki
Finland

Loikkanen, Heikki A.
Department of Geography, University of Helsinki
P.O. Box 17 (Arkadiankatu 7), 00014 Helsinki
Finland

Lundström, Stellan
Division of Building and Real Estate Economics, Royal Institute of Technology
100 44 Stockholm
Sweden

Maclennan, Duncan
Department of Urban Studies, Glasgow University
25 Bute Gardens, Glasgow G12 8RS, Scotland
UK

Martellato, Dino
Department of Economics, University of Venice Ca Foscari
Dorso Duro 3246, 30123 Venice
Italy

Niebuhr, Annekatrin
IAB Nord, Regional Research Network of the Institute for Employment Research
Projensdorfer Straße 82, 24106 Kiel
Germany

Nordvik, Viggo
Norwegian Building Research Institute
PO Box 123, Blindern, 0314 Oslo
Norway

Pettersson, Lars
Department of Economics, Jönköping International Business School
P.O. Box 1026, 551 11 Jönköping
Sweden

Piesch, Christian
City of Munich, Department of Urban Planning and Building Regulation
Blumenstr. 28b, 80331 Munich
Germany

Rietveld, Piet
Faculty of Economics, Free University
De Boelelaan 1105, 1081 HV Amsterdam
The Netherlands

Rossi, Angelo A.
The University of Applied Sciences of Southern Switzerland (SUPSI)
Galleria 2, 6928 Manno
Switzerland

Skifter Andersen, Hans
Danish Building Research Institute
Dr. Neergaards Vej 15, 2970 Hørsholm
Denmark

Strömquist, Ulf
Temaplan
Peter Myndes Backe 16, 118 86 Stockholm
Sweden

van der Vlist, Arno J.
Business Economics Group, Wageningen University
P.O. Box 8130, 6706 KN Wageningen
The Netherlands

Wilhemsson, Mats
Centre of Excellence for Science and Innovation Studies, Royal Institute of Technology
100 44 Stockholm
Sweden

Index

I

Printing: Krips bv, Meppel
Binding: Stürtz, Würzburg